THE ARCHAEOLOGY OF RELIGION

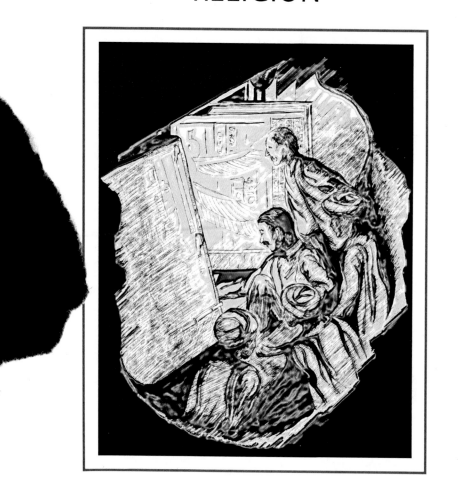

For

Rose and the Lord of the Mountain

THE ARCHAEOLOGY OF RELIGION

CULTURES AND THEIR BELIEFS IN WORLDWIDE CONTEXT

Sharon R. Steadman

Left Coast
Press Inc.

Walnut Creek, California

Left Coast
Press inc.

LEFT COAST PRESS, INC.
1630 North Main Street, #400
Walnut Creek, CA 94596
http://www.LCoastPress.com

ISBN 978–1–59874–153–7   hardcover
ISBN 978–1–59874–154–4   paperback

Library of Congress Cataloguing-in-Publication Data
Steadman, Sharon R.
  Archaeology of religion : cultures and their beliefs in worldwide context
/ Sharon R. Steadman.
     p. cm.
  Includes bibliographical references and index.
  ISBN 978-1-59874-153-7 (hardback : alk. paper) -- ISBN 978-1-59874-154-4
(pbk. : alk. paper)
  1. Archaeology and religion. 2. Religions. I. Title.
  BL65.A72S74 2009
  200.9--dc22
                            200901303
Printed in the United States of America

09 10 11 12 13 5 4 3 2 1

TABLE OF CONTENTS

ILLUSTRATIONS

ACKNOWLEDGMENTS

This book could not have been written without the assistance of numerous people. First and foremost are the art and map specialists who illustrated this book: Tiffany Edwards, Mary Jean Hughes, and Rebecca Jennison. They made this volume much better through their work. Various scholars reviewed portions of this work and offered invaluable comments: Jennifer Ross, James Weinstein, and Mike Smith. I also thank Dave Whitley, who has guided me through this entire process. Mitch Allen, Carol Leyba, and everyone at Left Coast Press also provided invaluable assistance, with kindness and professionalism. The Archaeology of Religion class of 2006 gave me valuable comments on an early version of the book, and I thank them for their guidance. Support from friends, colleagues, and family has been a constant companion as well, one without which this project would never have come to fruition.

PART 1

METHOD, THEORY, AND THE STUDY OF RELIGION

1

INTRODUCING
THE ARCHAEOLOGY OF RELIGION

" Can you see anything?" asked Lord Carnarvon. "Yes, wonderful things," answered Howard Carter as he gazed upon the contents of King Tutankhamun's tomb in 1922 (Figure 1.1). The methods used by Howard Carter in the early twentieth century and those employed by twenty-first century archaeologists differ greatly. Not only are the methods used divergent from a century ago, so are the motivations behind archaeological research. Nineteenth- and early twentieth-century seekers of ancient cultures too often sought to increase their own fame and fortune via their "archaeological" discoveries; artifacts and sometimes portions of entire buildings were whisked away to a foreign land for display and study. The objects themselves were deemed the vehicles by which ancient cultures would be revealed.

Archaeology in the later twentieth and twenty-first centuries has changed immeasurably from those early days. While artifacts and features remain important, it is their context that is recognized as the vehicle into the past. This, combined with scientific methods and anthropologically driven interpretive frameworks, has allowed archaeological researchers to skillfully reconstruct past cultures in sometimes surprisingly intimate detail. What is it that inspires archaeologists to undertake the challenge of reconstructing the past? Furthermore, what responsibilities are embedded within these challenges? This opening chapter seeks to answer these questions as well as another: why is the archaeology of religion important? A final section describes the themes and subjects found in succeeding chapters.

Why Archaeology and Why Religion?

Why should archaeology be considered an important field of study in the larger scheme of this increasingly globalized world? Many suggest that the most basic reason to study the past is to better understand the present, even to avoid "making the same mistakes twice." One archaeologist suggests it is informative to use the present as an interpretive tool for the past (Binford 1983), creating a connective loop of

15

Figure 1.1. Carter and Carnarvon look into King Tut's Tomb. *(M. J. Hughes)*

human experience. Humans seem to be curious about what their predecessors did; and archaeology seems to be the discipline best-suited to satisfy that curiosity. The answer to the question of why archaeologists do what they do is linked with the answer to why archaeology is considered a legitimate discipline for study: human curiosity. However, it is a curiosity paired with a desire to embark on the unique challenge of compiling disparate clues, derived from multiple sources, and using them as the foundation—usually one missing many footings—to recreate the structure of an inhabited past. The archaeologist's role, most simply stated, then, is to offer informed interpretation of the past.

In recent years archaeologists have made tremendous efforts to include some discussion of the target culture's religious beliefs. The reasons for this are both cultural and practical. On the cultural end, archaeologists have long known that the linkages between religious belief and daily life are indiscernible in many, if not most, cultures. However, the tools, methodologies, and interpretive frameworks to illuminate past belief systems have been longer in the making; while far from perfected, using the methods of scholarly inquiry outlined in this book, bolstered by elements of psychology, sociocultural anthropology, and religious studies (Bertemes and Biehl 2001), archaeologists have proceeded in their endeavors to describe ancient beliefs.

A second reason the archaeology of religion has grown in importance is due to increasing levels of cultural sensitivity by archaeologists. Every discipline has its standard of ethics unique to that field. Sociocultural anthropology has a strict code of ethics guiding the field anthropologist's behaviors and what it considers appropriate actions regarding informants in the cultures under study. However, archaeologists have come to realize that, just like anthropologists, they also deal with the living every time they are in the field excavating a site, whether with local residents or the descendants of those cultures they investigate. In those settings they are bound by the same ethics as any sociocultural anthropologist. Even those working in their home countries must remember they are a guest in someone else's place, whether it is in the next-door neighbor's field or in a far-flung state or province.

Practically speaking, archaeologists are *encountering* past religions on a frequent basis. The combination of national infrastructural development and an increasing interest in cultural resource management (CRM) has led to the growth of a CRM field that undertakes archaeological investigation of many places destined for large-scale building projects. Many countries have enacted regulations requiring their own versions of CRM work to be accomplished prior to the commencement of a project, or to be performed should cultural resources be discovered during a project. In 2005 a Turkish government project to build an underwater tunnel linking the European and Asian sides of Istanbul was virtually halted by the discovery of a Byzantine port, and a large-scale excavation was launched. The building project, including an intended subway, has been revamped to accommodate the excavation of this enormous port and the planning of a new museum. Such stories are becoming increasingly common as nations take a greater interest in preserving their cultural past. As more excavations are undertaken, archaeologists face a greater need to properly excavate, and interpret, sensitive cultural materials, particularly those pertaining to belief systems. Additionally, a growth in the worldwide practice of archaeology has created a priority to revisit, and reinforce, ethical concerns within the field.

Ethics, Archaeology, and Religion

When archaeology and ethics are mentioned in the same breath, the first thought centers on the serious issues of site looting, the black market trade in stolen antiquities, and the inappropriate curation and display of cultural objects (Vitelli 1996; Zimmerman, Vitelli, and Hollowell-Zimmerman 2003). However, embedded within the archaeology of religion are some further, field-specific, ethical concerns that must be considered.

The Ethics of "Proving" the Past

Those undertaking archaeological investigation must maintain absolute objectivity when interpreting the material culture within its context, particularly if there is other evidence available that pertains to the same culture, time period, or region. What has occasionally proved to be too tempting, particularly for archaeologists in earlier centuries, was to "prove" the past according to written records. This was particularly prominent in the field known as Biblical Archaeology in the nineteenth and twentieth centuries. Important archaeological material was discarded because it didn't "fit the texts" and thus contradicted what was assumed to be true based on biblical accounts (Bergquist 2001; Insoll 2001). Archaeologists must certainly be familiar with any written records pertaining to their research area, and should even be guided by such records, but they must also recognize when the data derived from the material culture diverges from that written in the texts. The material culture is the purest record of the past; the discipline of archaeology, therefore, must maintain that purity as much as possible in presenting that past.

The Sacred Past

As travelers, when we enter a building or locale sacred to another culture, we think nothing of abiding by the behavioral codes practiced in that culture. Those who don't are considered rude and disrespectful. What were the behavioral codes associated with sacred places and things in the past, and how can we as archaeologists abide by them and still do our work? In general, these are unanswerable questions because in order to abide by behavioral codes, an archaeologist must discern what they were; and the method by which he or she learns them (i.e., by excavating sacred places and things) is almost certainly a violation of those codes. Where is the happy medium between the scientific investigation of the past to inform the present, and preservation of the sacred past by leaving it undisturbed?

For now, archaeologists are guided by the living descendants of past cultures. The Native American Graves Protection and Repatriation Act (NAGPRA) mandates behavioral codes for any archaeologist dealing with Native American sites, especially regarding any aspect of the material culture that may be considered "sacred." In the Middle East, archaeologists are cautioned to be cognizant of burials on high mound sites, especially if they are quite close to the surface. The reason for this is that often Muslim families will decide to bury a loved one not in the local cemetery but on a high place, with the deceased facing east (or toward Mecca). It is not only illegal, but inappropriate, to excavate such burials, and if they are discovered on an archaeological site, that area is left alone and the presence of the burials made known so that future excavators can also leave them undisturbed.

These are but two examples of principles regarding the proper treatment of sacred objects and places that help guide archaeologists in the field. Note, however, that in both cases these guidelines were set out by descendants of those past cultures. At issue, then, is how can archaeologists be guided when there are no descendants to set down rules?

We must adhere to our own internal ethics while still striving to present, in objective fashion, the results of our discoveries to the public. It is an imperfect solution to the problem of appropriate behavioral codes and the sacred past—but the best we have nonetheless. Its success depends on the professionalism of the archaeologist and the appropriateness of the display of the retrieved material culture (i.e., in a museum or other public venue). If both of these factors are satisfactory, then the beauty of that ancient culture and its beliefs will themselves rekindle the appropriate behavior in everyone who sees them.

Cultures and Their Beliefs in Worldwide Context

Which cultures should be explored in a book on the archaeology of religion? Ideally, all of them—but of course this is an impossible task. Inevitably someone's favorite ancient society will be absent from the coming chapters (this is true for the author herself, who painfully decided that the religions of Neolithic and Chalcolithic Anatolia were a bit too remote for presentation). Certain discussions are a must, given their popularity: the Egyptians, the Aztecs. Other chapters focus on lesser-known but equally fascinating past belief systems (Great Zimbabwe, Neolithic Southeast Asia). The author, and those who choose to read this book, can perhaps be comforted by the fact that there are a growing number of excellent treatments on the archaeology of religion (see Chapter 2), and it is certain that in some of these, one's favorite past culture and religion are profiled.

This volume seeks to go beyond simply presenting a shopping list of past cultures and their religions, interesting though that may be, to examine what religions can tell us about human culture as a whole. A few theoretical frameworks, introduced here and explored in more detail later (see Chapter 2), offer some methods for interpreting past, and present, religions as lenses on the prism of belief systems and how they function in society.

In general, four interpretive frameworks will be employed, to greater or lesser extent, as approaches for understanding the cultures and belief systems explored throughout the book. The first, and perhaps the most often evident, is the model that dictates the reflective nature between religion and culture. The overall structure of a society, as well as its most crucial institutions, values, and ideals, can often be clearly observed in its belief system, in effect mirroring the culture. A second, related model examines the interrelationship between religion and environment. A culture is most certainly shaped by the environment in which it is located, and so too is its religion. In many cases it is possible to discern how important a healthy ecological balance is to a culture by examining the significant focus on environment in the belief system.

A third interpretive framework sees a more proactive use of religion as a powerful method to control society. This becomes particularly prevalent in more complex societies when ruling elites seek to keep a tight reign on their peoples; however, such methods crop up in other societal structures as well. Finally, several chapters (especially Chapters 13 and 18) examine the role religion can play as a method to rebel against oppressive regimes and foreign or hostile powers and as a mode to revitalize a culture in crisis.

There are countless other models that may be employed to understand religions past and present, many of which are found in Chapter 3. The four interpretive frameworks outlined here are broad in their scope and thus allow us to see how deeply intertwined religion is in virtually every aspect of the human experience on earth.

Chapter 2 lays out an anthropological history of the study of religion. Archaeologists cannot hope to interpret past belief systems without the aid of their sociocultural compatriots who have studied it in its living form. Chapter 3 demonstrates how archaeologists have used the theories generated by these sociocultural anthropologists (as well as sociologists and psychologists) to build interpretive frameworks for the archaeological past. The innovative thinking of these researchers is not only fascinating, but it is at the heart of what makes a book such as this one possible.

Part II offers an exploration of shamanism, followed by a study on the emergence of religion among humans, and concludes with an overview of rock art in both Africa and Australia. At first glance these three topics may not appear to be interrelated, but indeed they are. How soon after the first spark of religion began did the first religious practitioners begin their work? Perhaps nearly simultaneously with those earliest beliefs. Whenever such practitioners began their work, we can be certain they were shamans—hence the placement of a chapter on these earliest religious specialists in this section. In addition to burials, covered extensively in the Neanderthal chapter (Chapter 5), rock art may be one of the earliest archaeologically visible signs of religious belief. Often, though not always, the art is the product of cultures that practice a hunting-gathering lifestyle, and this is certainly true of those profiled in Chapter 6. That this is the most ancient of human economic strategies, and that rock art has such an ancient tradition, allows this chapter to fit quite comfortably in the section discussing the emergence of religion in human culture.

The following four sections are organized according first to a geographical and then a chronological theme. In some cases the presentation of material in later chapters builds on what was offered in those earlier in the same section (such as Chapters 16, 17, and 18 on the ancient Near East), while others, such as Chapters 9 and 10 on the Aztecs and Inka, describe contemporary but largely unrelated cultures. In many of these chapters artistic renderings of ancient rituals and ceremonies bring the archaeological data to life, which is, after all, our ultimate goal as archaeologists.

USEFUL SOURCES

Brian Hayden, *Archaeology: The Science of Once and Future Things*, 1993.

Christopher Scarre and Geoffrey Scarre (eds.), *The Ethics of Archaeology: Philosophical Perspectives on Archaeological Practice*, 2006.

Alison Wylie, *Thinking from Things: Essays in the Philosophy of Archaeology*, 2002.

2

ANTHROPOLOGY AND THE STUDY OF RELIGION

One important step in any scholarly endeavor is to review past work that led to the present state of the topic. This chapter begins with perhaps the single most difficult feat in the entire book: the definition of *religion*. This is followed by a discussion of anthropologists, past and present, who have shaped the discipline's view of this concept and how to study it.

Defining Religion

The anthropological definition of religion has changed drastically over the last two centuries because anthropology and its theoretical approaches have changed. With so many definitions, how does one achieve an unbiased understanding of religion? Most of the cultures discussed in this book never attempted to define religion because they did not recognize its existence. In other words, their belief system was just that, theirs, and their place in the universe was explained by their own cosmology, mythology, and rituals. What was there to question? Rather, with notable exceptions such as Confucius, it is primarily Western intellectuals (including the ancient Greeks) who have sought to explain religion as a phenomenon of human society.

The desire to define religion anthropologically began essentially with the origins of the discipline itself. Edward B. Tylor's 1871 book outlined religion as a belief in supernatural beings. Definitions have become somewhat more complex in the century or so since that publication. Perhaps the best-known explanation of religion comes from a contemporary anthropologist, Clifford Geertz (1926–2006), who suggested that religion is

> (1) a system of symbols which acts to (2) establish powerful, pervasive, and long-lasting moods and motivations in men by (3) formulating conceptions of a general order of existence and (4) clothing these conceptions with such an aura of factuality that (5) the moods and motivations seem uniquely realistic. (1973:90)

This interpretation recognizes the symbolic role of religion in that myths, rituals, and supernatural beings are representative of crucial aspects of social, economic, and even political behaviors within a culture. On some levels, however, Geertz's definition fails to yield insight into the *meaning* of religious traditions within a culture. The correlation of symbol to social fact does not leave much room for understanding how religious beliefs explain the universe to their adherents. It is toward this end that Lehmann and Myers offer a broadened definition:

> Expanding the definition of religion beyond spiritual and superhuman beings to include the extraordinary, the mysterious, and unexplainable allows a more comprehensive view of religious behaviors among the peoples of the world and permits the anthropological investigation of phenomena such as magic, sorcery, curses, and other practices that hold meaning for both preliterate and literate societies. (Lehmann, Myers, and Moro 2005:3)

This definition certainly addresses the aspect of what religion *means* in culture, but moves further away from Geertz's symbolist explanation. Perhaps it is best to follow the advice offered by John Bowen, who writes, "I view religious traditions as ever-changing complexes of beliefs . . . practices (including formalized rituals), and social institutions. . . . I thus refrain from giving too precise a definition for religion" (2005: 3–4). This is indeed the most cautious approach in a broad-based study, especially when entire books have been written on the origin and definition of religion.

For instance, Raymond Firth's book *Religion: A Humanist Interpretation* (1996) is based on a lifetime of research on the subject. In it he suggests that

> [religion] fits the highly complex world of human imagining, and serves an array of human purposes not always consciously realized by people themselves. It corresponds in figurative and symbolic language to an attempt to meet basic human problems involved in mental and physical anxiety and pain, the certainty of death, the uncertainties of life in the complicated relations with other human beings. (1996:11)

In this we can recognize some of the well-known explanations for the existence of religion discussed in the next section—that is, as relief to anxiety and uncertainty, as a social bonding device, and as a psychological response to external stimuli. A slightly different tack is taken by Paul Boyer who, in his book *Religion Explained: The Evolutionary Origins of Religious Thought*, suggests humans have religion because it is how our brains are hard-wired:

> The explanation for religious beliefs and behaviors is to be found in the way all human minds work. I really mean all human minds, not just the minds of religious people or of some of them. I am talking about human minds, because what matters here are properties of minds that are found in all members of our species with normal brains. (2001:2)

Thus Boyer defines religion as a complex system generated within the context of human evolution. Religion is a collection of inferences, emotional responses, reason, moral judgments, and so on, developed over eons and bundled together to create human *belief*.

In *Ritual and Religion in the Making of Humanity*, Roy Rappaport suggests that religion "grew up" with humans. More specifically, Rappaport argues that language allowed humans to escape from the confines of here and now and explore the unseeable, the imagined; this ability sowed the seeds of religious thought and action (1999). Rappaport notes that "it is in the nature of religion to fabricate the Word, the True Word upon which the truths of symbols and the convictions that they establish stand" (1999:20). He believes that the performance of ritual stands at the heart of human religion and is the impetus and carrier of emotion, unquestioning belief, and social unity, which make religion such a powerful human institution.

How, then, does one define *religion*? Should we chalk it up to human evolution and language development and be done with it? Perhaps, but we are still in need of a basic definition from which to examine past religions as they are demonstrated through material remains. Therefore, shamelessly drawing upon foregoing anthropologists who devoted their scholarly careers to the understanding of religion, a brief definition can be offered here:

> Religion is a system of beliefs that posits supernatural beings and resolves mysterious or unexplainable phenomena; it is a set of practices and associated trappings that allows believers not only to engage the supernatural world but also to demonstrate their devotion and faith in it. It is intricately intertwined with every aspect of culture that shapes social structure, while it also in turn is shaped by it.

This may sound suspiciously broad and non-specific, but there are several items of importance relevant for an archaeological study of religion. One of these is the "associated trappings" that comprise the material remains archaeologists must rely on to inform them about past cultures. A second is the fact that these trappings, and what they represent, are certainly indicative of emotion, devotion, conviction, and faith on the part of the believers who manipulated them. The imprint of these emotions and feelings may very well have been carried down through the centuries in the way such objects were handled, stored, or left in place. Finally, and perhaps most important, is the fact that we cannot separate religion from the rest of the culture. Religion, in the past and today, permeates every aspect of how humans construct their social institutions—from art, to marriage, to politics. This definition, with its focus on material culture and a holistic approach, will suffice as a working platform for the exploration of past religions.

Early Anthropology and the Origins of Religion

The mid-nineteenth century was a time of Western imperialism, when a deluge of new societies and cultural practices were revealed to European and North American intellectual circles. The wide diversity of such practices and cultural types was a puzzle that needed solving. Herein lies the birth of the anthropological discipline and the desire to explain cultural diversity. Early theories were shaped by the ethnocentric thinking of the time, skewed by interpretations based on a sliding scale of the value of cultural types. Nonetheless, nineteenth-century scholars made important contributions to the understanding of cultural structure and diversity. Many of these breakthroughs form the underpinnings of the anthropological discipline today.

Evolutionary Approaches to Explaining Religion

In the mid-nineteenth century, Charles Darwin and other naturalists offered explanations of the human past from scientific, orderly, and rational perspectives. This ideological milieu had an impact on how early anthropologists such as Edward Tylor and James Frazer sought to explain the origin and ubiquity of religious belief systems.

Tylor (1832–1917) was appointed a professor of anthropology at Oxford in 1884, the first such position in Britain. He was a "prototypical Victorian armchair anthropologist" (Erickson 1998:50), meaning he developed his interpretations using secondary sources rather than by visiting the cultures himself. While today this would seem the height of shoddy anthropological methodology, in the nineteenth century it was the norm; those with actual fieldwork experience, such as Lewis Henry Morgan (1818–1881), who studied Iroquois ritual in order to help them win a land claim court case, were the exception. Morgan later went on to do fieldwork across North America and eventually published his magnum opus, *Ancient Society*, in 1877. Classical cultural evolutionists such as Tylor and Morgan created a sliding scale of human cultural structure, reasoning that in the past, all cultures were deeply "primitive," and over time many evolved into more sophisticated social systems. One school of thought, known as *unilinear evolutionism*, viewed cultural structures and institutions as progressing from "savagery" to "civilized," passing through stages of "barbarism" along the way.

Tylor was particularly interested in magico-religious belief systems, and in his well-known 1871 book, *Primitive Culture*, he outlined theories on the origins of religion and its evolution from primitive stages to more sophisticated systems. Tylor believed early cultures took a rational approach to explaining the unexplainable—things like strange events in dreams, waking visions, hallucinations, and shadows—by adopting the belief that spiritual energy was responsible. He suggested that early cultures believed this energy derived from humans and animals and was responsible not only for dreams, visions, and hallucinations, but for all phenomena that made up the natural world. Tylor labeled this belief system *animism*, from the Latin for "soul." He speculated that as societal structures "evolved" into more complex systems, belief in simple spirits also progressed into a more complicated structure involving individualized spirits, and finally gods and goddesses. Tylor posited that the origin and development of religion came from humankind's ability to logically reason out an explanation for a world beyond the normal earthly plane of existence.

Following on the heels of Tylor was Sir James Frazer (1854–1941), author of *The Golden Bough*, a twelve-volume set published over a course of twenty-five years (1890–1915; with a condensed version appearing in 1922). Frazer, a unilinear evolutionist, was taken with the idea of animism; in *The Golden Bough* he advanced the theory that much of early religion relied on a belief in magic *prior* to the development of animistic systems. He suggested that early cultures used magical practices to "solve problems" such as finding enough food and remaining safe, and to punish misbehaviors. These magical practices, Frazer asserted, preceded initial notions of "religion" and so were really the first human foray into supernatural belief and practice.

To categorize these behaviors, Frazer advanced the term *sympathetic magic*, which is divided into two types: *imitative* (also known as *homeopathic*) and *contagious*. The "Law of Sympathy," as Frazer termed it, is based on the notion that like produces like—that carrying out a magical act will cause a corresponding action; for instance, a ritual sprinkling of water on the ground will bring rain. Contagious magic dictates that once something is part of an entity, it remains spiritually connected even when irrevocably separated. Thus, a lock of human hair inserted into a doll enables someone to carry out actions on the doll and expect corresponding reactions in the human from whom the hair was taken. Eventually, according to Frazer, humans determined the Law of Sympathy did not always work. People then turned to a belief in "religion," such as animism, and later a recognition of more individualized beings such as gods and goddesses. These, Frazer suggested, provided a more satisfactory explanation for the unexplainable, leading to the emergence of complex religions as practiced today.

Max Weber (1864–1920), a German sociologist, also had views rooted in evolutionary thought, and his goal was to explain the presence of today's world religions, including Christianity, Judaism, Islam, Hinduism, and Buddhism. He contrasted these, which he termed "historical religions," to those of earlier cultures that he called "traditional." Weber believed that societal structures and their belief systems were the products of cultural value systems, and even further, of the individuals within the cultures; the collective group of people in a culture had unique ideas, beliefs, and modes of thinking that produced their own structures and, therefore, a unique religion (see, for instance, his *Sociology of Religion*, 1922). Thus religion and cultural institutions were interactive, providing feedback and reinforcement for each other.

Weber was not terribly concerned with explaining the "origins" of religion, nor with describing those he termed "traditional"; these latter, he believed, were cultures that had practiced various forms of animism and magical rituals reflective of simple societies with uncomplicated value systems. As societal structure grew more complex, Weber argued, so did its religion. What was once a traditional system of beliefs and values that could be passed orally from generation to generation became a complex collection of institutions with divergent but interconnected domains. Members of cultures began to take a more "rational" and even scientific approach to understanding their cosmos, while also embedding ethical and moral codes within the belief system. They created a set of core values, an *ethos*, that could be recognized and followed by all members of the culture, no matter their function and status in the society. Eventually supernatural actors (deities) were so complex they necessitated human intermediaries to assist believers (i.e., priests and priestesses), who served to interpret sacred texts and difficult religious concepts for the masses.

Emile Durkheim (1858–1917), a French sociologist and contemporary of Tylor and Weber, took a somewhat different tack in his efforts to interpret the role of religion within culture. In his 1915 book *The Elementary Forms of Religious Life*, Durkheim put forth the idea that a culture's religion is the manifestation of social action and thought. Religion is not an intellectual attempt to explain the world, a product of the rational mind, but rather a system of collective beliefs and actions that are symbolic representations of mores, values, and ideals considered most crucial to the survival of a society. Because religion is fashioned from the symbolic representations of the social foundations within a culture, it serves to reinforce these foundations, while creating a harmony of belief and behavior. This is one of the core principles of Durkheim's interpretation: "Religion is a unified system of beliefs and practices . . . which unite into one single moral community" (Durkheim 1915:62). Religion, therefore, at its origin and in its continuance, serves as the interconnective tissue to continually reinforce basic societal norms and mores within the social framework.

Durkheim believed the earliest notion of religion did not rely on the "unseen" or "illusion" (such as spirits) but rather on reality as each culture understood it. Therefore, depending on a culture's worldview, customs, and value system, the world was divided into two categories of *sacred* and *profane*; because cultures vary, the things in these two categories varied as well, thus explaining diversity in religious beliefs. Things that are profane are ordinary everyday things that do not require special treatment or thought. Sacred things are special and represent important aspects of social consciousness; they are either forbidden or worshipped, and in all cases are inspiring of deep emotion and awe. As individuals understand and internalize the categories and take part in rituals or other specialized behavior celebrating the sacred, the community becomes more tightly bound in a solidarity of belief and action.

Durkheim felt that *totemism*, a system in which ancestral spirits are symbolically represented by animate or inanimate objects (such as a bear or a mountain), was illustrative not only of original religions, but also of sacred and profane divisions and their power to unite a community. Durkheim used Australian Aboriginal cultures and their totemic beliefs to demonstrate his ideas. Members of Aboriginal clans are kin-linked by an original ancestor, represented by an animal or a plant. Families united under this clan symbol share a sense of unity that ties them closely together, reinforcing their view of what is sacred and what profane; anything associated with the clan totem is sacred, treated with great respect and celebrated by ritual actions. Durkheim argued that events such as an annual ceremony in which the totem was ritually killed and consumed by the entire clan served to tie members of the clan together in an even tighter bond, making them part of the ancestor and part of one another. As members of the society were united, so was the societal structure, ensuring the continuance of a well-structured and cohesive cultural entity.

Durkheim suggested that totemic beliefs preceded animism, and in an evolutionary process, cultures and their belief systems grew more complex, eventually incorporating gods, goddesses, priests, temples, and the like. However, Durkheim argued that, at their core, all religions maintain the dichotomy of sacred versus profane and the unity that comes from following the strictures associated with these categories. Thus, all religion, no matter its form or beliefs, serves to unite communities and provide a method to reinforce basic principles, mores, values—in essence, the social consciousness of the culture.

Religion as Psychological Need

Although he doesn't fit into the category of "evolutionist" or even "anthropologist," Sigmund Freud (1856–1939) offered important ideas on the origins and development of religious systems. Freud wrote on religion in several books, including *Totem and Taboo* published in 1913 and *The Future of an Illusion* in 1927. In the former he attempted to explain the origins of religion and other basic human behaviors; in the latter he focused more on the universality and function of religion in human culture.

In *Totem and Taboo*, Freud drew on the concept of early totemistic religion, suggesting that younger males in early human cultures developed feelings of anger and resentment toward elder males (including their fathers) over sexual access to females and aspects of power and control. In a frenzy of revolt, the youths murdered and consumed the elder males and subsequently experienced feelings of intense remorse and guilt. From this event, according to Freud, developed the totemistic belief system in which the elders were held up as the original ancestors, to be revered but yet ritually consumed at periodic sacred rites (thus recalling the original events). While most anthropologists do not subscribe to this Freudian explanation of totemism (in fact, it is unclear whether Freud actually advocated that these events were real), many find merit in the suggestions he made regarding the function of religion in human culture, concepts he explored in *The Future of an Illusion*.

In Freud's thinking, humans face a tremendous number of frightening and dangerous things that promote feelings of anxiety, fear, and helplessness, and could render humans incapable of action and unable to maintain a solid cultural structure. However, the existence of religion, which not only explains the universe (where did we come from, where do we go after death, why do children die, etc.), but provides comfort and calm, formed a necessary "illusion" to allow humans to carry on with their daily lives. Echoing Durkheim, Freud also asserted that in following the customs and "laws" set down by supernatural beings, humans not only felt safe and comfortable in their lives, but they also could live together in harmony, as all were cognizant of, and intent on following, culture-wide codes of behavior. Thus, in Freud's thinking, religion functions to soothe human anxiety and satisfy emotional and psychological needs, while simultaneously reinforcing cultural norms and values.

New Views in the Twentieth Century

It wasn't long before monolithic models for cultural diversity were discounted as too simplistic and also insensitive. The realization that evolutionary models ranged dangerously close to being racist also spurred new and more enlightened directions of exploration and thought. The early twentieth century saw the rise of influential thinkers whose research and theories literally shaped the foundations of modern anthropology.

Anti-Evolutionism and the Birth of Cultural Relativism

Franz Boas (1858–1942) did not subscribe to the same overarching ideas about cultural evolution as did Frazer, Tylor, and Durkheim. Born in Germany, Boas began conducting research in both Canada and the United States, and then settled in New York where he later became the first professor of anthropology at Columbia University. Boas argued against generalized explanations that sought to describe all human culture, past and present, in one tidy package. He asserted that each culture was unique, a product of its individual history, and that one must study each culture, personally and intensively—only then could one make inferences about that culture. This interpretive framework has come to be known as *historical particularism*. Boas rejected unilinear evolutionism as haphazard, lacking in empirical evidence, and even prejudiced in its terminology and comparative method of evaluating "savage" cultures as lesser than "civilized" ones. Boas asserted that "armchair anthropology" must be abandoned for dedicated fieldwork and that it was senseless to judge cultures that were innately unique and thus incomparable. This point of view has become a main tenet of anthropology and is invoked in the concept of *cultural relativism*.

Boasian ideals became embedded in North American and European anthropology in the early decades of the twentieth century. His approach, embraced by many contemporaries and successors, allowed anthropologists to evaluate religions individually and avoid offering a universal "culture and religion" explanation. By insisting on culturally relative, non-ethnocentric views of culture, and by instilling the necessity of ethnographic fieldwork, Boas almost single-handedly reoriented the field of anthropology into a structure we recognize today as modern anthropology.

Religion, Functionalism, and Societal Needs

Boas was not the only one who became increasingly uncomfortable with notions of cultural evolutionism. Several European scholars were also searching for alternative frameworks to explain cultural diversity. Prominent among these was Branislaw Malinowski (1884–1942), a Polish-born scientist educated in physics and mathematics who, after reading Frazer's *The Golden Bough*, changed career paths to study anthropology in Britain. Like Boas, Malinowski saw the efficacy of fieldwork and departed for the Trobriand Islands in Melanesia to conduct his studies. He ended up staying in the islands for the duration of World War I. His nearly four years of fieldwork offered him oceans of data from which he built his interpretations of cultural structure.

Like Boas, Malinowski rejected evolutionism and theories extolled by nineteenth-century scholars. He considered them uninformed, lacking empirical data, and essentially wrong-headed—they were not only inaccurate, but offered the worst kind of *etic* (outsider) view of culture. Malinowski stressed the need for sustained fieldwork in which an anthropologist not only learned the language, but obtained as much of an *emic* (insider) view as possible. Malinowski's main theoretical model is known as *functionalism*. This school advocates that cultural institutions are totally integrated; a single institution such as marriage cannot be understood in isolation but only in the context of the culture's economy, family structure, religion, and so on. Furthermore, institutions are structured in order to meet societal needs such as safety, reproduction, nutrition, and education, and to address other basic aspects of human behaviors. The organization of these cultural institutions, and actions associated with that organization, serve these needs for every individual in the society. In this way Malinowski felt he had not only unlocked the mystery of cultural diversity, but essentially explained how all cultures worked: human needs are satisfied by the construction of cultural institutions that are intimately integrated.

Malinowski addressed the issue of religion in his book *Magic, Science, and Religion, and Other Essays* (1925). He insisted that preliterate cultures were pragmatic, even scientific in their approach to religion. Non-Western peoples were not wild-eyed superstitious savages, as earlier thinkers had proposed. For Malinowski, religion, and the rituals, myths, and events associated with it, were ordered and structured in ways that allowed individuals within the society to live productive and relatively fearless lives. Birth rituals, and particularly death rituals, relieved anxiety and fear of the unknown, thereby allowing individuals to proceed with necessary activities that might result in death (warfare, hunting, childbirth, etc.). Magic, Malinowski asserted, took over where a culture's technical or natural understanding of the world ended. In one of his best-known examples, Malinowski used Trobriand fishing practices to illustrate his ideas: when fishing in calm waters where technical knowledge was sufficient, no magical rituals were necessary, but when going out to the open sea or in stormy weather, magic was performed (rites, incantations, etc.) in order to keep the fishermen safe. Such magical rites gave the fishermen a feeling of safety and protection, allowing them to go out to complete their task; in this way magic functioned to satisfy their needs of safety and comfort. Although all humans had the same basic needs, different cultures structured their institutions uniquely to serve those needs. Thus cultural diversity and differing forms of religion were, in Malinowski's thinking, logically explained by a functionalist approach.

Several decades later, another anthropologist employed a functionalist interpretation to understand religion and ritual, but added an ecological dimension to his model. Roy Rappaport (1926–1997) worked among the Tsembaga of New Guinea and then advanced the theory that Tsembaga ritual is derived from societal needs and ecological balancing. An example illustrating his theory is found in *Pigs for Ancestors: Ritual in the Ecology of a New Guinea People* (1968). The pig, in Tsembaga and other New Guinean cultures, is a symbol of wealth and status and as such it is not casually slaughtered and eaten. However, ritual feasts are certainly an occasion for pig roasts, and in one case that Rappaport observed, the Tsembaga slaughtered well over 100 pigs, leaving only 60 alive (Rappaport 1967). The slaughter and consumption of pigs has cosmological meaning in Tsembaga culture, but Rappaport noted that the timing of the feasts also corresponded with two ecological and social needs. First, ritual feasts occurred when the pig herd had nearly reached or achieved unmanageable size. For instance, in the example cited above, Rappaport noted that the pig herd was consuming over half of the garden product of sweet potato and manioc. Second, Rappaport suggested that such feasts happened after the stress of warfare had created a need for the protein and other nutrients supplied by meat, an otherwise rare food item in the

Tsembaga diet. Rappaport thereby added an ecological component to his functionalist-based interpretation of religion.

The Structure of Culture and Religion

The final break from cultural evolutionism was accomplished by the introduction of yet another theoretical approach known as *structuralism*. Primarily the brainchild of French anthropologists, structuralism was first built on the notion of reciprocal exchange as a method for creating staunch interpersonal relationships and connections within a culture. This idea, advanced by Marcel Mauss in his book *The Gift* (1924), was adopted and further developed by Claude Lévi-Strauss (1908–2005). Lévi-Strauss was a prolific author, publishing on kinship, food, and the interpretation of religion. Two of his books, *The Raw and the Cooked* (1969) and *The Savage Mind* (1966), employed his structuralist interpretations of culture. The goal of structuralism is to identify the organization and meaning of the cultural institutions underlying any society. Once identified, the overarching and confusing differentiations across cultures can be better understood and cultures can be more productively analyzed in comparative analysis. Thus, in constructing his theory, Lévi-Strauss was engaged in building an interpretive model that could be applied to any culture and could delve below superficial diversity to the structured underpinnings beneath.

Lévi-Strauss believed that religion is a representation of a society's structural make-up, including beliefs, values, and customs, and that these could be most clearly identified in its myths. In this interpretation, societies and their religions are structured according to "binary oppositions," a concept he derived from structural linguistic studies. In structuralist theory, binary oppositions refer to the polar opposites that make up the human cultural experience: life and death, raw and cooked, east and west, culture and nature, and the like.

In his analysis of myth, Lévi-Strauss found good examples of how structuralism works; every culture has unique myths seemingly different from other cultures. But this superficial diversity can be stripped away when analyzing the underlying structure of myths and the binary oppositions they display. Creation myths, for instance, though varied across cultures, relate to the same underlying human concerns: where did we come from, how did our environment emerge, what happens when we die, and so on. As these myths are passed on from one generation to the next, so is the underlying societal structure that maintains and reinforces cultural integrity. Thus, the same elements of human culture are encoded in myths, but one must strip away the layers of culture-specific details that conceal the actual structuralism underlying the myth. Though scholars today continue to use some aspects of structuralism, the concept has been widely criticized as too narrow and confining to serve as an all-inclusive interpretive framework.

Contemporary Anthropological Theories

In a continued effort to understand religion and its place within the human cultural framework, anthropologists working in the last several decades have offered interpretive schemes built on those proffered in the past and have forged new ones of their own as well. All have fundamentally contributed to our ability to explain religions both present and past.

Symbolism Comes to the Fore

E. E. Evans-Pritchard (1902–1973) would have been discussed in the previous section had he not altered his thinking in the latter twenty years of his career. Evans-Pritchard studied under Malinowski and became a disciple of the functionalist approach. Like Malinowski, Evans-Pritchard believed in extensive fieldwork, and he spent years working with several cultures in Africa, including the Azande and the Nuer. He published an important work on religion entitled *Witchcraft, Oracles, and Magic among the Azande* (1937) in which he described how a belief in witches and witchcraft served to explain unpleasant events such as death, illness, and other examples of ill fortune. A few years later he published an almost scientific study of the Nuer (1940) that focused on the political and socioeconomic activities of this cattle-herding culture, detailing how the structure of Nuer culture satisfied needs in order to produce a smoothly functioning community.

However, in the early1950s Evans-Pritchard underwent a sea change in his approach to cultural interpretation and the role of the anthropologist. He began to assert that anthropology was better housed in the humanities than in the social sciences, and that it had a particularly close relationship to the field of history. He embarked on a program of interpretation that employed history combined with intuitive understandings of the meaning underlying the religious practices and associated beliefs found in a culture. In two later publications on religion, *Nuer Religion* (1956) and *Theories of Primitive Religion* (1965), Evans-Pritchard's altered interpretive framework is clear. He eschewed the functionalist or structuralist approaches and warned against the temptation to explain religion using facile interpretations based on sociology or psychology. Evans-Pritchard argued that anthropologists must take an *emic* approach to understanding a culture's religion; they must delve deeply into the symbolic meaning represented by every element within a religion and then seek a method to translate this effectively back to the anthropologist's own culture. During his lifetime Evans-Pritchard journeyed from an almost scientifically based functionalist approach to an interpretive framework that serves in part as the basis of the symbolic anthropological approach employed by many anthropologists today.

It is perhaps Mary Douglas (1921–2007), a student of Evans-Pritchard, whose work is most closely associated with *symbolic anthropology* as an interpretive approach. Douglas also worked in Africa, but it was her theories on cultural analysis rather than her ethnographic work that catapulted her to international status. Douglas's books *Purity and Danger: An Analysis of Pollution and Taboo* (1966) and *Natural Symbols* (1973) continued the arguments made by Evans-Pritchard—namely, that religion and ritual consist of symbolically meaningful components that represent a culture's most basic values and worldview. Only with extensive field research and a concerted attempt to gain an insider's view can an anthropologist hope to unravel the meanings underlying the actions, myths, and rites that make up the religion.

In *Purity and Danger*, Douglas explored the presence of taboos in various cultures. She theorized that all cultures harbor notions of ritual purity and ritual contamination, or pollution; what is pure versus impure varies across cultures—though she did find that cultures commonly viewed aspects of the human body as "impure." By unraveling the symbolic meaning underlying the pure/impure classification, one could extrapolate an understanding of the culture, its structure, and worldview. An example of this comes from a Hindu myth of creation. A deity is killed by other gods, and from his mouth comes a group of humans that become priests; his arms become warriors; merchants spring from his thighs, and laborers from his feet. Feet touch the earth, which is unclean, while learning and religious devotion are pure. Thus this myth symbolically represents the ancient Indian caste system in which priests are ranked at the top (i.e., the head of the slain deity) and laborers at the bottom (the feet).

Although symbolic anthropology gained enormous popularity as a method for understanding belief systems, it was not an interpretive framework embraced by all. An almost diametrically opposite approach was offered by Marvin Harris (1927– 2001). In his various works, including *Cows, Pigs, Wars and Witches* (1974) and *Cannibals and Kings: The Origins of Culture* (1977), Harris advanced the interpretive model known as *cultural materialism*. In this approach Harris disavowed the notion of otherworldly symbolic meanings to things, places, or concepts considered sacred in a culture. Rather, he suggested a more pragmatic approach: cultures arrange their religious beliefs (and other cultural institutions) according to modes of production and reproduction—that is, methods of work, population maintenance, and ecological management of the environment. In a somewhat Marxist approach, then, Harris asserted that cultures organize behavior, religious and otherwise, to support these underlying infrastructures, which in turn shape the overarching sociopolitical economy and finally the overall cultural institutions (which Harris calls "superstructures"). In this way religion is simply a response to the material conditions existing in that culture's environmental sphere.

In one of his better-known examples, Harris explained why cows are sacred in India and pigs are forbidden in Judaism and Islam. Harris argued that as humans became more dependent on agricultural products (which co-occurred with population increases), cultures had to make intelligent decisions about the economic management of food resources. Humans could *directly* eat agricultural products, whereas animals had to be fed and nurtured before consumption. It therefore made sense to put more effort into agricultural work and less into animal husbandry. However, some animals needed to be maintained for meat sources as well as for draft labor. But animals that could not effectively serve humans economically, such as pigs, were banned as unneeded. Cattle, which were very useful to humans, could be kept, not for eating but rather for working. One way to ensure the maintenance of cattle, but also guard against the eating of one's work animal, was to make it sacred and thus taboo for consumption. Harris argued that anthropologists could discover, using similar reasoning, the materialistic reasons underlying the superstructure of any culture, including its religious beliefs, economic endeavors, or political institutions.

The Symbolism of Ritual and the Community

Mary Douglas was not the only voice advocating the symbolic approach. Victor Turner (1920–1983) made extremely important contributions to this field, particularly in his analysis of the role ritual plays in cultural constructs. Turner conducted fieldwork among the Ndembu people of eastern Africa, from which he produced his best-known work, *The Forest of Symbols: Aspects of Ndembu Ritual* (1967). For Turner, symbols are both cognitive and emotional responses, "units of meaning" representative of the entire cultural structure. Some symbols are perhaps more straightforwardly understood in that they represent lines of cognitive thought. In Christianity, for instance, the cross represents the wooden structure on which Jesus died. In the Ndembu culture, the white sap of the Mudyi tree represents the breast milk a mother provides her infant. However, each of these central symbols leads to other, more abstract meanings that are a compilation of many important concepts. The reasons underlying Jesus' death are represented by a simple cross, which in turn symbolizes a constellation of important Christian ideological concepts; mother's milk represents fertility, the mother-child bond, and thus the institutions of marriage and family, and the interrelationship these have with other aspects of Ndembu societal structure. Thus, by understanding the cognitive relationship between symbolic meaning and object or place, one can then trace the interconnections within the societal structure.

Turner suggested that each symbol has a "polarization of meaning," in that the symbol represents something physiological, on one hand—such as Jesus' blood on the cross, or mother's breast milk—and the ideological content, such as selfless giving or parental love, on the other. In this way each symbol has what Turner calls a "multivocality" of meaning: individuals or groups may interpret the symbol differently because they are accessing it at different points on the polarization of meaning. However, everyone understands the entire "forest of symbols" and their range of meanings, and this unites them into a community of believers sharing a complex system of symbolic meaning.

In addition to his writings on the interpretation of symbols, Turner made important contributions to the anthropological understanding of ritual. In his book *The Ritual Process: Structure and Anti-Structure* (1969), he described the stages a participant in a rite of passage travels through during the ritual. Rites of passage are rituals that advance a participant from one position in life to another, as from childhood to adulthood, novice to apprentice, and so on. Turner suggested that rite-of-passage participants enter a *liminal* stage, which is a period of marginalization from their society. During this liminality, individuals are neither what they were prior to the rite nor what they will be afterward. Because they have no recognizable position in society, they are often secluded or even ignored. That being the case, all those going through the process together, especially as they experience liminality, bond with one another. All are expected to follow the rules and guidelines of the rite, to heed the directions of their elders, and generally navigate the ritual process as successfully as possible. Those who follow the process together achieve a lifetime bond of unity that Turner called *communitas*. Finally, all the participants emerge from the rite of passage to the other side, shedding their liminal status but retaining their bonds forged in *communitas*.

The Cognitive Science of Religion

One of the most recent explorations into the study of religion takes an overtly scientific approach, seeking to understand how religious belief works within the human mind. Scholars from scientific fields such as neurobiology and zoology collaborate with psychologists and anthropologists to examine how the human mind *believes*—that is, how humans understand religion cognitively. The cognitive evolution of religion was briefly addressed at the beginning of this chapter in the discussion of Boyer's suggestion (2001) that religions emerged from early human emotional and intellectual responses to the challenging and dramatic, and mundane and routine—events and occurrences in an alternatively dangerous, beautiful, unexplainable, but always experiential world.

This idea is echoed in Atran's study (2002) in which he argued that religion developed in an evolutionary "landscape," built from human experiences and perceptions of what they were facing "out there" in the world. Paleolithic peoples, in order to deal with the fear involved in hunting large creatures (or being hunted by them) and engaging in other rather daunting survival strategies, responded by developing a belief in the supernatural, especially spirits; the invention of such beings, events, and actions arose from psychological responses to environmental stimuli that, reinforced through group interaction and passed generationally, became embedded as belief systems. Atran developed his argument to show how humans can be so devout that they are willing to make extraordinary sacrifices for those beliefs, including giving up their own lives (Atran 2002).

A concrete example of studies in the *cognitive science of religion* (see the International Association of the Cognitive Science of Religion website to confirm this field has become well embedded in the field of anthropology; and see Whitehouse and Laidlaw 2007; Whitehouse and Martin 2004; Whitley 2008) was offered by Whitehouse's work on *imagistic modes* (2000, 2004a, 2004b). Whitehouse contrasts this with the *doctrinal mode* in which religious practice is repetitive and routinized, completed according to (often written) direction and thus accomplished almost automatically, without substantial emotional or intellectual investment (2000:154–56). Such practices are the norm in organized religions: Catholic mass, Islamic prayer at specified times, chanting in Hinduism, even proper meditative techniques in Buddhism. Imagistic modes are much more individualistic and therefore elicit a far greater range of responses. The imagistic mode is initiated by a person's experience of a memorable event, a rite of passage or other ritual that incites an exceptional emotional response, such as terror or awe, often accompanied by a physical response such as pain. Since the experience is unique to the individual, the mind must search for and construct a response, a way to understand the experience (Whitehouse 2000:7–9). The event is encoded in the memory in a way that is relevant to that individual only, making the transmission of that experience to others in the same age set, and to those in the next generation, distinctive. The imagistic mode, practiced primarily in small-scale societies, creates a religion unified by the fact that most believers experience the same or similar events; however, each has an individualistic response to them. Believers in such religions live in a more spiritually charged world, since even everyday routines are psychologically translated within the context of their encoded memories of these past experiences; the transmission of religion from one generation to the next, therefore, creates new participants who expect an overwhelming religious experience without guidance as to a specified response. A Religion based on imagistic modes operates on principles of unity in that everyone experiences the religion, but it retains an element of variability in that individual adherents believe based on their powerful memories of their own participation in shared events.

A number of scholars ask why imagistic modes appear to be at the heart of the earliest religions, and by far the more common type practiced throughout human history, while doctrinal modes are found in more recent systems of religious belief. One astute suggestion is that doctrinal modes emerged with the written word (Goody 2004). It is far easier to institutionalize a ritual or religious action when it is written down so that all may follow the prescribed practice. While agreeing that literacy is an important factor, Whitehouse suggested that another human invention, the domestication of agriculture, had a powerful impact (2000, 2004b). As humans all felt the urgency to ensure a fertile earth and a successful harvest, this unity of belief engendered "routinized orthodoxies" (Whitehouse 2004b:228) within increasingly complex societies that relied on agrarian production. Individualistic responses to ecstatically charged events became less important than the need by a majority of the worshippers to engage in the "proper" ritual, led by someone knowledgeable about what the gods required, and to accomplish it without fault. Thus the doctrinal mode was born within the emergence of a unified human need to collectively ensure continued nourishment.

The cognitive science of religion moves the study of humans and their beliefs into the scientific realm, while allowing it to stay firmly anchored in cultural structure. As research continues, the complex intersections of psychology, science, culture, and religion will continue to reveal insights into the origins, and continued practice, of religion in worldwide contexts.

Anthropology and the Study of Religion

There are, of course, dozens of other anthropologists who have offered various models for the interpretation of religion and ritual. Some of these will be introduced in the next chapter, and some of those discussed above will reappear there. By this point, however, a reader has obtained a fairly comprehensive understanding of the various anthropological approaches to understanding religion. This is a crucial underpinning to any archaeological approach that seeks to illuminate a culture's religious belief system. Failing to understand how the anthropological discipline interprets *living* religions is a prelude to interpretive mistakes in understanding those in ancient times. The next chapter reviews how archaeologists have built on these interpretive frameworks to explain the past.

USEFUL SOURCES

Fiona Bowie, *The Anthropology of Religion*, 2006.
Brian Morris, *Anthropological Studies of Religion: An Introductory Text*, 1987.
Harvey Whitehouse and James Laidlaw, *Ritual and Memory*, 2004.

3

INTERPRETING RELIGION
IN THE ARCHAEOLOGICAL PAST

While Chapter 2 featured anthropological theories about religion, this one focuses more on archaeological approaches. The various components that make up belief systems are defined, and methods for recognizing their material manifestations are outlined. In the final section, the theoretical underpinnings employed in this book, briefly mentioned in Chapter 1, are discussed.

Cosmology, Myth, and Ritual

Understanding the meaning of these three terms—*cosmology*, *myth*, and *ritual*—and how the concepts function within cultural contexts is a first crucial step in understanding past or present belief systems.

Cosmology and Worldview

Cosmology is a word that describes the less tangible elements of a belief system. Another phrase with a similar connotation of intangibility is *religious worldview*. *Worldview* refers to a culture's perception of reality: how do people and society fit into the workings of the world, and how, in fact, does the world work? Some cultures have a *naturalistic* worldview, believing that humans exist as one part of a vastly complicated natural system. Alternatively, the Western worldview would perhaps be described as "scientific," in that physical and logical laws are at the basis of how the world works; if these laws can be understood and mastered, then the world can be controlled, and humans are in a unique position to sit at the helm of the controls. A culture's cosmology refers to its religious worldview, including the workings of the supernatural world and how humans fit into and interrelate with it. A culture's cosmology is expressed in its myths and rituals, and it is through these that researchers grasp a culture's perception of the supernatural and natural world.

Myth

Myth is a common term that is often misunderstood to mean "fictional" stories. Myths are the sacred stories that explain the basis of a culture's belief system. Mythologies contain creation stories, describe what happens after death, reveal how supernatural beings came about, and explain all elements necessary for understanding the universe. Here is where ethnocentrism must be kept to a minimum and cultural relativism ratcheted up to maximum, as these sacred stories are believed to be describing true events by the culture with which they are associated.

Myths also reveal a great deal of important information about the culture. Past events often become embedded in mythical stories; these give the researcher important clues to cultural history and also yield insight into occurrences that might have shaped the culture's worldview. For instance, ancient Middle Eastern mythological stories tell of a terrible flood that devastated humankind. In fact, the widespread presence of flood myths in Western Asian mythologies has led scientists to search for clues to just such an event.

Myths are part of a larger oral tradition (which sometimes becomes written) that also includes folklore, the latter describing stories and legends considered secular but which may have "larger than life" or even magical and supernatural occurrences contained within the account. Folkloric stories are usually about past events with human actors and may have embedded important cultural information about historical occurrences, and cultural values, mores, and ideals. In this way they reinforce the subtexts offered within many of the culture's myths. Researchers interested in a culture's religion are wise to acquire knowledge not only about the myths, but about the folkloric tradition as well.

Beyond simply learning the meaning of myths, researchers must seek to understand their function within the society. For instance, Durkheim and Malinowski take a functional approach to myths; they and others suggest that myths maintain societal structure by reminding believers of the crucial codes of behavior, value system, and morality that shape the culture as a whole. Structuralists such as Lévi-Strauss assert that analyzing the mythic structure yields clues to the underlying configuration of the society; more important than the story itself is what elements are in opposition to each other, which figures work together, and so on. For instance, a myth that portrays a great deal of tension between male and female supernatural beings is indicative of the same oppositional structure within the society. Other scholars focus more on the symbolism contained in sacred stories. For instance, in Greek mythology, Demeter's daughter, Kore, is taken down into the underworld. There she consumes some pomegranate seeds and so cannot return permanently to the upperworld. Kore ascends to spend spring and summer with her mother and descends in the fall, staying through winter. In this way she symbolizes the birth and growth of the agricultural cycle and the dormancy of the earth in the winter months. These were crucial concepts to the agriculturally based ancient Greeks.

Ritual

Although we associate the word *ritual* with religious behavior, it can have a secular meaning as well. In general, a ritual refers to repetitive and routinized behavior. Children in a U.S. elementary school who stand, place hands over hearts, and recite the Pledge of Allegiance every morning are performing a secular ritual. Rituals are repetitive in that the process of events is the same, and usually there are no surprises in store. All the children know what they are supposed to do and say and roughly when it is supposed to happen.

Rituals are, of course, one of the core components of a culture's religion. They are closely tied with the culture's mythology and are often structured according to guidelines in a myth. Performers in the ritual may even act out the story contained in a myth. Rituals may be held frequently, or at special times; they may be public or private, elaborate or simple, led by an official, or performed individually. Rituals can be examined and categorized in terms of *when* they are performed, which helps us get partially at the *how* and *why*. Some rituals happen frequently and at particular times, such as the prescription that Muslims must pray five times a day at set intervals. Such rituals might be easier to recognize in the archaeological record because paraphernalia associated with such frequent activities might have some permanent material culture associated with them. Other rituals are more situational, in that they are occasioned by a crisis or unexpected event (Stein and Stein 2005). A good example of this is a series of protective rituals performed when a culture is under attack and must send out its warriors. A third category of rituals comprises those that are infrequent but still happen at particular times, perhaps according to an annual cycle. A harvest festival, the Christian celebration of Christmas, or the Muslim pilgrimage to Mecca are good examples of such periodic rituals (Stein and Stein 2005). Because such rituals tend to be rather extensive, they too might be detectable in the archaeological record.

Determining the reason for a ritual is perhaps even more important than identifying its frequency. Some rituals are meant simply to pay tribute to a supernatural being. In propitiating the supernatural world, the performers are also ensuring continued goodwill and protection from the "rulers" of their universe. Other rituals are directly related to specific tasks such as food acquisition. These might be *nature* rituals that are performed to keep the natural world functioning properly, or to fix a problem such as drought, pestilence, or other anomaly. Rituals may be performed to ensure a successful hunt, to bring about a fertile crop cycle, or to keep a herd healthy and safe from evil. Another category of rituals is aimed more at humans and can be deemed protective in nature (Stein and Stein 2005). These would take place before dangerous activities, to protect children from evil, or when a group fears an external threat such as attack. Healing rituals are a type that is quite commonly found. A final specific category of ritual that should be discussed is the rite of passage.

As already outlined in Chapter 2, rites of passage are rituals that stand at the intersection of one individual's or group's stage of life and the next. Passing though the rite of passage advances the participant into a new life stage. A few rites of passage can be elaborate and can last hours, days, months, and even years; during this time participants are symbolically removed from society, existing in a liminal state, as described in Chapter 2. Participants complete the rite of passage feeling newly born into their society and having formed more tightly knit ties with their age group (*communitas*; see Chapter 2) who endured the experience with them.

Functionalists such as Malinowski viewed rituals as methods to relieve anxiety and offer comfort to performers, and Durkheim interpreted rituals as methods to ensure social order and reinforce important societal codes, allowing society to operate smoothly. Cognitive science studies suggest the practice of ritual is a deep-seated psychological response to a multitude of external stimuli (Sørensen 2007). The many approaches to understanding ritual demonstrate its vital role within religious systems.

Myths, Rituals, and the Archaeological Record

It is one thing to describe how anthropologists identify myth and ritual in a culture and another to knowingly observe remnants of such religious components in the archaeological record. Ritual behavior is easier to identify archaeologically than are myths, since ritual practices are more likely to leave behind material culture (e.g., altars, offering bowls, burned animal bones) (Figure 3.1). However, the old cliché in archaeology, "if you can't identify the artifact, it must be a ritual item," is both a truism and a trap. When dealing with artifacts, there is virtue in suspecting something unusual may have had religious/ritual uses. In part this is because archaeologists who are extremely well versed in material culture will recognize when an object may be non-utilitarian and thus possibly non-secular. However, it is easy to fall into the trap of automatically assigning an artifact to a "ritual" category and thereby failing to pursue other interpretations. Furthermore, "everyday"

Figure 3.1. Artistic rendering of a ritual. Note the presence of a stone basin, ritual vessels, and a stone platform for a table. (*M. J. Hughes*)

objects may also take on ritual meaning in religious contexts; the lunchtime soup bowl may become the depository for an offering to the ancestor at the evening ritual. The best advice for unusual artifacts is to keep an open mind while harboring a suspicion that a piece of the "religion puzzle" may be that very item.

It might be somewhat easier to identify locales where ritual activity took place, especially if there is some knowledge of what type of rituals were normally carried out in the culture. Regular and frequent rituals and major annual events will be more easily detected than crisis rituals which occur infrequently. Practices involving fire, water, animals, and other elements or materials that require built structures (such as altars or basins for water; see examples in Figure 3.1) or leave remains such as burned animal bones are obviously very useful in advancing the archaeologist's understanding of ritual behavior (Renfrew 1994). Areas of a settlement set aside for practices that seem other than domestic might have served ritual purposes. Clues to activities lie in features and artifacts found in such an area; interpretation is then aided by the archaeologist's deep-seated knowledge about the culture's behavioral patterns (Whitley 2005).

Retrieving myths archaeologically is far more challenging, especially if the culture was preliterate or nonliterate and the cosmology was transmitted orally from one generation to the next. At this point the archaeologist might well flap her hands in frustration and decide the mythology is beyond reach. However, it must be remembered that the cosmology and the myths that reveal it are part and parcel of everyday life and may very well be represented in both religious and everyday items. Naturally, special locations such as rock art sites would require particular attention; suspecting that a culture's myth is embedded in the message would be a logical inference. It would be a mistake, however, to designate the rock or wall paintings as religious and ignore the small story told on the shoulder of a ceramic pot, thinking instead it is "just decoration." The geometric figures carved on the handle of an adze may well be symbolic representations of important elements in the creation myth; the small bone carving of an animal could be a miniature of the sacred animal spirit rather than a child's toy. Clues could abound in the mundane, there to be revealed if the right interpretive framework is applied. The danger here, of course, is seeing representations of myth in things that are indeed only mundane, everyday tools without an ounce of religiosity about them, or, of course, ignoring something such as the soup bowl even though it becomes the ritual bowl a few hours later. Here the holistic approach is crucial. Examining the context of all the discoveries and making well-considered, evidence-based interpretations may allow an archaeologist a glimpse into a culture's sacred stories.

Supernatural Beings and Religious Specialists

In the study of any religion, it is important to understand the types of supernatural beings that occur in that religion and to know which beings are most common. This depends on a given culture's worldview and socioeconomic and political complexity. Identifying the types of specialists most likely to interact with the supernatural world is also crucial.

Supernatural Beings

There are several types of supernatural beings: spirits, ghosts, and deities (gods and goddesses). There are numerous ways to classify these supernatural beings, including whether they generally have human or non-human origins, what roles they play in a society, and which types are likely to be present in cultures of varying social, economic, and political complexity.

The broadest category of beings is the one known as *spirits*. In most belief systems, these beings, with the exception of ancestor spirits, have non-human origins. Spirits either predate the creation of the world or were created with it, and they usually had a hand in the creation of humans. Spirits generally inhabit the same world as humans but on a different plane, normally invisible to the humans around them. Various rituals and codes of behavior encourage favorable behavior toward humans. Hunting-gathering cultures are quite likely to have animistic belief systems, and such cosmologies can also be found in cultures practicing herding and small-scale cultivation economies. Spirits may also be more individualized, with specific names, and they may inhabit particular places considered sacred. Though spirits are usually well disposed toward humans, it is unwise to anger these beings by mistreating them or their domains.

A subcategory of spirits found in many cultures is sometimes referred to as *tricksters*—spirits who are overtly hostile to humans, although in some cases they can be cajoled into being helpful. Tricksters include such beings as leprechauns in Ireland, the Middle Eastern jinn, or the coyote of some Native American belief systems (note that some anthropologists consider tricksters a type of deity rather than a spirit [e.g., Stein and Stein 2005]). The function of trickster spirits is to cause problems for the unsuspecting human, particularly one who is misbehaving in some fashion. Tricksters are particularly useful in encouraging correct behavior in children and can also be blamed for seemingly undeserved misfortune.

Another category of spirits consists of the *ancestor spirits*. These spirits were once human and are closely associated with the familial unit from which they came. Ancestor spirits inhabit the homes or lands of their lineage and generally serve to guard and protect the family and its holdings. Shrines to the ancestors are built either in the home or in other sacred locations where prayers, offerings, and rituals can be performed to keep the relationship strong and healthy. Ancestor veneration is a widespread phenomenon, but it is most often found in societies with a strong lineage descent system, with inheritance rights involving lands, material property, and leadership roles.

Ghosts, another category of supernatural beings, are uniformly thought to have had human origins and, unlike most spirits, do not have the well-being of humans in mind. Ghosts can cause a host of problems for the families from which they came. Cultures with a strong belief in ghosts might exhibit *ghost fear*, patterns of behavior designed to minimize the impact ghosts of the recently deceased might have on the living. An example of this is the Navajo practice of closing up a *hogan* (house) in which someone has died. All the deceased's belongings are left there, and people refrain from entering the hogan in order to avoid infection from *ghost sickness*. A belief in ghosts and ghost fear can be found in many cultures regardless of their socioeconomic or political structure.

Deities, like spirits, are usually viewed as having had non-human origins, although this is not always the case. Some humans become deified, either by the action of the deities or through processes such as the automatic deification of rulers. Unlike spirits, deities usually reside separately from humans, not among them. They may inhabit an upperworld or underworld, a distant location such as Mount Olympus in the ancient Greek cosmology, or otherwise carry out their lives separate from humans. Deities are usually fairly individualized personalities, with names, characteristics, and agendas. Mythologies tell of their lives and how they interact with one another and with their human charges. Deities are often anthropomorphic in that they resemble humans and have emotional responses similar to those of humans in their culture. If the belief system is polytheistic, with a pantheon of gods and goddesses, there will usually be a hierarchy within the pantheon, with a supreme deity, or a group at the top, and other beings of descending importance, each responsible for some aspect of human existence (e.g., creation, fire, love, war, etc.). Religions identified as monotheistic, such as present-day Judaism, Christianity, and Islam, are less common than polytheistic systems. Religions that feature gods and goddesses tend to be associated with societies that have more complex sociopolitical and economic systems, such as chiefdoms and states. Such cultures may also recognize a collection of spirit beings, but in most instances they will be considered inferior in power and importance to their godly counterparts.

Religious Specialists

Although rituals and ceremonies can be carried out by individuals, it is common for specialists to assist believers. Specific terms to describe specialists are used here as technical anthropological terminology, but it should be kept in mind that individual cultures employ a variety of terms to describe their religious specialists.

Though the next chapter deals specifically with *shamans* as religious specialists, some general characteristics can be described here. Shamans do exist in highly complex societies, but they are usually secondary relative to priests, who are sanctioned by the government. The shaman is most likely to be the main religious specialist in hunting-and-gathering societies, small-scale herding and cultivating cultures, and other agrarian-based social systems. A shaman is often a part-time practitioner, meaning that he or she performs duties when called upon, but otherwise lives very much like anyone else in the culture. Shamans acquire their training either through natural ability—that is, they are imbued by the spirits—or by observation and sometimes apprenticeship with another shaman. The selection process for shamans is as varied as the cultures who have them, ranging from the recognition of innate abilities, to selection because of one's status or family. Shamans are sought out by their people to fix such problems as illness, misfortune, and environmental distress, and to counteract sorcery. Although shamans perform services for large groups, they are usually commissioned by an individual client. Shamans are generally thought of as acting beneficially toward their people, and successful shamans can amass a fair amount of power and status. However, shamans are also capable of casting ill on believers and thus tread the line between shaman and sorcerer in the minds of many. Indeed, it is not uncommon for a shaman to cure someone of illness cast by another shaman.

The religious specialists known as *priests* and *priestesses* are far more likely to be found in chiefdoms, states, empires, and other societies with complex sociopolitical and economic systems. Such cultures have a formalized religious structure, often with sacred written texts and sanctified buildings used only for religious purposes. In some cultures priests are selected much like shamans: by natural ability or by cosmological sign. In others, individuals choose the priesthood as a profession; some cultures require that families with multiple sons send one to enter the priesthood (Stein and Stein 2005). Because they operate in more populous systems, with more duties to carry out on a daily basis, priests tend to be full-time specialists. They are supported either by the government, by offerings from the people, or both. For the same reason, priests, and usually priestesses, receive specific and regularized training in preparation for their duties, including formal schooling and more individualized apprenticeships. As priests are full-time practitioners, they can usually be identified as such by their dress, accoutrements, or some other indicator of their position even in nonreligious settings. This is different from a shaman, who can usually only be identified when performing a ceremony.

Another difference between shamans and priests is their "clients." While individuals in the society are the shaman's client, priests exist to carry out the wishes of the supernatural beings, the gods and goddesses. In other words, the main role of priests and priestesses is to guide the behavior of the population according to the strictures set out in the sacred texts or oral tradition (mythology) of the culture. Thus, while shamans work on behalf of the needs of the people, priests labor on behalf of the desires of the gods. The priest's job is to interpret the will of the god(s), to help humans perform the proper rituals and ceremonies to honor the supernatural order, and to ensure that humans behave according to religious and societal codes. At times the work of a priest may conflict with the will of the people. However, because of their position and status, priests most often prevail, and the religion and its practice remains consistent and strong.

A final category of religious specialists is *witches and sorcerers* (either of which can be male or female). One of the main differences between the two types is that sorcerers are considered skilled at manipulating magic to carry out their wishes, whereas witches are born with the innate abilities to accomplish their goals. Both, in anthropological terms, are practitioners whose main concern is not the health and welfare of their culture. Rather, witches and sorcerers often *intend* to cause ill fortune for individuals, groups, or even the entire society. They carry out their work either for their own personal reasons (revenge, ill will, personal gain) or on behalf of a client. These specialists possess magic or innate abilities that enable them to exert control over certain supernatural powers (and thus are not like priests or shamans in this regard). Because of their dubious role in society, the identity of witches and sorcerers is often, but not always, hidden.

Though witchcraft and sorcery are usually used to cause problems, belief in such specialists and their crafts is fairly widespread in societies; they are commonly blamed for illness or other misfortune that seems unexplainable. Shamans might be employed to search out the witch, or the spell, and then effect a healing ceremony to bring about a cure (but note that shamans are also capable of using their power to cause misfortune). There are many anthropological explanations for the common belief in witchcraft and sorcery, but one aspect is clear: fear of angering a witch or sorcerer, or someone who has access to one, serves to keep improper behavior to a minimum. Individuals do not wish to risk the wrath of a witch or sorcerer and so refrain from acting in ways that are contrary to societal norms. In this way witchcraft and sorcery act as social controls for behavior.

One clarification regarding the term *witch* is necessary here, and that is in regard to the present-day religion known as Wicca. Wiccan practitioners generally refer to themselves as witches, and though they consider part of their ritual to include "magic," they do not conform to the anthropological definition of witch or sorcerer described above. The Wiccan religion is one that has a particular focus on nature and sees its roots in pre-Christian European practices that recognized the sacred essence of the earth. Wiccan magic and rituals are meant to bring about good and engender a healthy and harmonious life for its practitioners. The example of Wiccan "witches" serves to illustrate the differences between anthropological terminology and actual word use within cultures. An anthropologist studying Wicca might describe the religious specialists as shamans in an ethnography, thereby capturing the actual role a Wiccan witch plays in her society. In similar fashion, a culture might call its religious practitioner by a term that loosely translates to "priest," but anthropologically that individual may be described as a shaman, or perhaps a sorcerer. Careful use of anthropological terminology, therefore, with additional description and explanation, alleviates the types of confusion that might occur if an anthropologist is guided only by terms used *within* the culture.

Supernatural Beings, Religious Practitioners, and the Archaeological Record

It is sometimes difficult to find evidence of spirits and gods in the archaeological record, not to mention ghosts and tricksters. When is an ivory carving of a cow a representation of the Bull God and when is it a child's toy (or, as discussed earlier, when is it both)? Do cattle seem important? Were they hunted, used as crucial work animals, prevalent in the faunal record? Was the ivory carving found in what appears to be a normal household area or in a location that has been designated as "specialized"? One must also consider that its domestic location may not indicate a nonreligious use but rather its importance as a household deity. Other evidence makes it slightly easier on the archaeologist: half-animal/half-human representations can usually be safely deemed supernatural; humans represented with special paraphernalia (e.g., elaborate headdresses, or halos) or shown larger than those around them are often indicative of divinity. When such pieces of evidence are located and compiled with what is known about the culture's myth and ritual, though huge gaps may still exist, some aspects of the individual supernatural players in the cosmology start to become clearer.

It is admittedly much easier to identify a priest than a shaman, a shaman than a witch. Priests, because of their full-time status, specialized clothing, and symbols of office are more evident in the material culture left behind. This is particularly true if priests were housed separately from the nonreligious population, perhaps in specialized areas near or inside a religious structure. This does not mean that shamans are invisible.

Shamans, too, have their religious paraphernalia, their costumes, and tools of their trade. In excavating a domestic setting, the archaeologist who discovers items that are unusual, not found in other houses, would be wise to wonder, "could this be a shaman's house?" The same methodology used to identify the presence of a shaman might also be used to discover evidence of a witch or sorcerer, especially if the archaeologist suspects the culture under investigation harbored such practitioners. Unusual items, hidden away in a secret household compartment, might be a wonderful clue alerting an archaeologist to the possibility of a less-than-helpful religious practitioner. It is, however, most difficult to identify these practitioners in the archaeological record; while evidence of shamans and priests are often described in archaeological accounts, witches and sorcerers are peculiarly absent from the past. It is not that they weren't there; it is just that as they sought to remain hidden in their own cultures, so do they remain hidden from us.

Method and Theory in the Archaeology of Religion

The combination of archaeology and religion is nothing new. Finding the trappings of religion and ritual, and interpreting them, has been a mainstay in the field since its inception. A number of excellent treatises on mortuary practices and what we can learn from how a society treated its dead form important underpinnings to the study of religion (e.g., O'Shea 1984; Tainter 1978; Ucko 1969). In the last several decades, a number of well-regarded archaeologists have undertaken the task of not only investigating the religions of past cultures, but writing about how to do so. More recently, work has focused on a broader description of the *archaeology of religion* and has even elevated it to a subdiscipline within the larger field (Edwards 2003; Whitley 2005).

The first guideline in the archaeology of religion is, as Kent Flannery and Joyce Marcus remind us, that such an approach belongs firmly in the realm of *cognitive archaeology*, in that it comprises "the study of all those aspects of ancient culture that are the product of the human mind" (1993:264). This includes cosmology, religion, ideology, iconography, and any other product of human intellect and symbolic beliefs. The most successful cognitive archaeology takes place when there is a wealth of information already available about the culture; when little is yet understood, the archaeologist must proceed very cautiously to avoid misinterpretation and unintended misdirection. Cognitive methods allow the archaeologist to step beyond the object, to attempt to reattach the emotion, belief, and action associated with what are otherwise static material remains. Applied with caution, cognitive archaeology is one important key to the successful interpretation of past religions.

In a similar approach, Colin Renfrew's article "The Archaeology of Religion" (1994) begins by reminding the reader that religion is a product of the human mind and is only partially manifested in material remains. Renfrew insists that the archaeologist must recognize the mystery, power, and experience embodied in religious belief systems, and that the cognitive map of how to navigate mores, values, and ideals is embedded in that system. He recommends, for instance, that in addition to a ritual location—perhaps a natural place such as a cave or a human-constructed locale—the

researcher should seek attention-focusing devices that enclosed the participants physically and psychologically into a ritual performance. These sacred locations were often
considered the boundary zone between this world and the next; therefore, indicators
of purifying processes (e.g., basins) might be present. Renfrew directs our attention to
any symbols found in such a place; these, he asserts, are sure to provide insight into
who or what was the subject of adulation there. Finally, it is worthwhile to try to imagine the movements of the worshipper(s) during the ceremony; besides possible purification procedures, were food and drink consumed, offerings made, or ritual movements performed? Such questions will, Renfrew assures us, yield a deeper
understanding of the religion and ritual under consideration.

Cave and rock paintings are very productive areas of religion-related archaeological research. As the many authors in Whitley's (ed., 2001) *Handbook of Rock Art
Research* tell us, one must start not "with the pictures" but rather with the people who
made them. In the Western view of "art," artistic activity is considered a luxury rather
than an integral component of society; the messages embedded in Western art need
not represent larger cultural themes, either religious or secular (Chippindale 2001;
Lewis-Williams 2002). Western archaeologists thus must shed their preconceived
notions of artistic representations as "marginal" or "non-representative" and delve
deeply into what meanings were intended by the creators of images on rock faces and
cave walls. Instructions on how to interpret cave and rock art are myriad and are usually particular to the culture involved, their environment, and historical circumstances. For instance, an archaeologist should not be surprised to find boats drawn by
island cultures who may have origin myths recounting great travels across the sea
(such as the Maori culture and their origin story about the hero who traveled to the
"land of the long white cloud," that is, New Zealand). Nonetheless, cave and rock art
specialists caution us about over-interpretation: when is a hunting scene just a hunting scene, and when is it a shamanistic ritual to guarantee the success of future hunts?

The first step in interpretation is to ask, as one author puts it, "what is it a picture of?" (Chippindale 2001:254). Based on one's understanding of the culture and
ecological setting, the researcher might have already set up classifications for pictorial types, such as animal, human, geometric, and so on. One might then ask questions of the art: Is a story or myth being told? Were components added to the image
over time? Was it repainted repeatedly, perhaps at annual rituals? It is important to
remember that such art is a cognitive product, which is, at its most basic, an attempt
to express human consciousness as it struggles to understand a cosmological and
physical universe. Keeping that daunting notion at the forefront of all interpretive
efforts will lend depth to any archaeological analysis.

Sacred places that use architecture or natural monuments are also important targets of study in the archaeology of religion. Because each sacred space and the structures built or found upon it are products of the culture that revered them, the archaeologist must begin asking questions not about the space and the monuments but
rather about the culture that created them (Steadman 2005). This would include asking why that particular spot was important: was it chosen on account of economic fac-

tors, or can important natural landmarks be observed that might have influenced the choice of that locale (e.g., the confluence of rivers, a slight rise in a flat landscape, an unusual rock formation)? Another research direction asks who built the structure(s) or used the sacred space. Was it open to the entire community, particular kin groups, or only to elites? The important questions to ask are dictated by what the archaeologist already knows about the culture and its belief system.

The last fifteen years, and especially the last ten, have seen a number of books exploring the religions of cultures past (e.g., Fagan 1998; Insoll, ed. 1999, 2001; Whitehouse and Martin 2004; Whitley and Hays-Gilpin 2008), clearly elevating the archaeology of religion to a new level and focus. An expanded treatment on the subject, titled *A Prehistory of Religion: Shamans, Sorcerers and Saints,* by Brian Hayden, appeared in 2003. This book is really the soup-to-nuts treatment of the subject, with analyses ranging from the very origins of religion to the roots of the major traditions of today. Hayden approaches the study of past religions from two theoretical viewpoints. First, he believes that human emotion and its expression are central to the formation and structure of a culture's religion. Second, he asserts that ecological factors are equally important in a culture's religious belief system. A very recent publication on method and theory in archaeology includes a prominent chapter on "The Archaeology of Religion" (Whitley 2005), in which the author discusses the growth of the field, the difficulty of both defining religion as well as identifying beliefs in the past, and the methods archaeologists should employ to do both. There is no doubt that the archaeology of religion is alive and well as a research endeavor in the early twenty-first century.

Interpreting Beliefs in Worldwide Context

Each culture, including its religion, is unique in its mythology, cosmology, rituals, and other components. That said, however, general observances about the role religions play in societal structure can be discerned. An important observation about world religions is the remarkable level to which many mirror their cultural structures. That is, aspects of a culture's worldview, and elements of its sociopolitical or economic structure, are quite often easily identified in the cosmology.

One straightforward example of religion reflecting its societal structure can be found in the types of supernatural agents that exist in a culture's belief system. A hunter-gatherer society that is essentially egalitarian is likely to have an animistic religion featuring spirits of relatively equal power. Religious practitioners in such a culture will not hold exalted positions, and usually most, if not all, members of the society may act as intermediaries with the supernatural realm. By contrast, societies that are socially ranked tend to feature religions that have ranked spirits (ancestor or otherwise) or gods and may also believe in a high or supreme deity at the helm of the supernatural coterie (Swanson 1969). Such cultures may have full-time religious practitioners who occupy a special position in the society and who are essential to the successful enactment of public rituals.

In a similar vein, the economy and other important institutions can also be viewed as critical components in the belief system. For instance, the Inuit cultures of the Arctic Circle believe that all animals have souls. Much of Inuit religion involves elaborate rituals and taboos embedded in the hunting process so that animal spirits do not become angry and cause living animals to evade Inuit hunters (Pelly 2001). We are not surprised, therefore, when earth fertility is a focus in a culture that depends on cultivation, or when the appeasement of war gods is crucial to a frequently warring society.

Anthropologists have also observed that the level of external stress on a society seems to have a direct correlation to the amount of harm the supernatural world can visit on individuals. If a culture exists in a sociologically or ecologically "difficult neighborhood," one is likely to find that the supernatural world is a bit fickle and unpredictable as well. For instance, the Ik culture of Uganda, the subject of *The Mountain People* (1972) by Colin Turnbull, live in a harsh environment given to frequent droughts. Surrounded by other peoples who also need land and resources, the Ik constantly feel social as well as environmental stress. In their creation story, the creator deity becomes angered by Ik behavior and withdraws his attention from humans, leaving the Ik to fend for themselves without supernatural guidance. The Ik must not only survive in a "rough neighborhood," but also must navigate a supernatural world full of pitfalls and difficulties.

Cultures that live in a difficult and dangerous environment often take great steps to ensure supernatural support. For instance, on Easter Island, massive statues called Moai, dedicated to the ancestors, were erected by the Polynesian colonists. The effort to create and erect these statues was enormous, showing colonists' devotion to their ancestors. However, overcultivation and logging left the landscape treeless, which soon led to an environmental crisis. No trees meant no canoes for fishing and no escape from the island. Food shortages caused a deterioration in the societal structure which then led to internal warfare. Anger toward ancestors who failed to protect their descendants, as well as intra-island competition, caused inhabitants to topple the Moai and to behave increasingly violently, including, possibly, engaging in cannibalism. As the society became more aggressive, due to resource competition, so did the rituals and belief system practiced.

That culture and religion are reflective of each other is an important concept in the archaeology of religion, since archaeological endeavors often reveal a great deal about a culture's social, economic, and political structure; an understanding that religion reflects culture can serve as a crucial interpretive tool in revealing that culture's belief system. The following section explores three other interpretive frameworks that may serve as valuable aids for identifying the interplay between religion and culture. While not all of the religions discussed in this book conform to these interpretive guidelines, a surprising number of them do.

The Interrelationship of Religion and Environment

The concept of a human–environment balance is a common one in many of the world's cultures (see, e.g., Hayden 2003). A naturalistic worldview dictates that humans live *within* the ecological setting, that they are part of the whole. Quite often, methods of maintaining an ecological balance are embedded in the cosmology and enforced by the supernatural world, thereby ensuring complete cooperation on the part of the entire culture (Reichel-Dolmatoff 1976). An example of this comes from pre-contact Chero-kee culture. Prior to a successful deer hunt, a Cherokee hunter performed an impor-tant ritual that ensured environmental and spiritual balance and harmony, even with the loss of a deer. The arrival of European colonists who desired numerous deerskins (in exchange for cheap guns) caused the Cherokee to hunt so frequently and kill deer in such quantities that the balance and harmony ritual ceased to be performed (Ander-son 1991). This unbalancing of the relationship between humans and their environ-ment caused a great deal of anxiety among the Cherokee people.

Religion and environment may also serve as the basis for societal stability. For instance, the Wape of New Guinea, traditionally egalitarian, believe that lineage ancestors inhabit and protect certain areas of the forest; only descendants of that lin-eage can hunt successfully in that region. In this way the Wape ensure that all hunters have "protected" hunting grounds to provide for their families, thereby ensuring egal-itarianism (Mitchell 1987). Other cultures are more concerned with using religion to manipulate and control not only the environment, but also the humans in it. Compet-itive individuals or groups seek an advantage by which to rise to greater levels of pow-er than their rivals. Often that advantage is control of important resources found in the surrounding environment. Hayden and others suggest that the building of large stone tombs, a practice that emerged in the Bronze Age of the British Isles, was, in large part, an attempt to control a landscape that was becoming increasingly impor-tant to these early farming societies (2003). The elaborate burial of ancestors served to mark the land as controlled by descendants; the larger the tomb that could be built and the larger the tract of land controlled, the more important the living descendant.

All too often researchers into the past become too focused on material remains as keys to understanding the past. However, cognitive archaeology reminds us that cultures lived *within* an ecological setting and that the material data are simply important clues to how that culture related with its environment. This is one of the real keys to revealing a past belief system.

Religion and Social Control

Religion can be used as a method to control the actions of people and to coerce believers into behaviors and actions that are contrary to what is perceived as normal-cy; examples include the performance of tremendous labor without recompense, or the curtailing of previously enjoyed social freedoms. There are many methods that can be employed to guide human behavior: inspiring fundamentalist beliefs; instill-ing fear, awe, or unquestioning belief in a deified ruler; or convincing a population that certain actions will ensure the health of the entire community. Though not exclusive to them, many of these methods can occur in complex societies.

Fundamentalism

Religious fundamentalism can be considered a method of social control, not because some overarching authority demands compliance to fundamentalist beliefs (although that is often the case), but rather because the fundamentalists hold *themselves* to these behaviors and codes, with the fervent conviction that beliefs and customs constitute the true *essence* of religion. By adhering to their prescribed customs, they believe they will repel moral danger and cultural dissolution.

As the term implies, fundamentalists are known for belief in the absolute "basics" of their religion, what they perceive to be the original practice, undiluted by time and the impact of secular elements. Quite often fundamentalism develops when believers unite to act against something they perceive will threaten their culture and religion (Stein and Stein 2005; Crapo 2003). In the twentieth and twenty-first centuries, such threats would include modernity, secularism, "Westernization," and capitalism; in times past, the Enlightenment, the Scientific Revolution, and the Industrial Revolution spawned fundamentalist sects in Europe and the United States. The fundamentalist approach is authoritarian in that fundamentalist leaders insist on total obedience and adherence to accepted customs and codes as defined by their interpretation of the religion. At times the line separating religious fundamentalism and extremism is difficult to determine (Kimball 2003). In Taliban-controlled Afghanistan in the early 1990s, Taliban rules of conduct imposed on the people of Afghanistan went far beyond anything outlined in the Qu'ranic sacred texts of Islam. On the other hand, the Taliban did indeed view themselves as fervent religious believers who were trying to steer the people away from dangerous secularism, modernity, and Westernization, back to the fold of a Taliban version of proper Islam.

Though today we see fundamentalism as a reaction against elements of modernity, we should not discount the possibility that fundamentalist sects may have existed in past cultures. That is, fundamentalist tendencies could have developed if conditions were right for them. If conditions such as conquest and imperialism and forced cultural or religious conversion existed, and if material culture suggests a redoubling of traditional rituals and beliefs, then archaeologists should not dismiss as impossible the emergence of fundamentalist practices.

Religion and Politics: Pathway to Social Control

Most often, the combination of religion and political authority is accomplished in complex societies such as chiefdoms, states, and empires. Social control through religio-political means is achieved through the establishment of a *theocracy* in which the government is essentially one and the same with the religion, when ruling elites imbue themselves with divine characteristics, or both (Lewellen 2003).

We can turn once again to the example of the Taliban, who were on their way to establishing a theocracy in Afghanistan prior to their defeat in the U.S.-led war in 2002. Taliban "religious police" patrolled the streets of Kabul looking for violators of the stringent guidelines for behavior and appearance set out in many public announcements. The vast majority of the population complied not because they agreed with the fundamentalist (or, extremist) beliefs touted by the Taliban, but because they feared for their lives and the lives of their families if they did not. Taliban rule in Afghanistan is a prime example of how religion, politics, and threat can combine into an extremely effective method of social control. That most Afghanis are Muslim and therefore would have believed, to some extent, that they were following the wishes of their religion by complying with Taliban orders helped the process along.

Another successful method to achieve social control through religion is for rulers to declare themselves divine. The archaeological record shows us many such empires with deified rulers who portrayed themselves as intricately interwoven with the culture's cosmology. One short-lived example is the first Qin Dynasty ruler in China (221–210 B.C.E.), who came to power during a time of bloodshed and chaos. The Qin emperor vowed to restore harmony with the cosmos, essentially balancing the *yin/yang* which had been disturbed:

> The emperor was Man *par excellence* within the tripartite unity of Heaven, Earth, and Man which composed the cosmos. . . . Thus the macrocosm and the microcosm—humans, the state, and the natural order—were bound together into a single, complex, organic whole through the medium of the body of the ruler. (Yates 2001:367)

The people's belief in this gave the Qin emperor tremendous power over them. During his short reign he was able to compel them to carry out monumental building projects, including the completion of the Great Wall of China. The first Qin emperor is famous for his mausoleum, in which as many as 7,000 terracotta soldiers, along with horses, chariots, and other military equipment, were entombed with him. Laborers were forced to build this mausoleum and artisans to create the soldiers. Only a portion of the emperor's tomb has yet been excavated; it remains to be seen whether human sacrifice was also demanded.

Examples derived from cultures with written records have left explanations of their notions of a divine ruling class. Not all early complex societies were literate, though. For instance, the ancient Hawaiian chiefdoms and other Polynesian societies did not produce written records, and yet there is ample evidence that some may well have made use of religion as a method of social control. The archaeologist who finds a blurring of the lines between the supernatural world and the earthly ruler, combined with monumental works or other evidence of controlled labor, would do well to consider the possibility that the ruling elite used religion as a tool of power.

Religion as a Tool for Change

Fundamentalism can also be seen as a response to external stresses (Fogelin 2008). Anthropologists have found that the development of new or restructured religious systems are often the response to what is perceived to be overwhelming pressure on the culture; such pressures include forced acculturative change, oppressive laws, and the restriction of normal freedoms. These movements are in part a rebellion against that pressure and also may be an attempt to reinvigorate a culture and help ensure its survival. Sometimes such religions are called *cults*, a term generally referring to religious movements that run contrary to the ideologies of conventional religious traditions. However, the term *cult* has become very problematic in recent decades because it has been applied to highly publicized and extremely aberrant religious movements that employ mind control and illegal activities (for example, "The Heaven's Gate" cult in San Diego and Jim Jones's Peoples' Temple apocalypse at Jonestown, in which people took their own lives or the lives of others). However, anthropology continues to understand the concept of *cult* as a description of a reactionary belief in response to external stimuli.

An example of what might be termed "religious rebellion" can be seen in the various "New Age" religions that emerged in the 1970s. In general, adherents rejected the rigid practices of organized religion and focused instead on more loosely defined religious concepts such as spirituality, the environment, or the feminine principle. Such movements were primarily reactions against the "establishment" in the 1960s by North Americans and Europeans (Brown 2000; Puttick 1997). Young adults rejected an establishment that had initiated decades of war (WW II followed by the Korean War and then Vietnam); instead they sought a peaceful, harmonic, and unified society. The feminist movement also developed in this milieu, as women rebelled against all values and behaviors perceived as patriarchal, including organized religion. Out of this social rebellion emerged numerous new "spiritual" movements now termed *New Age*. The overarching conviction within these belief systems is that a new and better world will emerge if enough believers seek equality, spirituality, and personal growth (Morris 2006).

Past cultures have also turned to religious movements for revitalization when their very survival was in question. Well-known revitalization movements include the nineteenth-century Native American "Ghost Dance" and the Melanesian "cargo cults" of the last half-century (Kehoe 1989; Morris 2006). Such movements feature the expectation that some type of savior will arrive or supernatural event will occur that can erase the source of stress and free the society to return to their traditional ways; the forces of oppression or external stress will be eradicated and the culture will return to a "golden age" of customs that they themselves have designed. There is every reason to suspect that some of the world's past religions began for the very types of reasons outlined here: in rebellion to internal or external societal stresses or to revitalize an endangered cultural entity.

Conclusion

A great deal of information has been covered in this chapter, much of it theoretically and methodologically based. While the ideas and methods outlined cannot begin to act as a "field guide" for an archaeologist intending to reveal an ancient belief system, they are useful for understanding the material presented in the book and how valuable a holistic approach to the study of past cultures and religions can be.

USEFUL SOURCES

Richard Bradley, *The Past in Prehistoric Societies*, 2002.
Ian Hodder and Scott Hutson, *Reading the Past: Current Approaches to Interpretation in Archaeology*, 2003.
Andrew Jones, *Archaeological Theory and Scientific Practice*, 2001.

PART II

THE EMERGENCE OF RELIGION IN HUMAN CULTURE

4

THE WORLD OF THE SHAMAN

The religious practitioners known as *shamans* warrant an entire chapter because of the antiquity of the shamanistic practice and the complexity of the shaman's role in human cultures both past and present. Given the assumed ubiquity of shamanic presence in past cultures, archaeologists might expect to find more evidence of shamans than of priests, witches, or sorcerers in their excavations. This chapter delves into the nature of the shaman and discusses the shamanic ritual activities that might be recognized in the archaeological record.

The Nature of the Shaman

The word *shaman* comes from a Tungus word used to describe this Siberian culture's religious agent (Howells 1948). Archaeological evidence indicates shamans have been present in this region for at least 2,000 years, and probably much longer (Rozwadowski 2008). The term *shaman* has come into common usage in anthropology, uniformly replacing terms such as *medicine man* or *witch doctor* found in much older anthropological texts and "B" movies about "tribal" cultures. In such movies, the person in this role most likely wore an outlandish costume, carried a staff, rattle, or other non-utilitarian item, and engaged in some strenuous body movements; he may have mixed potions and probably chanted loudly. Strange as it may seem, some or all of these behaviors are indeed found in shamanistic practices throughout the world (Winkelman 2008). The wild-eyed, head-weaving, nonsensical guttural chants might not be accurate depictions, but costuming, paraphernalia, and spoken and performed rituals are certainly the norm. Early anthropological accounts suggested these "shamans" were mentally unbalanced and thus capable of extraordinary psychotic behavior (e.g., Narby and Huxley 2001). By the twentieth century, while it was clear that shamans were indeed unusual characters, anthropologists recognized them as extremely talented and skilled practitioners rather than as people on the brink of insanity.

Though not all anthropologists agree that the term *shaman* should be applied to practitioners who are not priests, witches, or sorcerers (Kehoe 2000; Townsend 1997), archaeologists cannot afford to be so nuanced in their distinctions, being lucky even to find remnants of religious behavior in the material record. For the purposes of this book, and as is generally found in archaeology, the term *shaman* is used to describe the actor who carries out numerous religious services for his or her culture but is not cast in the role of priest. By examining the role of the shaman, and the material culture associated with the shaman's activities, we can identify methods for recognizing the presence of such practitioners in the archaeological record.

Who Becomes the Shaman?

As described previously, shamans are chosen according to the custom in their cultures. Among the Kalahari Bushmen of Africa, half of the people in an entire band might become shamans. More often, however, shamans are fewer in number and are selected by some process other than their own personal choice. The position might be inherited, father to son, or less often, mother to daughter. A propitious birth, special abilities in a child, or a simple apprenticeship with a shaman are all possible paths to shamanism. Although shamans are more commonly male, many cultures also recognize female shamans. In smaller societies in which there is a single unified belief system, males tend to be the religious practitioners; in larger, complex societies practicing multiple religions, women tend to act as the shamans while men become the priests (Townsend 1997). In small-scale farming and market cultures practicing a single or multiple religions, either or both sexes may become the shaman-healers. An example of this is found in India where, in the Sora culture, shamans are usually female. Sora little girls who will become shamans are visited by spirits and taught how to enter the underworld; as adults, in addition to diagnosing and healing, their most important duties are as intermediaries between the living and the recently dead, especially to encourage the deceased soul to journey on to the underworld (Vitebsky 1993).

In Korea, shamans are traditionally women known as *mansin*. They are considered divinely inspired and called to their profession by the gods; they act as both healers and seers (Choi 2003; Kendall 1985). Clients come to the mansin and explain their problem; the mansin then uses her clairvoyance not only to interpret the client's problems, but to discern the proper path to dealing with it (Choi 2003). The mansin then carries out *kut*, rituals to solve the problem. If help is needed, the mansin may bring in others of her profession to take part in the kut; and, in addition to the client, there may be others who observe the ritual (Kendall 1985). For the Korean mansin, the clients are always female, but Sora Indian female shamans may be called to help either males or females.

Beyond the notion that the shaman acts or thinks differently from the norm, quite often the male shaman is seen as possessing a dual gender or as transgendered in some way. This is particularly true in Siberian shamanism, where religious practitioners are considered androgynous and able to change their sex with the aid of spiritual helpers (Balzer 2003; Stutley 2003). Religious practitioners capable of understanding both the male and female perspective due to their dual gender can also be found among Native American, Southeast Asian, and African cultures.

The Role of the Shaman

One of the reasons it takes an entire chapter to explain this religious practitioner's role in society is that it is so varied. We can use the following terms to define the role of the shaman: healer, medium, problem-solver, diviner, sorcerer, pharmacologist, and entertainer. These are not mutually exclusive, and in fact in many cultures the shaman is expected to embody many or all of these roles. It takes a skilled shaman indeed to be successful in any of these endeavors and gain the trust and respect of his or her people.

In most cultures, the shaman is expected to be the *healer*. Some cultures believe that spirits cause illness, while others attribute it to magic, sorcery, or witchcraft, or even to actions by another shaman. People may fall ill because of inadvertent contact with some polluting substance or person, or even because of their own intentional but inappropriate actions. In many cultures it is the person's soul that has become ill, in turn causing the physical body to succumb (Stutley 2003). Once the shaman-as-healer has entered the picture, he or she must first determine the cause of the illness: did it come from spirits, sorcery, actions by the victim, or by other magical or human means. Next the shaman must determine how to heal the victim: what are the proper ceremonies, medicines, performances, prayers, or actions to drive out the illness and restore the soul and body to health. In the South American Shuar culture, the shaman ingests a drink in the late afternoon and evening; this drink allows him to see into the victim's body and determine the cause of the illness (Harner 1968). Among the Shuar, illness is usually caused by sorcery produced by an invisible dart shot into the victim. The shaman extracts the poisoned item and the victim should return to health. In many cultures, counsel from the supernatural world is needed to determine the cause of illness and the appropriate cure; it is here that the shaman often calls on his or her role as *medium*.

A medium can act as a conduit between "this" world and the "other," whatever that other is in any given culture. The shaman may serve not only as conduit but as host. While acting a medium, which usually involves a trance state, the shaman can speak *for* or *as* the supernatural agent (Lewis 2003; Narby 2001). In this way the shaman can bring the supernatural world to that of humans, imparting messages and even carrying out acts that spirits cannot do in their own world. Beyond this, however, the shaman can send his or her own soul into that other plane and interact with souls and spirits, both imparting and retrieving information. In some cultures the shaman helps the souls of the recently dead find their way to the world of the dead, or shamans "scare away" souls or ghosts who are unwilling to depart (Hutton 2001). Because of their intimate interaction with the supernatural, shamans run the risk of being accused of bringing illness or other ill will to stricken victims; there is often a fine, even imaginary, line between shaman and sorcerer.

When adversity strikes, people turn to the shaman to alleviate the problem. If a rash of unpleasant events occurs in a village and sorcery is suspected, the shaman is called upon to discern the source—perhaps a neighboring village, recent visitors, or rival shamans. The shaman is expected to know what actions to take to counteract the sorcery. Among the Kalahari Bushmen, shamans will take action if, for instance, seasonal rainfall is late or insufficient, or the hunts have been unsuccessful. Shamans enter a trance that takes them into the supernatural world where they can determine the problem and negotiate a solution (Lee 1984). Shamans also perform ceremonies to head off such problems. In some Siberian cultures the shaman carries out a "good luck" ceremony prior to the major hunting season (Hamayon 2003). This ritual ensures the coming hunts will be successful and that the cosmological balance will not be upset by the death of the animals. Should the ritual not occur, not only would the hunters be unsuccessful, but animals would fail to reproduce and real destruction might rain down on the culture. The shaman, then, is the ultimate problem-solver.

Often the shaman is able to retrieve information about or even predict the future through the process of *divination*, a method also used to acquire information such as how to heal someone, how to deal with a crisis, which are proper future actions to take, and so forth. The shaman usually uses divination objects such as bones, the internal organs of recently sacrificed animals, or ritual objects made of wood, metal, and other materials specifically intended for the divination process. There are many paths to divination; in Thailand a shaman might use astrology, numerology, the number and pattern of facial blemishes, and dream interpretation to offer information on everything from suitable marriage partners and future pregnancies, to diagnoses of illness (Heinze 2004). In the African cattle-herding Samburu culture, in order for the *laibon* (shaman-diviner) to determine what type of sorcery has caused someone to fall ill, he must cast divination stones and read the patterns (Fraktin 2004). The laibon not only divines the ensorcelment, but also concocts a medicine to cure the problem. The example of the laibon also illustrates the shaman's knowledge as herbo-pharmacologist.

Anthropologists have long known, and pharmaceutical companies are realizing, that members of indigenous cultures have a tremendous store of knowledge about the healing properties of plants (Davis 1995). When a shaman determines the cause of an illness, he or she often prescribes a cure or prepares the medicine for the victim. Sometimes plant properties are known to everyone in the culture. Most often, however, the secrets of which plants, the amounts needed, and the proper mixtures are known only by trained indigenous healers, making this knowledge a mainstay in their power as healers.

Another role the shaman plays is entertainer and storyteller. In order to interact with the supernatural world, the shaman must either go to that world or else bring members of it to the shaman's plane of existence. In the former case, the shaman usually uses trance, either drug-induced or through self-hypnosis, to travel to the spiritual plane. The shaman's entrancement may be something of a public spectacle, offering a type of visual entertainment for spectators who might even take part on some level. Kalahari Bushmen carry out a "trance dance" which includes music and chanting and dancing around a campfire until the dancer-shamans fall into a state of hypnotic exhaustion; during this time they can discern the cause of an illness and attempt to cure it. Non-dancers clap, sing, and provide music, in this way taking part in the healing ceremony. In other cases, it is not so much the process of attaining the trance that

Figure 4.1. Artistic rendering of an entranced shaman attempting to heal a victim of sorcery. (*M. J. Hughes*)

is the "show," but the healing of the victim. Like the Shuar culture, many Amazonian cultures believe illness results from invisible darts shot by sorcerers into their victims. The shaman must first determine the type of dart (and possibly the identity of the sorcerer) through interaction with the supernatural world. The shaman ingests a hallucinogenic drink commonly called ayahuasca or yage and then enters a trance (Harner 1968; Johnson 2003; Rogers 1982), which allows him to acquire the necessary information and determine the location of the dart(s) in the victim's body (Figure 4.1). The following account from one anthropologist describes the theatrical nature of the search for and extraction of these darts:

> As darkness fell upon us, the patients and their kin waited for Yankush [the shaman] to enter into a trance induced by a bitter, hallucinogenic concoction he had taken just before sunset (it is made from a vine known as *ayahuasca*). While the visitors exchanged gossip and small talk, Yankush sat facing the wall of his house, whistling healing songs and waving a bundle of leaves that served as a fan and soft rattle. Abruptly, he told the two women to lie on banana leaves that had been spread on the floor, so that he could use his visionary powers to search their bodies for tiny points of light, the telltale signature of the sorcerer's darts. As Yankush's intoxication increased, his meditative singing gave way to violent

retching. Gaining control of himself, he sucked noisily on the patients' bodies in an effort to remove the darts. (Brown 1989:8)

During the ceremony, family and visitors shout encouragement to the shaman and generally take part as non-healing bystanders. Eventually, after several hours the shaman extracts the darts and sends his patient home with recommendations for herbal medicine. In some cultures the shaman actually "spits out" the darts, either as a bit of blood or as an actual object; this allows the audience to observe that the source of illness is now gone from the victim. In large part the success of the shaman is derived from how convincing the performance is.

The Successful Shaman

Claude Lévi-Strauss perhaps said it best when he declared "Quesalid [the shaman] did not become a great shaman because he cured his patients; he cured his patients because he had become a great shaman" (1963:180). Quesalid, a Kwakiutl shaman, lived in British Columbia in the early twentieth century. Interestingly, he did not believe in the power of his native shamans, and so he undertook an apprenticeship to prove their falsity. He learned some "shamanic tricks" but before he could proclaim shamans as frauds, he himself was called to heal a sick person (Lévi-Strauss 1963). Quesalid went on to have a great career as a healer but realized that much of his skill came from the fact that his patients *believed* that he *would* heal them, not because of the "trickery" he used in the healing rituals. This is one of the key concepts in successful shamanism as well as the efficacy of sorcery—the belief that it is real.

Given this essential belief in a shaman's abilities, not just anyone can be a successful shaman. First of all, the shaman must take steps to either maintain or attain reputable standing in the community. Then the shaman must be proficient not only in herbal lore, chants and rituals, and other skills normal in the culture, but he or she must be able to perform so that all witnesses are convinced that cures or problem-solving has taken place. This means that an expertise in sleight-of-hand, acting ability, and showmanship are a must.

An anthropologist in Nepal experienced a shamanic healing ceremony (Hitchcock 2001). Sakrante, the village blacksmith, had donned his shamanic costume and extracted evil substances not only from the anthropologist, but from other attendees as well. His entire performance, consisting of bodily movements, drumming and singing, and mediumistic activities and spirit possession, included searching out witches and predicting the future. The anthropologist says of the performer, "I remember that even after Sakrante had removed his costume, slowly and carefully putting each item away in the wicker basket, the spell cast by his drumming and singing remained on us all" (Hitchcock 2001:2–3). The title of the article about Sakrante, "Remarkably Good Theater," illustrates a main tenet of the successful shaman.

This aspect of shamanic healing is not terribly different from that of modern Western medicine. Everyone has heard of an ill person who took "medicine" and later learned, after the problem had disappeared, that the patient had taken a placebo. Simple faith in the power of Western medicine and its drugs is a powerful element in the successful efforts of Western doctors, just as belief in the power of the shaman is crucial in traditional religions. Unfortunately, this faith is not visible in the archaeological record, but the items the shaman uses to carry out performances and reinforce that faith sometimes are.

The Shaman's Tools

Shamans frequently have spirit helpers who assist them in their travels to and within the supernatural plane, and even guide the shaman back to the world of humans. In many cultures the spirit helper is considered the alter ego of the shaman, and in fact it is the spirit helper's form the shaman takes during his or her travels to the supernatural world. In the Sora culture, shamans are guided by the spirits of earlier shamans (Vitebsky 1995), while in other cultures spirit helpers come in the form of animals. Powerful shamans may have more than one animal spirit helping them, each responsible for different courses of action—one to chase away evil spirits, one to help with healing, and so forth (Hutton 2001). Besides assisting the shaman, helper spirits guard against attack from hostile spirits or other forces bent on impeding the shaman's work.

In many cases the shaman's costume may reflect the nature of the spirit helper. If the spirit helper's animal form is, for instance, a snake or a bird, the costume may consist of snake skins or feathers. In other cultures the shaman's costume may contain images or purported parts of mythical animals, as well as noise-making objects such as rattles and bells, and other items considered sacred or magical (Stutley 2003). The shaman wears the costume only when engaged by a client to carry out his or her performance.

Music often accompanies the shaman's work. Drums are common accoutrements in Siberia, while shamans in the Amazon make use of a flute. Rattles of various types are used throughout the Americas, and the Sora shamans of India use the sound of horns. Songs and musical chanting are also commonly used in the shamanic performance. Besides music, the shaman makes use of a variety of other tools, depending on what the culture perceives as sacred or magical. The Samburu laibon uses his sacred stones for divination; other paraphernalia such as sticks, baskets, beads, animal skins, crystals, and any other manner of things might be in the shaman's tool kit. In many cases these items are sacred and are therefore handled only by the shaman; but in others it is the shaman's skill that ignites the power in what is otherwise a mundane object found in any household.

Whether a culture's shaman is a healer, medium, diviner, or all of these, in order to enter the spirit world or to invite spirits to the human plane, the shaman usually must be in a *shamanic state of consciousness* (SSC), also known as an *altered state of consciousness* (ASC). To achieve ASC, the shaman might use a type of self-hypnosis, including physical exhaustion (as in the Bushman trance dance), hyperventilation, some type of meditation, or another physical activity designed to induce trance. More

often, though, hallucinogenic plants or other consumable or inhalable items that produce altered states can be used. Hallucination-aiding products include alcoholic
drinks, mind-altering drugs, tobacco smoke, and foods that have trance-inducing
properties (such as mushrooms).

In most cultures it is only the shamans who enter ASC, because it is generally considered that during this period of time their soul leaves the body and embarks on a journey to the supernatural world. Many cultures, especially those with practicing shamans,
envision the universe as multilayered. The human world occupies one layer, but the others are often places of great danger, inhabited by supernatural beings who may or may
not be friendly to those who dwell in the human layer. Not only is passage from one layer to another difficult, but surviving in a non-human layer is also a serious challenge.
While there, the soul might be in some danger, and if injured, killed, or otherwise
detained, the shaman's life is also forfeit. Even with the aid of a spirit helper, it is only
the skilled practitioner who can navigate the treacherous landscape of the spirit world
and return with the necessary information, or even the necessary spirit, in tow. For
instance, when the Siberian Yakut shaman is ready to embark on his ASC, he dons his
costume and is then strapped to a tent pole or other object to keep his body in this
world and prevent the spirits from carrying him off, literally body and soul (Grim
1983). In many cases there are physiological alterations in the shaman's body while in a
trance; sometimes the pulse races madly, while other shamans exhibit such slow breath-
ing and heartbeat their bodies appear to be on the threshold of death. In most cultures
the shamanic ASC and trance journey is considered a stressful and difficult undertaking, and only the most powerful of shamans can accomplish this task regularly.

Other tools may be individual to that particular culture. For instance, North
American Ojibway shamans keep records of their performances. Symbols of the
shaman's chants are etched into birch bark, acting not only as a mnemonic device for
the spoken invocation, but also as a type of story of the ritual (Grim 1983). Inside an
Ojibway shaman's lodge, then, numerous pieces of birch bark scrolls with pictographic
symbols can be found. Such tools would be unique to the shaman and probably would
not be part of the archaeological assemblage from the average non-shaman household.

Finding Shamans in the Archaeological Record

Finding the shaman when you enter a village for your ethnographic fieldwork is one
thing; identifying them in the archaeological record is another entirely. Statues and
drawings of religious practitioners that have labels inscribed in the culture's language
are great, but more often than not, these depict priests rather than shamans. Shamans
are far more elusive, in part because their part-time status makes them look, archaeologically, pretty much like everyone else. Armed with the type of knowledge described
in the foregoing sections, archaeologists have made great strides in highlighting possible evidence of shamans in their ancient contexts. The following section profiles
some methods that have been used to track the presence of shamans through the
extant material record.

Shamans and Rock Art

The literature on rock art research is vast, in part because such images are ubiquitous, appearing on all of the inhabited continents. What was the ancient motivation to create such art? Some researchers have recognized the historical narrative aspect of the art, which details great battles and other events worthy of memory (Klassen 1998), while others have suggested that rock art can function as territorial markers (Bradley 1998). Using an ethnographic approach, Layton notes that a few examples of rock art may be nothing more than someone's doodles scratched or painted while stuck inside a cave on a rainy day (2001). However, most agree that the vast majority of rock art has religious significance, and in many instances it is related to shamanic activities. Several world-class researchers have advocated a slow and systematic analysis based the structuralism of Lévi-Strauss. Before even attempting interpretations, such scholars undertake detailed study of images, their placement relative to one another, and their context (i.e., cave, landscape), their form, and many other aspects of the art itself (e.g., Clottes 1998; Conkey 1989, 2001; Leroi-Gourhan 1965). It is, they suggest, this careful analysis of form that provides a platform for interpretation that can include function and meaning.

As Clottes notes, there are three basic tools for interpreting rock art: "ethnological analogy, the subjects and the way in which they are depicted, and their location" (2002:115). Ethnography, through direct interpretation by living informants, can be very informative for archaeologists. In some cases, however, the rock art was made so long ago that the time lapse between the original artists and their descendants living today may nullify any possible interpretive analogy. Relying on ethnographic analogy can be a double-edged sword; important clues are indeed often gleaned, and at other times the myriad interpretations offered by various informants may serve only to muddy the picture, so to speak. In places where there is virtually no connection between the living population and the rock art artists—for instance, in Europe or Central Asia—archaeologists must rely on other lines of evidence while using ethnographic analogy only in the most general sense of "why people decorate rocks" in that region of the world.

As outlined in Chapter 3, one of the first questions an archaeologist asks of a painting is "what is it a picture of?" The archaeologist must then identify the images based on classifications of image types. It is in these categories that evidence of the shaman may emerge. The first and perhaps most suggestive category of images is that of *therianthropes*, or combination beings, usually of animals and humans. Such images may depict a being that is a true combination, anatomically half-human and half-animal. In other cases the artist has made a clear attempt to show that the image is human but is wearing an animal costume, or perhaps is in the mid-stages of transformation, as seen in the Paleolithic French example in Les Trois Frères cave (Figure 4.2). Some suggest this human-animal connection in rock art depicts a totemistic system. In Australia, living informants have described the images of therianthropes as ancestral figures, or clan totems (Layton 2001). In this scenario, then, therianthropes do not depict shamans but rather represent a cosmological figure in the sense that

Figure 4.2. Therianthropic figure painted in Les Trois Frères Cave. The figure has human legs and feet and wears an animal headdress and skins over the torso. (*R. Jennison*)

kinship and cosmology are inextricably intertwined in Australian Aboriginal culture. Another explanation for this imagery relates more directly to shamanistic activity—namely, that it depicts the shaman's journey to the spirit world or the spirit inhabiting the shaman's body in this world. The animal represents either the shaman's hybrid spirit or his spirit helper. Images depicting a transformation (or costuming) could be interpreted as the shaman in his costume or in the actual throes of spirit possession (Aldhouse-Green and Aldhouse-Green 2005; Lewis-Williams 2002; Whitley 2006). Totemistic representations and a shamanic journey are only two possible explanations for the fairly frequent depiction of therianthropes. However, these are admittedly curious images, and since they fit nicely with ethnographic accounts regarding the close ties between animals, animal spirits, and shamans, such images do give pause for thought.

A second category involving the human form is that of *anthropomorphs*. These are figures that appear human but may depict some aspect that implies the subject is "more" than just a normal human being. Examples of anthropomorphs might include humans with oversized body parts such as hands, head, or torso. In other cases the figure may have a body part that appears like another object, such as sun rays extending from the head, or an arm that merges into a sword or other weapon (Figure 4.3). In such anthropomorphic imagery, odd-looking heads or other body parts have been interpreted as part of the shamanic costume (Devlet 2001). A subcategory of anthropomorphic figures comprises images known as *X-ray style*. These figures appear to show the person's internal organs or skeletal structure. X-ray-style figures are found in Asia and Siberia, in North American rock art, and are quite common in Australia. One interpretation for the "transparency" of these figures is that their transformation into a spiritual being is being depicted (Boyd 1998). Another is that shamans, while in their trance-based journey, are in a near-death state, and this x-ray imagery depicts their position between the world of the living and the world of the dead (Devlet 2001).

The same arguments for therianthropic figures are made for the depiction of animals, especially when they are associated with humans. Obviously there is a very wide range of explanations that might be applied to animal imagery on rock art. The depiction of animals may reflect the practice of sympathetic magic rituals: drawing the animal may be seen as a way to ensure a successful hunt, increase the herd, or represent some other aspect of subsistence strategy. In southern Africa, the Kalahari Bushmen speak of a "rain bull," an animal depicted in art when rainmaking ceremonies occur; in some instances of Great Basin rock art, the mountain sheep serves the same function (Lewis-Williams 1981, 2002; Whitley 1994, 1998). This would explain the ubiquity of these animals in their respective settings, given the importance of rain in these fairly arid landscapes. In other cases the depiction of animals may herald the transformation of the shaman into an animal spirit or represent his spirit helper. Animals may also represent totemic ancestors, as is often the case in Australian rock art.

Perhaps the most controversial images are those that fall into the category of *geometric* art. This category includes dots, wavy lines, squares and rectangles, circles and ovals, and various abstract forms. A major school of thought in rock art research identifies these images as shamanistic in origin. This explanation rests on the idea that the human nervous system responds in a limited and predictable set of ways when one enters a trance-like state, producing visions that include these geometric figures (Lewis-Williams and Dowson 1988). This explanation, known as a *neuropsychological* model, describes these visions of geometric figures and abstract forms as

Figure 4.3. Sketch of North American anthropomorphic petroglyph figure with rays extending from the head, executed in X-ray style showing internal organs. (*S. R. Steadman*)

entoptic phenomena, meaning a type of internal vision (Lewis-Williams 2002, 2008; Pearson 2002). This theory suggests that all humans see these types of images as they enter trance states because we all share an identical central nervous system. However, in each culture these figures seen by the entranced individual have different meanings within the cultural construct. In one culture a circle might represent a hole out of which all life came; in another the circle is the entrance to a tunnel through which one passes to the spirit world. Wavy lines might represent snakes in one culture and water in another. This theory would explain why geometric and abstract figures occur in rock art across the world, but it does not help archaeologists with their interpretation; that interpretive framework must be drawn from the culture's own belief system and cosmological explanation of the symbols.

The assumption that shamans are the likely authors of the rock art stems from the theory that it is they who took the journey represented, witnessed the images later drawn, and had the cosmological and symbolic knowledge to interpret the meaning of what they saw (Dowson 1998a; Lewis-Williams 2002; Whitley 2000). As already discussed, trance states are often considered dangerous and should be attempted only by those who know how to travel to the spirit world and return successfully with the desired knowledge; the person who can accomplish such a feat and remain alive is the shaman. It is, therefore, the shaman who records the journey on the face of the rock. It should be noted that the neuropsychological model and its interpretation of geometric figures as entoptic phenomena is not a universally accepted explanation (e.g., Bahn 2001; Solomon 1998, 2001). However, the majority of scholarship on rock art interpretation recognizes the merit in the neuropsychological model; archaeologists are discovering greater levels of interpretive opportunities when they apply the model to examples of rock art all over the world.

Interpreting rock art and its symbolic meaning is fraught with difficulties for the archaeologist interested in identifying religious belief systems in general, and tracing the presence of shamanistic activities in particular. The best bet is to go in armed to the teeth with the requisite research on how to interpret the art from all perspectives, combined with as much knowledge as possible about the culture that produced it. The first step is to classify and categorize the images, yielding not only a list of images, but perhaps clues as to the story or setting depicted. If possible, living informants, or those only slightly removed from the artists, can be consulted with tremendous success. Failing this, ethnographic analogy based on informants long descended from the earlier artists, or even present-day artists from nearby cultures in similar environments, may yield very useful insights. Finally, if the archaeologist suspects the culture under consideration had practicing shamans, the neuropsychological model may help to analyze all the images, especially those that are not therianthropic or anthropomorphic but instead are abstract or even geometric. The latter (abstract and geometric images) may well depict the entire journey a shaman undertook on behalf of his people. With such information, the archaeologist might be able to take the interpretation of the rock art beyond just the date, the method of producing it, and the categorization of "what it is a picture of."

The Shaman's Artifacts

Besides rock art, there are any number of items found in archaeological contexts that might indicate shamanic presence in the culture. The earlier section on "The Shaman's Tools" outlined the sorts of things a shaman typically uses while working. Clothing, of course, does not reliably remain in the archaeological record, but parts of musical instruments might, as could other accoutrements like the Ojibway birch bark mnemonic device. Objects with geometric forms etched or painted onto them would be good candidates for analysis regarding entoptic phenomena; the material, provenience, and rarity of an item or group of items, such as a collection of semiprecious stones or a cache of quartz crystals, might aid in interpretation (Whitley et al. 1999). Therianthropic statuettes and figurines might be indicative of the shamanic role in a society, and the same can be said for anthropomorphic figurines with overemphasized features or strange body parts (e.g., Fedorova 2001; Sutherland 2001). However, once we move beyond items that are unusual or clearly representations of, at the very least, some aspect of a culture's cosmology, we find it much harder to categorize shamanistic artifacts.

The best approach is to be open-minded but cautious. If the culture under investigation is likely to have had shamans, then the occasional hint as to their presence should be anticipated. Hints might include any of the types of artifacts suggested above, or perhaps a larger house with an unexplainable open area (where the shaman carries out performances and healing rituals?), a house with secret compartments and unusual layout, or even unusual containers that might have held the shamans medicines or trance-producing potions or drugs. One must, however, guard against the tendency to over-interpret something that might well be a basic utilitarian item. Cautious and careful analysis, with the addition of a detailed understanding of the world of the shaman, may indeed yield some fascinating insights into a culture's religious practitioners.

USEFUL SOURCES

Graham Harvey (ed.), *Readings in Indigenous Religions*, 2002.
Neil Price, *The Archaeology of Shamanism*, 2001.
Robert E. Ryan, *The Strong Eye of Shamanism*, 1999.
Edith Turner, *Among the Healers: Stories of Spiritual and Ritual Healing around the World*, 2006.

5

THE FIRST SPARK OF RELIGION
THE NEANDERTHALS

As the title suggests, this chapter examines the earliest evidence for religion. Did *Homo sapiens* invent religion, or should we attribute it to our forebears on the human evolutionary ladder? Evidence indicates that the boast of "first religion" belongs to our evolutionary cousins, the Neanderthals (*Homo neanderthalensis*), and possibly to even earlier ancestors.

Human Evolution: *Homo Erectus*, Neanderthals, and Modern Humans

The controversy involving the identity of the Neanderthals vis-à-vis modern humans fills many books. We cannot hope to solve such issues here. However, the undisputed fact of Neanderthal existence in human evolutionary history allows us to contemplate the evidence for their ritual behavior. To understand the Neanderthals in Europe and the Middle East, we must step back along the evolutionary path to their ancestors in Africa.

Homo Erectus *Out of Africa*

Who the Neanderthals were and how they are related to modern humans is a controversy that stems from another puzzle—namely, the connection between *Homo erectus* and *Homo sapiens*. There are two prevailing theories regarding the evolution of modern humans. One, known as the *multiregional hypothesis*, asserts that roughly 1.5 million years ago *H. erectus* migrated out of Africa, probably in multiple waves, to populate the European and Asian continents. There is no doubt that *H. erectus* did exactly this, since archaeological work has found their fossils and settlements stretching from France and Spain to China and beyond. This hypothesis goes on to stipulate that *H. erectus* then evolved in place into modern humans—that is, in "multiregions" (Thorne and Wolpoff 1992, 2003). In these areas, *H. erectus* evolved until eventually modern *Homo sapiens* emerged in each region. In the multiregional hypothesis, the Neanderthal is one of the intermediate phases between *H. erectus* and *H. sapiens*, the species that immediately precedes modern humans in Europe and Western Asia. Similar intermediate stages of hominids would have existed in other regions of Asia and Africa as well, though the fossil record of Neanderthals is much richer. In this scenario *H. sapiens* emerged, through extensive gene exchange, as a single, but diverse, species across Asia, Europe, and Africa.

The other hypothesis is known as the *Out-of-Africa* or *replacement theory* (Stringer 1990, 2003). This explanation starts off exactly as does the multiregional: *H. erectus* left Africa roughly 1.5 million years ago to populate Europe and Asia and did indeed continue to evolve into other hominid species. This same process took place in Africa and, according to the Out-of-Africa model, it is in Africa, and Africa only, that *H. sapiens* evolved. Here this model diverges from the multiregional hypothesis. In the Out-of-Africa model there is a *second* wave of migration out of Africa, this time of *H. sapiens* (Figure 5.1). Approximately 150,000 years ago, early *H. sapiens* (often referred to as "archaic" *H. sapiens*) spread out from Africa to Europe and Asia. There they encountered the various descendants of the original *H. erectus* migration, including the Neanderthals in Europe and Western Asia. Over time, archaic modern humans (who, of course, became modern *H. sapiens*) "replaced" these species who were their evolutionary cousins. What method of "replacement" was responsible—violent eradication, a simple case of survival of the

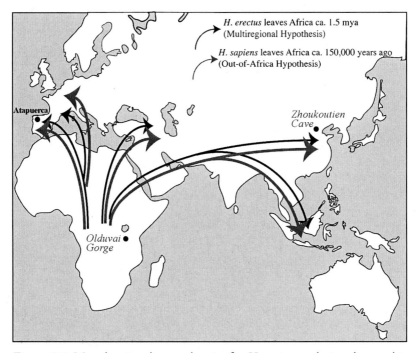

Figure 5.1. Map showing the two theories for *H. sapiens* evolution discussed in the chapter. (*S. R. Steadman*)

fittest, or even interbreeding—is a major area of controversy in present-day Neanderthal studies (Arsuaga and Martínez 2006).

The majority of anthropologists working on hominid studies today subscribe to the Out-of-Africa model as the most accurate, based on available fossil evidence. In part this is due to a separate evidence stream based in biology: molecular analyses of mitochondrial DNA (mtDNA) over the last 20 years. MtDNA is found in the outer part of human cells, and it contains a small portion of DNA that is more easily analyzed than that found in cell nuclei. Another interesting component of mtDNA is that it is passed down only though the female line; thus the mtDNA of modern females allows scholars to trace mutation strings back to the original *H. sapiens* carrier of mtDNA. In short, this research has shown that the last common *H. sapiens* female ancestor lived in Africa somewhere between 100,000 and 200,000 years ago. More recent analyses of Neanderthal DNA, though in early stages, suggest that Neanderthals and *H. sapiens* were different species altogether (Dumiak 2006). Such studies strongly support the Out-of-Africa model for the origins of modern humans. Clearly, in one way or another, Neanderthals were earlier relatives of modern humans, and we can now address the subject of first religions.

First, it is relevant to ask whether any evidence for pre-Neanderthal ritual behavior exists. Some of the most suggestive evidence comes from Atapuerca Cave in Spain (Figure 5.2) where two sets of fossils raise interesting questions. One set of fossils from an area known as Sima de los Huesos, the "pit of bones," dates to about 400,000 years ago (Figure 5.3). These are tentatively identified as *Homo heidelbergensis* (the probable direct ancestor to Neanderthals in Europe). In this "pit," a vertical shaft roughly 40 feet deep, were the remains of at least 30 hominids, along with bones of cave bears, foxes, lions, and other carnivores . While the animals may have fallen into the pit accidentally, there is some speculation that the hominids were thrown in by other hominids, per-

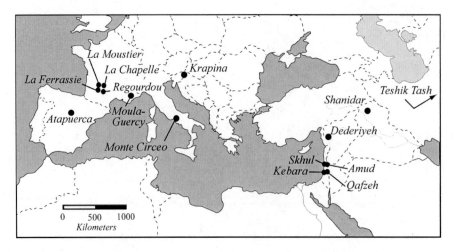

Figure 5.2. Map of sites discussed in the chapter. (*T. Edwards and S. R. Steadman*)

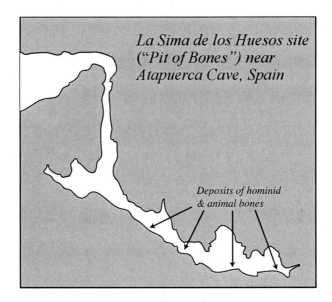

La Sima de los Huesos site ("Pit of Bones") near Atapuerca Cave, Spain

Deposits of hominid & animal bones

Figure 5.3. Sketch of the Atapuerca "Pit of Bones" (La Sima de los Huesos) site. (*S. R. Steadman*)

haps as an attempt to bury them. Not far from the pit of bones is a cave site known as Gran Dolina, where hominid fossils dating to 780,000 years ago have been recovered. These fossils, probably *Homo antecessor* (a species predating *Homo heidelbergensis*), show evidence of intentional butchering; meat was removed from the bones by stone tools, and marrow was extracted from bones. The inhabitants of Gran Dolina were apparently cannibals (Arsuaga and Martínez 2006). Other sites with *H. erectus* fossil remains, such as Zhoukoutien Cave in China, have also offered evidence of cannibalistic behavior, but this is disputed (Tattersall and Schwartz 2000). It might be a stretch to suggest, without additional evidence, that the tossing of hominids down a shaft, or eating the flesh of a fellow hominid, is ritualistic. It is enough, perhaps, to acknowledge that the first spark of religion may one day be proven to rest with hominids who even predate the Neanderthals.

Who Were the Neanderthals?

While we cannot yet definitively state whether Neanderthals were our direct ancestors or our cousins (though it is most likely the latter), we can offer a pretty good description of what the typical Neanderthal was like. The old view of brutish, lumbering, and stupid cave-dwelling creatures, so popular in "B" movies of a half-century ago, is a far cry from the actual truth of the strong, intelligent, and inventive hominids they were.

The misguided views of Neanderthals as more beast than human resulted from a set of fossils examined a century ago. The "Old Man of La Chapelle," discovered at a French site in 1908, was a Neanderthal male of about 40–50 years of age. The

French paleontologist Marcellin Boule, who examined the La Chapelle bones in 1910, chose to emphasize the apparent deformities of the skeletal remains to make them seem as far removed from modern humans as possible, using words such as "beastly," "brutish," and "stupid" in his descriptions. His report created the image of a "man-beast" in the minds of those interested in early human research (Figure 5.4). Over the next decades, however, several hundred other Neanderthal bones were analyzed by other researchers, and in the 1950s the La Chapelle fossils were reexamined. The "Old Man" was found to have suffered from crippling arthritis, causing misshapen bones and indeed making him look quite different from a healthy modern human. By 1960, anthropologists and anatomists had revised their opinions of Neanderthals, with many suggesting that if a cleaned-up Neanderthal man sat beside you on a bus in Paris or the subway in New York, no one would notice he or she was any different from the many denizens of these two cities (Figure 5.5). This "new view" of the Neanderthal has, however, been slow to make its way into the public's imagination.

Fossil evidence suggests Neanderthals came on the scene of Europe and Western Asia by about 200,000 years ago; we see the last of them by about 30,000 years ago. In the latter stages of the Pleistocene (Ice Age), Europe and Western Asia were much colder than today, though some areas such as France, Spain, and Israel were certainly warmer than other places, such as Germany. Neanderthals had stockier bodies than those of modern *H. sapiens*, and had larger nose cavities that served to warm the air they breathed before it hit their lungs. Their skulls sloped back over braincases that

Figure 5.4. Artistic rendering of "bestial" Neanderthal as described by Boule. (*R. Jennison*)

Figure 5.5. Artistic rendering of more modern interpretation of Neanderthal appearance. (*R. Jennison*)

housed a brain larger than that of modern humans. One of the best-known features of the Neanderthal is the prominent brow ridge, which some describe as resembling McDonald's "golden arches" (Tattersall and Schwartz 2000:198). This feature gives the Neanderthal face seemingly deep-set eyes. Other than these facial features, longer and thicker fingers, and a shorter and stockier frame, there is little in the Neanderthal appearance that would be noticeable in a large crowd of modern humans. Neanderthals made use of a stone tool kit known as *Mousterian* which included cutters, choppers, scrapers, and points that may have been hafted onto hand-held spears. Many Mousterian tools show evidence of sharpening and refashioning for reuse. Neanderthals understood the utility of reshaping a larger tool into a smaller one when the larger had become too dull or otherwise useless.

Neanderthals were big-game hunters who lived in mobile groups, inhabiting rock shelters and caves as well as open campsites across the landscape. It is unclear whether Neanderthals built shelters in the open, though something resembling a tent stake was recovered from a French site. They did appear to organize their space in caves, making distinctions between areas where "trash" was deposited and where cooking and storage took place. We do not know how Neanderthals divided up labor, though based on present-day hunter-gatherers, we may speculate that women did the majority of gathering and men the hunting. How much plant foods contributed to Neanderthal diets is an ongoing subject of research. Hunting of small and medium-sized animals may have been accomplished in groups rather than individually, but large-game hunting was almost certainly done in groups. One reason Neanderthals may have hunted in groups is because they did not possess throwing spears but rather used short ones that had to be thrust into an animal. This meant Neanderthals had to get up close and personal with their prey. Even deer can have sharp horns that can easily eviscerate a hunter if he is inattentive. Several Neanderthals simultaneously attacking an animal would mean a quicker kill with less chance for injury.

One major controversy about Neanderthals concerns their ability to communicate with one another. While they must have had some method of communication in order to work together as hunters and to perform other activities, they most likely did not have the same type of vocal language abilities of modern humans. Some speculate that it was the superior communicative abilities of *H. sapiens* that doomed the otherwise intelligent and successful Neanderthals to extinction.

Neanderthal Sites in Europe and Western Asia: Rituals in Caves?

Our main information about Neanderthals and their potentially ritualistic behavior comes from burial sites in France, Iraq, and Israel, with a few scattered sets of data from other sites in Europe and Russia. A study sometime ago documented at least 59 intentional Neanderthal burials (Belfer-Cohen and Hovers 1992; Smirnov 1989), but few of these sites are without controversy. While some consider the Neanderthal sites to exhibit incontrovertible evidence of intentional burial and ritual behavior, others explain away the evidence as postdepositional natural actions of wind, rain, and rodent activity (Chase and Dibble 1987; Gargett 1989), though this is a minority view. Most archaeologists who study European and Western Asian Neanderthal sites argue that the evidence is certainly indicative of some level of religious or symbolic belief system. Answering the question of what specific beliefs existed in Neanderthal communities is where the greatest difficulty lies. While accepting that we will probably never know in detail what Neanderthal rituals and beliefs might have been, we can certainly follow the evidence toward measured and evidence-based speculations. The following discussion examines Neanderthal burials and sites with an eye toward determining whether Neanderthals might have practiced some sort of animal-based belief system, if they engaged in death rituals, and whether they had shaman-like religious practitioners or perhaps practiced some type of ancestor veneration.

Animal Cults and Totemism

The idea that Neanderthals believed in animal cults was first introduced by discoveries at Drachenloch Cave in the Swiss Alps, excavated by Emil Bächler from 1917 until 1921. Inside the cave he found Mousterian tools and thus declared that Neanderthals had lived there. Beyond the tools, though, Bächler found numerous cave-bear bones, a formidable Ice Age species. Bächler reported that these cave-bear fossils were not just scattered around the cave, but that the skulls were contained in stone-lined cists, sunk into the cave floor and then capped with a stone slab. Bächler interpreted these as evidence of a "bear cult," ritualized behavior involving these large and fearsome creatures. Though Neanderthals might well have treated cave bears with fear and respect, the evidence from Drachenloch has been largely discounted. Bächler's excavation techniques were sorely wanting, and in a reexamination of the evidence, most believe that natural taphonomic processes created a collection of stones and bones in depressions in the cave floor. However, other more carefully excavated sites offer suggestive evidence.

The French site of Regourdou was first excavated in 1957 and again from 1962 to 1965. A number of interesting discoveries were made in this cave. One pit, Va, was considered intentionally dug because it cut through naturally laid stratigraphy. At the bottom was a brown-bear skull accompanied by two bear leg bones, one crossed over the other and propped up by a small stone. The pit was intentionally filled (according to the excavator, Eugène Bonifay); halfway through the filling process, a stone with an intentionally made hole was deposited. The excavator as well as others (Hayden 2003) believe that this pit and assemblage of bear bones was intentionally constructed by Neanderthals.

In another part of the cave, Neanderthal remains were found apparently associated with bear bones. This burial dates between 60,000 and 70,000 years ago. Two shallow pits were dug near each other, with a type of rock wall between them (apparently built of stones that came out of the pit). Another rock pile rested at the other end of one pit. In this latter pit was a nearly complete skeleton of a bear, over which rested a heavy stone slab, each end placed on the rock walls. In the other pit was an adult Neanderthal, lying on flat stones and then covered by a small slab of stone.

Interred with this Neanderthal were two bear leg bones; on top of the stone slab were Mousterian tools and another bear leg bone. This entire deposit was then covered by cobblestones (Hayden 2003). It is difficult not to find this evidence compelling.

At the Amud Cave site in Israel, excavated during the 1960s, a number of Neanderthal fossils, dating between 50,000 and 40,000 years ago, were recovered. One of the most recent discoveries, known as Amud 7, was made in the early 1990s. An infant, approximately 10 months old, was found tucked into a niche in the cave. Resting on the hip was the jawbone of a red deer, a circumstance unlikely to have occurred naturally (Rak, Kimbel, and Hovers 1994).

Another interesting discovery in 1938 was made in a cave known as Teshik Tash in Uzbekistan. Here a young male, 8–10 years of age, was buried in a shallow pit. The excavator reported that the burial was surrounded by ibex (wild goat) horns, planted in six pairs (points implanted in the ground) around the burial. However, ibex was a regular food item for the Neanderthals, and it is entirely unclear whether the horns associated with the burial were placed intentionally or there by accidental circumstance (Chase and Dibble 1987).

The evidence for Neanderthal/animal symbolism is certainly mixed. The case for a cave-bear cult at Drachenloch is all but disproved, and the evidence from Teshik Tash is certainly questionable. Stronger cases for Neanderthal/animal associations in burials can be made for Regourdou and Amud 7, but these are few examples indeed. Perhaps it is more productive to ask why Neanderthals might have engaged in some animal-based belief system. First of all, animals made up much of the world Neanderthals inhabited. Animals lived in caves also frequented by Neanderthals, and some animals might have made quite an impression, such as cave bears and hyenas, both dangerous to a hominid population. Meat and the hunting of it was important to Neanderthal survival, though we don't know how frequently they were successful at acquiring fresh meat. As has already been advanced, more often than not a culture's cosmology is reflective of the daily world that culture inhabits. Why would the Neanderthals have been any different? A second item to consider is the burial practices of early anatomically modern humans. In several examples, such as in Qafzeh and Skhul caves in Israel, modern humans, dating to as much as 100,000–120,000 years ago, were buried with animal bones. At Qafzeh a child was buried with a deer skull and antlers, and at Skhul one adult was buried holding a wild boar skull in his hands and another male was found with a cow skull (Parker Pearson 1999; Tattersall 1995). Controversy over the relationship between Neanderthals and modern humans aside, intentional burial with animal skulls was practiced by at least one of these groups. This naturally leads to the question, "what symbolic meaning was attributed to the animals?" Here we enter the unadulterated realm of pure speculation.

Bächler had no trouble believing in a Neanderthal cave-bear cult; cave bears were huge creatures and were certainly a constant threat to any human crossing their path. Why wouldn't a survival-minded people engage in efforts to soothe the spirit of such a fearsome beast by making altars, offerings, and carrying out rituals to honor it? Alternatively, perhaps the association of different animals with different individuals is indicative of the tie between that animal and that human. Perhaps the red deer with Amud 7 and the ibex horns with the Teshik Tash boy represent the totemic ancestor associated with these children. We know nothing of Neanderthal kinship structures; perhaps here are clues to clan-based totemic systems.

If we take the opposite approach and ask why *wouldn't* Neanderthals engage in an animal-based belief system, we are back to the old days of stupid, brutish, monstrous cave dwellers. The view of such creatures, solely engaged in finding food and copulating between bouts of violence with one another, has been convincingly dispelled by Neanderthal studies of recent decades. These large-brained, sturdy, resilient, and resourceful humans might well have been capable of symbolic thought and action.

Neanderthal Death Cults and Cannibalism

The notion of Neanderthal cannibalism isn't so far-fetched, given the evidence from Gran Dolina and numerous ethnographic reports of ritual cannibalism in past or present cultures. What is at issue, of course, is whether the cannibalism resulted from a Neanderthal need for a meat source or from ritualistic and symbolic behavior.

Claims of Neanderthal cannibalism have been common for decades. Many believed the first sure evidence of cannibalism was found in an Italian cave called Monte Circeo. In 1939 a worker on the Guattari family estate fell through the roof of the cave and then scrambled around in a bit of entrepreneurial exploration. Inside he discovered a skull, rocks, and other debris. A well-known fossil aficionado, Alberto Blanc, was staying on the estate and was called in to have a look (Trinkaus and Shipman 1992). What Blanc observed when he entered the cave was a broken Neanderthal skull resting upside down, apparently within a circle of stones. Blanc immediately put the word out that evidence of ritual cannibalism had been discovered in Monte Circeo. The living, he suggested, had extracted the brain from the deceased Neanderthal and then carefully placed the skull in a "ring of stones" as a sort of testimonial. As even the most novice archaeologist would recognize, the discovery of the Monte Circeo skull was fraught with problems. Did the original discoverer move the skull, put it upside down, accidentally kick it while scrambling around in the dark? Were the stones in an intentionally placed circle, or just a random circumstance from natural processes? These are the types of questions later archaeologists asked, and then answered. Reexamination of the cave site and the skull have led most to suggest the stones were simply the result of natural taphonomy and the break in the skull as likely to have resulted from a rockfall as a Neanderthal-induced blow. The rejection of the Monte Circeo "evidence" of cannibalism, however, does not mean that such practices did not exist.

In contrast to the Monte Circeo discovery, the 1899–1905 excavations at the site of Krapina, near Zagreb, Croatia, were systematic, scientific, and carefully recorded. The excavator, Gorjanovic, was fastidious in keeping notes on his stratigraphic excavations, detailing the discovery of human and animal fossils in each layer; Gorjanovic collected hundreds of Neanderthal bones ranging in date from 127,000 to 115,000 years ago. Most of these specimens were broken and disarticulated, and their presence among other animal bones, along with their fragmented state, caused Gorjanovic to suggest they resulted from cannibalism. The carefully excavated remains from Krapina make this claim far more plausible than the suspect Monte Circeo evidence.

A more recent discovery at the Moula-Guercy shelter in France lends credence to the cannibalism theory. Excavations in the 1990s revealed nearly 80 Neanderthal bones that exhibited stone tool cut marks; further analysis suggests that at least six individuals were represented, and that the cut marks on their bones resembled those on red deer that were likely consumed by Neanderthals (Klein and Edgar 2002).

Neanderthal Burials: Shamans, Ancestors, and the Concept of Death

The most extensive evidence for Neanderthal ritual behavior is found in burials that appear intentional. Living Neanderthals apparently dug a "grave" or intentionally piled stones or other materials over someone who had died. The important question here is what might have motivated Neanderthals to exert themselves for the dead. Of course, the most prosaic explanation is that they were simply getting the body out of the way or even burying it to cut down on the smell. However, simply removing the body to somewhere outside the living area would have accomplished the same goal.

Several examples of intentional burials have already been described, including the Neanderthal burial at Regourdou, possibly accompanied by bear bones and tools. The Old Man of La Chapelle was laid within a pit, on his back, with his head facing west. The pit in which he rested had been filled with soil different from that surrounding the burial, indicating intentionality in the creation of his resting place and the infilling after he was placed in it.

The evidence at the French rock shelter site of La Ferrassie offers not one burial but seven. Two of these burials were adults, a male and a female; the rest were children ranging in age from a post-natal fetus to 5–7 years. They were interred between 65,000 and 75,000 years ago, in separate pits covered by mounded earth, in flexed positions, with the adult male and female lying head to head. The flexed position of the skeletons, particularly the female who was tightly flexed, leads some to suggest that the bodies may have been bound before burial (Jordan 1999). Flint tools accompanied the adult male burial and several of the children; other pits had been dug, apparently empty of anything or containing only animal bones. Perhaps the most remarkable feature in this set of burials was the treatment of one of the children, aged approximately 4 years. The skull in this burial had been removed and buried a short distance away. Lying over the skull was a large triangular slab; on the underside, eight pairs of cup-like depressions had been carved, with two other depressions in separate positions, for a total of 18 on the slab. The burials at La Ferrassie have raised numerous questions, including whether this is a "cemetery" for a "family," and great curiosity over why the skull of the child was removed and buried separately. Was this young child special, and if so, why? Had he been heralded as a potentially important individual in the future and his death at such a young age dictated special treatment? Was the stone carved to mark his skull for continued ceremonies even after his death? Unfortunately, none of these interesting theories can be confirmed with the present evidence and thus remain in the realm of speculation.

Another example of the intentional burial of a child is found at Dederiyeh Cave, in Syria. A young child, approximately 2 years of age, was buried on its back with its legs flexed. Accompanying the toddler was a rectangular limestone slab placed at the child's head, and a piece of flint, triangular in shape, placed over the child's heart (Akazawa et al. 1995). An adult male burial in Kebara Cave in Israel is also worth noting. Excavated in 1983 in an intentionally dug pit, this burial of an adult male dates to 60,000 years ago. The skeleton was on its back, with one hand placed across the body on the opposite shoulder, the other resting on the stomach. The most interesting feature is the missing skull. The fact that the rest of the skeleton was not disturbed, and that it showed no animal teeth marks, indicates to the excavators that the skull was intentionally removed by humans rather than by animals. Furthermore, it appears that the skull was removed after the flesh of the body decayed, meaning that Neanderthals returned to the burial much later with the intention of removing the skull.

Perhaps the most spectacular evidence of Neanderthal intentional burial comes from Shanidar Cave, in Iraq. There are several burials at this site that bear consideration. The cave, excavated by the Soleckis in the 1950s and 1960s, offered nine Neanderthal burials (referred to as Shanidar 1–9), five of which were individual burials, the other four possibly representing a group burial. Shanidar 4, 6, 8, and 9 were buried either at the same time or one shortly after another. These burials were superimposed on one another, with Shanidar 4 lying atop the others. These burials date to approximately 50,000 years ago. Shanidar 4 was an adult between 35 and 40 years in age and probably male, though the bones were in very poor shape and thus sex assignment is only provisional (Trinkaus 1983). Shanidar 6 and Shanidar 8 have smaller bones than Shanidar 4, with Shanidar 6 having the smallest skeletal structure of the three. Shanidar 6 was an adult, perhaps 20–25 years in age, but the Shanidar 8 bones were too fragmented to yield age or sex evidence except to say that it was probably a young adult. Both Shanidar 6 and 8 were most likely females (Trinkaus 1983). Shanidar 9 was an infant, perhaps 2 or 3 months in age. This collection of individuals is interesting in and of itself, especially if they were intentionally buried together, either simultaneously or as they died. It highlights the same type of "Neanderthal family structure" question that the burial group at La Ferrassie raised. However, perhaps even more interesting is what pollen samples from the Shanidar 4 burial show: flowers were apparently buried with this individual (Solecki 1975). Studies show the pollen was ancient (therefore not a result of present-day contamination), and it was deposited in quite large quantities, far more than windblown action or animal disturbance of the grave might have caused. Shanidar 4, an adult male, possibly buried with two younger females and an infant, was laid to rest and then covered in spring flowers (Figure 5.6).

The other remarkable burial in Shanidar Cave is not notable because of any grave goods accompanying the burial, but for the skeletal remains. The Shanidar 1 burial was later in time than Shanidar 4, perhaps between 10,000 and 15,000 years later. Shanidar 1 was an adult male approximately 40–45 years in age, a rather long life in the difficult world of the Neanderthals (Trinkaus 1983). What is remarkable about Shanidar 1 is not his long life, but the injuries he sustained during it. Trinkaus notes,

Figure 5.6. Artistic rendering of Neanderthal "flower" burial of Shanidar 4. (*M. J. Hughes*)

"Shanidar 1 was one of the most severely traumatized Pleistocene hominids for whom we have evidence. He suffered multiple fractures involving the cranium, right humerus, and the fifth metatarsal, and the right knee, ankle" (1983:401). The injuries to his right arm were so severe that the lower portion atrophied and was entirely unusable. Several joints showed degenerative disease resulting from these injuries. It is unlikely that this individual could have walked without help, or used his right arm; furthermore, an injury to the left side of his head, perhaps from a different time than those sustained on the right side of his body, left him blind in his left eye. What is remarkable is that this individual survived these injuries, not just by a few weeks, but by *years*. Certainly this person could not have hunted or taken part in any vigorous daily activities in which Neanderthals must have regularly engaged. Theories as to what caused Shanidar 1's injuries include a crushing injury, perhaps from a rockfall (a perpetual danger of cave life), or perhaps by a fall down a very rocky slope or even a cliff (Trinkaus 1983). The upshot of Shanidar 1's survival is that as he became increasingly infirm, he certainly required help; someone had to provide food for him, and perhaps even help him move from place to place and provide warmth in the form of campfires or blankets. Shanidar 1 was not left to die after his injuries, but survived them for years while receiving care from fellow Neanderthals. It is worth noting that the same might be said of the Old Man of La Chapelle, who was of a similar age and who suffered from severe arthritis, possibly limiting his contribution to group survival. Evidence, therefore, teaches us that some of the old and infirm were not left to die but were cared for until, presumably, they died of natural causes.

The various examples of intentional burials lead us to several avenues of speculation. Specialized treatment of the dead, and the depositing of goods such as tools, suggests Neanderthals conceived of something "beyond" death, along the lines of an "afterlife." Also relevant is the question of why some Neanderthals received such treatment and others did not. At least three burials feature old men who needed assistance: La Chapelle, Shanidar 1, and the Kebara Cave male whose skull was much later carefully removed. Such treatment of these individuals possibly suggests that they were important to the living, though the reasons why are lost to us. Perhaps their roles as shamans or living (and then dead) ancestral leaders is not beyond the realm of conjecture. Whether the specialized treatment of "shamans" or "ancestors" at death heralds a belief in an afterlife or just respectful handling of important individuals after they cease to exist cannot be determined. The same question applies to the multiple burials at La Ferrassie and Shanidar. Were these families who were buried together so that they would be united in whatever comes after? Why did one child at La Ferrassie receive specialized burial, and what meaning did flowers have in Shanidar 4? While the reasons for such actions cannot be confirmed, they do add to the mounting evidence that Neanderthals conducted specialized burials for reasons that smack of ritual symbolism and notions of a world that contained more than just the next meal.

Conclusion: Did the Neanderthals Really Have Religion?

This chapter has explored the evidence for the first occurrence of religious practice or at least the glimmerings of symbolic thought. None of the evidence is incontrovertible, but there is enough to suggest that modern humans were not the first to contemplate a world beyond life on the physical plane with its needs for food and procreation. If we accept most of the evidence above, then the Neanderthals practiced animal cults or held totemistic ancestors in reverence; they also cared for the elderly and infirm and may have then engaged in ancestor veneration at the time of their burial. Some individuals, even young children, were singled out as special, perhaps because they had been chosen as future shamans or leaders. Families were buried together, perhaps in hope that they would live united in what came after; others were given tools or symbols of their totemistic ancestor to carry with them to the beyond. Finally, special individuals were partially consumed in ritual ceremonies, not to supplement a meager diet, but because consuming their flesh meant keeping their spirit alive in those who consumed it. It is nearly certain that not all of these explanations of Neanderthal behavior are true, but it is almost equally certain that Neanderthals believed something. However, what the first spark of religion was remains, at present, in the realm of supposition.

USEFUL SOURCES

Christopher Stringer and Clive Gamble, *In Search of the Neanderthals*, 1993.
Christopher Stringer and Peter Andrews, *The Complete World of Human Evolution*, 2005.
James Shreeve, *The Neanderthal Enigma*, 1995.

6

ROCK ART AND RITUAL IN AFRICA AND AUSTRALIA

Some of the most elusive religions to track archaeologically are those practiced by mobile cultures which typically leave behind little in the way of material remains. Hunter-gatherers fall perhaps into the "most difficult" category, since tracing even their campsites archaeologically is often a challenge. Present-day informants have greatly aided archaeologists in the interpretation of a major feature in hunter-gatherer religion: rock art. Exploring the artistic representations of hunter-gatherer cosmology offers unique insight into how humans interrelated with their environment.

Cultures of the Kalahari

The Kalahari Bushmen live in the desert of the same name; Bushman cultures are found scattered across the modern nations of Namibia, Botswana, and South Africa (Figure 6.1). The Bushmen have been known by a number of culture names: Khoisan, primarily referring to their language group; San, a Tswanna word meaning "primitive"; and various ethnic group names such as !Kung. One of the most distinctive aspects of Khoisan languages is the audible click sound that is part of normal speech. The Bushmen are an ancient culture and in fact are often referred to as the "First People" of Africa, having lived in the same region and practiced their hunting-and-gathering lifeways for tens of thousands of years. Recently anthropologists and archaeologists have begun to address the plight of the Bushmen in their struggle to retain their lifeways and their lands (Hitchcock and Koperski 2007; Hitchcock and Osborn 2002; Isaacson 2001).

As discussed in Chapter 3, the best approach to interpreting rock art is to understand the culture that produced it. Since most archaeologists agree that the rock art in southern and southwestern Africa was created by ancestors of the Kalahari Bushmen, it is this culture that is profiled here. However, present-day ethnographic data does not guarantee precision of insight into the exact societal structure that produced the artwork.

The Kalahari Bushmen are traditionally mobile hunters and gatherers, living in small kin-related bands of anywhere from 15 to 50 individuals. In their movements across the landscape, the Bushmen follow a seasonal cycle that roughly corresponds to the path they followed in previous years; in general their movements are dictated by

Figure 6.1. Map of African region where rock art associated with the Kalahari Bushmen occurs. (*S. R. Steadman*)

the rainy versus dry season; bands either disperse more widely or aggregate more closely depending on water availability (Kent 1992). In this way a particular group becomes associated with a particular territory, although there is no sense of "ownership" of that territory, just familiarity and association with it (Lee 1984).

Bushman males are renowned hunters and hunt in a cooperative group. Small game is often hunted with traps; for larger game, bow hunting is the norm. Bushman hunters are superb trackers and possess terrific physical endurance. Arrows tips are dipped in a slow-acting poison that may not bring the animal down for hours or even days, depending on the size of the prey. Not only must the hunter track the animal as it flees, but he must eventually butcher it and carry it back to camp, which may be quite a distance away. All parts of prey are used: bones make tools, while skins and internal organs are used for clothing, bags, containers, and blankets. Typical prey includes zebras, giraffes, deer, and antelope, and smaller creatures such as porcupines, hares, tortoises, and snakes. Bushmen whose territory includes rivers will regularly exploit fish as well. That said, most of the Bushman diet consists of plants gathered by the women, although if an opportunity presents itself, a woman will also trap or snare a small animal. Bushman women exploit over 100 different types of plant products, including nuts, fruits, tubers, and roots. They use a digging stick for extracting deeply buried plants, and carry everything, children included, in their *kaross* (animal-skin bag).

Anthropologically, hunter-gatherer bands are described as *egalitarian* with regard to the ownership of materials and the decision-making process. This is more or less true of the Bushmen when it comes to group or band-wide decisions (versus individual decision-making within a nuclear family group). Perhaps the best word to describe the decision-making process is *consensus*: there is no single leader who can make decisions for the group irrespective of the opinion of others. Though there may be a "headman" or "headwoman" in the band, this is generally an honorary title given either to the eldest member or perhaps to the members of the family most closely associated with the region in which the band hunts and gathers. With regard to the sharing of resources, the Bushmen are scrupulously careful about the equal distribution of hunted and gathered foods and the sharing of tools and necessary goods.

The Bushman kinship system can be considered *universal* in the sense that everyone is classified as some type of relative, whether blood-related or not. When Richard Lee (1984), an ethnographer who studied the Dobe !Kung Bushmen, finally received his "name" and thus entered the kinship system, he instantly possessed relatives, including fathers, mothers, and even wives! Bushman kinship consists of two basic categories—"joking kin" and "avoidance kin"—which dictate all social relationships, the selection of marriage partners, and essentially with whom you spend the majority of your social time. Joking kin, which have a more easygoing and natural relationship, encompass grandparents and grandchildren, spouses and spousal relatives (with some exceptions), and the individual's siblings and some cousins. Those in the "avoidance" category include parents and children, those who are classified as parents (such as aunts and uncles), and some in-laws, such as the mother of one's spouse. There are formal rules of behavior for avoidance kin that reinforce lines of respect between individuals who live in an egalitarian society.

The collective religions of the Kalahari Bushmen cultures are perhaps our best key to interpreting the rock art of the region. The Bushmen believe in a supreme being who was responsible for creation, though his nature and his role in daily life differ somewhat across the cultures. In some cases, the supreme being is male and has a consort or wife; in others he is dual-gendered. Some believe he is purely good, locked in combat with evil forces, while others believe he represents both good and evil, alternately helping and harming humans. Another deity named Kaggen, sometimes associated with the preying mantis, is often credited with the creation of various things such as the moon and the eland (one of the larger antelopes of southern Africa and a common actor in Bushman rituals) (Vinnicombe 1976). Kaggen is a trickster deity who does not always have the best interests of the Bushmen at heart. Quite often Kaggen tries to thwart the efforts of the Bushmen in their rituals, especially when such rituals involve the eland (Lewis-Williams 2001).

Common among Bushman groups are initiation ceremonies for both males and females and a ritual specifically for healing purposes called the *medicine dance* or *trance dance*. In the male initiation ritual, the process culminates with the boy's successful hunt. He is expected to kill a large animal, preferably an antelope or eland, in order to achieve full adulthood. At their first menstruation, girls are isolated and women relatives perform the Eland Dance, where they imitate this animal's mating behavior. The eland also appears in the marriage ritual, during which the groom gives eland meat to the bride's parents, and the bride is later adorned with fat from the eland.

Illness is thought to result from a spirit shooting invisible poisonous arrows into the victim. The trance dance has the dual purpose of healing the victim by drawing the arrows out, as well as discovering the reason for the illness in the first place. The ritual starts at sundown; a group of Bushmen gather around a fire and begin to clap and sing to musical accompaniment. Those who are shamans, usually males and some elder women, begin to dance in a circle around a fire. They dance for hours until they fall into an altered state of consciousness which ignites the healing medicine, known as n/um. This boils in their stomach and moves upward to their head, causing great pain as it does so. Shamans frequently experience stomach cramps as the n/um activates. Another common side effect is bleeding from the nose when they enter the trance, perhaps a result of changes in blood pressure as the shamans' bodily functions alter.

When n/um is activated, the healers then lay hands on the patient(s) and draw out the poisonous arrows; shamans' souls can also leave their bodies and travel to the spirit world to try to discover the reason for the attack on the victim. Only very skilled shamans attempt this journey, as it is believed that the soul might become lost and never return. One enters the spirit world through holes in the ground or through pools of water into which the shaman's spirit travels (Dowson 1998a); there the reason for the illness may be discovered. Besides those who are obviously ill, the healers may lay hands on others sitting in the circle to bring well-being to their souls. Although anyone may become a shaman, some are considered more skilled than others, and these shamans achieve an element of renown. While the trance dance is one of the main methods used for healing, the Bushmen also have a deep knowledge of the healing properties of plants and make use of a variety of herbs and potions to treat all sorts of ailments. Women are particularly skilled in the use of plants for healing purposes.

In Bushman culture there are generally three categories of shaman: *healers* such as those already described, *game shamans* (discussed below), and *rainmaking shamans*, all of whom use the trance dance in their work. Every shaman is considered to have expertise in one of these three areas. Some believe that very powerful shamans have the ability to turn themselves into animals, essentially into what might be considered their "familiars" or representatives in the spirit world.

Like any other culture, the Bushmen have a rich cosmology, with many myths explaining the universe. Many of the myths involve Kaggen and his exploits. Original creation, illness, and death are attributed to the supreme being described above. Places that are cool and water-filled, such as caves, pools of water, and holes in the ground, are thought of as the entrance place to the spirit world (Dowson 1998a), and so such places should be approached with extreme care.

The rainmaking ritual takes several forms, but all forms include a *rain animal*. According to informants, the animal can be a hippopotamus, but the eland is considered the most powerful rainmaker. Snakes, because of their close association with water, may also be rain creatures. One method to induce rain is to capture a powerful rain animal while it is at the watering hole and then lead it to the area where rain is needed. Slaughtering the animal there and letting its blood fall to the ground will bring rain. However, it is unclear from ethnographic accounts of this ritual whether the action takes place on the earthly plane, physically carried out by a shaman, or on the spiritual plane and accomplished by the shaman's spirit or familiar.

Southern African Rock Art

Rock art images have been found across the breadth of southern Africa, created by ancestors of the people today known as the Bushmen. The art is either painted on the rock face or engraved into it. Engraved images have a longer life span, but the painted art is more ubiquitous. Earth tone colors—dark red, white, black, brown, and orange—are the norm. White is frequently used to represent magical substances, such as the n/um in the shaman's body, as well as to show lines emanating from an entranced shaman, depicting his spirit leaving his body bound for the spirit world. Red usually indicates blood, while black, orange, red, and various shades of brown are used for the bodies of animals, humans, therianthropes, and anthropomorphs. The mixing of red and white yields light reds and pinks that can indicate color variations on animals. The depictions show great skill and an eye for depth perception and overall scene setting.

Without a doubt, Bushman rock art is reflective of their culture and environment. Some scenes show events of everyday life. In others, a more nuanced interpretation offers insight into Bushman religious belief and ritual. Actions depicted are often ones that are meant to put the environment to rights in a world where rain and meat are sometimes too scarce. The Bushman rock art is an ideal example of the intersection between culture, religion, and environment.

Dating the Art

Dating rock art is difficult because often there are no associated sites nearby, and the art itself doesn't always offer datable materials. Even if there are associated material remains, one must wonder whether it was the artists themselves who built that campfire or used those tools. There have been cases in which the pigment, which might include animal blood, plant fibers or hair (from the brush), or charcoal, can offer radiocarbon-dating opportunities (Rowe 2001). In other circumstances, later stratified layers covering the art can give a *terminus ante quem*. Occasionally it is the scenes themselves that offer relative dates; an image featuring a covered wagon or a human wearing recognizable dress (such as a soldier's uniform or a bustled dress), domesticated animals or plants, or other datable activities or objects can usually be placed within a century of its creation. Nonetheless, even with such methods, some rock art remains undated. However, the scholars who have devoted their lives to studying these images have determined with some certainty that the majority were created in the last several millennia, many having been painted within the last 500 years (Dowson 1998b; Solomon 1998). Several other sets of paintings, however, have been tentatively dated to over 25,000 years ago (Garlake 2001; Solomon 1998).

Rock Art Images

While much of the art has been interpreted as representing various aspects of Bushman cosmology and shamanic activities, other scenes may simply display everyday activities.

Many examples of southern African rock art can be placed into type categories. One category depicts food-acquisition activities, including hunting and gathering. Depictions show women with digging sticks and a kaross heading out in groups or singly, or squatting to dig up a root plant. More common are images of men engaged in hunting. These scenes show every stage of the hunting cycle, including groups going out on the hunt, the approach to the animal, and the toting of the kill back to camp (Vinnicombe 1976). Some scenes show groups of men running with their bows, perhaps chasing an animal that has been hit with a poisoned arrow. A few scenes appear to depict the butchering process as well. Fishing scenes are also found on rock faces near rivers. These images are, without much doubt, depictions of the daily lives and activities of the ancient Bushmen of the region. A few scenes in which a single hunter successfully brings down a large animal may represent the "first kill" manhood initiation rite of young Bushman males. The young man's triumph, in this case, is forever commemorated on the rock face for all to see.

In addition to the manhood ritual scenes, other depictions appear to take a step beyond routine activities into the realm of religion and ritual. The general consensus among rock art scholars is that many scenes represent shamanistic activities, the most frequent of which is the process of rainmaking. In these scenes, a rain animal has been captured and a human (shaman) leads it by a rope. Most commonly the rain animal is an eland, an animal thought to have much magical power, but other animals appear in such scenes as well. Often the animal appears to be bleeding. An example of such a scene is shown in Figure 6.2. Here, the rain animal (eland, bull?) is led by a thong or rope, while the spray of paint emanating from the animal suggests liquid flying off its hide (sweat, water, or possibly blood). Most likely the animal is being led to the place where rain is most crucially needed; the majority of its blood will be let there by the shaman or shamans, who may be male or female (Tedlock 2005), involved in the rain-making ceremony.

A second category of depictions shows people in attitudes of dance. These images are almost certainly renderings of the trance dance ceremony, probably for healing purposes. Some people, often women, are seated and clapping, while others are dancing. Sometimes the dancers have lines extending from their noses, which likely indicate the nosebleeds so common when entering the trance. In some scenes the dancers also have white-painted lines extending upward from their heads. These depict the shaman's spirit leaving his body for the spirit world; in some cases an animal or therianthropic figure is shown in the background, probably representing the shaman's spirit form as it enters the spirit world. Occasionally dancers are shown bending over in attitudes of pain, demonstrating the activation of the n/um. Without knowledge of present-day Bushman religion and ritual, the rich detail of the rock art images would certainly be lost to us.

In some examples, therianthropic humans are featured, sometimes with animals or other images. One example (Figure 6.3) shows a figure with human legs but an

Figure 6.2. People leading an animal (possibly a "rain eland") by a rope (the dotted line at the top). (*Photo courtesy of D. Whitley*)

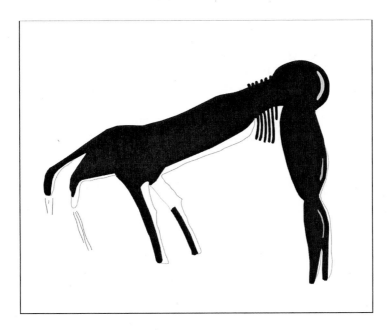

Figure 6.3. A therianthrope.
(*Sketch based on D. Whitley's photo of Willem's Shelter painting*)

animal torso and head. The depiction here represents the shaman's journey in his spirit form, and his triumph over the eland. Other drawings show humans with animal characteristics that may represent costuming. Men with antelope (probably rhebok) horns or ears may be game shamans, responsible for making game available to the hunters. While entering the trance, the game shaman dons costuming of this animal which he intends to lure to the hunting arena (Challis 2005).

One other interesting set of images includes geometric images, dots, zigzags, grids, and curvy lines. Many scholars, including Lewis-Williams, believe these geometric figures are images seen by shamans entering a trance. In the neuropsychological model discussed in Chapter 4, this is a phenomenon known as *entoptics*. In the first, or lightest, stage of entering a trance, all humans visualize geometric images (Lewis-Williams 2002, 2008). The second stage of the entoptic process, which Lewis-Williams calls *construal*, is to interpret these images. Thus, since every culture has different symbolisms, environments, and experiences, these images are variously interpreted by informants. In southern Africa, construal circles can represent the holes though which one enters the spirit world; zigzags might represent a zebra or zebra-like creature present in the spirit world, and crescent-shaped lines with associated dots are often interpreted as beehives. The neuropsychological model, combined with ethnographic data, is an invaluable interpretive tool for understanding Bushman rock art.

Conclusion

Although the nuanced messages these paintings were meant to impart may be lost, ethnographically based insight drawn from Bushman religion and ritual offers numerous clues. Many images represent the shamanistic journey in a trance state; the beings the shaman encounters (fantastical animals and other shamans), the actions he undertakes, and his own spiritual form are all rendered on the stone face. Various lines of evidence suggest these paintings were visited, touched, added to, and perhaps served as the sites of additional shamanistic journeys (Lewis-Williams 2001). The rock art in southern Africa is indeed "art" but is also a crucial key to unlocking the rich ritual behaviors and religious beliefs of the ancient inhabitants of this region. One overall message in the rock art is that religion was an important element in helping the inhabitants of a challenging environment cope with the dangers of scarce rain and minimal game. The intersection between religion and environment is clearly played out in the rock art of southern Africa.

Religion and Rock Art in Australia

The original inhabitants of Australia, collectively known as Aboriginals, arrived on the northern mainland at least 50,000 years ago. No land bridge to Asia has existed for millions of years, but during the Pleistocene epoch (1.8 mya to approximately 12,000 years ago) sea levels dropped, creating a land mass stretching from Tasmania in the south to New Guinea in the north. This continent is known as Sahul (Figure 6.4). Sahul was separated from the enlarged Asian continent (called Sunda) by only 50 kilometers of open water. The first inhabitants probably came in small groups, either intentionally or as a result of unexpected currents or inclement weather that made a short inter-island trip an unwanted adventure to a new land.

New residents slowly spread across the continent. The Lake Mungo site in New South Wales dates to approximately 26,000 years ago. The settlement at Lake Mungo, now a dry lake, featured a number of hearths where residents cooked their meals and made stone tools. Two burials, a female dating to ca. 26,000 B.P. and a male buried ca. 30,000 B.P., both received specialized treatment. The male was laid on his side with clasped hands; ocher was sprinkled over his body, eternally staining the soil around him pink and eventually his bones as well. The female was first cremated, and then her bones were smashed. Her remains were then buried in a small pit (Flood 1983). It is

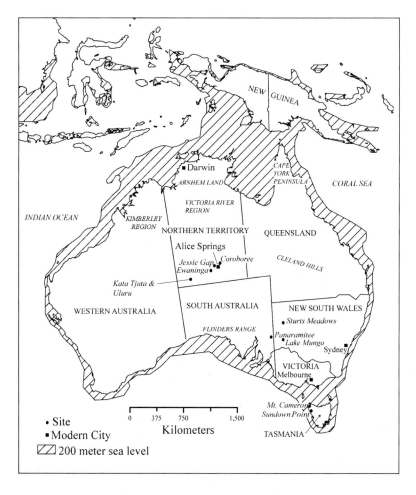

Figure 6.4. Map of sites discussed in the chapter, and area of Sahul and Sunda.
(*T. Edwards*)

probable that these burials were not unique, but the difficult climatic conditions of the Lake Mungo region do not preserve organic remains well. The site does, however, indicate that rituals may have accompanied death in Aboriginal Australia as long ago as 30,000 years.

Aboriginal Social Structure

At the time of European arrival there were roughly 250 different, mutually unintelligible, languages spoken in Australia, each with several or more dialects. Although nearly all these languages are from the same language family known as Proto-Australian, the separation of culture groups made them quite distinct. As many as a thousand distinct cultures may have existed in pre-contact Australia; thus only the broadest overview can be offered here.

Traditional Aboriginal economy relied on the hunting-and-gathering model. The ecosystems in Australia include desert, tropical coast, rainforest, alpine mountains, and open scrub. Because there are a variety of ecosystems, cultures used different methods to acquire their food, ranging from extensive fishing on the coast to large-game hunting (kangaroos, emus) in the interior, substantially supplemented by plants and insects. Aboriginal groups had intimate knowledge of the landscape and everything in it, allowing them rich and satisfying diets. The Aboriginal men and women tended to collect food in family groups. Though they might come together with other family groups (some probably kin-related) to camp at the end of the day, food was consumed by each individual family rather than shared among the entire collection of people.

The majority of the hunting was carried out by the men, though women sometimes came home with game if such became available on an outing. The main hunting weapons were the spear and the club, which were also used in warfare. Aboriginals made extensive use of spear throwers, which allowed hunters to throw farther and with greater accuracy. The other weapon, now famous to most of the world, was the *boomerang*, a throwing stick that required much skill to throw accurately. The most famous boomerang is the one shaped like the wings of an airplane. This is known as the "returning" boomerang, and if thrown properly will fly in a high circle and return to the thrower. This was used in games but might also be thrown to bring down a bird. More common in hunting was the non-returning or hunting boomerang, which is not symmetrical but looks more like a capital *L*, with the short leg angled upward by a few degrees; the hunting boomerang also functioned as a weapon in combat.

The majority of the Aboriginal diet came from the plant foods gathered by the women, who have been called the "chief breadwinners" for the group and family (Berndt and Berndt 1983:66). A day of gathering might also net a small animal or eggs, thereby providing protein in the diet as well. On their gathering expeditions, women carried digging sticks and wooden bowls, and net bags or baskets to collect food.

As is the case with many foraging societies, the Aboriginals were highly nomadic. They built branch huts (today known as *wurlies*) used mainly for storage of their foods and belongings, and perhaps to provide a bit of shade for children during the hottest part of the day. They were careful land managers and took pains not to over-hunt or deplete the landscape in any way. For instance, the honey ants in central Australia store honeydew in their abdomens, creating a pea-sized sack of nectar. Women dig down for these ants' nests and then remove the sack from the ants but leave the insects alive because the sack will develop once again.

In the more temperate and tropical regions in the north and along the western coasts, where freshwater rivers and lakes can be found, water is in regular supply. However, in the arid center and east, intimate knowledge of the location of water holes is an essential component of Aboriginal survival. Though the surface may be dry, digging down a meter or so often reveals a source of water. Aboriginals will examine the landscape for signs of where animals have dug down and follow suit in the same place, using the the animal kingdom's innate knowledge for their own survival as well.

The hundreds of Aboriginal cultures are mainly defined by their language, territory, and social ties of kinship and clan (Berndt and Berndt 1983). Kinship groups were unilineal, with some cultures practicing patrilineal descent and some matrilineal; a few used both systems, but children would belong only to one descent group. The choice of marriage partners was carefully monitored so as to avoid incest in what were essentially very small communities. Marriages were usually arranged by the family, and in most cultures men could take more than one wife, while women were restricted to a single husband.

Another important aspect of Aboriginal social structure is their belief in totemic ancestors. Aboriginal totemism rests on the principle that all life is connected spiritually. Totems are drawn from all the plant and animal life in Australia, as well as from important natural features such as lightning, water, and clouds. Individuals may have links with several totems; they acquire their links by virtue of their kinship relationships, their mother's pregnancy, as well as other factors (Berndt and Berndt 1983). For instance, when a woman becomes pregnant, the child immediately acquires the totemic relationship with whatever ancestral being is associated with the place where she first realized her pregnancy. Totemic beings associated with the sacred sites in a group's landscape are worshipped as well.

Australian Aboriginals practice their religion in an all-encompassing manner:

> For Aborigines in any given region, religious commitment was something that involved the whole community. Everyone was caught up in it, actively, or passively, not only from birth but from the moment of conception, or even before that in one mode of reckoning. Traditionally, nobody could opt out. (Berndt and Berndt 1983:60)

When sacred rituals were to be carried out, everyone was involved (usually excluding children). If a ritual took place at a site sacred to one part of the kin group (for instance, at the emu totem), then those who were most closely associated with that ancestor led the ceremony; at the kangaroo ritual the following month, others were the leaders. Some locations were for "women's business" only and thus could not be visited by men, and vice versa. At many places the sacred stories associated with the site were known only to those who were initiated there and belonged to that totem; these stories were passed on to initiates at the time of their rite of passage, but were not bandied about at general storytelling sessions. They were the secret and sacred knowledge of the select few associated with that place.

Dreamtime and Religion

The Aboriginal religion, awkwardly translated as "Dreamtime" or "The Dreaming," encompasses dimensions of time, space, locality, and kinship, among many other elements.

The Aboriginal understanding of time is not linear but rather transcendent. For instance, an event that happened in the past, such as the creation of the landscape, is also viewed as happening now and in the future (Stanner 1987). Aboriginal religion is one of the most difficult of religions for anthropologists to adequately describe (Swain 1998); one scholar defines Dreamtime this way:

> an understanding and explanation of the world and how it works, a moral code, law and love. It relates to the creation of the world, to a timeless past when "people" and "animals" and all things animate and inanimate were more or less free to wander the cosmos and act, not having yet attained their defining features. But it is also a time when these defining features were obtained. (David 2002:17)

These defining features, and the cosmos itself, were created by ancestral beings who were responsible for the creation of the landscape and the creatures in it. There is a Dreamtime myth for every aspect of this creation, explaining how and why it happened and how it links Aboriginals, specific animals, and places together.

Dreamtime stories recount events such as the movements of Rainbow Serpent across northern Australia; as he wound his way across the landscape, the movements of his body created topographical features that became sacred to the cultures living in those areas. Other stories describe the actions of animals in specific places. Aboriginal kin groups hold both place and animal sacred, carrying out rituals there and reciting the Dreamtime stories that made the locality a religious setting.

One way to visualize these stories is as *tracks*. As the ancestral beings moved across the landscape, they created such features as trees, water holes, and rock formations; their mythic events became recorded in Dreamtime stories that formed tracks or *songlines* across the territory of one kin group and often into that of the next. Thus the landscape exists in the resident's mind as a mental map of lines and places that make up the past, present, and future of existence (Smith 1999). A woman sitting on a rock rests on a piece of her ancestor or totem, a location where some important part of the Dreamtime associated with her kin group occurred (Lawlor 1991).

Sacred places are found at nearly every natural setting or geographical feature, as small as a pool of water or as large as Uluru in central Australia (Figure 6.5). Because individual Aboriginals are associated with several totems, they travel across the landscape with a mental map. This map provides a network of sacred places and Dreamtime stories that explain their creation, important events, and inter- and intra-kin relationships, but the map grows fuzzier the farther they range from their ancestral land. This map floats in a temporal continuum that brings ancestors and living Aboriginals together. Myths are passed down within clans, orally through song and recitation, and through rock art. If a clan dies out or is unable to live in their territories (as has happened since the European colonization of Australia), these stories of Dreamtime are lost, as are the specific explanations of the rock art images found in those sacred places.

As noted above, everyone except uninitiated children participated in Dreamtime rituals and ceremonies. There were Aboriginal male and female specialists, shamans who were capable of performing many services for their people; female shamans most often served as midwives and healers (Tedlock 2005). Men trained as apprentices and underwent more severe initiation rites to gain status as specialists in their communities (Elkin 1977). They could be called on to perform a number of services, including healing, especially if the sickness was thought to have been caused by sorcery; they were also capable of mind reading, predicting future events, and divining other information such as the identity of a killer, as gleaned from the soul of a murder victim (Elkin 1977). In general, shamans were

> recognized by their tribe or community as possessing the power to outwit malign spirits and persons, to control the elements, to have foreknowledge of an enemy's approach, and to keep pestilence away from the camp. (Elkin 1977:11)

The source of the shaman's power may spring from one or more of the Dreamtime beings, such as Rainbow Serpent (discussed below); sometimes the spirits of the dead may impart power. Shamans were "made" through a variety of rituals, depending

Figure 6.5. Uluru monolith in the "Red Center" of the Northern Territory in central Australia. (*Photo by S. R. Steadman*)

on the culture, which took place at sacred places on the Dreamtime landscape. In most of these rituals a Dreamtime supernatural being, or an ancestral spirit, was an integral participant in the creation of the religious specialist. It is possible, perhaps even likely, that such rituals were preserved in the art painted and engraved on the Australian landscape.

Embedded in Aboriginal life and Dreamtime are other rituals marking important points in the life cycle and the reenactment of Dreamtime stories; they also serve to maintain the natural world and ecological balance. Rituals performed to reenact activities of totemic ancestors take place at sites sacred to these beings; rituals may celebrate important events such as the very creation of a place, a battle there, or even the totem's death. Ceremonies may include the recitation of songs or stories recounting the events; if rock art is associated with the site, repaintings might also be important components.

Many rituals include initiation rites which mark the passage in the life cycle from one stage to the next. Aboriginal men may have numerous initiations during their lifetime, depending on the culture. Sites where such initiations take place are sacred to men; only initiated men or those undergoing the rites are allowed to go to these places. There are also many places sacred to women, where "women's business" is carried out and men are not allowed to go.

Another ceremony is known as an *increase ritual*, though one scholar notes this is a bit of a misnomer (Stanner 1998), because they are really intended to *maintain* an ecological balance rather than increase the animal or plant population; he suggests that *maintenance rite* is a better name for these rituals. Such events take place at Dreamtime locales sacred to the target of the ritual (i.e., animals such as kangaroo, or elements such as water).

Stone Monuments, Rock Art, and Dreamtime

Because Australia is far larger than the Kalahari Desert, and it has a far greater variety of ecosystems and cultures, the sheer quantity of rock art and motifs is much greater. A great deal of work over the last century has been devoted to finding and classifying these styles and motifs for more concentrated study and interpretation.

Styles, Motifs, and Dating

The three main methods of rock art decoration are stencils, engravings, and paintings. Stencils usually depict hands. In these, the hand is placed on the rock face and then the paint (ocher) is blown onto the rock face and hand, leaving the hand image on the bare rock surrounded by red ocher. The engraving style was usually accomplished using a pecking method. The earliest engraved art is known as the *Panaramitee style*, named for the location where it was first observed in central Australia. Often images consist of animal tracks, which make up approximately two-thirds of the Panaramitee style, and geometric forms, which constitute the other third (Morwood 2002). Often many separate images were pecked onto a single rock face (Figure 6.6).

Researchers have had some success dating this earliest rock art using both relative and absolute techniques. The most common type of relative technique is measuring the patina on the engraving or painting. In the Australian desert regions and elsewhere, a type of varnish builds up on rock faces over time. To create an engraving, the artist pecks through the existing varnish or paints over it. After the engraving or painting is completed, the patina begins to develop once more, thinner on the art than on the surrounding rock. Comparisons with varnish of known date, such as is found on the Egyptian pyramids, can offer a roughly older or more recent date for Australian engravings. Many exhibit thicker patina, suggesting they are at least 5,000 years old or more. Patina comparisons suggest Panaramitee tracks and geometric images are the oldest styles of art.

Another dating method is by the content of the images themselves. Some depict animals now extinct, giving a *terminus post quem* for the images. Others depict animals

Figure 6.6. Rock engravings at Ewaninga near Alice Springs.
(*Photo by S. R. Steadman*)

such as the dingo, the indigenous canine of Australia; the dingo came to Australia about 4,000 years ago, giving a *terminus ante quem* for these depictions.

Absolute dating methods are used on organic material such as that contained in mudwasp nests built over artwork, again giving a *terminus ante quem* (Morwood 2002). Naturally laid deposits covering rock art can also yield the *terminus ante quem* when properly dated. If cultural materials are located near the art, dates from such sites can also be used, though an assumption that there is an association between the two must be made. Some of the earliest art has been dated as long ago as 40,000 years B.P.

A second style of art, which probably developed after the Panaramitee style, is known as the *Simple Figurative style* and includes both engravings and paintings. These are images produced in a naturalistic style. Humans are rendered frontally, and animals are shown from the side or from the perspective of looking down on them (Morwood 2002). The Simple Figurative style seems to be the most common around the edges of the continent, with the majority occurring near Sydney and the Cape York region.

The third and most recent painting style is known as the *Complex Figurative style*, found mainly in northwestern Australia, in the Arnhem Land and Kimbeley regions. The Complex Figurative style includes fascinating images that are neither human nor animal but rather are beings from Dreamtime. Paintings from various areas have acquired particular style names because they are unique to the region. The *Mimi style* in Arnhem Land shows small figures, usually red, in naturalistic poses or appearing to move across the landscape. Also in Arnhem Land are the slightly more recent *X-ray-style* paintings. In the Kimberley region a set of paintings in the *Bradshaw style* show humans in what is probably ceremonial dress and attitudes of dance.

Sacred Landmarks

Australia is a geologically fascinating land, with otherworldly land formations and evocative stone monuments. It isn't surprising to discover that a culture as spiritually oriented as Aboriginals would find such places sacred. The scarcity of·water in vast regions of Australia adds to the need to be intimately familiar with the earth and its secrets.

The most dramatic land formations are in a region known as the Red Center in the Northern Territory, an area named for the brick red color of the earth (from large amounts of iron in the soil). The city of Alice Springs serves as the largest modern settlement in the state. The Red Center is home to Uluru and Kata Tjuta, two large natural rock monuments which draw half a million visitors every year. However, nearly every landscape feature across the breadth of Australia has a Dreamtime story associated with it. For instance, Dreamtime stories explain that the mountains and river valley known as the Flinders Range in south Australia were created by a large snake. One story tells that the snake, known as Akurra, was thirsty and drank all the water in a lake. His distended belly carved out a river valley, and everywhere he stopped he created water holes (Tunbridge 1988). This snake is part of the Adnyamathanha culture's Dreamtime. The water holes and valley created by Akurra are sacred to this culture, and certain areas belong to various clans of the Adnyamath-anha. More intimate details of Akurra's exploits are known only to adult men and women of those clans, passed down to the next generation at appropriate points in initiation rites of passage.

Another place near Alice Springs known as Coroboree (Figure 6.7) offers a similar example, this one from the Arrernte culture which dominates the region. Dreamtime stories explain that Coroboree, meaning "meeting place," was created by a perentie, similar to a monitor-type lizard, which can grow to 6 feet in length or more. It is an important site for Arrernte men's initiation rites. At different points around Coroboree, a boy will have a tooth knocked out, be circumcised, and have his thigh cut by a spear. This entire process, in traditional times, took weeks. During these days and nights the boy was instructed by his mentor in Dreamtime mythology, warfare methods, hunting techniques, marriage, and everything else he needed to know in order to survive in the challenging landscape of central Australia.

Certainly the most famous natural monument in Australia is the massive monolith known as Uluru (Figure 6.5) in the Red Center. This single sandstone rock, which stands approximately 1 kilometer above ground and extends as much as 5 kilometers below, rests at an intersection of several Dreamtime tracks across the landscape. The rock itself extends across the territory of several kin groups collectively known as the Anangu. Stories in Anangu Dreamtime tell of the creation of the land, how all the plants, animals, and humans came to be, and hand down law and custom to the Anangu.

Four well-known stories associated with different parts of Uluru incorporate many creator beings, including hare wallabies (small kangaroo-like animals), pythons, poisonous snakes, blue-tongued lizards, the Kingfisher bird, and red lizards. An Anangu becomes associated with one of these Dreamtime tracks depending on events such as where one's umbilical cord drops after birth; other life events associate the Anangu with additional Dreamtime tracks (Layton 2001). Siblings, therefore, may have separate creator beings sacred to them, and learn different aspects of the myths at their individual initiations.

Some of the rock paintings at Uluru recount Dreamtime stories that explain natural landmarks. The story of Kuniya Woman is associated with a gorge on the

Figure 6.7. Coroboree rock near Alice Springs. (*Photo by S. R. Steadman*)

south side of Uluru. Kuniya Woman, a python, was traveling with her nephew to Uluru, carrying her eggs on her head. At the east end of Uluru, they were attacked by the Liru people (poisonous snakes), and Kuniya Woman's nephew was killed. Later on, she engaged a Liru warrior in battle on the south side of Uluru. In the gorge where the battle took place are two natural black marks on the east side rock face, which the Anangu say depict the two snakes in battle. On the west face are two natural linear gouges that represent Kuniya Woman's skillful and powerful attack on Liru, where she lunged with her weapon and struck the rock. The "Hunter's" rock shelter near the mouth of this gorge displays a panoply of rock art (Figure 6.8), some of which certainly tells elements of this myth. These linked concentric circles are thought to portray either Kuniya Woman's journey, or perhaps the eggs she carried (Layton 1992).

The lesson of the Kuniya Woman story is that the archaeologist seeking the sacred past must look not only at what is excavated, painted, or engraved, but at what occurs naturally as well. Without the oral tradition of the Anangu, we would never be able to interpret the black marks and gouges on the walls of the gorge. The presence of the art in a nearby rock shelter bearing images similar to those occurring naturally should alert us to the importance of not just the rock shelter, but of the entire landscape. Religious belief comprises the painted or engraved image, as well as the myriad physical, spiritual, and symbolic components it represents.

Figure 6.8. Rock paintings at Hunter's Cave near Uluru in the Northern Territory. (*Photo by S. R. Steadman*)

Rock Art and Dreamtime

The inhabitants of each area in Australia produced unique images and styles, corresponding to their particular Dreamtime tracks. Some art is considered public and can be viewed by anyone, including children and the uninitiated (Morwood 2002). This type of art occurs at public places, such the Uluru Hunter's Rock Shelter, so-called because hunters waited here for game exiting from a water hole in the gorge. While waiting, the hunters created art to while away the time, tell stories, decorate, and communicate information. The subjects portrayed were a mix of "doodles" and public Dreamtime stories, such as that of Kuniya Woman, told to children before their initiation. The majority of Aboriginal art is placed in locations sacred to individual clans and kin groups and portrays elements of important Dreamtime tracks.

The following section surveys the art found in various regions; in some cases informants offer clues to interpretation, and in others interpretation comes from the realm of informed archaeological conjecture.

Engraved Rock Art

The majority of engraved art is found in the arid heart of Australia. Given the antiquity of many of these images, some at least 14,000 years old, their interpretation is "not susceptible to analysis in semantic terms unless indigenous exegesis is available" (Layton 1992:142). In other words, without living informants, these images are quite a challenge to interpret accurately. The geometric and figurative engravings have been assessed as to frequency of occurrence and measured in order to classify shapes into categories that may then be interpreted (by archaeologists) based on what they look like (as discussed in Chapter 3) (e.g., Layton 1992). In addition, contemporary Aboriginals have been asked for their interpretations of the art. For instance, an engraving classified as "concentric circles" might be identified by Aboriginal informants as portraying either a meeting place or a water hole, depending on the region.

Many engravings have been interpreted as depictions of animals tracks, and some appear to show human footsteps. The animal tracks (e.g., emu, kangaroo, crane, dingo, and others) might suggest a number of meanings: (1) the artist saw the animals in the area; (2) the artist successfully hunted the animal(s); (3) they are iconic representations of animal creator beings in a Dreamtime story; or (4) engraving them serves as a type of "increase" or "maintenance" ritual device. That some are found in association with engravings thought to represent boomerangs may suggest a secular hunting scene, but then again, the boomerang might have also been part of the Dreamtime story.

The antiquity of these engravings presents a real challenge to interpretation. An engraved rock site with multiple images, such as at Ewaninga near Alice Springs (Figure 6.6), may have been created over thousands of years by as many artists, who may have been male or female, depending on whether the site was sacred to men, women, or both (Hays-Gilpin 2008). Images and their meanings may have changed subtly or even drastically over time. This is one of those points at which researchers may well want to throws up their hands in frustration; fortunately few have done so.

The Red Center

The antiquity of Red Center engravings is demonstrated by the figurative images at Cleland Hills east of Alice Springs. At this site, 16 "smiling faces" may date to 22,000 years ago (Figure 6.9). Not all of them are "smiling," and even their identification as faces is controversial. One has arms and legs, and several express emotion; thus they were initially thought to portray human faces. However, further work suggests they appear more owl- or emu-like (Flood 1997). The presence of an emu Dreamtime story associated with a sacred place to the north may be relevant. Perhaps Cleland Hills recounts the same story or represents another stage of the emu dreaming farther along the track.

Returning for a moment to the Ewaninga engraved art, we find a similar difficulty in offering interpretations. The engravings here are in Panaramitee and Simple Figurative styles and are found on a set of sandstone outcroppings that was probably once a rock shelter that collapsed. It is likely that these engravings were made over a long period of time, perhaps by different artists. The date of these engravings is not known, but it is likely that they are thousands, rather than hundreds, of years old. Like Hunter's Cave at Uluru, the Ewaninga rock art was located near a water source, a clay pan that acted as a type of artificial lake holding water after significant rains. Using the Uluru scenario, Ewaninga may simply be the "doodles" of hunters waiting for an opportune moment to obtain an excellent meal. However, if we wish to speculate further that these engravings relate more directly to Dreamtime mythology, we can identify some of the potential characters by the animal tracks, which include kangaroo (or perhaps wallaby) and emu. We might then begin with investigating the Dreamtime stories of the cultures in the region. At Jessie Gap near Alice Springs, about 40 kilometers from Ewaninga, there is an important Emu Dreamtime site associated with the Arrernte people (Figure 6.10). Perhaps their ancestors knew of additional emu activities at Ewaninga and recorded these on the rock face. Alternatively, this might have been an important "increase ritual" site meant to maintain the animal and plant populations of this arid region. Our knowledge of such rituals, and of the Emu Dreamtime site nearby, allows us to speculate that these interpretations might be the most likely for Ewaninga; confirmation, however, is unfortunately beyond our grasp.

Figure 6.9. Cleland Hills "faces." (*R. Jennison*)

Figure 6.10. Artistic rendering of ancient Aboriginal man painting at Jessie Gap. (*M. J. Hughes*)

Southeastern Australia and Tasmania

If we turn to the very southeast of Australia, including the island of Tasmania, we find some interesting engraved art and a suggestive Dreamtime story. At a site known as Sturts Meadows, several examples of Panaramitee-style engravings depict animal tracks and additional geometric forms such as clusters of circles (possibly emu eggs to go along with emu tracks), wavy lines, and other designs. Many of these occur on some dark-colored rocks jutting from the surface of this somewhat arid region. These rocks are known as "whale backs" because they resemble just that, as if the creatures were rising from the ground's surface rather than from the sea. The more unusual engravings are circles with a wheel-shape or starred design inside. Some researchers have interpreted this as a sun image. These engravings may date as early as 10,000 years ago.

Turning to the island of Tasmania, we find, in the Mount Cameron region and at Sundown Point, a range of engraved art, including animal tracks and geometric figures. The most common motif, however, is circles; some are empty inside, others have an interior circle, and some have dots inside. These motifs occur nearly at the water's edge, not in rock shelters or caves, but on outjutting rocks rising from the beach sand near the sea. The first arrivals to Tasmania came during the Pleistocene, before the waters rose between Australia and Tasmania and it was still part of Sahul. It is possible that these engravings date to that later Pleistocene period, or perhaps somewhat after, when waters began to intercede between the Australian mainland and what became the island of Tasmania. Hopes of acquiring explanations of Tasmanian rock art are forever dashed, as European colonization of Tasmania had a hugely detrimental effect on the indigenous population and there are no living informants left on the island.

Although any sure explanation of Tasmanian engraved art is lost, we might consider the "wheel" circles at Sturts Meadows and other circle engravings at places such as Flinders Range. A Dreamtime story associated with a coastal culture known as the Tharawal (in the Sydney region) recounts the earliest animal arrivals to the region; they came from the sea. The "Whale's Canoe" tells how the animals, in human form, wanted to cross the water to a new land and needed a canoe. They wanted to use the large canoe that belonged to the whale, but he would not lend it to them. The little starfish volunteered to help the animals and perched on the whale's head, removing lice and telling stories, to distract the whale while the animals sailed away. Eventually the whale noticed the canoe's disappearance and in a fit of anger attacked the starfish and tossed it from his head. The abrupt departure of the starfish created the hole in the whale's head; the whale's attack so wounded the starfish that he now stays on the sandy bottom of the water, away from danger. This Dreamtime story explains the whale's appearance, the behavior of starfish, and how animals came to, presumably, the western coast of Australia. With regard to rock engravings, it might be interesting to consider whether engraved circles are meant to represent the whale's blowhole. Though not in the present-day range of the Tharawal culture, could the circular "wheels" at Sturts Meadows, engraved on "whale backs," be the legs of the starfish rather than wheels or sun rays? Finally, could the circles on the northern coast of Tasmania be meant to convey the whale and starfish role in the movement of animals? All these are highly speculative and can never be confirmed with any certainty, especially given the great antiquity of these engravings. However, the point here is to take into consideration the archaeological and ethnographic evidence and offer educated speculation as to how the two might mesh together to better explain the sacred past.

Painted Rock Art of North and Northwestern Australia

North and northwestern Australia offer the best-known examples of painted rock art. Some of the discussion here focuses on the more complex and recently rendered paintings. Because they are more recent, many of the paintings still have Dreamtime stories attached to them. Using these, we can then make some attempts to extrapolate back in time to interpret far older images elsewhere.

Rainbow Serpent

The Dreamtime myths featuring Rainbow Serpent are some of the most widespread, occurring across a significant expanse of northern Australia and in several cultures' sacred Dreamtime tracks. Rainbow Serpent stories are found from the Victoria River region and south of Darwin in the Northern Territory, all the way to the northern reaches of Queensland. Such widespread belief in this creator being is significant, indicating the great antiquity of a snake-like ancestor and the extensive contacts among north Australian cultures. Rainbow Serpent stories are particularly prevalent in coastal regions and date as far back as 6,000 years. One theory for the ubiquity of the Rainbow Serpent is a precipitous rise in sea levels at that time, bringing numerous sea creatures, including snakes, farther inland (Morwood 2002). The idea of waterborne snakes essentially traveling across what was once dry land may have been a very evocative image, creating powerful stories of landscape creation.

It is not only in the (sub)tropical north that snakes are associated with water, but all over Australia, especially in the arid center, though they are not necessarily known as Rainbow Serpent in these other regions. Ethnographic accounts associating paintings of snakes with water could give us clues for interpreting older paintings. That snakes live in the water, come up out of the ground as does water (at a spring or water hole), and leave a trail in the sand that resembles the path of a river or ripples on a lake are all good reasons to make an association between snakes and water in an arid or even tropical region. Here we see the role of environment in Aboriginal religion. Rainbow Serpent mythology may coincide with a surfeit of water in northern Australia; snakes are important creatures in the arid center where water is constantly scarce. I visited a site near Alice Springs where there were two sets of rock paintings. The first featured faded paintings of several geometric figures. One appeared to me to look very much like a snake winding across the rock face. The second was a sacred men's site, so only my two male companions went on to visit those paintings. I was not surprised when they later reported to me that there was a large water hole at the site, along with more elaborate and intricate paintings. Though I do not know the Dreamtime stories lodged at this site, the close proximity of a painting that resembles a snake and a water hole seems to fit right in with the association between this creature and an element so vital to life in the arid center.

The Bradshaw and Mimi Paintings

The Bradshaw paintings in the Kimberley region are some of the earliest found in the northern reaches of Australia, dating to more than 16,000 years ago (some suggest as much as 20,000 years ago). Painted rock faces have been dated to as much as 40,000 years ago (Morwood 2002), so an even earlier date for the Bradshaws is not untenable. They were named after an early explorer who first discovered them in the nineteenth century. These paintings depict human figures in elaborate dress, including headdresses, aprons, tassels, and armbands. Painted with red ocher (they may have once been bichrome, but other colors have disappeared), these figures are often in attitudes of dance or perhaps celebration. They hold spears or boomerangs and other weapons, ceremonial gear such as dancing sticks (a short stick with feathers adorning one end), or what may be musical instruments. Interestingly, boomerangs are not used by present-day Aboriginals in the area, nor have they been for as much as 3,000 years. Aboriginals in the region believe the paintings were made by a bird and depict the "first people" created.

The Mimi art, also known as the *Dynamic style*, is found in Arnhem Land and is similar to the Bradshaw paintings in form and content. They are red in color, but the great antiquity of these paintings leads many to believe that other colors may have faded away. The Mimi art may be more than 10,000 years old. These are called "Mimi" images because the Aboriginal cultures in the region say that the Mimi spirits who inhabit the area were the authors of the paintings; the humans claim no knowledge of the artistry or its meaning. One of the main differences from the Bradshaw figures is the more energetic movements of the Mimi figures. Many appear to be in full sprint, and there are some scenes that indicate a battle is taking place. Other scenes appear to depict everyday activities such as hunting and gathering (Flood 1983), and images of animals and animal tracks abound. Another interesting feature of the Mimi images is the depiction of dots and lines that denote the issuance of sound from mouths; this is a unique feature in Aboriginal rock art. The presence of therianthropes and anthropomorphs suggests Dreamtime stories were an important part of the Mimi art of Arnhem Land.

What can we learn from the Bradshaw and Mimi paintings? Basic archaeological evidence of tools and weapons is readily apparent; clearly the boomerang is a weapon of great antiquity in northwestern Australia, but one no longer used in the region. Another interesting feature is the elaborate dress of the figures, particularly their headdresses. Several researchers have noted that Aboriginal groups in these regions still wear dress at important sacred rituals that strongly resembles that in the Bradshaw and Mimi paintings. But what is even more interesting is that some cultures on the island of New Guinea also have similar dress. At the time these paintings were created, Australia and New Guinea were connected by land. Perhaps the Bradshaws are indicative of widespread ritual practices; one could imagine that if the rocks under the sea were suddenly exposed and magically restored, thousands more examples of such dancing figures would give us much more insight into the extent of what is now exclusively called "Aboriginal" religion.

The warring figures in the Mimi art are also interesting because they show rather significant battles taking place. The Mimi paintings may be more or less contemporary with the end stages of the Pleistocene and rising sea levels. Is it possible that battles over decreasing amounts of land were occurring? One scholar suggests that it is during this time that clan totemism became ensconced in Aboriginal culture, used as a method to mark territories for clan and kin groups, something perhaps unnecessary in earlier periods when land was more plentiful (Layton 1992). Perhaps the Bradshaw and Mimi images recount an early history of the region: peaceful intercultural religious events, followed by wars between peoples desperate to protect their hunting-and-gathering territories, and the introduction of sacred landscapes made venerable by important totems associated with individual groups who claimed those territories.

X-Ray Figures

A more recent style of painting in the Arnhem Land region, dating primarily to the last 3,000 years, is the X-ray style of images. These paintings depict animals, humans, and human-like creatures. X-ray-style paintings use a variety of colors, and the images are less stylized and more naturalistic. Some of these images are very bright and seem almost to shine. Some analysts suggest that the paintings that are monochrome and do not show internal organs represent dead animals, whereas the x-ray paintings that detail the animal in its habitat going about its business represent living creatures. The meaning of these x-ray figures, beyond the notion of "dead" and "alive," is not understood. As noted in Chapter 4, some researchers suggest the X-ray style depicts the shamanic journey to the spirit world; animals represent the spirit helper. Another theory is that the detailed depiction of the animal's internal organs, somewhat stylized, signifies different kin or clan groups and their territory (Layton 1992), similar to that described for the Mimi art. This explanation does not stretch, perhaps, to the more human and human-like images, but oral traditions of the region, once fully explored, might help to better explain these figures.

Conclusion

The antiquity of African and Australian rock art makes nuanced interpretation of the images an impossibility. Ethnographic accounts and scientific research offer us many insights into the possible meanings embedded in the art, but these can take us only so far. However, our study of the depictions does reveal how intertwined these rituals and myths were with their environment. The depth of belief in the spirits and beings of the supernatural world who created and sustained these ancient peoples is displayed clearly, in bright colors, across the rock faces of Africa and Australia and many other regions of the world. Investigation into the religion expressed in these beautiful images remains one of the most intriguing fields in the archaeology of religion.

USEFUL SOURCES

Josephine Flood, *Rock Art of the Dreamtime*, 1997
John Mulvaney and Johan Kamminga, *Prehistory of Australia*, 1999.
Graham Connah, *Forgotten Africa: An Introduction to Its Archaeology*, 2004.

PART III

RELIGIONS IN THE AMERICAS

THE MOUND-BUILDING
CULTURES OF NORTH AMERICA

Who were the first humans to arrive in North America? This is a subject of tremendous controversy. Humans crossed a land bridge called Berengia (now the Bering Strait), between Siberia and Alaska, as early as 40,000 years ago, but it is unclear whether these migrants continued southward or remained in the northern reaches of the continent. The first unequivocal evidence of human occupation in North America comes from sites spanning the region from Montana to Texas, dating to ca. 11,000 B.C.E. However, recent discoveries in Oregon suggest humans may have been in North America as early as 14,500 years ago, although more evidence is necessary to confirm the data from a single site (Curry 2008). More numerous sites dating to approximately 13,000 years ago exhibit *Clovis* technology, referring to a particular type of fluted stone projectile point suitable for large-game hunting. By 12,000 years ago, the North American continent was widely inhabited by a population known as the *Paleoindians*; the Paleoindian period dates from ca. 11,000 until approximately 7000 B.C.E.

Paleoindians exploited a variety of subsistence sources in a hunting-gathering economy, including big-game hunting as well as reliance on smaller animals and aquatic resources (Anderson 2005). Since the Pleistocene Ice Age was still in relatively full swing 11,000–10,000 years ago, Ice Age animals such as the giant sloth, the giant beaver, mammoths, and mastodons, now extinct, roamed the landscape. Sites show evidence of cooperative game-hunting in which numerous animals were killed and slaughtered at a single event. As time progressed, however, these large animals died out, probably from a combination of warming trends in the Holocene (the geological epoch following the Pleistocene) and over-hunting by the relatively newly arrived human population. By the close of the Paleoindian period, indigenous North Americans lived in a different landscape than had their forebears. Tool technologies were adapted to smaller animals, and there was an increasing reliance on plants, as warmer climates made habitation of additional North American regions possible.

Foraging, Agriculture, and Trade

The period following the Paleoindian age is known as the Archaic and dates from 9,000 until about 3,000 years ago. It is during the Archaic period that several species of plants, including squash, sunflowers, and other seed plants, were domesticated in several different places; maize became an important crop roughly 2,000 years ago.

Poverty Point

Even though some populations were in the process of cultivating plants in the late Archaic period, other residents were content to continue a foraging-based economy. The residents at the site known as Poverty Point, in the lower Mississippi Valley (in Louisiana), practiced a mainly foraging economy and yet lived in semi-sedentary villages and engaged in extensive regional trade (Figure 7.1). Residents at Poverty Point also engaged in the construction of earthworks. Although not the earliest mound-style earthworks, those at Poverty Point are the largest in the later Archaic period. Construction of the mounds began as early as 1800 B.C.E. and continued until the settlement began to decline around 700 B.C.E. Poverty Point's location on the Macon River allowed for trade both upriver and down; stone artifacts were made of materials whose source is over 600 miles away. It appears that the stone, including chert, steatite, jasper, hematite, and slate, arrived in raw form and was then worked into tools, animal-shaped amulets (especially birds), and jewelry by Poverty Point residents.

The earthworks at Poverty Point fall into two main categories: individual mounded structures, and sets of semicircular concentric ridges, broken into sections (Figure 7.2). Post holes, hearths, and other domestic materials suggest that residents may have lived atop these concentric mounds (Gibson 2000). West of the concentric ridges is a large, unusually shaped mound attached by a long ramp. Someone standing on top of this mound can see the sun rise over the river and ridged mounds on the vernal and autumnal equinoxes; it would be quite a coincidence if this were simply accidental. Survey work has revealed smaller, non-mounded settlements in the vicinity of Poverty Point which housed fewer than 100 residents, while estimates of Poverty Point's population range in the hundreds.

Careful examination of these mounds has revealed that they were created by emptying individual baskets of clay and dirt. It had to have taken a great deal of organization and dedication to create these mounds using such methods. Rough estimations suggest that it took 1,000 workers nearly 300 days to construct Poverty Point. Such an enormous investment of labor at this settlement indicates that earthworks were essential components in this later Archaic culture's societal beliefs and ideology. Whether they were built for purely cosmological purposes, or also demonstrated the burgeoning ability of some to control the labor of others, or a combination of the two, is as yet uncertain.

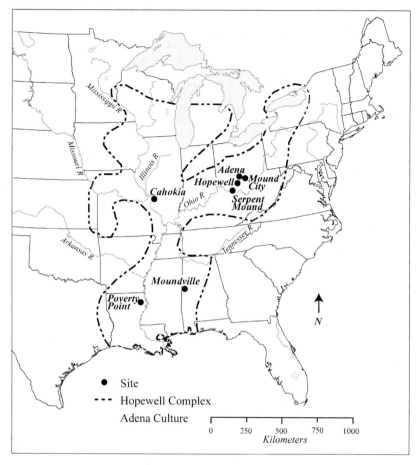

Figure 7.1. Map of sites and regions discussed in the chapter. (*T. Edwards*)

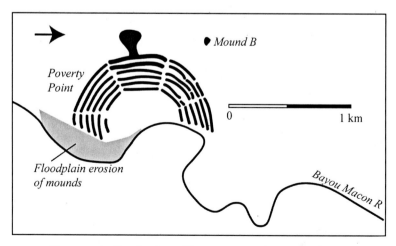

Figure 7.2. Sketch plan of Poverty Point. (*S. R. Steadman*)

The Adena Complex

As the settlement at Poverty Point was fading, the Adena culture in the Ohio River Valley was developing long-distance trade networks, exchanging everything from stone tools to copper artifacts. The Adena culture, named for the estate on which a site was excavated in the early twentieth century, was cultivating food plants and using pottery containers, all suggesting that residence was partially, if not wholly, sedentary. Some of the most evocative artifacts associated with the Adena culture are their stone *effigy pipes*, demonstrating the practice of smoking tobacco, probably in ceremonial contexts. The few known pipes are in the shape of humans. The tobacco used at this earlier time was considerably stronger than varieties today and was capable of producing a significant narcotic effect. Pipes, discovered in burial mounds, may be indicative of shamanistic practices or, at the very least, of ritual activities using tobacco.

The earthen-mound tradition continued in the Adena culture in the form of large burial mounds and earthen enclosures situated near the Adena settlements. These earthen enclosures were made by piling up basketfuls of soil in circles, squares, and even in a type of pentagonal shape; others were irregularly shaped, following the ridgeline of hills. The soil came from the interior of the enclosures, making them look like moats or pools on the inside. The interiors of these earthen enclosures do not appear to have been occupied and may have been more ceremonial in nature. The burial mounds contained, in most cases, multiple burials, some in simple graves, others in log coffins or tombs that could hold several people (Milner 2005). Many of the exchanged goods were found in these burials, presumably as burial gifts, and some individuals had been sprinkled with ocher. Also buried in these mounds were individuals who had been cremated. Burial mounds grew up "organically," in that as more burials were interred, the mound grew bigger. Some smaller mounds contained only one or a few individuals. Why some mounds are small and others large, and why some are actually inside earthen enclosures, and others are not, are still questions requiring answers. It is possible that as the Adena culture became more involved in long-distance trade and expanded cultivation, the notion of more firmly envisioned territoriality initiated the burial of family members in places that would establish control of an area (Yerkes 1988). Possibly the most powerful members of the society were destined for mound burial and others were disposed of elsewhere. Whether for power and control, or purely religious reasons, or a combination of these, the Adena culture firmly established mound-building as a mainstay of North American ritual behavior for centuries to come.

The Hopewell Culture

The Hopewell tradition, named after a site excavated in Ohio, possessed all the elements of the Adena but in much greater size and quantity. Hopewellians developed a very fine tradition of metalworking, producing gorgets and chest ornaments, many in animal motifs. Like the Adena, the Hopewell culture constructed elaborate earthworks, but the latter are much larger and more elaborate in scope. The traditional date for the appearance of the Hopewell culture is 200 B.C.E., in a core area encompassing parts of present-day Ohio and Illinois. For over 600 years the Hopewell culture extended across much of eastern North America in a complex trade network that also carried with it Hopewellian ideology. Although the Hopewell complex is called a "culture," it is more like a connection of cultures that interacted through trade and the exchange of ideas. Many of the artifacts associated with the Hopewell core area, as well as Hopewell-style burial mounds, spread across an enormous region stretching along the river valleys that run from the Great Lakes and Canada down to the Gulf of Mexico (Milner 2005).

Unfortunately, very little is known about Hopewell settlements, as these were located away from the mounds, and it was the mounds that drew the attention of earlier archaeologists. Recent work reveals that residents preferred to live along the rivers and waterways, which also served as their means for transporting goods. Houses, constructed of posts and covered with a variety of organic materials, tended to be oval or round in shape, but some were rectangular. Hopewell residents cultivated a variety of plants, supplemented by the gathering of wild species. Hunting provided meat, most prominently deer; but other animals, including waterfowl and freshwater fish, also contributed to their diet.

There is little doubt that there was some type of rank-ordered social hierarchy in the Hopewell core culture. The organization required to construct earthen works, direct the very lively exchange system, and make the stunning examples of copper and stone burial and exchange goods certainly called for some type of leadership system. However, whether leadership was rooted in kinship lines or in other criteria is a subject of controversy. The labor investment in the burial mounds suggests a practice of ancestor veneration which would support kin-based and social hierarchical ranking, but this is only speculative. Further evidence, some of which is discussed below, sheds a bit more light on the inner workings of Hopewell social structure.

The Hopewell earthworks, like those by the Adena, featured large, square, circular, octagonal, or generally geometrical enclosures inside of which were sometimes burial mounds, inner earthworks, and open ground suitable for ceremonial activities. Less frequently, "effigy" earthworks in the shape of animals were built. One famous example is the Serpent Mound in Ohio. A snake winds along a 400-meter distance, with a tightly coiled tail and a mouth opened, apparently, to consume an oval mound.

In many cases, circular and square mounds are located near one another, sometimes connected by a causeway. The reason for these earthworks has been a long-standing subject of inquiry. Some form complexes of mounds and earthworks that extend for several miles; many have been lost to agriculture and construction. However, these earthen works fascinated nineteenth-century geographers and archaeologists, and so many were mapped. Astonishingly, many of these circles, separated by hundreds of kilometers, are of exactly the same size and dimensions; in addition, groupings of earthworks of differing shapes could have been "nested," in that one would fit perfectly inside the other (Romain 2000). It is clear that Hopewellian architects had a very firm grasp on geometry and built these structures with certain principles in mind. Researchers have also noticed the intersection between these earthworks and astronomical mechanics. Precise measurements of relatively undamaged mounds and earthworks reveal that from certain locations, one can observe the rising and setting of the moon according to a lunar calendar, as well as watch the winter solstice sun set (Hively and Horn 1984; Romain 2000). Such research suggests that at least one important function served by these earthworks was observation of the lunar cycle, likely an important factor in a society moving steadily toward full-scale agriculture.

A Hopewellian desire to observe the sky and track the movements of the heavenly bodies explains the need to build mounds, but not their geometrical shape. Most scholars believe there are deep symbolic meanings in these shapes, but unraveling those meanings is challenging, to say the least. One archaeologist suggests the symbolic meanings attributed to squares and circles by present-day Native Americans are relevant (DeBoer 1997). He observed that in many cultures, winter structures tend to be circular, while summer houses are rectangular, expressing a type of duality with regard to season. Hopewellian earthworks built in the summer may have been square, and those in the winter round; burials in each season were located in or near appropriate earthworks. The octagonal shapes might therefore have been inter-seasonal, built on the cusp of change between summer and winter.

Also drawing on Native American beliefs, in which the earth is envisioned as circular, another researcher suggests that the square earthworks are representative of the sky, and circular ones denote the earth (Romain 2000). Strategic placement of burial mounds at the center of these circular earthworks might convey earthbound symbolism, perhaps representing mountains or the original creation of land surrounded by water.

Two types of artifacts regularly found in Hopewell burials are platform pipes and beaten copper ornaments. The platform pipes are also known as *effigy* pipes because they usually have an animal form perched on top of the pipe's platform (Figure 7.3). Usually the animal faces the smoker, but occasionally it faces outward. These pipes may have played a role in ritual or shamanistic activities. The tobacco most likely smoked in these pipes was capable of producing trance states and was probably a hallucinogen of some form (Brown 1997). If the pipes were viewed as the vehicle though which the shaman (or smoker) achieved trance and entry into the spiritual realm, then the animal effigies, including frogs, panthers, birds, beavers, and other creatures of the region, may have represented the spirit guides particular to the shaman utilizing that pipe (Brown

Figure 7.3. Stone effigy pipe from Hopewell Culture. Note the beaver perched on the pipe faces the smoker. (*R. Jennison*)

1997). Alternatively, animals may have represented different aspects of the trance state, such as the feeling of flying (birds), swimming (frogs, beavers), or moving stealthily through the spiritual realm (panthers). Another possibility is that these pipes might have played a dual role in both religion and diplomacy. Hopewellians, well entrenched in a long-distance trade network, may have needed to engage in regular interactions with traders and middlemen and even to negotiate disputes between villages and regions. One scholar suggests these effigy pipes served as "peace" pipes during these negotiations, but also as passive weapons of war in that the pipe represented a weapon known as an *atlatl* or spear thrower (Hall 1977, 1997). The atlatl, common in the weapon assemblages of native North Americans, is a long stick with a hook at the end to hold the spear. That hook was often shaped in the form of an animal. The animals on the effigy pipes, then, could represent the animals at the end of the atlatl, just as the platform of the pipe represented the shaft (Hall 1977). In this way the pipe could symbolize both peaceful negotiation and threat of war should talks fail.

Hopewell copper ornaments have added tremendously to our understanding of trade patterns since sourcing analyses can trace the movement of these items from their original ore source to their final destination. However, the meaning of these copper effigies is far from clear. That some mirror the types of animals found on effigy pipes suggests a spiritual basis for interpretation; they may have functioned in a similar fashion to the platform pipes, calling to or representing important animal spirits during religious ceremonies (Milner 2005). However, this leaves unexplained those that are fashioned in human images, unless they were meant to represent the human (shaman?) undertaking the spiritual journey.

Since the majority of Hopewell residents were cremated, those who were buried in mounds received specialized treatment. Even within the mounds, there are different levels of labor associated with various burials. Some mounds were built atop charnel houses. Huts were erected for the dead in which cremated remains and uncremated bodies were placed. Once the building was full, it was burned down and an earthen mound built over it. Other mounds had tombs at their base. These tombs were wooden boxes into which one or a few burials were placed. Other burials were placed on top of or beside the tomb, and eventually earth was mounded over the entire collection. Who was buried in these mounds? Almost certainly they were special individuals, given the labor that went into the construction of their burial mounds, and the goods in them, including the effigy pipes and copper ornaments. What types of individuals required such elaborate and richly adorned burials?

One common explanation is that those buried in the mounds are important members of kin groups who then became "revered ancestors" in a society in which the most important social connection was family. The mechanism that selected who was mound-bound and who received simple cremation is, at present, beyond archaeological reckoning. Another theory suggests that the Hopewell culture was one in which sociopolitically complex systems were emergent. Various social groups, perhaps kin-based, competed for power over territory, trade connections, and perhaps even control of the religion. The ability to command the building of a tomb and subsequent mound upon one's death, with the requisite burial goods, may have served as a method of demonstrating status and power (Seeman 1979). One study of the skeletons themselves suggests that there was a hierarchy of important individuals buried in the mounds; tomb types were ranked from 1 to 6, Type 1 being the most labor intensive (the wooden tombs) and Type 6 being a simple burial in the surface of an already constructed mound. Skeletons in Type 1 tombs had less joint wear and disease than those in other tombs, indicating they did less of the manual labor in the society (Tainter 1980). This might indicate a higher status in a society in which elites were released from the normal daily duties that everyone else carried out. Perhaps those in the Type 1 tombs were leaders, elders, the shamans, or a combination of these.

Hopewellians concerned themselves with astronomical observations, engaged in animal imagery, and invested considerable labor in the burial of their dead. Clearly they had a rich and complex belief system that archaeology has only begun to reveal.

The Mississippian Culture

Although the Hopewell complex had faded by the middle of the first millennium, the practice of mound-building had not. The *Mississippian culture*, spread along the Mississippi River, had a much greater dependence on maize agriculture than previous cultures. Inhabitants were more sedentary in their settlement structure and therefore able to store greater amounts of surplus foods. The stability of a reliable food source allowed for larger population centers to emerge in the Mississippian period (ca. 750–1500 C.E.). Another development in this period was the use of the bow and arrow as a weapon, largely replacing the spear and atlatl. The bow and arrow served as a more effective hunting device but was also useful in a society that had come to expect more regular hostile attacks. Warfare was a fairly frequent occurrence in the Mississippian culture.

There are countless settlements that date to the Mississippian period, but the most extensively excavated, and certainly the best known, is the large center known as Cahokia, located across the river from St. Louis, in southern Illinois. Cahokia rests in a region known as the American Bottom, where three major rivers—the Mississippi, the Missouri, and the Illinois—all come together. This is a lush area very suitable for agriculture, thick with flora and fauna. In addition, the rivers allowed for extensive travel and trade; artifacts are made of materials that come from the Great Lakes, the southeastern coastal region, the upper Midwest, and from the Gulf Coast. It is an ideal location for settlement, and the Cahokians took full advantage of their landscape in order to build a spectacular center.

Cahokia is the largest known Mississippian settlement, with a complex of plazas, ceremonial and burial mounds, walls and palisades, and residential areas that sprawl across well over 15 square kilometers. At its height in around 1000 C.E., Cahokia may have had a population as high as 35,000 people. The elites lived in the settlement's enclosed center, while the vast majority of the population lived farther out in the countryside. Archaeological investigation of the residential area of Cahokia and other outlying communities offers very illuminating insight into the average Mississippian's life.

In the earliest stages of the Mississippian period (750–950 C.E.), residents built small rectangular huts with small storage pits in the inside. These huts were arranged around central courtyards that gave household residents access to communal storage pits, often arranged in a four-cornered pattern. Communal activities and perhaps ceremonial events took place in the central courtyards (Mehrer 1995). As time passed and population and social complexity increased, settlement structure altered. Larger and more well-built rectangular and circular structures included sizable internal and exterior storage pits. Communities grew in size, with some towns building mounds and small ceremonial areas. In many cases, households were no longer built in a collective gathering but rather were dispersed. *Homesteads*, consisting of several buildings and private storage, were built some distance from other homesteads, presumably near the agricultural fields belonging to that family. In more rural areas, one homestead served as a *nodal household*, larger and with extensive open areas suitable for hosting a large gathering of people at ceremonies or other public events (Mehrer 1995).

At the height of the Mississippian period (1050–1250 C.E.), the landscape consisted of a few large *temple towns* such as Cahokia, as well as smaller towns with mounds and moderate ceremonial areas, and smaller outlier communities consisting of dispersed farmsteads with nodal households. These outlying communities were probably important suppliers of subsistence products to the temple towns but in other ways appear to have functioned with a fair amount of autonomy. The nodal households served as locales for ceremony, relieving residents from having to travel to distant centers such as Cahokia. Residents of the nodal households demonstrated greater wealth in the size and outfitting of their domestic structures, reflective of their sociopolitical, economic, and apparently religious role in their community. The evidence from these first 500 years of the Mississippian period clearly demonstrates an increasingly complex structure with religious, political, and economic power being consolidated into fewer hands and larger settlements.

As study of Mississippian culture has proceeded, most scholars have come to believe that the temple towns such as Cahokia make up North America's earliest chiefdom (Milner 1998; Pauketat and Emerson 1997). The Cahokia complex includes nearly 120 earthen mounds, many with burials, others supporting buildings. At the center of the settlement is a plaza surrounded by a wooden palisade, with guard towers built at intervals along the wall; besides its defensive role, it also served to control public access to the plaza, apparently keeping unwanted Cahokians out. This palisade took enormous effort to build. The entire structure consisted of approximately 20,000 wooden poles requiring more than 150,000 person-hours to build; this means that nearly 2,000 people, working all day long, would have needed at least a week to build the palisade. Clearly some individuals within the Cahokian society were able to command large amounts of labor for significant periods of time.

Inside the central plaza was the Monk's Mound, the largest earthen structure in pre-colonial North America. The plaza also contained other mounds, some conical, some with a square base and shaped like pyramids; residential structures belonging to Cahokian elites and religious personnel rested on flat-topped mounds. Other mounds supported buildings that were public or religious in nature, apparently for the exclusive use of those who lived inside the plaza walls.

Another feature inside the Cahokian center was the set of woodhenge structures. These consisted of wooden poles erected in a circular form; one henge had one pole in the middle. The number of poles in each henge (five have been discovered) was based on multiples of 12: one had 24 poles, another 36, another 48, and then 60; the smallest had only 12 posts. The function of these woodhenges appears to have been astronomical, as the summer and winter solstice sun can be seen rising over the central pole. Like the henge monuments in Britain, these woodhenges probably served to mark important points on the agricultural calendar (Pauketat 1994). Perhaps the number 12 was meaningful in time-keeping, or it may have been a sacred number in Cahokian cosmology. The woodhenges must have served some important service, as the effort needed to construct and maintain them was not insubstantial.

Burial of the dead is an important indicator of social stratification in the Mississippian culture. The upper strata of society were buried in mounds that held numerous and valuable grave goods: marine shell beads, copper and mica items, and chert tools and weapons made of materials derived from long-distance sources. Some graves included non-utilitarian items that may have had ritual significance, including rattles, copper plates made to look like turtle carapaces, scarifiers, and stone ornaments. One adult male grave contained 20,000 marine-shell beads, among other goods. Certain mounds, or areas, appear to have been controlled by kin groups who had the right to be buried there. Some mounds were created by the collective burials of various individuals over time, eventually creating one giant mound. One mound held several hundred individuals (Milner 1998). Other mounds were large but held only one or two individuals, perhaps indicating their greater importance. Burials of lower-status people were found in simple mounds in town, but also out on the riverine floodplain. When simple burials did contain goods, which was not often, the offerings were utilitarian items such as pottery or tools.

Cahokian elites were also occasionally accompanied by human sacrifice. Though this doesn't appear to have been the norm at the death of every high-ranking individual, it is clear that some were awarded the death of others upon their own. In one burial collection known as Mound 72, several mass burials suggest the practice of human sacrifice. In one portion of the mound, a pit held 50 young women laid in rows, stacked one atop the other. Three other pits contained over 60 other young women, some buried with marine-shell beads, arrowheads of chert and bone, and ceramics. Also in Mound 72 were four young men who had been beheaded and behanded (the head and hand are prominent in Cahokian iconography, perhaps indicating these features held special powers), all perhaps sacrificed in honor of the death of a Cahokian elite (Fowler 1991). It is possible that the sacrificial victims were not Cahokians but rather those captured through attack on other regions; alternatively, victims may have come from the lowest echelon of Cahokian society. It is unclear how sacrificial victims were chosen or which Cahokian elites were deserving of such accompaniment at death. What is clear is that a society in which human sacrifice can be commanded by a few is one in which the elite class wields a substantial level of power.

The building of Monk's Mound demonstrates the ability of a few to control many. The base of the mound, roughly square, covers approximately 14 acres. It has four levels that give it a height of approximately 100 feet, each constructed separately over a period of several hundred years, beginning around 900 C.E. It is possible that each terrace was added at the time of the accession of a new ruler or a change in dynasty. Monk's Mound (so-named for the nineteenth-century occupation by a group of Trappist monks on its summit) would have required well over 1 million 5-hour days of labor to construct its over 20 million cubic feet of volume (Milner 1998). It, like the palisade, demonstrates the ability to control labor as a resource. On the highest level of Monk's Mound was a wooden building measuring approximately 100 × 50 feet. This may have been a ceremonial center where the leader or religious officials performed rituals or other duties related to Cahokian religion (Figure 7.4). It may have also served as the residence for the leader of this temple center.

Without written texts, the certainly complex belief system of the Cahokians can only be described in broad strokes of the archaeological paintbrush. Landscape archaeology, careful analysis of Mississippian artifacts, and ethnographic information from Eastern Woodlands and Southeastern Native American cosmologies lead us to some insights into Cahokian beliefs. Drawing on present-day Native American beliefs, archaeologists suggest Cahokian cosmology featured a four-sided, four-quartered world. Referred to as *quadripartite*, this cosmology views the world as four-sided, divided by symbolic axes that run either on the cardinal points (i.e., north to south, east to west) or slightly off these points, creating diamond-shaped quadrants (Emerson 1997a). Such beliefs would explain the squared bases of so many Mississippian mounds (though their tops had a variety of shapes). The large central plaza at Cahokia, laid out on a north/south, east/west orientation, is itself four-sided, with Monk's Mound resting at

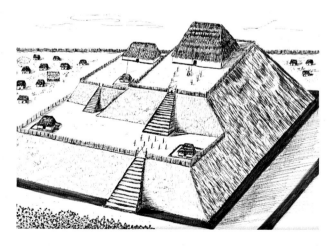

Figure 7.4. Artistic rendering of Monk's Mound at Cahokian center. (*M. J. Hughes*)

its northern end. Three additional small plazas, outside the palisade (simply named North, West, and East Plazas), are also four-sided; mounds of various types also surround these plazas. The exact meaning of the quadripartite symbolism is presently unknowable, but it is not far-fetched to connect it with Cahokian beliefs about the creation of the world.

The quadripartite mounds and plazas represent a "horizontally based" cosmological symbolism, while the height of the mounds offers a vertical aspect of Cahokian beliefs. Again relying on ethnographic data, archaeologists familiar with Mississippian settlements suggest that mound culture cosmology featured a system of layered worlds, including an upper, lower, and middle world (Emerson 1997a); thus, just being in Cahokia allowed one to visually experience Cahokian cosmology (Emerson and Pauketat 2008). This vertical cosmology may have also been reflective of the social hierarchy: the upper social stratum embodied by elites, nobles, and religious specialists, who were closest spatially (i.e., living on top of mounds) and spiritually to the upperworld. Most Cahokians probably lived in the middle (earthly) world, with houses on ground level. But even here we might discern different levels: some "ordinary" Cahokians may have lived in or near the plazas and town center, while others resided in the lower "bottomlands" of outlying regions. Perhaps individuals ranged in "levels" both spiritually and socially.

Other aspects of Cahokian religion seem to have focused on human activities— namely, agriculture and warfare. Agricultural symbolism seems more closely linked to non-elite farmers in Cahokian society, the same individuals who lived in the lower "bottomlands" of the earth and closer to the underworld. Warriors may have been drawn from the higher levels of Cahokian society and were socially closer to the elites and spatially closer to the upperworld (Emerson 1997b). Discoveries of Cahokian figurines have gone far in helping to substantiate these interpretations. In particular, there seems to have been an agriculture cult, which was perhaps the most widespread element in the Cahokian belief system, spanning all levels of society.

At a site near Cahokia several figurines were discovered in the temple mound. One, known as the Birger figurine (Figure 7.5), is made of red stone and represents

Figure 7.5. Birger figurine. (*R. Jennison*)

important symbolic notions of the underworld and its constituent elements, including serpent monsters, water, and fertility. The female in the Birger figurine kneels on a circular base with one hand on a feline-headed snake, the other holding a hoe that touches the snake's back. The snake's body transforms into vines that issue gourds near the woman's feet and at her shoulder. This combination of images suggests water (the snake represents a water serpent in Native American cosmology), the agricultural cycle (the vine, gourds, and hoe), and finally, the Earth Mother in the form of the keeling woman (Emerson 1997b). The Birger figurine is joined by several others depicting similar motifs of females, serpents, plants, and the growing cycle. Several clearly represent cornstalks rather than gourds, suggesting a Corn Mother association with the Earth Mother (another common belief in Native American religions). Recent analysis has shown that these figurines were made in the Cahokian region (and therefore were not products acquired through trade from elsewhere); they are therefore likely representations of Cahokian supernatural beings and symbolism, as well as of shamans, elites, and other important members of Cahokian society (Emerson et al. 2003). Cahokian ceramics with similar decorations may have been used at public ceremonies at which all social classes came together to celebrate the agricultural cycle and the fertility of the earth (Emerson 1997b).

While analysis of Native American cosmology provides clues to Cahokian belief systems, archaeology offers a more nuanced view of how these belief systems may have been managed within the Mississippian society. In the emergent period of the Mississippian culture (ca. 750–950 C.E.), an agricultural fertility cult seems to have been prominent in rural settings, based at the household level, while elites in more populous towns were concerned with warrior cults and the building of Mississippian political and economic power bases through diplomatic trade or hostile interaction with regional neighbors (Emerson 1997a). Commoners and farmers in outlying towns and villages, and even those living nearer the large towns, were far less involved in the elite warrior cults, as these did not impact the daily and annual cycle of farming and the important elements of water, sun, and fertility.

Between 950 and 1050 C.E., as social complexity and population increased, ritual activities in more rural settings were transported out of the individual household to nodal households of the wealthier and socially elevated residents of outlying communities. Such nodal households had larger courtyards sufficient to encompass community residents in public ceremonies led, perhaps, by a resident of the nodal household. Residents living closer to temple towns could access ceremonial activities at these centers.

At the height of Mississippian power (1050–1250 C.E.), the elite class appears to have been in complete control of the religion, including both warrior and agricultural cults. Whether in temple towns such as Cahokia or in the countryside, ceremonial centers dominated religious practice. In fact, settings such as Cahokia's central plaza appear to have restricted access to the ceremonial center, implying that elites controlled and carried out ritual on behalf of the entire society (Emerson 1997a). Mississippian elites had wrested the commoner's cult right out of the household and embedded it in the hands, and localities, of the uppermost stratum of society. The success of the agricultural cycle, fertility symbolism, and the proper management of the upperworld and underworld had become far too important to the Mississippian power structure to leave in the hands of the lower stratum of society, the farmers. The success of this cycle was, however, also the lifeblood of those commoners who produced the food for the elites as well as for their own families. The appropriation of the agricultural cult by the elites allowed them to take control not only of this widespread belief system, but of the people as well, while essentially excluding them from ceremonies celebrating and ensuring the fertility cycle. By consolidating their power over the commoners, elites could then command the building of large public works such as woodhenges, palisades, and temple mounds. Even the requirement of human sacrifice at the death of an important elite may not have been beyond the power of those in charge of the religion. Mississippian religion became a vital tool in the elite effort to ensure a continued expansion in power over the region and an effective method of controlling Mississippian society.

Conclusion

North American mound cultures emerged in concert with two important developments: the establishment of agricultural cultivation and the appearance of politically and/or economically elite classes. It cannot be a coincidence that these three elements came together to create the fascinating cultures of the North American river valleys. As agriculture became increasingly vital, religious beliefs highlighted the importance of fertility and the growing cycle. Mounds built to observe the skies and bury the ancestors who protected lands and ensured healthy harvests aided residents in their need to celebrate the earth. This is a powerful example of the intersection of religion, the society that practices it, and the environment. As agricultural production outstripped warfare in importance, so did the agricultural cult become more important, as it was literally removed from the commoners and installed in the temple towns. The building of mounds and other monuments also demonstrates the power of religion to motivate people to accomplish tremendous feats. When power structures emerge in a society, what was once a communal effort quickly becomes co-opted labor to celebrate not only the supernatural world, but the elites as well.

Useful Sources

Thomas Emerson and R. Barry Lewis, *Cahokia and the Hinterlands*, 1999.
Christopher Carr and D. Tony Case, *Gathering Hopewell: Society, Ritual and Ritual Interaction*, 2006.

8

PUEBLOAN CULTURES OF THE AMERICAN SOUTHWEST

At roughly the same time as the Mississippian culture was rising to prominence, the Puebloans in the American Southwest were building a substantial cultural complex. The origin of those who became the "Puebloans" is still unconfirmed; they most likely originated in the Great Basin area to the north. Two thousand years ago they occupied the Four Corners region of the Southwest. Hunter-gatherers, they wove beautiful baskets and began to experiment with plant cultivation. By roughly 800 C.E., the first Pueblo communities were scattered across the region, and residents were fully engaged in subsistence farming and building pit houses and large circular structures that functioned as places of worship. For the next several hundred years, their population increased, more villages and larger towns appeared, and long-distance trade networks were developed with Mexico and regions to the north and east. By the mid-twelfth century, larger and more socioeconomically complex settlements existed in the American Southwest. Three distinct cultures were spread across the landscape: the Hohokam in southern Arizona and northern Mexico, the Mogollon in eastern Arizona and western New Mexico, and the culture long known as the Anasazi, in northern Arizona and New Mexico, and regions of Colorado and Nevada. It is the Anasazi culture that will be the focus of the following discussion (Figure 8.1). One of the great mysteries of ancient America is the complete abandonment of nearly all of the Puebloan settlements by 1400 C.E. Why the inhabitants left and where they went are enduring questions in Southwestern archaeology.

The term *pueblo* refers to the adobe structures built by Native American cultures in the Southwest today (e.g., the Tewa, Zuni, Hopi, and Pima). Many believe that the ancient Puebloans are the ancestors to these cultures, though this remains controversial since the gap in occupation offers no continuous connection between ancient and modern cultures. However, the similarities in material culture and even belief systems have encouraged many archaeologists to use modern Puebloan cultures for insight into interpreting the past.

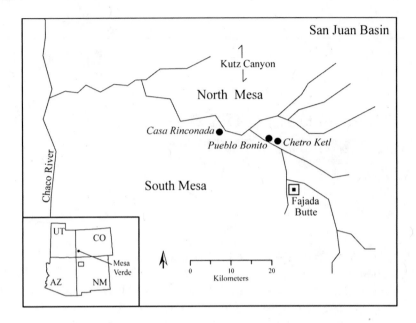

Figure 8.1. Map of sites and regions discussed in the chapter. (*T. Edwards*)

The Hisatsinom (Anasazi)—Early Settlement

Anasazi is a Navaho word meaning "ancestors of our enemies" (a reference to the uneasy relationship between the Navaho and Puebloan cultures of more recent history). Today archaeologists use *Hisatsinom*, a Hopi word meaning "ancient people," to refer to the ancient Anasazi Puebloans. The Hisatsinom built remarkable settlements at Mesa Verde, where the structures are known as *cliff dwellings*, and in Chaco Canyon, where the enormous *great houses* at sites such as Pueblo Bonito are monuments to architectural innovation.

The earliest Puebloan settlements are called the Basketmaker cultures. They emerged when villages were first forming and residents constructed strikingly beautiful basketry but no ceramics. The Basketmaker II period extends from 1 to 400 C.E., and Basketmaker III from 400 to 750 C.E. (Stuart 2000). During the Basketmaker II phase, residents continued to forage and hunt but were also engaged in regular cultivation of maize and other plants. Houses are termed *pit houses* because floors rested as much as 2 meters below the surface. These houses were circular or squarish, with rounded corners. Walls were constructed of horizontal wooden beams, branches, and reeds, covered with mud, and then plastered; the dome-shaped roof was supported by vertical wooden beams. Most houses had an interior hearth; some had interior storage pits, while others had even larger external storage areas. It is possible these settlements were occupied for only part of the year, perhaps during the fall and winter; during the warmer seasons, residents may have been more mobile, making use of the natural landscape for their subsistence (Wills and Windes 1989).

By Basketmaker III, more substantial houses and rudimentary ceramics made their appearance, settlements increased in size and were more permanently occupied, and a wider variety of plants was cultivated. Pit houses were larger than those in Basketmaker II, sometimes twice as big (5 or more meters across, as opposed to the 3 or so of Basketmaker II). Pit houses also often featured a type of antechamber, which provided entry from ground level as well as additional space for storage. One unusual feature in these pit houses was a small circular hole in the floor, usually near the hearth and northernmost wall. Most believe this is an early version of similar holes found in later Hisatsinom houses and religious structures that represent a symbolic passage into the spirit world. Burials were found more frequently, some in the middens outside the pit houses, and others in abandoned storage pits both outside and inside houses (Stuart 2000). Burials were accompanied by goods such as shell and stone ornaments, and pottery. The ceramic assemblage primarily consisted of storage and cooking vessels, a few with white and black paint. The Basketmaker III ceramics, however, do not rival the beauty of the later Hisatsinom pottery.

Chaco Canyon and Pueblo Bonito

The "Pueblo" phases began in the eighth century C.E. Pueblo I (700–900 C.E.) was a period of continued population increase, larger villages, and ceramic innovation. Villages averaged 20–30 houses rather than the 5–10 of the Basketmaker III phase (Stuart 2000). Population movement to higher elevations, out of canyons and valleys, may have resulted in these larger communities. In higher elevations, away from the lower and less-watered valleys, rain-fed agriculture was more easily accomplished, though in a shorter growing season. In addition, while Puebloans were still building semisubterranean rooms, some houses had above-ground attached rooms. However, near the end of the Pueblo I phase, residents began moving into the lowlands again, especially into the San Juan Basin and the Chaco Canyon region. The reason for this movement may have been competition over land resources, internal strife, or climate change that decreased crop output.

It is during Pueblo II (ca. 900–1100) that the Chaco Canyon settlements reached their zenith, and in Pueblo III (ca. 1100–1300) that the abandonment began. One of the most interesting, and debated, aspects of Chaco Canyon settlement is the different kind of architecture at the settlements. Rather than the square or circular semisubterranean detached houses described above, the Chacoan great-house architecture consists of masonry-built structures in the shape of the letters *D*, *E*, or *L*, or in geometric forms (circles, squares). All the rooms are connected, and the structure can be several stories high. By 1100 C.E. the Chaco great-house style was adopted by settlements outside the canyon, in villages in the San Juan Basin and beyond to the Mesa Verde region (Kantner 2004). The architecture, and most probably the ideology, of the Chaco Canyon ancient Puebloans had spread far and wide.

Chaco Canyon provided good farming opportunities, as it received springtime runoff from the surrounding higher mountains. Residents built channels, dams, and canals to direct water to their maize crops in order to make the most of the modest (less than 10 inches a year) rainfall. Maize was their staple crop, but small gardens provided additional plant foods such as beans and squash; hunting remained the norm for meat acquisition. Over the centuries Chaco residents had to weather seasons of lower rainfall which affected food production. In part they managed food shortages through their extensive social and economic networks.

Chaco residents were engaged in trade networks with other Puebloans across the Southwest, extending as far as northern Mexico. Trade was an essential component in Chaco society, demonstrated by the items that moved around the region. Though clay and chert sources were available in Chaco Canyon, households possessed pots and stone tools made from sources outside the valley (Toll 2004). Residents also acquired wood for building their great houses from distant sources, and enjoyed more exotic items such as turquoise from the Texas region and copper bells from Mexico. Chaco residents also had a penchant for the brightly colored tropical macaw bird from Mexico. Food was an essential trade item. When rainfall was insufficient for a good crop in the canyon, other areas of the Southwest that had adequate or even abundant rainfall could provide both plant food and meat to Chacoan trading partners to tide them through a difficult season (Toll 2004).

People traveled to Chaco on an extensive roadway system that included *line-of-sight topographical features* along which signal fires might have been used to send messages. Roadways were constructed by deliberately removing the top layer of ground to a depth of as much as 50 centimeters, to a more compact, less sandy level; they were bordered by earthen berms or sometimes by low stone walls. The labor investment to build these roads was considerable, and a number of communities cooperated in the efforts. They led out of Chaco in all directions, sometimes directly to other communities, while some led to other canyons or high buttes (Kantner 2004). Shorter roads connected Chacoan great-house communities within the canyon. While these roadways (some over 20 feet wide) may have been constructed to allow for easy trading connections, they could well have served religious or symbolic functions as well.

Best known among Chacoan trade items is pottery. Painted Chaco pottery is most commonly a black-on-white ware with geometric, spiral, zigzag, and original designs, as well as occasional human figures. Particular to Chaco are tall cylindrical jars (Figure 8.2); other decorated forms include mugs with handles, jars, bowls, and ladles. Chacoans also used a type of gray pottery for cooking and storage, but even some of these more utilitarian vessels were acquired through trade connections.

One of the largest and best-known settlements in Chaco Canyon is Pueblo Bonito (Figure 8.3); it is masonry-built, D-shaped, and nestled against the canyon wall. At its height in the late eleventh century, it featured approximately 800 rooms and nearly 40 circular structures known as *kivas*, a Hopi word for similar buildings. Pueblo Bonito's great house was built in stages, beginning around 875 C.E., with subsequent portions added on for the next 250 years (Lekson 2004). There is only one main entrance into the settlement, near the mid-point in the southern wall. The entire structure appears defensive in nature, though whether Pueblo Bonitoans feared frequent attacks is unknown. The entire complex is divided into two sections, each with a large plaza and kiva. Interspersed throughout the rectangular rooms are circular ones, typically also called kivas. These circular structures were long thought to have a religious function, perhaps serving as the family "temple" (in modern Pueblo communities, the circular kivas are used for rituals).

Figure 8.2. Chacoan tall black-on-white cylindrical jars. (*R. Jennison*)

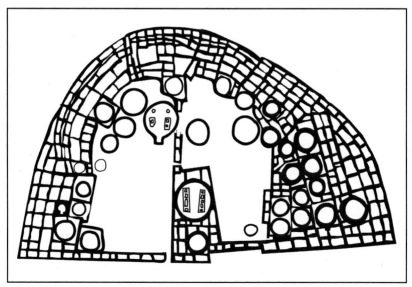

Figure 8.3. Sketch of D-shaped Pueblo Bonito in Chaco Canyon. (*S. R. Steadman*)

Originally it was thought that great houses were like enormous apartments, housing hundreds and even thousands of people. However, more recent work has suggested that a majority of Chaco great houses were not entirely residential, or at least not fully occupied at any one time. In fact, based on analysis of the presence of hearths and other domestic items, several archaeologists have suggested that only about a dozen families may have lived in Pueblo Bonito at any given time (Kantner 2004). Much of the space in the Pueblo Bonito great house was devoted to uses other than actual housing. Many of the spacious rooms were probably used to store crops and other items. Exotic import items were found in some rooms, including vessels with stone mosaics on them, carved wooden objects, effigy pots from the Mississippian region, shell trumpets from the southwestern coast, and copper bells from Mexico (Kantner 2004). One room held over 100 of the cylinder jars seen in Figure 8.2, and brightly colored macaws imported from tropical Mexico resided in several Pueblo Bonito rooms. Some of the rooms may have functioned as places where guests could stay during events at Pueblo Bonito, though this is a subject of debate, given the lack of "creature comforts" in such rooms.

Great houses such as the one at Pueblo Bonito may have functioned as central locations for public events both ceremonial and religious. This coincides with the growing conviction that the relatively few families who occupied Pueblo Bonito and other great houses were elites who were very important in Puebloan economy, politics, and possibly religion (Lekson 2004). These elite families merited enormous houses not only to store their goods, but to host the periodic events at Pueblo Bonito. That residents in outlying villages had a stake in preserving the architecture at Pueblo Bonito is established by the simple fact that they must have contributed to its construction. A dozen families, or even a few dozen, could not have built the massive structure at Pueblo Bonito; rather, they may have organized the labor and directed others in the building of these elite residences (Lekson 2004). While even the largest great houses such as Pueblo Bonito cannot rival the immensity of Cahokia in the Mississippian culture, evidence from these Chacoan settlements indicates there was a definite element of class differentiation between those who inhabited the great houses and those in the other settlements with single-household structures. The relationship between the elites and the rest of the population rested within networks of economic, political, and, it seems, religious ties that knitted the peoples of the entire canyon into one large societal structure.

Chacoan Social Structure

Two of the major questions in Southwestern archaeological investigations ask what type of sociopolitical structures existed in the Chacoan culture, and what happened to that culture in the twelfth and thirteenth centuries. Was Chaco a chiefdom, or a loose confederation of cooperating kin groups? Or did a more egalitarian political structure operate within the Chacoan communities? The fact that great houses such as Pueblo Bonito apparently housed very few people leads some to suggest that these inhabitants were the caretakers of this religious center, akin to priests whose duties included overseeing important rituals and ceremonies (Renfrew 2004). In this scenario, socioeconomic and political differentiation among Chacoans was not really the issue, since the main distinction was one of religious position. Locations such as Pueblo Bonito would have been visited by a steady stream of pilgrims, directed in worship by the resident Bonitoans. In this interpretation, the monumental architecture of the great houses was a testament to "high devotional expression" rather than political or economic power (Renfrew 2004). In this view, Chaco's great houses were the cathedrals of the Southwest.

However, most suggest there were elements of social stratification based on the evidence of architecture, the burials discovered in places such as Pueblo Bonito, and the presence of exotica in the great houses. Scholarly debate centers not on inequality versus egalitarianism, but on whether Chaco Canyon was an economic or political center, and what role religion may have played *within* such structures. One explanation notes that Chaco residents had greater access to more productive farmlands than did surrounding regions. The great houses at Pueblo Bonito and elsewhere, even in their early Pueblo I and Pueblo II stages, had large storage areas for surplus crops. In an early incarnation of a *reciprocity* system, Chacoans were in a position to be more generous as givers and less often the takers in a regionally based exchange system. Over time this might have led to a situation in which Chacoan "generous givers" coalesced into powerful Chacoan "lenders" to whom everyone was beholden, placing Chacoans in a position of superiority (Sebastian 1992). By approximately 1000 C.E., Bonitoans might have become true political leaders, able to marshal large labor forces, dictate building and other activities (such as roadway construction), and perhaps even regulate participation in major and minor religious ceremonies. Various great-house communities in Chaco may have competed with one another for surplus and control of ever greater areas. By the end of the eleventh century, however, when climatic change began to affect food production, a Chacoan control of surpluses would have slipped, and it is in fact at this time that we see the Chaco era coming to an end (Sebastian 1992).

Another explanation of the Chaco system suggests a similar structure of leaders living at great-house communities such as Pueblo Bonito, but the method of control relied less on subsistence resources and more on trade goods. Some argue that Chaco Canyon great-house communities were the center of a *redistributive* economy, in which goods, both utilitarian and exotic, were collected and stored. Goods would have arrived via trade networks and as gifts and donations from pilgrims attending major religious events at the great kivas. Great-house residents in charge of a vast redistributive economy would have wielded rather substantial power and influence. Their greatest influence may have rested in their control over the prestige goods such as turquoise, macaw feathers, copper bells, and other long-distance trade items (Lekson 1999). Residents in a great house such as Pueblo Bonito could have controlled access to such exotica, dictating which lesser great-house communities, or even small outlying villages, received particular (political and/or religious) items of power. Commanding the redistribution of subsistence and prestige goods would have placed Chaco great-house residents in a strategic position of power, bolstered by the importance of great kivas in the ancient Puebloan belief system. Using the power of a redistributive economy, the building and maintenance of great houses and kivas, roadways, and other projects could easily have been accomplished.

Burials at Pueblo Bonito and other great-house sites, in contrast to those in smaller communities, also suggest social, political, and economic ranking in ancient Chacoan society (Atkins 2003). Burials at smaller communities were generally either in middens or under the houses of floors and were often accompanied by utilitarian items such as cooking pots. Over 130 burials were excavated from the Pueblo Bonito ruins; one group was in the western area of the great house, and one was at the center arc of the D-shaped structure. Individuals in both of these burial clusters were taller and healthier than people in smaller communities, indicating better nutrition and a more stable food source. Pueblo Bonito burials also had more plentiful grave offerings that were of higher quality than those in the smaller communities. Burials in the western cluster were laid in constructed chambers in interior rooms and contained ceramics and jewelry, baskets, and some items that may have been for ceremonial use. Those at the center arc were buried in an even more elaborate, sealed location with no obvious external access; they were accompanied by more numerous goods, including turquoise objects, jewelry, cylindrical jars and other ceramics, and many other items that were probably of great value, such as *prayer sticks* (wooden sticks with carvings or designs and knobs on one end, which may have had religious purposes). Similar objects are used during ceremonies in present-day Puebloan cultures. The differing labor invested in the actual burial places of the three groups, and the varying number and value of grave offerings, suggest that there may have been two different social groups resident in, or at least buried at, Pueblo Bonito, and a third comprising people in smaller outlying communities. If there were two classes of individuals buried at Pueblo Bonito, this may in fact reflect the types of sociopolitical and economic structures described above; perhaps one group represented political or economic elites while the other held religious offices.

Whether the sociopolitical structure in ancient Chaco Canyon may be called a "chiefdom" or not continues to be a subject of debate. That the residents of settlements such as Pueblo Bonito were living more privileged lives than those elsewhere, however, is not seriously contested. Were the residents benevolent dictators, high religious personnel, rich elites, or did they have some other constellation of purposes? These are questions that scholars continue to pursue.

Chacoan Religion

Modern Puebloan religions are well known for the religious buildings called *kivas*. Initially archaeologists believed the ancient kivas were strictly for religious purposes, but more recent investigation has suggested that they may have also served as permanent or temporary residences. Typically kivas were stone-lined, with log-built roofs. Entrance was by wooden ladder through an opening in the roof, which also provided ventilation. Around the interior was a low stone bench upon which items could be placed or people could sit; hearths were situated in the center. Some kivas had grooves or vaults in the floor, perhaps for storage or religious purposes. Most had a small hole in the floor, believed to represent the *sipapu*, or "place of emergence" in Hopi. The

Hopi believe that people first ascended from the spirit world to this layer of the world through a hollow reed. The hole in the floor of the Chaco kivas could be a symbolic representations of the sipapu through which the original people came.

At Pueblo Bonito the smaller kivas within the great house were probably associated with particular kin groups. Household ceremonies may have been carried out in these structures on a daily or frequent basis (Figure 8.4). Outside the great house are the structures known as the *great kivas*, significantly larger than other kivas (as much as 45 feet in diameter) and probably used for more public gatherings. Great kivas were similar in structure to the smaller kin-group kivas, but entry was usually through an attached antechamber leading from ground level downward into the central kiva area, giving the great kiva a keyhole shape when viewed from above. During special ceremonies, great kivas may have been used by everyone inhabiting Pueblo Bonito. They may have also been used when visitors came to celebrate important ritual events in the ancient Puebloan calendar.

As is so common in Native American beliefs, present-day Pueblo cultures view their cosmos in vertically and horizontally layered segments, with a center place balancing all six directions (the four horizontal and two ends of the vertical) in harmonious symmetry. Archaeologists have noted that such notions of balance and center place appear to be reflected in the ancient Chacoan architecture and landscape (Van Dyke 2004). Chacoan roadways may have served both as pathways to facilitate networks of exchange as well as symbolic representations of ancient Puebloan cosmology. The roadways didn't always connect important trade partners or great-house communities. Many archaeologists believe that while the roadways were most likely used by traders, they were constructed for other purposes. Two major roads emanate from Chaco Canyon, one to the north and one southward, each extending at least 30 miles. The northbound roadway leads to an area known as Kutz Canyon, a lower depression in the landscape possibly representing the lower layer in Chacoan cosmology. The south road leads to a place called Hosta Butte, a very high point on the landscape visible from Chaco and possibly representing a higher layer of the cosmos (Van Dyke 2004). These two major roads, then, may have represented both the north/south cardinal directions as well as the vertical dimension. Chaco Canyon itself is on an east/west axis, thus representing the fifth and sixth directions. That Chaco was the symbolic center place must have made large settlements like Pueblo Bonito particularly important not only to Chaco Canyon residents, but to those beyond as well.

Besides the multilayered cosmos, ancient Puebloans may have also been concerned with astronomical observations, especially those relevant to the agricultural cycle. This makes perfect sense, as the uncertainties of the dry climate made farming a sometimes difficult undertaking. One widely cited example of a device used by ancient Chacoans for tracking the movements of the sun and moon is the Sun Dagger at Fajada Butte, roughly 6 kilometers southeast of Pueblo Bonito. Three slabs of stone rest against a rock face that has two spiral designs—one large, one small—pecked onto it. At the solstices and equinoxes, sunlight in the shape of a ragged dagger shines between the slabs onto the pecked spirals (Sofaer 1997). During the summer solstice the dagger bisects

Figure 8.4. Artistic rendering of ritual in Pueblo Bonito kiva. (*M. J. Hughes*)

the larger spiral exactly, and during the winter solstice two daggers frame it. During the two equinoxes the dagger is slightly off-center of the larger spiral and bisects the smaller one (Figure 8.5). This is only one of several points on the Chacoan landscape in which the movement of the sun, signaling seasonal changes, can be tracked. Archaeologists have speculated that within settlements, important solar and lunar events might have been observed using built structures. For instance, a strategic niche in the roof of a kiva would have allowed sunlight to shine on a kiva wall. If the wall's interior had important drawings or designs on it, the sun's movement across the sky could be tracked. This appears to be the function of a niche in a great kiva at a site called Casa

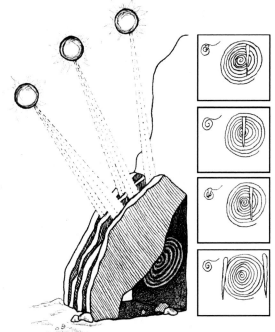

Figure 8.5. Artistic rendering of the sun daggers at Fajada Butte. (*R. Jennison*)

Rinconada, "where a beam of sunlight thrown on an interior wall could have marked certain days" (Malville 2004:90). That the plaster has decayed off the walls of most kivas, and the roofs have caved in, impedes archaeologists from documenting whether some or even all great kivas were used as astronomical devices to mark ritually important points on the calendar. Clearly the Chacoans believed most strongly that keeping track of the sky was a vital component to the success of their agricultural cycle.

The End of the Chaco Era

The Pueblo III period (1100–1300 C.E.) saw the end of the Chaco era. After 1100, great houses ceased to be built or even maintained. Trade fell off substantially, so that Chacoans were forced to obtain their own raw resources from more local sources (Kantner 2004). These events coincided with a period of drought that began early in the Pueblo III period. Prior to the drought, a period of increased rainfall probably allowed residents to build up their surpluses. If Chaco great-house communities had been controlling surrounding regions through redistribution of crop surpluses, the period of good climate may have weakened that control somewhat. The subsequent drought, when Chaco centers could not support themselves, much less others, might have further eroded Chacoan power. By the mid-twelfth century, Chaco Canyon was essentially deserted. Puebloan society continued outside the canyon, and some settlements even built Chaco-style great-house communities with similar architecture and goods; it is possible that Chaco residents left the canyon to resettle elsewhere and built communities in the style they had always known.

However, even these regions could not sustain the difficulties of continued drought. Another downturn in rainfall occurred in the thirteenth century, causing another phase of abandonments. By the end of the Pueblo III period in 1300 A.D., the entire San Juan Basin was essentially deserted. Hisatsinom culture had dispersed, though Puebloan culture and beliefs endured, carried on in the living traditions of inhabitants today.

Though there is still much to be learned about the Hisatsinom and their neighbors, it is clear that their beliefs included astronomical observations, and it is quite possible that their socioeconomic and political structures were intimately tied to the vagaries of the Southwestern environment. The ability to build crop surpluses might have maintained the hierarchical social structure, allowing elites (whether secular or religious) to command labor to build great houses, kivas, and roadways. Religious personnel may have been charged with ensuring the rains and helping to maintain the balance between the horizontal and vertical worlds, doing so at public ceremonies in the great kivas. Our evidence to date reveals that ancient Puebloan society is an excellent example of a culture displaying the intersection between environment, power, and religion.

USEFUL SOURCES

Brian Fagan, *Chaco Canyon*, 2005.
Steven Lekson (ed.), *The Architecture of Chaco Canyon, New Mexico*, 2007.
Stephen Plog, *Ancient Peoples of the American Southwest*, 2008.

9

MESOAMERICA AND THE RELIGIONS OF EMPIRE

The Aztecs are perhaps the best-known culture of ancient Mesoamerica, in part because of the dramatic stories associated with their demise at the hands of the Spaniards, and in part due to their spectacular sacrifices of human victims. The Aztecs burst on the Mesoamerican scene in the twelfth century C.E., reaching the pinnacle of their civilization in the fifteenth and early sixteenth centuries. However, they were not the first to build grand structures and carry out human sacrifice in Mesoamerica. A long succession of fascinating cultures preceded their arrival.

Prelude to the Aztecs

Nearly 2,000 years before the Aztecs, a culture known as the Olmecs occupied a significant swath of Mesoamerica. The Olmecs (ca. 1500–400 B.C.E.) are best known for the large, sculpted stone human heads scattered across their landscape (Figure 9.1). However, there was much more to Olmec civilization, including a rich religion. Two main Olmec cities were San Lorenzo and La Venta (Figure 9.2), each with populations in the thousands; their buildings were adorned with sculpture, and large areas were available for public ritual. Each city also boasted monumental works, built by residents at the direction of their rulers. At San Lorenzo, sculptures adorned nearly every edifice, and a vast aqueduct carried water throughout the settlement, particularly to important ritual locales within the city. At La Venta, sculptures also abounded, and there were also several pyramids. The grandeur of these cities demonstrated the ability of Olmec leaders to command considerable labor from their residents. Religion as a method to control the actions of the population was part and parcel of this early civilization in Mesoamerica.

Our understanding of Olmec religion derives primarily from iconographic representations and from archaeological discovery of ritual areas. Olmec and later Mesoamerican religion is explained by the *continuity hypothesis*, which states that most of the elements of pre-Columbian religious tradition in Mesoamerica are interrelated, based on original myths first found in Olmec religion (Joralemon 1976). Much work on the religions of post-Olmec cultures does show similarities in cosmologies, as well as in the nature and deeds of their major deities. Whether the

Olmecs were the progenitors of these myths, or inherited them from even earlier cultures, is as yet undetermined.

Archaeology has provided the images of Olmec deities, but their functions in Olmec cosmology have been harder to come by. Three deity types have emerged as primary gods in the Olmec cosmology: the were-jaguar (known as the Olmec Dragon), the

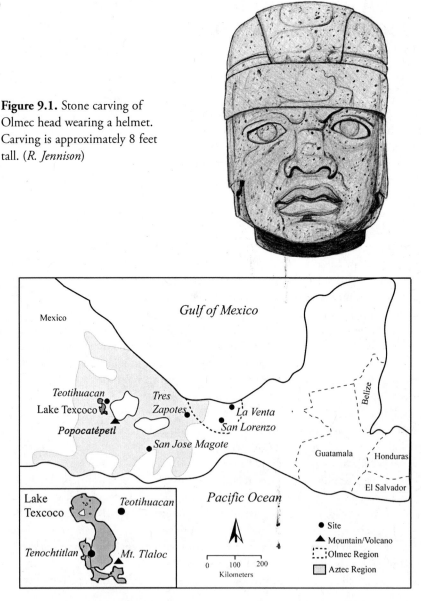

Figure 9.1. Stone carving of Olmec head wearing a helmet. Carving is approximately 8 feet tall. (*R. Jennison*)

Figure 9.2. Map of sites and regions discussed in the chapter. (*T. Edwards*)

Bird Monster, and the Fish Monster (Diehl 2004). Each of these presides over its own region of the cosmos: the Dragon over the earth and its functions, the Bird over the sky, and the Fish over the waters. As noted above, the roots of later Mesoamerican deities are found in these gods. The Olmec concept of a three-layered world (an upper layer in the sky; the earth and its humans; and a layer below the earth), oriented according to the four cardinal directions and connected by a vertical axis, is something found in Aztec and Maya belief systems as well. As farmers, the Olmecs' daily life depended on the agricultural cycle, which was featured prominently in their belief system; the Olmec Dragon was responsible for agricultural fertility, in combination with an Olmec maize god and a water/rain god.

The Olmecs relied on religious practitioners, including shamans and priests, to guide them in their ceremonies. Olmec art depicts therianthropes, usually human-jaguar combinations, which probably represent the process of a shaman entering a trance, induced by the ingestion of hallucinogenic drugs, and his travel to another layer (upper or lower). Priests may have been the more formal figures depicted in Olmec art, perhaps responsible for public rituals.

The Olmecs also believed their leaders played an important role in their religion. Rulers carried out rituals, and by the height of the Olmec period they also served as "chief priests" in important public rituals (Diehl 2004). Whether rulers claimed a divine nature is not clear to us from Olmec art, but their role in Olmec religious belief was undoubtedly of significant importance.

By their height, ca. 1000 B.C.E., the Olmecs were building temples and large plazas for their ritual activities. Other ceremonies apparently took place at natural settings such as caves and freshwater sites. One other sacred area seems to have been the ball court where the earliest version of the Mesoamerican ballgame was played. Players represented various deities and played a game in which the goal may have been to ensure future prosperity for the winner; there is some evidence to suggest that the loser lost not only the game, but his life as well (Diehl 2004). The Olmec head in Figure 9.1 may show a player in his helmet. The ball court and associated game continued to be an important aspect of Mesoamerican religion in succeeding centuries and cultures.

By 400 B.C.E. most of the major Olmec settlements were abandoned, and the ubiquitous Olmec art was no longer produced. The cause of the collapse is a subject of continued investigation, but a combination of environmental difficulties and internal systemic disorder was probably at the root of the disintegration of the first Mesoamerican civilization.

Hundreds of kilometers to the west and several centuries later, another city was rising to prominence. Teotihuacan lies in the Basin of Mexico and rests at an elevation of over 2,000 meters. The basin is surrounded by volcanoes, now dormant, which made obsidian a plentiful item thousands of years ago. Near Teotihuacan is Lake Texcoco, originally a network of connected lakes creating a border region full of marshes. These are now gone from the modern Mexican landscape, having been drained by the Spaniards after they colonized the region.

By the beginning of the first millennium C.E., Teotihuacan was a large city with a population as high as 150,000 spread across a settlement of nearly 20 square kilometers. The city was a center of commerce, with neighborhoods occupied by merchants and craftmakers from regional and distant areas (Millon 1976). Teotihuacan was the center of the Mesoamerican world in the early centuries of the first millennium, but by 800 C.E. this metropolis was all but abandoned.

At its height, Teotihuacan was a city to be marveled over. At its center were monumental buildings and pyramids, workshops and markets, and elite residences nearby. The city boasted many pyramids, but the most remarkable of them are at the ceremonial center, lying on the 5-kilometer-long Street of the Dead. The largest structure, and one of the earliest, is the Pyramid of the Sun (Figure 9.3), standing 70 meters

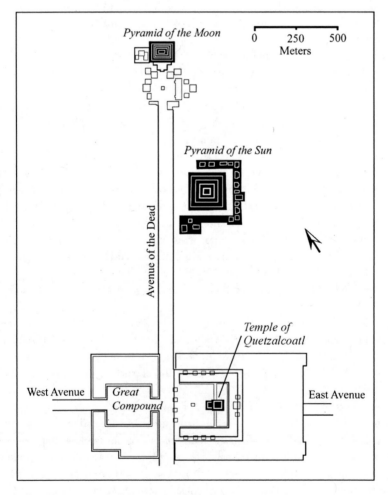

Figure 9.3. Sketch of Teotihuacan center. (*S. R. Steadman*)

high and built of adobe and rock. Since the few recovered Teotihuacan hieroglyphs are mainly calendrical, we have no written records detailing the role of this or other apparently religious buildings. However, the pyramid is built over an underground chamber, perhaps created much earlier by the quarrying of stone. A tunnel built from the Pyramid of the Sun leads down to the chamber. This chamber may have been a sacred place even before the city grew there, its importance eventually marked by the main temple built over it. Given the importance of the underworld in Mesoamerican religion, it is possible that this underground chamber was considered an entrance to that world.

At the northern end of the Street of the Dead stands the Pyramid of the Moon, and farther to the south is a structure known as the Temple of Quetzalcoatl. Like the Pyramid of the Sun, these buildings were once brightly painted, and the Temple of Quetzalcoatl especially was decorated with stone reliefs of what must have been Teotihuacan deities. Using knowledge of Olmec religion, and extrapolating back from later cultures such as the Aztecs, archaeologists have identified the iconography of several gods who were worshipped at Teotihuacan. In Aztec times these gods were known as Tlaloc, god of the rain, Miclantecuhtli, who presides over the underworld, and Quetzalcoatl, the Feathered Serpent, whose image appears on the temple named for him at Teotihuacan.

By the middle of the eighth century, residents were abandoning Teotihuacan. Climatic change, depletion of the environment, invasion, and infrastructural collapse have all been offered as explanations to describe the rather rapid disintegration of this major center. Whatever the cause of the collapse, Teotihuacan's importance remained in the minds of those who came later: the Aztecs considered it a sacred "city of ghosts."

The Aztecs

One of the best-known Mesoamerican civilizations is the Aztec Empire which rose to power in the early fifteenth century and was destroyed by the Spaniards in 1521. Though short-lived, their empire was powerful; at the heart of it were their superb warriors and their deep belief in the power of their gods.

Aztec Origins

Aztec origins are not fully understood by archaeologists. People think of the Aztecs as those who occupied the city of Tenochtitlan in Lake Texcoco. However, this area was occupied by numerous ethnic groups who had differing traditions and followed leaders other than Aztec kings. These groups shared language and belief systems, but were not united politically (Smith 2003). The name *Aztec* is derived from *Aztlan*, a place in the north from which they came; *Aztec* is apparently a corruption of this name and was not how the residents of Tenochtitlan referred to themselves (the Spaniards called the peoples in this region the "Mixtece"). The location of Aztlan is debated among scholars. Some locate it far to the north in the southwest of the United States or northern Mexico, while others suggest it was only a place of myth in the

Aztec cosmology. There is, however, some consensus that in the late twelfth century, the Aztecs came from the north to settle in the Valley of Mexico, with several waves coming over the next half-century. Aztec myth recounts that the god Huitzilopochtli urged the Aztecs to leave their homeland for the Valley of Mexico. This god, who figures in the creation myth, may have been an early Aztec leader or priest named Huitzil, deified at his death (Moctezuma 2003). The Aztecs wandered for some time, finally settling in a marshy area called Chapultepec, or "Grasshopper Hill," because the better locations were already occupied by previous migrants and other indigenous groups. After several violent encounters with neighbors, the Aztecs were driven out to wander yet again; mythology tells us that Huitzilopochtli revealed to his people that their new homeland would be marked by an eagle standing atop a cactus. When they spied this sight in 1325, they founded their new homeland and named their city Tenochtitlan, derived from their setting (*tenoch-tetl* meaning "cactus-rock") (Smith 2003); this scene now decorates the flag of Mexico. Their new homeland was in the swampy area ringing the great Lake Texcoco, surrounded by many other city-states that did not cast out this small group who chose to live in such an inhospitable place.

The Rise of the Aztec Empire

Though their new homeland offered neither solid ground nor good building materials, and agricultural land was inadequate at best, the Aztecs persevered and built a grand city. Residents hunted and fished and traveled by canoe to develop trade that helped supply their needs. Through trade and hard work, the Aztecs acquired building materials for their city and constructed *chinampas*, or agricultural lands built on the freshwater edges of the lake.

With a stable place to live, the Aztec population began to grow, and Tenochtitlan residents built more extensive trade networks with surrounding city-states. By the later fourteenth century, Aztec elites were intermarrying with those from surrounding regions. Aztec society was divided into two groups: those who governed (the *pipiltin*), and the commoners (the *macehualtin*). At the head of the pipiltin was the *tlatoani*, or "speaker," who was not only a great warrior, but had to be well versed in Aztec religion and ritual as well (Moctezuma 2003). The nobility, or pipiltin, had many privileges, including the right to wear certain clothing, ownership of land, and possibilities of advancement to leadership roles. Warriors who excelled on the battlefield could be elevated to pipiltin status, but the majority of warriors came from the commoner classes. Besides peopling the war machine, macehualtin commoners included craftsmen, farmers, artisans, and slaves. The macehualtin had to pay a type of tax to the tlatoani, and this was usually given in the form of cotton textiles and labor; commoners built temples, palaces, courts, and other building projects in the service of the Aztec leader. The pipiltin nobility also paid tax, and their service as leaders on the battlefield was considered a type of payment to the state (Smith 2003).

All Aztec boys who did not enter the priesthood received training to become warriors. As youngsters, boys entered the House of Youth, where they learned the labors and arts of adult Aztec men, including the methods of warfare and the rules that bound behavior on the battlefield (Clendinnen 1985). By the teenage years, boys had learned much of what they needed to know to perform Mesoamerican warcraft. Most then turned to the work of their fathers, whether it was farming, trading, craftmaking, or performance of some other service in Aztec society. These commoners were essentially the foot soldiers of the Aztec army in that they were not full-time warriors but only came when called for battle. In a young man's first battle, he assisted a more seasoned warrior, but by his second time on the battlefield he was expected to fight. As noted above, a commoner who performed well in warcraft might advance in Aztec society. One of the most important measures of success was not how many enemy combatants were killed, but rather how many were taken captive (Clendinnen 1985). Captives taken on the battlefield made up a large proportion of the human sacrifices carried out in Aztec rituals. Taking captives was an art, as they needed to be virtually unharmed in order to be unblemished offerings to the Aztec deities. Herein is an intimate interconnection between warfare and Aztec religion, a concept explored more fully below.

By the early fifteenth century, the Aztecs had gained substantial territories and thus became the recipients of tribute from these regions. Their power base in the Valley of Mexico was quickly growing; it would soon rival the most powerful city-states of the time. Over the next decades, more wars brought more tribute-paying regions under Aztec control and more chinampas available for cultivation. Wealth and trade allowed the Aztecs to continue building their capital city, establishing vast palaces, shrines, and imposing temples. The tribute and lands from conquered regions not only enriched the Aztec elites, but allowed them to develop a system of land tenure. Warriors and elites became the stewards of various tracts of land on which they built impressive homes befitting landed noblemen in a powerful empire (Smith 2003).

By the mid-fifteenth century, the Aztec Empire was well established as a powerful entity in the Valley of Mexico; in 1440 Motecuhzoma I came to power and expanded the empire substantially. Under this ruler the Aztecs perfected their military tactics, used not only to conquer but to enforce rules of tribute-paying and to resist rebellion. The empire commanded respect and fear from its conquered territories. Much of their success had been built on warfare, and thus the warrior class, and the deities associated with warfare such as the sun god, were very important in the Aztec cosmology. During the fifteenth century, Aztec rulers mounted building campaigns to erect Aztec monuments in the capital city and throughout all their conquered lands. These projects, undertaken by workers from the commoner classes, included ceremonial centers, temples, forts, and religious monuments. In this way the Aztecs were able to reinforce their belief systems and practices in outlying territories, which may have had similar methods of worship but also adherence to local deities.

The Aztecs developed a type of writing system that included both hieroglyphs and pictorial representation. The latter recorded events, people, and the gods through the representation of images that carried symbolic meaning. An example of this is the picture of a temple afire, which could represent the Aztec victory over a neighboring city (Smith 2003). The image really functioned as an ideogram, since the reader would need to know the context of the picture, including which region was conquered, by which warriors, and so on. Thus, this type of Aztec writing was more of a mnemonic device than a document one would "read." The Aztecs also employed hieroglyphs that had to be learned by scribes in order to be used correctly. These glyphs represented calendrical dates, names of individuals, ritual events, and other categories of information. Temple personnel and the elite were taught to read and write these hieroglyphs; commoners could "read" the pictorial writing but not the hieroglyphs. When the final Aztec independent ruler, Motecuhzoma II (grandson of Motecuhzoma I) came to power in 1502, he ruled the second largest empire in the Americas, surpassed only by the Inkas to the south.

Aztec Religion

Aztec religion is a complex mix of numerous myths, deities, and concepts, some of which seem to contradict one another or give entirely separate explanations for the same person or event. This confusion arises from a melding of the original Aztec (Aztlan) beliefs from their homeland and the existent belief structures the Aztecs found on their arrival in the Valley of Mexico. Many of the Aztec myths and deities are drawn from those found represented on the temples at Teotihuacan, a city the Aztecs considered very sacred. Another source of confusion is the imperfect understanding Spaniard chroniclers had of the Aztec religion, recording information not from priests but from whomever would talk to them (Carrasco 2000). It is not surprising, therefore, to find gods with two versions of their births, and myths describing the same events in two different ways. Despite these discrepancies, archaeologists have provided much insight into Aztec belief and ritual, and we learn much about how religion was effectively used to rule a people.

The Aztecs conceived of a multilayered world composed of an upper or celestial level, the middle world inhabited by the Aztecs, and an underworld. The Aztecs believed they were living in the fifth recreated world, after destructions of four previous worlds; they called their world the Fifth Sun age. The previous four suns were worlds inhabited by people who had differing subsistence strategies; in one sun, people ate seeds; in another they subsisted on acorns. In each age, a different Aztec god presided over the people and the Aztec pantheon; each previous age was destroyed by a cataclysm. The Fifth Sun was peopled by those who ate maize and was presided over by the sun god (Tonatiuh); this age would also someday end in cataclysmic destruction, the date of which was unknown (Taube 1993). In Aztec mythology, the destruction of the Fifth Sun can only happen at the end of a 52-year-long cycle based on two separate Aztec calendars (see below). Therefore, when one cycle ended and the world was still intact the following day, a grand ritual to celebrate another 52 years of existence took place. One can only imagine the anxiety Aztecs must have felt in the days and weeks before the end of each cycle, and the subsequent intense relief at seeing the sun rise on the first day of the new cycle.

Though there are variants, the main mythological thread of the creation story rests with the actions of a god who possessed both male and female characteristics and who therefore could give birth. Four children produced from this divine unity became principal gods in the Aztec pantheon: Quetzalcoatl (the Feathered Serpent, god of creation and of priests), Xipe Totec (god of agriculture), Tezcatlipoca ("Smoking Mirror," god of all power, and of the nobility), and Huitzilopochtli (god of war, and patron god of the Aztecs). These four proceeded to create the earth, animals, plants, the four elements, and, eventually, people (Taube 1993). People in the world of the Fifth Sun were created from the bones of the ancestors in the previous age that Quetzalcoatl had retrieved from the underworld. The gods then shed their own blood on these bones and the Aztecs were created. Later, the gods met in the sacred city of Teotihuacan to decide who would light the newly created fifth earth. Two gods, Tecuciztecatl and Nanahuatzin, came forward as contenders, and so two hills were built upon which they would prepare themselves for the difficult feat of becoming the sun. In the Aztec cosmology, these two hills became the Temple of the Sun and Temple of the Moon at Teotihuacan. When they were prepared, the two gods approached the sacred fire; first Tecuciztecatl attempted to enter the fire but was driven back by its ferocity. The other god, Nanahuatzin, jumped directly in it; Tecuciztecatl, inspired by the fortitude of Nanahuatzin, followed him in. These two gods then rose in the sky; Nanahuatzin became the sun god Tonatiuh, and Tecuciztecatl the moon. However, in order to cause the sun and moon to follow their patterns of rising and setting, the remaining gods had to offer a blood sacrifice. Embedded in these two myths is the explanation of the need for bloodletting, an important aspect of Aztec ritual (Taube 1993).

As already noted, the Aztecs conceived of time as ordered by a calendar. The calendar operated on the basis of two counts: one was a 260-day ritual cycle, and the other was a 365-day solar count, the latter important for the agricultural cycle. The 52-year cycle is based on both calendars; only once every 52 years did the two calendars conclude on the same day, offering the possibility that the world would end. The 260-day calendar had a complex system of naming and numbering: each day received a name, such as Rabbit, Flint, or Jaguar, and a number between 1 and 13; the name of each day was unique, allowing for precise recordkeeping concerning important rituals and other events. This calendar was divided into 13-day segments, constituting the Aztec "week," and each of these weeks was the responsibility of a different Aztec deity. Aztecs could go to professional diviners to determine the best day in this calendar to undertake an important event, and predictions about a newborn could be sought out (Smith 2003). The 365-day calendar was divided into 20-day segments, totaling 18 months. This calendar was important for the agricultural cycle, for scheduling market days, and for keeping track of public ceremonies that occurred on a monthly basis. In a similar fashion to the shorter calendar, the 365-day count also designated names for each day. Thus, when the two calendars were combined, each day had two names, making it utterly unique within the 52-year count. In this way the Aztecs could keep track of events in the past and predict the precise timing of events that were foreseen to come.

In addition to a very sophisticated reckoning of time, the Aztecs also viewed the landscape around them as imbued with sacred meaning. As was the case with earlier

Mesoamerican cultures, caves and unusual formations on the landscape were considered sacred and often functioned as the setting for important events. Of particular importance to the Aztecs were mountains, especially Mount Tlaloc to the north. This mountain was said to be the origin of rain, mist, snow, and the clouds that produce these; it may have also influenced the orientation of Templo Mayor at the center of the Aztec ceremonial precinct (Aveni et al. 1988). Temples were not just religious buildings in the Aztec landscape, but also represented important aspects of Aztec mythology. The Aztecs conceived of their world as surrounded by water; at its edge it rose vertically to connect the Aztec world with the upper layer, where the gods resided. Upon the inhabited earth, the connectors between the human world and the one above were mountains; the Aztecs believed mountains could provide rain, cause disease, and harbored the deities (Broda 1991). The Aztecs built temples in their cities, in the countryside, and on mountaintops as well (one was built on Mount Tlaloc at an elevation of over 13,000 feet); these functioned as destinations for sacred pilgrimages at important points on the calendar (Townsend 1991). Therefore, a temple like Templo Mayor served not only as a religious landmark, but as a representation of a sacred mountain connecting the Aztec world to that of the gods.

It is the Aztec rituals of bloodletting and sacrifice that captured the widest attention from the Spaniards who conquered them and continue to intrigue students and scholars today who study them. Public rituals took place on the tall and beautifully built temples such as Templo Mayor at the center of Tenochtitlan (Figure 9.4). These rituals were presided over by priests, each of whom was dedicated to an Aztec god and served the deity at the temple built for that god. There was a ranked hierarchy among priests, beginning with the two highest and most sacred Quetzalcoatl Priests, followed by the Fire Priests near the top of the hierarchy, down to the newly initiated Little Priests at the bottom (Smith 2003). Only the Fire Priests could oversee the most important and sacred ceremonies involving human sacrifice.

At the center of Aztec ritual beliefs were several concepts: sacred blood, sacred body, warfare, and death. Each of these was found in the grandest of the Aztec rituals. Bloodletting was an integral part of most Aztec rituals, at which priests cut themselves to bleed for the gods. The Aztecs believed each human possessed *tonalli*, a divine force derived from the heat of the sun and from fire. Tonalli resided in the head and body of each Aztec; the human body also contained *teyolia*, a different divine force, closer to the notion of a "soul," and this resided in the heart (Carrasco 1990; Ingham 1984). Humans had differing levels of teyolia in their hearts; priests, great warriors, artists, and those who represented the gods at festivals and ceremonies held the most. The belief in the existence of these two substances in the head and heart illustrate why bloodletting from the head, and the removal of the beating heart from a sacrificial victim, were the most sacred activities accomplished for the gods.

The blood sacrifice was seen as a reenactment of the bloodletting done by Tezcatlipoca and Huitzilopochtli to create humans. Priests were responsible for offering their blood to the gods on a daily basis, by piercing their ears, tongue, arm, or genitals with a sharp thorn. In some ceremonies, a string was pulled through the wound to

Figure 9.4. Scene of human sacrifice on Templo Mayor. (*R. Jennison*)

bloody it, after which it was then offered to the gods. Priestly devotion could be seen on their very bodies, which bore many self-inflicted wounds; their long hair was matted with blood (Smith 2003). The offering of blood, especially from the head, gave not only blood but tonalli to the gods. However, as all blood was sacred, it was not just the priests, but all Aztecs who bled themselves at various times. They gave a blood offering when they wished to make a request of an Aztec god, such as for a successful harvest.

The Aztecs are perhaps best known for their human sacrifices. Such events were very public and, with only a few exceptions, took place at the pyramidal temples. Attendees watched as sacrificial victims were laid out on a stone altar where Fire Priests used a ceremonial knife (Figure 9.5) to open the victim's chest. The heart was removed while still beating and offered to the sun god Tonatiuh. The victim was then rolled down the steps so that the blood from his chest ran down the stairs and coated the walls of the temple, thereby feeding the sacred house of the god. At the end of the ceremony, when all the victims rested at the bottom of the stairs, the priests removed their heads and placed them on a "skull rack" near the temple (Smith 2003).

The selection of sacrificial victims depended on the needs of the god to whom the sacrifice was to be dedicated. The majority of those sacrificed were prisoners of war, taken on the battlefield for this very purpose. The Aztecs believed that the sacrificial victims were a personification of the god for whom they died, and therefore

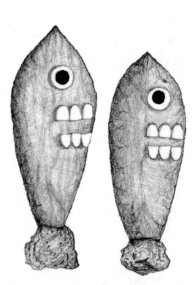

Figure 9.5. Ritual knives used to cut the hearts from sacrificial victims. (*R. Jennison*)

needed to have the appropriate characteristics acceptable to that deity. The sun god Tonatiuh required warriors captured in battle; these enemy soldiers were kept as "guests" of the Aztecs, housed, fed, and treated very well until the time of their sacrifice. Besides male warriors, other members of Mesoamerican society were acceptable sacrifices; Coatlicue and Yeuatlicue, the wives of important Aztec gods, accepted only female offerings (Broda 1991). The important Aztec god Tlaloc, responsible for rain and the earth in general, required a fairly regular diet of child sacrifices, usually accomplished by decapitation. Sometimes children who had been sold into slavery, or additional (secondary) children of nobles, would be chosen as suitable offerings to Tlaloc. These sacrifices often took place out in the landscape, on hills, in valleys, or in other places sacred to Tlaloc; such places were considered the "mouths" of the earth, allowing the blood and flesh of the children to feed the god and give him the power to keep the rains and earth functioning properly. Tears of the children, and the weeping of the attendees, were seen as symbolic of the rains Tlaloc would bring (Arnold 1999).

Some ceremonies needed an enormous amount of preparation. The important god Tezcatlipoca, translated as "Smoking Mirror," god of power and of the nobility, required a "perfect" young man, chosen from the warriors captured on the battlefield. This man had to be handsome and free of imperfections in body or face. It took a full year for this man to be transformed into the earthly version of Tezcatlipoca. During this time he was housed and cared for, treated as if he were actually the god. He was adorned with fine clothing, given ornaments and decorations to wear, and attended numerous public ceremonies where, as representative of Tezcatlipoca, he interacted with the Aztec people (Carrasco 1999). During the last month before the sacrifice, he was returned to his previous warrior status in appearance, thereby representing this aspect of the god as well. He was then given four women to act as the god's wives in the last weeks before the ceremony. On the appointed day in the month of May, the representative of Tezcatlipoca proceeded to the temple at Chalco, a city south of Tenochtitlan, where he mounted the steps and was then sacrificed by heart extraction (Carrasco 1999). After his heart was offered to the god, his head was placed on the skull rack; his blood renewed the sun, earth, god, and Aztec alike.

Not all sacrifices involved the removal of the heart at the top of a temple. The most notable yearly sacrifice to Xipe Totec (The "Flayed Lord"), responsible for agricultural success, involved a mock battle in front of the temple dedicated to him. Xipe Totec's priests wore the flayed skins of warriors whose hearts had been removed and offered to Tonatiuh at daily events during the ceremony. The priests resembled Xipe Totec, who was always depicted wearing a flayed skin, symbolizing earth's new "skin" exhibited every spring by new growth. At the beginning of the planting cycle, in the spring, the sacred Feast of the Flayed Man was held. In this ritual, only the finest enemy warriors were selected for sacrifice, and their captors were honored and given opportunities for advancement in rank. On the appointed day, the sacrificial warriors were stripped of the finery they had worn preceding their sacrifice and dressed in a loincloth. Tied by the waist to the "gladiatorial" stone set on a pedestal at the base of Xipe Totec's temple, warriors were given a battle club. However, this club had not obsidian blades in it, but feathers. One at a time, four Aztec warriors approached the captive, each with a real club, to engage in battle (Figure 9.6). The captive was expected to fight as if in real battle, and because he was on an elevated stone he was sometimes able to "defeat" (probably strike) the Aztec warriors from above (Clendinnen 1985). Eventually the captive was felled, and a priest of Xipe Totec opened his chest, removed his heart, and offered it to the sun; the head was removed and placed on the skull rack next to the temple. The captor who originally offered the warrior was then allowed to flay the skin and wear it, and dismember the body, part of which would be featured at a feast in the captor's house. This feast was attended by the captor's family, who acted as mourners for the sacrificed warrior they had housed and cared for during his captivity. They mourned him as a "family member" as they consumed his body. The actual captor, however, did not partake of the feast, as eating the captive's flesh would be like eating his own (Clendinnen 1985).

How many people were sacrificed on an average ritual day in Aztec ceremonies? Estimates vary widely, and the count may have depended on the number of warriors in captivity. In addition to the special enemy warriors who died "in battle" at the Xipe Totec gladiatorial stone, more traditional sacrifices (simply removing the heart and casting the body down the temple steps) took place on the god's temple each day of the multi-day festival. One scholar estimates that approximately 60 victims were sacrificed each day of the Xipe Totec ritual (Clendinnen 1985). As there were numerous festivals to the multitude of Aztec gods throughout the year, if such numbers were typical for each ritual, this could easily add up to hundreds of victims each year, or many more. This leads to obvious questions: why so much death, why so much blood, and why did the heart and head become so important?

Figure 9.6. Artistic rendering of Xipe Totec gladiatorial ritual; the priest wears a flayed skin and watches the battle. (*M. J. Hughes*)

Explaining Aztec Religion

One theory offered to explain the significant level of human sacrifice involves the rite of cannibalism. Michael Harner suggested that the minimal level of protein available to Aztecs was responsible for the human sacrifices which then led to cannibalistic consumption of the victims' bodies (Harner 1977). This interpretation was immediately countered by others who view ritual cannibalism as rooted more deeply within Aztec society. Price suggested that cannibalism functioned to reinforce the sociopolitical hierarchy existent in the empire. Kings, nobles, and heads of households were responsible for the provision of necessary and luxury goods to their families and other dependents; these would include precious stones and metals, feathers, and human flesh (Price 1978). The consumption of a captive's flesh meant people were ingesting the essences of tonalli and teyolia residual in it, adding an important symbolic and religious aspect to cannibalism far beyond a need for protein. In addition, many argue that there was sufficient protein from beans, insects, meat, and fish to more than satisfy human nutritional needs, and thus the cannibalism was better explained by more ritual and symbolic motives (Ortiz de Montellano 1978; Smith 2003).

The Aztec focus on the human head, heart, and blood and the practice of ritual cannibalism are readily explained by Aztec cultural history and their environmental setting. Two themes are prominent: nearly everything the Aztecs achieved was through aggression and warfare, and their precarious position in swamplands at the edge of a lake made successful agriculture both difficult and an absolute priority. In the sun-drenched landscape of the Aztec homeland, rainfall was a crucial element in chinampas-style agriculture. It is not at all surprising, therefore, that Aztec religion featured a strongly rooted belief in the power of warfare and warriors, the fertility of the earth, and the need to ensure the continued success of both. The most prized sacrificial victims were those captured on the battlefield, carrying powerful teyolia in the heart, with concentrated tonalli in the head and body, both sacred and nourishing to Aztec gods. Not only did warriors give up their hearts as well as provide impressive contributions to skull racks in devotion to the gods, they reenacted the actual act of battle in the Flayed Man ritual dedicated to Xipe Totec. Warfare, so crucial to the origins and success of the Aztec Empire, played an integral role in their religion as well.

Blood, shed on the battlefield at death, was a life-giving force for the gods and the earth. Priestly bloodletting not only demonstrated devotion, but also provided the deities with a steady diet as well as ensured the continued health of the earth. The blood that sprang from the opened chest of sacrificial victims, spraying the temple as the body tumbled down the steps, symbolized the feeding of the gods, especially the sun, who in turn ensured a fertile and productive earth. In the same fashion, drops of blood and tears, essential human liquids, symbolized the rains falling upon the earth to feed the crops. Even in Xipe Totec's ceremony that featured a ritual battle, the notion of fertility is apparent in the flayed skin of humans, which represents spring renewal, new growth, and sustenance. At the heart of Aztec religion was a reflection of those things most crucial to their continued success in the region, mastery of the battlefield, and the acquisition of sufficient resources to feed a large, and growing, population.

In addition to utter belief in the power of blood and heart to ensure Aztec survival and success, ritual sacrifice in their religion served a somewhat more secular need as well: establishing and maintaining control over both the Aztec population and those cultures and kingdoms surrounding the empire. Although many of the neighboring cultures practiced human sacrifice, not all did, and few were as prolific in their ritual sacrifices as the Aztecs. Nobles and leaders from nearby and more distant regions were periodically invited to visit Tenochtitlan and attend one of the many elaborate ceremonies. Occasionally an attendee witnessed the sacrifice of some of his own warriors captured in battle (Smith 2003). That Aztec gods demanded so much of their people, and that Aztecs were so faithful, demonstrated not only the power and ferocity of the Aztec deities, but the dedication of their people as well. Furthermore, that Aztec rulers could command such utter compliance from their subjects, both elite and commoner alike, was testament to the power of the Aztec leadership over people and region. The bloody and elaborate ceremonies may have given significant pause to any enemy, or ally, thinking of defying the hegemony of the Aztec king and empire. That one's warriors, or even the ruler himself, might be featured at a future ritual may have helped to suppress thoughts of refusal to pay tribute to the Aztec coffers. In this way the Aztec religion may have functioned as a very effective control over those subsumed into the Aztec Empire.

Aztec religion also served to control its own people. Aztecs believed utterly in the power of blood and the importance of sacrifice, but that did not mean they were anxious to give up their own lives at future rituals. However, in addition to enemy warriors, Aztecs themselves were featured at ritual sacrifices, including women and children, drawn from both the slave and commoner classes and very occasionally from the elites. If you were not from the slave class, the most efficient road to becoming a sacrificial victim was to cause a problem in Aztec society: commit a crime or some sort of moral infraction, fall into debt and need to sell a family member or oneself for sacrifice, or indeed, defy in some way the Aztec leadership. To satisfy a debt or rectify a legal or moral transgression, the Aztec state deemed sacrifice a noble repayment, as one was giving one's own teyolia, tonalli, and lifeblood to the gods (Graulich 1997).

However, ritual sacrifice served not only to suppress problematic behavior among Aztec subjects, but also to elevate individual status in society. Capturing an enemy warrior or providing a human for sacrifice (one's slave or family member) was an important method of gaining status in Aztec society and perhaps advancing into and upward through the ranks of the elites (Ingham 1984). Nobles (pipiltin) who captured a brave enemy warrior, unblemished and well-cared for until the appointed ritual, stood to gain position in the Aztec social hierarchy, especially if the captive was deemed suitable for special recognition in, for instance, the Xipe Totec Flayed Man gladiatorial ritual. Offering sacrifices was, in addition to serving on the battlefield, a type of pipiltin "tax" payment to the state (Ingham 1984). Providing a sacrificial victim, whether captive, slave, or family member, showed one's dedication to the religion as well as to the health and power of the state and rulers. Thus, not only did human sacrifice glorify the power and control of the Aztec state and its rulers over the people, but it served as a vehicle for lesser nobles and even commoners to advance in that social hierarchy, ensuring their continued quest for suitable sacrifices to the Aztec religious machine. Aztec notions of blood, warfare, fertility, and power were inextricably bound with the Aztec view of their own society.

Conclusion

How far might the Aztecs have spread their empire? Geographically they were bounded by a fierce desert to the north and the lowland region ruled by the Maya to the south and east. Many other cultures resided in the highlands and lowlands of Mesoamerica about which we know very little. The expansionary dynamics carried out by the Aztecs in the fifteenth century may have continued well into the sixteenth, had not disaster, in the form of Hernando Cortés and his conquistadores, descended in 1519.

The Spaniards, with their cannons, guns, metal swords, and horses, used fighting techniques and strategies unheard of, and insurmountable, by Mesoamerican cultures. Furthermore, the Spaniards fought with no regard to preserving the life of their enemy warriors, a practice of great importance to the Aztecs. Upon his first visit to Tenochtitlan, Cortés took Motecuhzoma II captive and took over the rule of the city. It was not long after this that Motecuhzoma was killed under suspicious circumstances. In the early months of 1520, the Spaniards were forced to flee the city but only after terrible battles and much bloodshed. Cortés regrouped, aided by additional Spanish soldiers and many thousands of Mesoamerican warriors, mainly from lands conquered by the Aztecs, who had been required to pay heavy tribute to the Aztec state. Cortés and his army laid siege to Tenochtitlan in the summer months of 1521, and by mid-August the city had fallen (Smith 2003). The superior Spanish weapons and horses, and disease, mainly in the form of smallpox, defeated one of the greatest armies of ancient Mesoamerica. The Spanish zeal for spreading Catholicism quickly set about destroying Aztec sacred monuments and replacing Aztec rituals and beliefs with Catholic practices. Most Aztecs who did not succumb to disease or war were enslaved. The Spanish built the capital city of their colony, New Spain, over Tenochtitlan. Today that city is known as Mexico City.

USEFUL SOURCES

David Carrasco, *Daily Life of the Aztecs*, 1998.
Richard F. Townsend, *The Aztecs*, 2000.
Dirk Van Turenhout and John Weeks, *The Aztecs: New Perspectives*, 2005.

10

LORDS AND MAIDENS: RELIGIONS OF SOUTH AMERICA

The west coast of South America offers a beautiful but formidable landscape. A narrow strip of desert hugs the coast, while roughly 100 kilometers inland the Andes begin their rise to peaks that reach over 6,500 meters. Rivers originating in the snow-covered peaks created deep valleys where humans settled, domesticated plants and animals, and developed material cultures, religions, and buildings that are today known as the ancient cultures of the Andes.

An Early Andean Center: Chavín de Huántar

By 8,000–6,000 years ago, ancient Peruvians were domesticating peanuts, cotton, and manioc (a tuberous root crop); very recent evidence suggests that squash may have been cultivated as much as 10,000 years ago (Dillehay et al. 2007). By 4,000 years ago, residents were living in fairly permanent settlements, had begun making ceramics, and were building ceremonial centers in U-shaped patterns. These buildings consisted of a flat-topped pyramid at the bottom of the U-pattern, with two long structures extending from either side of the building to form the U. Such a structure is found at the center of Chavín de Huántar, built in approximately 900 B.C.E. (Figure 10.1). The Chavín culture is important to Andean culture history not just for its architectural elements, but for its art as well. Like the Olmec for Mesoamerica, the residents at Chavín seem to have set the standard for iconographic representation of Andean religious imagery.

The valley in which Chavín is situated rests at an elevation of 3,000 meters. Residents had access to good agricultural lands and ample water from two rivers. Chavín also rested along an important trade route, offering residents access to various goods passing from highland to desert and providing them with a rich selection of raw resources, food items to supplement their diets, and constant exchange of information with travelers along the route.

The original Chavín ceremonial center consisted of the Old Temple, built when the settlement was first constructed. The original U-shaped Old Temple had a northern wing wider than the southern one, making the arms of the U asymmetrical. In

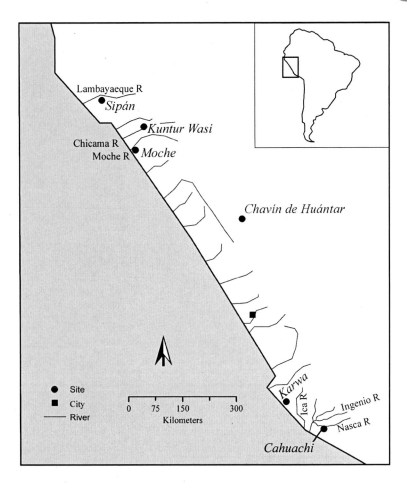

Figure 10.1. Map of Pre-Inka sites and regions discussed in the chapter. (*T. Edwards*)

front was a rectangular courtyard in which a sunken circular plaza was centered. This stone structure had walls that soared up to 16 meters high with no evident doorways in the outer walls. The only doorways into the Old Temple were inside the U; these led to various galleries, named by archaeologists according to features found within them (Figure 10.2). Thus, the Gallery of the Labyrinths is a complex maze of passageways, and the Gallery of Offerings, underground beneath the courtyard, provided hundreds of ceramic vessels as well as partially burned human and animal bones (Burger 1992). One of the most important of these galleries, known as the Lanzón Gallery, was at the center of the temple. Inside this gallery was a carved granite stone, the Lanzón; this now-famous stone is over 4.5 meters tall and tapers to narrower points at each end, to resemble a knife (Figure 10.3). The top of one end fit into a notch in the gallery ceiling, and the other rested in a floor notch. Carved on this stone is a human figure with feline fangs, adorned with necklace and ear plugs, and a belt displaying snake-jaguar images. The placement of this stone at the center of the temple suggests it was the focal point, displaying the principal deity or cult image to which the temple was dedicated (Burger 1992).

Archaeologists have offered various interpretations for the numerous temple galleries. Some suggest they were for storage of perishable goods in a difficult climate, while others assert they were reserved for rites and ceremonies; a third possibility is that they served as housing for religious personnel or initiates, perhaps as a type of cloister to remove them from the community for a period of time (Burger 1992). The later Inka culture built structures where initiates were housed, so it is indeed possi-

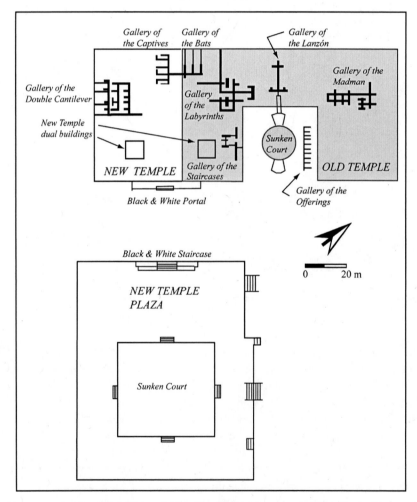

Figure 10.2. Sketch of Old and New Temples with courts at Chavín de Huántar. (S. R. Steadman)

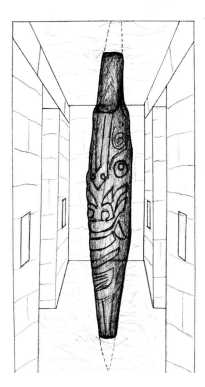

Figure 10.3. *Left:* A roll-out drawing of the carvings on the Lanzón statue. *Right:* The Lanzón statue in the center of the Chavín temple. (*R. Jennison*)

ble that those associated with ritual and belief at Chavín were housed within this temple. Human bones discovered in the galleries are sometimes carved, sometimes burned (such as those in the Gallery of Offerings). This leads some to suggest that the practice of sacrifice or perhaps ritual cannibalism took place, but neither interpretation is supported by additional evidence.

The exterior of the Old Temple is decorated with carved reliefs on black limestone and white granite quarried from outside the Chavín Valley; this suggests these colors and stone types were important elements in the religious imagery. The meaning and mythology of the sculptures are presently lost to us, but there is little doubt they tell the complex story of Chavín religious beliefs. There was clearly a significant component of animal symbolism in Chavín mythology; represented on the temple walls are carvings of anthropomorphic figures and animal combinations, including elements of snakes, jaguars, raptors, and caymans (alligators), along with geometrical forms carved in complex patterns. Several scholars suggest that the deity represented on the Lanzón was their supreme god, reigning over a pantheon of supernatural beings (Burger 1992). This would make feline/jaguar and snake/serpent imagery preeminently important in the Chavín belief system.

Sometime after 500 B.C.E. the New Temple was added to one wing of the original temple. This was a time of population growth at Chavín, due to their expanding trade-based economy and increased agricultural output. At this time the southern arm of the Old Temple was enlarged to become a massive rectangular structure. A large plaza was created in front of this new building, with an interior rectangular sunken court. On top of the new building were two identical structures, each two-roomed and easily visible from the plaza in front of the New Temple. It is here that important ceremonies probably took place (Burger 1992). To reach these buildings, one passed through a complicated set of passageways inside the New Temple; this limited access suggests that only special personnel could gain entrance to the rooftop buildings. Inside the New Temple were galleries and halls like those in the Old Temple; again their function is not entirely clear. On the eastern side of the New Temple, facing the plaza, was a portal built of black limestone and white granite; 20 meters east was a black and white stairway leading into the plaza.

The exterior of the New Temple is also covered in carvings, exhibiting the same themes as those represented on the Old Temple. However, the degree of complexity has increased to the extent that it is difficult to pick out individual components in some parts of the relief. Nonetheless, residents at Chavín almost certainly recognized the meaning behind these carvings on their central temple. The only clearly new iconography in the New Temple carvings are the depictions of a monkey, a non-raptor winged creature, and a viscacha (a rodent resembling a rabbit). Whether these are new deities or only more detailed representations of ancient Chavín myths is unknown.

Little is known of the specifics in the Chavín belief system, but the god represented on the Lanzón, or a cult of the Lanzón, appears to have been fairly widespread. At the site of Kuntur Wasi, several hundred kilometers northwest of Chavín, are several U-shaped complexes with sunken courtyards, decorated with sculpture in the Chavín style. Hundreds of kilometers to the south, a coastal site called Karwa offers a very important discovery: a tomb containing several interments along with numerous fragments of cotton textiles. On these textiles were painted symbols identical to carvings on the Chavín Old and New Temples, including representations of the Lanzón deity (Burger 1992). This discovery led scholars to believe that the Lanzón cult was spread across the Andean region through representations on cloth. The Karwa textiles also portray some images not found at Chavín, suggesting that the Lanzón cult may have been merged with local beliefs and deities. These are just two examples from a number of sites at which Chavín-style sculpture, architecture, or symbolism has been found.

Growing evidence suggests that along with increasing population and economic success, class stratification was also developing at Chavín, tied closely to the expanding power of the Lanzón cult, the control of which may have rested in the hands of a growing elite class (Rick 2004). Burials discovered in Chavín-period settlements show an increasing level of social stratification within communities; the wealthiest individuals were buried with Chavín-style iconography on goods and on textiles (Burger 1992). As the Chavín cult spread, those who sought leadership roles discovered that if they associated themselves closely with the religion, they could attain superior wealth and power within their societies. It is here in the Chavín period that religion and power became irrevocably linked in Andean culture.

At the end of the third century B.C.E., the Chavín cultural complex began to unravel. In the preceding century, a number of hilltop forts had been constructed, indicating Chavín residents began to feel a strong need for defense. Trade relationships, threatened by hostile action, broke down, and the Chavín economy began to suffer. By approximately 200 B.C.E., either actual attack or fear of it had caused residents to abandon their homes. Some suggest that the nature of the social stratification at Chavín de Huántar was partially responsible for its demise. If priests and religious personnel constituted the elite class, and an accompanying warrior class had not developed, then the Chavín culture may have been ripe for attack and conquest (Burger 1992). That a new population entered the valley at this time is suggested by the fact that much of the ceremonial architecture was dismantled, and some of the sacred relief carvings were incorporated into newly built house walls. Nevertheless, the influence of Chavín beliefs and artwork persisted into later Andean culture.

Precursor to the Inka: The Moche and the Nasca

As Chavín power and influence faded, other cultural complexes began to emerge, both in the Andean valleys as well as along the coast. On the northern Peruvian coast, the Moche culture began to rise approximately 2,000 years ago and persisted until its demise at the end of the seventh century. Far to the south was another culture known as the Nasca, which appeared by 200 B.C.E. but collapsed in concert with the Moche.

The Moche

Situated on the Moche River, the Moche site represents the first archaic state society in the Andes (Stanish 2001). By 400 C.E. the Moche controlled much of the northern Peruvian coast; Moche pottery and architectural styles dominated at settlements to the north and south. What had been dispersed agricultural settlements prior to Moche domination had become larger population centers (such as Sipán, described below) controlled by local Moche or Moche-loyalist rulers.

The Moche culture used canal-based irrigation agriculture to grow a variety of crops; they hunted for meat and had domesticated llamas and guinea pigs. The construction and constant maintenance of their irrigation system required enormous labor, almost certainly controlled by the state. The same can be said of the construction of the enormous religious buildings at the Moche capital.

The Moche are known for their extraordinary skill in producing such crafts as metalwork in gold, silver, and alloys, but they are perhaps best known for their ceramics. Moche vessels depict scenes from daily life, ceremonial events, religion, and warfare. A great deal of what we know about Moche culture and religion is derived from the images on their ceramics, which are echoed in the murals on their temple walls. There are many elements in Moche culture that indicate a strong belief in symbolic duality (Bourget 2006). The dualist principles appear to represent opposites: sun and moon, man and woman, fresh and salt water, and even life and death. Dualism is found in later Andean religions, including those of the Inka; possibly such beliefs had their origins in the Moche culture.

The two large religious buildings at the Moche center, known as *huacas*, are platform structures. The larger, Huaca del Sol, was built near the river and today stands 40 meters high, though it was likely much taller during Moche times; it spans the length of nearly four football fields (340 meters) and is wider than three put side by side (160 meters). Huaca del Sol was built in increasingly higher sections, with the highest, in the center, mostly likely the location of the most important ceremonies. The bricks used to build the platforms bear maker's marks so that the various stages of construction could be organized according to Moche work group (and today traced by archaeologists). Contained inside the platforms were rooms, courts, and burials. A combination of environmental destruction and Spanish looting (shortly after colonization) has left Huaca del Sol in ruins. The other platform structure, Huaca del Luna, stands 500 meters away near the slopes of the inland mountain range. The rocky outcrops of the mountain range, visible behind the platform, are found on Moche pottery depicting scenes of ceremonies and sacrifice (Moseley 2001). This complex also featured courts on the platform summits, decorated with murals displaying Moche deities and ritual scenes. High-status burials were also found in this complex, but far fewer than those in Huaca del Sol. Huaca del Luna may have been used specifically for ritually based activities, perhaps reserved for burials of religious personnel, while Huaca del Sol may have been used for more secular or state ceremonies and events, serving as burial grounds for the royalty and elites. One area of Huaca del Luna yielded evidence of child burials, possibly sacrificed during times of torrential rains (caused by the El Niño phenomenon), perhaps to urge the deities to cease the onslaught from the skies (Bourget 2001). Spread between the two huacas were numerous buildings. Many were residential compounds housing extended families; others were dedicated to craft production but may have also been the homes of the craft makers (Moseley 2001). Unfortunately, like Huaca del Sol, much of this portion of the Moche capital is lost to environmental damage and Spanish destruction.

One of the clearest indicators of social stratification in the Moche culture is the differentiation in tomb construction and goods buried with the dead. The power and wealth of the Moche lords are demonstrated by the burials at Sipán, several hundred kilometers up the coast from the Moche Valley. At Sipán, a burial containing the "Old Lord" and a younger man approximately 40 years of age was discovered in the late 1980s. This younger man may have been a "warrior priest" like those depicted on Moche ceramics. Burial gifts in these tombs were fabulously rich, including items of gold and silver, ceramics, textiles, and various items of clothing adorning the noble burials. Next to the warrior priest tomb was the burial of a man whose feet had been cut off; the excavator determined this individual was meant to guard this lord's tomb, hobbled perhaps to keep him from abandoning his post. Other burials of both men and women surrounding the main tombs were most likely servants meant to attend the lords in the next life.

The notion of duality discussed above is clearly expressed in the Sipán burials. The burials accompanying the warrior priest consisted of two women, one at his feet and one at his head, and two men, one on each side of him; individuals of the same sex face in the opposite direction from each other. These four burials therefore represent the duality not only of gender, but of space and direction. Within the nobles' burials there was a visual duality in the placement of the grave goods. Gold objects (possibly representing the sun) were placed on the right side of the body, silver (possibly symbolic of the moon) on the left side. Duplicate objects in both gold and silver, including many ornaments, accompanied the lords, and many objects were made of equal parts of both metals (Bourget 2006).

Depictions on Moche vessels appear to show important ritual activities and, perhaps, mythic themes. It is difficult to understand all the symbolic elements represented, but the actions portrayed are a trove of information about Moche daily life and ritual activities. One theme involves the capture of enemy warriors who are then led to a huaca for sacrifice. A Moche warrior, grasping a rope tied around the naked and painted or tattooed captive's neck, leads him to the top of the huaca, where the victim's throat is cut. These scenes portray real events, as sacrificial victims have been excavated near the Huaca del Luna complex. Large ceremonial goblets found in the Sipán tombs and elsewhere may have been part of this sacrifice ceremony (Figure 10.4). In depictions on vessels and murals, an important personage holds the goblet and appears to capture blood from the slain victim; interestingly, study of these scenes indicates the person holding the goblet is female, identified as a "priestess of the moon" (Cordy-Collins 2001). Possibly, like the Aztecs, the Moche believed the human body, and perhaps specifically the blood, contained powerful qualities and was thus consumed by Moche elites during these ceremonies.

As in the Chavín culture, Moche mural and ceramic artworks depict a number of supernatural beings that combine human and animal elements. However, one of the difficulties in identifying Moche deities is that some of the anthropomorphic forms illustrated on ceramics may instead represent humans with supernatural or animal characteristics (Bourget 2006) or people wearing costumes during certain ceremonies. Three deities that appear regularly are Wrinkle Face and his companion Iguana, and the Decapitator God. Wrinkle Face and Iguana, anthropomorphic beings, have important roles in the burial of important personages (Donnan and McClelland 1979). Not only do they lower the casket into the ground, but they also assist in any sacrifice of other humans accompanying the dead. The Decapitator God is found in mural art and on ceramics. He is usually shown as a human/spider combination but sometimes has wings or other animal characteristics. He is recognized by what he holds in his hands: a human head in one and a knife in the other. He may be the god that oversees the ritual sacrifice of enemy warriors and thus was a very important deity.

By 700 C.E. the Moche culture had essentially collapsed. The destruction of this early Andean state appears to have been caused by environmental factors commencing

Figure 10.4. Artistic rendering of Moche sacrifice of warriors. A Moche lord prepares to drink from the goblet that holds the victim's blood. (*M .J. Hughes*)

in the late sixth century, including drought and torrential floods caused by El Niño weather patterns. These events damaged crop production, and flood damage eroded trade and travel routes. The Moche center itself suffered a flood that buried much of the settlement under silt and debris. Nearly a millennium later, Spanish conquistadors completed the almost total destruction of the Moche capital in their search for gold.

The Nasca

The core of the Nasca culture lies in the Ica and Nasca valleys at the southern extent of the upper Andes region, a very dry and difficult landscape. The Nasca (ca. 200 B.C.E.–700 C.E.), like their Moche counterparts, made beautifully decorated pottery and textiles. However, it is their geoglyphs for which they are most famous. These lines are carved into the desert landscape between the Nasca and Ingenio valleys. They depict geometric forms, animals, plants, and a few humanlike creatures, many of which are hundreds of hectares in size. The Nasca religion was focused less on anthropomorphic deities and more on a spirit world inhabited by creatures of the earth; it is these that are most commonly found in their art and geoglyphs.

In adapting to their dry environment, the Nasca had developed sophisticated drainage systems that fed water into their agricultural fields. Nasca homes were built on the valley slopes, leaving the flatter valley floors available for farming. In the mid-sixth century, a drought (the same one that affected the Moche) caused the Nasca culture to fade from prominence.

The Nasca capital, Cahuachi, rested on the banks of the Nasca River approximately 50 kilometers inland from the ocean. Unlike the Moche capital, Cahuachi featured many mounds and ceremonial structures. Builders made use of the naturally hilly landscape, piling up debris on an existing hill and then facing it with adobe bricks to create a small or medium-sized huaca. Cahuachi was largely uninhabited and functioned as a ceremonial center to which people made pilgrimages for rituals, feasts, and ceremonies (Silverman 2002). Huacas held graves, provided platforms for ceremonies, and contained large vessels for the storage of ceremonial items, including textiles. The largest huaca, known as the Great Temple, was at least 20 meters high and featured rooms, courtyards, and a large central plaza. Excavations revealed evidence of feasting at which hundreds of llamas and guinea pigs were sacrificed and then consumed. Cahuachi was probably chosen as the sacred center of the Nasca culture for two reasons: the natural hilly topography looked ready-made for the construction of numerous huacas, and the water table, so near the surface here, made it seem as if water sprang from the earth (Silverman and Proulx 2002).

Disparate evidence from the Nasca region has led archaeologists to believe that, unlike the centralized leadership system of the Moche, the Nasca operated more like a confederacy of allied groups. These groups, probably kin-related, lived in small settlements along the Nasca and Ingenio valleys, where they practiced agriculture, made crafts, and then gathered at Cahuachi at specified times. This does not mean, however, that the Nasca did not possess a warrior class. They were indeed capable of defending themselves, as images on their pottery attest.

Like Moche ceramics, Nasca vessels portray people in many different settings. Pots show male farmers in loincloths and caps, and war scenes in which face-painted warriors in tunics carry clubs, spears, and atlatls; at times they sport elaborate headdresses (Silverman and Proulx 2002). Unlike the Moche and the Aztecs (see Chapter 9), the Nasca apparently did not care about capturing enemy warriors alive for later sacrifice. Rather, the Nasca practiced the taking of trophy heads, demonstrated in their art and in archaeological remains.

Excavations at Nasca settlements have recovered human skulls with holes drilled in the cranium for inserting a cord, held in place by a toggle inside the skull, presumably for ease in carrying; thorns were used to pin the lips shut, and the skull was stuffed with cloth and plant matter (Proulx 2001). Ceramics depict the beheading of warriors and adult males carrying trophy heads. Interestingly, some Nasca burials contain headless skeletal remains, perhaps victims of the head-taking practice. In some of these burials, Nasca *head jars*, vessels that are roughly head-shaped and depict a human face, are possibly meant to "replace" the head of the deceased. The meaning of trophy heads is not clearly understood, although they sometimes appear painted on vessels with plants growing from their mouths. This leads some archaeologists to suggest that the Nasca believed the human head carried a great deal of ritual power and that trophy heads were an important part of ceremonies influencing fertility, rain, and successful crop yields (Proulx 2001). In other cases, trophy heads appear in ritual scenes that seem to be funereal, suggesting that some type of ancestral importance should be attributed to this practice, although heads taken on the battlefield seem to belong to those from more distant regions. However, head-taking may have been practiced off the battlefield as well, since skulls from women and children have also been recovered (Silverman and Proulx 2002). After their use, trophy heads were buried in caches: in one case 48 were found together (Silverman 2002). In addition to taking the head of a valiant enemy warrior, retrieving heads from departed kin members may have been part of Nasca ancestor veneration. In this complex Nasca belief system, trophy heads seem to have tied together the dual notions of ancestral veneration and the health and fertility of the earth and the living.

Nasca deities are depicted on ceramics, and though the symbolic meaning behind them is unknown, we can be certain that animals were important in the cosmology. One powerful supernatural being, called the Anthropomorphic Mythical Being by archaeologists, combines characteristics of humans and many animals. Other important beings include the Killer Whale, the Horrible Bird, and the Spotted Cat. Nasca burials have provided evidence that humans, perhaps shamans, may have dressed as representations of these beings (Silverman and Proulx 2002). In an examination of the ritual scenes depicted on vessels, especially those in which these supernatural beings appear, it is clear that one of the main concerns of the Nasca people was agricultural fertility. Water, a crucial resource in such a dry climate, was represented by the Killer Whale deity; the sky, provider of sun and water, was overseen by the Horrible Bird god (various types of raptors); and the earth from which healthy plants grew was represented by the Spotted Cat, or jaguar (Silverman and Proulx 2002). It is not surprising to find people who were dependent on rain-fed agriculture in a desert landscape worshipping deities who would ensure that the agricultural cycle remained secure and fertile.

The famous Nasca geoglyphs were carved into the desert pampas between the Nasca and Ingenio valleys. The pampas are covered with thin, pebbled topsoil overlying a white alluvial layer. By removing the topsoil, bright white lines emerged, visible from miles away. The simplest are straight lines, some 20 kilometers long, connecting two points; others, however, create giant images that make sense only when viewed from above. Some geoglyphs were created over older ones, possibly representing the intersection of two symbolic messages, or perhaps the older geoglyph was no longer relevant. Animal and anthropomorphic images, depicting such creatures as birds, a monkey (Figure 10.5), several Killer Whale images, and a figure known as Astronaut or Owl Man, are quite complex but are created without distortion or

Figure 10.5. Photos of Nasca spider and bird *(Jarnogz/Dreamstime.com).*

mistake, even though some are as much as 200 times the size of the animal itself (Silverman and Proulx 2002).

What the meaning and function of these drawings were is a subject of great debate. Several scholars have suggested that the lines were created by Nasca feet, worn into the alluvium by people on pilgrimage or in ritual performance (Silverman and Proulx 2002). The fact that some lines portray images of supernatural beings also found on Nasca pottery suggests that some or all of the images were meant to represent important elements in Nasca cosmology. Perhaps they demonstrated dedication to the gods and point, in some cosmological way, to important and sacred places (the sky, mountains, valleys) that provided the crucial water for Nasca crops. Recent research offers an explanation both cosmological and geological. Some of the geoglyphs coincide with subterranean aquifers and water channels that eventually led to Nasca settlements and their agricultural fields (Johnson et al. 2002). The geoglyphs in this scenario embed, iconically, images of their belief system onto the actual sources of life-giving water, perhaps ensuring its continued flow and the earth's fertility. Research will undoubtedly continue to develop explanations for these extraordinary images carved into the earth's face.

A Patchwork of Andean Kingdoms

While the Moche and Nasca built their cultures close to the coast, another culture was building its first state in the Andean highlands. On the shores of Lake Titicaca, the settlement called Tiwanaku emerged around 200 C.E. (Figure 10.6). The Tiwanaku culture developed widespread trade networks and farmed agricultural fields stretching around the city for many kilometers. The Tiwanaku ceremonial center consisted of a temple within a large enclosure ringed by carved stones. A doorway into the complex has a relief of an anthropomorphic god above the entrance, perhaps the Tiwanaku creator god known as Viracocha (Davies 1997). A rain-fed moat surrounded the enclosure. Archaeologists believe this was meant to recreate, symbolically, the Island of the Sun in Lake Titicaca, a place considered sacred by many Andean cultures. The Tiwanaku, like their Andean neighbors, practiced human sacrifice and had animal imagery, particularly raptors and jaguars, embedded in their cosmology. By 1000 C.E. the Tiwanaku economic system had collapsed.

Meanwhile, farther north but still in the Andean highlands, another center rose to prominence around 500 C.E., though it was more short-lived than Tiwanaku. The Wari were heavily involved in trade and eventually expanded their territorial holdings to cover a large region, including that which is later part of the Inka Empire. The Wari also celebrated a supreme deity who has iconographic similarities to Viracocha. By 800 C.E. Wari settlements were abandoned. Their demise may have been due to internal revolt or perhaps to growing tensions generated by increasingly aggressive neighbors.

As the Tiwanaku and Wari power structures subsided, many small kingdoms scattered across Andean valleys began competing for access to trade goods and arable land. In the north a large state known as the Chimú arose around 1000 C.E. in the region previously controlled by the Moche. The Chimú, with their capital at Chan Chan, became the dominant force on the north coast over the next four centuries. As the Chimú state expanded southward in the fifteenth century, it began to encounter some of the smaller kingdoms that had developed in the wake of the Tiwanaku and Wari collapse, including a people known as the Inka. In the 1460s the Chimú and Inka fought many battles, and eventually the Inka prevailed. The Chimú, by 1470, became part of the expanding Inka Empire.

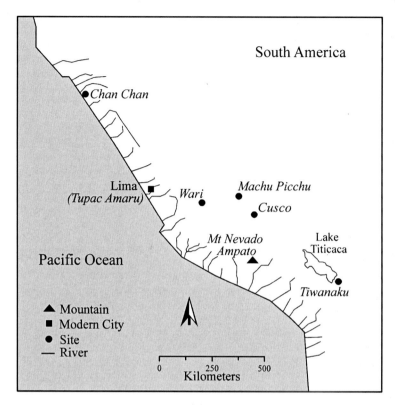

Figure 10.6. Map of Inka period sites and regions (*T. Edwards*)

The Inka Empire

The Inka were one of the many small kingdoms vying for power in the eleventh century. They were located in the region north of Lake Titicaca, in the valleys surrounding their later capital at Cusco. Inka origin myths assert that a creator called Viracocha, born from Lake Titicaca, created the Inka (Urton 1999). Viracocha drew the sun, stars, and moon from the Island of the Sun, making this island sacred to the Inka. The humans created by Viracocha fanned out across the landscape, and they called out others from the earth (from crevices, caves, and springs). These newly emerged peoples were the ethnic groups that later made up the Inka Empire (and thereby, cosmologically, they were "Inka"). These features in the landscape became sacred to the peoples inhabiting it and were often the site of rituals and ceremonies. The people brought forth from the region near Cusco were the greatest of the humans, later to become the ruling Inkas.

Inka chroniclers provide accounts of early rulers. At least seven rulers led the Inka people in the early centuries of the second millennium C.E. Several of these, such as a ruler named Qhapaq Yupanki, substantially increased the area controlled by the Inka, mainly through military means (D'Altroy 2002). However, our understanding of succession from one ruler to the next is confused for several reasons: accounts come mainly from later Spanish chroniclers relying on older oral traditions; and rulers named their sons for brothers, uncles, and fathers who had ruled previously. Which was a previous ruler and which an offspring sometimes became confused in the oral accounts recorded by the Spaniards.

Inkas kept their own records through the use of *quipus*, cords with a system of knots that acted as mnemonic devices. Each cord on the quipu held different styles of knots in different positions, and cords were dyed different colors; each of these characteristics contained information that could be "read" by an Inka. Quipus were used to record census information, keep track of amounts and types of materials stored, or reckon how many soldiers were needed and what equipment was required to outfit them (D'Altroy 2002). These devices also kept track of calendrical events, including when important rituals were to take place. Quipus also functioned as memory devices for oral traditions and myths, genealogical records, and property lists. While some quipus could be read by a number of people, others were individualized by the keeper, based on a code developed by the maker of that quipu. These latter are nearly impossible for modern scholars to crack, but even those meant to record public records are difficult to decipher. Symbolic interconnections between colors, knot styles, cord lengths, and Inka cultural knowledge are impediments to our understanding of how to read these cord documents.

The Rise of the Empire

In approximately 1400 C.E. an Inka ruler named Viracocha came to the throne. Viracocha apparently reconquered some regions that had rebelled under previous rulers and further expanded the Inka Empire as well (Davies 1997). It was Viracocha's son, Pachacutec, however, who set the Inka Empire on the road to supreme power in the Andean region. Early in Pachacutec's reign (approximately 1438), the Chanka culture to the north (not yet securely located archaeologically), which had plagued the Inkas during Viracocha's time, attacked the Inka heartland at Cusco. After several battles Pachacutec defeated the Chankas and rebuilt Cusco, not as a town, but as the seat of a great empire (Davies 1997). After the victory, Pachacutec set out to aggressively expand Inka holdings. Following Pachacutec came four more Inka rulers, each from Pachacutec's family. These rulers continued expansion until the last of them, Atahualpa, ruled an empire that stretched nearly the length of the Andes region. Atahualpa ascended the throne in 1532 after defeating his brother Huascar in something of a civil war. However, Atahualpa was not even finished celebrating his victory before he got word that a group of foreigners, riding large beasts, approached the boundaries of his lands. The Spanish had arrived and the demise of the Inka had begun.

In addition to expanding the empire, Pachacutec made several other changes to Inka rulership. Though perhaps regarded as divine in earlier periods, Inka rulers were certainly considered gods by Pachacutec's time. When a ruler took office he was anointed by Inti, the Inka god of the sun and their most powerful deity. However, new Inka rulers, known as *Sapa Inka* ("Unique Inka"), did not inherit the wealth of the previous king, due to a system known as *split inheritance*. In this system, whatever wealth a king had built up during his leadership remained in his possession even after his death. That is, the deceased king was mummified, and his wealth and property passed to his family and descendants (though not to the new ruler, even if he was the king's son), who managed his wealth and cared for him, including dining with him and treating him as if he were still alive (D'Altroy 2002). Meanwhile, the new ruler had to build up his own store of wealth to enhance his reputation and power and also provide for his family, descendants, and himself after his death. Newly crowned Inka rulers did this through two processes: by conquering more regions, expanding the empire, and acquiring wealth from new lands, and by enforcement of *mit'a*, a labor-based tribute system.

Inka subjects gave their *mit'a*, or tribute, according to their skills. Cloth and crafts were made by women and used by Inka elites as gifts to high-ranking visitors and as rewards to people within the empire. Men performed services such as mining, building roads and structures, or when necessary, soldiering. However, the Inkas were careful not to overburden their people; only a few men from a village or region were taken for service at any given time. While absent, other residents were required to keep up the fields and homes of those performing mit'a. Tasks that were dangerous or difficult, such as mining, required shorter terms of labor, so that no individual Inka gave more effort than any other. While serving their mit'a, laborers were housed, fed, and given whatever tools or goods were needed to perform their service (Davies 1997). It was a system that worked well for the Inka elites and helped build an extensive empire.

The Inka capital was at Cusco, divided into a lower and upper city, each with temples and important elite residences. Cusco rested at the heart of an empire composed of four districts to the north, south, east, and west of the city. Each of these regions was overseen by a governor who reported back to the king in Cusco. Split inheritance created a Cusco full of palaces, temples, plazas, and compounds built by each preceding emperor. Though these edifices were built by mit'a labor, only elites, religious personnel, and their servants were allowed to enter these areas of the city (Davies 1997).

Rulership was technically a monarchy in which power passed from father to son, but the Inka political machine was far more complicated than a simple dynastic monarchy. Each emperor had a *panaqa*, a group of aristocratic kin associated with his reign who were later responsible for the upkeep of his mummified remains (and thereby inherited his wealth). Below these were various groups: the "Inkas by privilege," consisting of various ethnic groups in Cusco; the *yanakuna* or lower nobility; the lower classes, including a group of specialized servants trained to serve the empire in many capacities; the religious personnel; and the commoners (D'Altroy 2002). Though the Inka emperor headed up the political hierarchy, he had to negotiate with the panaqa who sometimes resisted the Sapa Inka's decisions. Added to this mix was the advice and information gleaned from the four district governors, who also impacted the Inka ruler's decision-making power. Members of the panaqa and privileged elites vied for power in the emperor's court, formed alliances and pacts against others, and plotted for ever greater political office and wealth. Two consistent problems plagued the Inka Empire: constant rebellion and the rule of succession. Because the empire had expanded so rapidly, not all of the conquered peoples were successfully incorporated into Inka ideology; when the Inka army expanded the empire northward, groups in the southern part would stage a rebellion, and vice versa. The king and his army spent nearly as much time quelling revolts as expanding the empire. Perhaps even more problematic for the Inka infrastructure was the process of royal succession. Though rule passed from father to son, this inheritance did not always correspond to the strict biological relationship. Rather than to the eldest son, rule passed to the male relative deemed by the kin-based aristocrats to be the best choice to become Sapa Inka. Therefore, each family in the panaqa schemed to have its own choice in line for succession, creating a competitive and confusing process of succession at the death of the current emperor.

The Religion of the Inkas

Inka religion was complex and diverse, made up of an imperial ideology featuring Inti, overlying the indigenous and local beliefs of the many ethnic groups in the empire. Archaeologists have discerned many aspects of Inka state religion, but that of the local populations has been harder to uncover.

Like the Aztecs, the Inkas believed the world had been recreated several times and that they were living in a fifth age. In the previous four ages, Viracocha had created humans that were unacceptable. In the fifth, the age of the sun, he created the Inkas, who were the best of the previous creations (Urton 1999). In this myth, the importance of the creator god Viracocha and Inti the sun god is evident. A third important Inka deity was Illapa, the god of thunder, responsible for controlling the weather. Illapa was envisioned as a warrior, the wielding of his weapons causing thunder and lightning in the sky. In a region of the world where drought was always a concern, the god who controlled the weather was extremely important. The Inkas also recognized female deities, including Mama-Quilla ("Mother Moon") and Pachamama, a goddess of the earth (D'Altroy 2002). Mama-Quilla was Inti's wife; gold was thought to have originated from the sweat of the sun, and silver from the tears of the moon goddess. Pachamama was responsible for healthy crops and a successful harvest; she was especially important to farmers, who made regular offerings to her at stone altars in their fields. Many other lesser deities made up the Inka state pantheon, and temples to them were built in Cusco so that no deity was overlooked and balance and harmony could be maintained.

The Inka ceremonial calendar was keyed to the agricultural cycle, with major seasonal rituals set at times of planting and harvest. Not a month went by without some ritual celebration. Rituals in Cusco were held in open plazas so that the populace could attend. *Inti Raymi*, the "Warriors' Cultivation," occurred in June at the winter solstice (D'Altroy 2002). At sunrise the Inka ruler, elites, and religious personnel all proceeded to an open area of Cusco and began to sing praises to Inti; the singing went on until sunset. Also in attendance were statues of previous Inka rulers; these statues included bits of the ruler's hair and fingernails. The entire complement of divine Inka rulers, therefore, attended this important ritual. During the day, offerings of meat and other items were sacrificed, and llamas were loosed for the commoners to catch and offer to the god. Inti Raymi lasted for over a week, and at its conclusion the agricultural fields were plowed in order to begin the planting season.

Statues of Inka rulers, as well as their mummies, resided in temples in Cusco, constructed while the ruler was still alive. So far, archaeologists have identified several sacred precincts in Cusco where Inka deities and previous rulers could be worshipped. Other temple complexes in the city were dedicated to individual deities such as Viracocha, Inti, and Illapa the thunder god. Scattered throughout the larger Cusco environs were smaller shrines and sacred places that could be visited by the Andean commoners. Besides the royal residences, panaqa elites and Inkas of Privilege had grand residences in the city as well as "country estates" out in the landscape. The magnificent architecture at Machu Picchu, including residential compounds, magazines, fountains, a temple complex, and an open plaza, may have been one of these country villas.

Religious matters were overseen by priests who had considerable power in the Inka political system. Willaq Umu, the high priest of Inti, was responsible for anointing the new ruler as emperor; these priests may have also served as warriors in charge of the Inka army. Other priests assisted with sacrifices, led prayers, performed divinations, and offered oracular pronouncements. They were assisted by *mamakuna*, or virgin priestesses, who lived in compounds not unlike convents. At age 10 girls were chosen from families in the empire to become *aqllawasi*, or "chosen women." They then lived together and were instructed in Inka religion and important crafts. When they reached adulthood, some went on to become mamakuna and others married important Inka panaqa or other elites, given as a type of reward for loyalty and dedicated service (Silverblatt 1987). Mamakuna wove textiles and made *chicha*, a maize-based fermented drink consumed during ritual activities.

The Inka apparently believed very firmly in an afterlife, and archaeological evidence from a cemetery outside Lima, Peru, suggests that it was important for kin members to advance into the afterlife together. Happily for researchers, the dry climate allowed the extraordinary preservation of more than 2,500 individuals in *mummy bundles*, excavated under the Tupac Amaru shantytown on the outskirts of Lima (Cock 2002). Archaeologists discovered that multiple people, probably from the same family, were buried together in these bundles. Many bundles were topped by "false heads," cloths stuffed with cotton to mimic a human appearance. Individuals were bundled together with grave goods that would be useful in the next life, including utensils, food offerings, and more exotic items. The bundles were then completed by wrapping individuals together with plain cotton or finely woven and colorful wool. Archaeologists estimate this cemetery was used by every social class, from the most common Inkas to the elites of the region. The work to unwrap these bundles is underway in Peru, as are DNA studies to track kin relationships of those bundled together. Although archaeologists believe that less than 50 percent of the cemetery was actually excavated, continued study of these mummy bundles should reveal a great deal about Inka burial rituals, social class structures, and even kinship relationships.

Like their Andean predecessors, the Inkas also practiced human sacrifice. There were two main types of ceremonies that featured human sacrifice: the *Itu*, carried out when needed, and the *Qhapaq Ucha*, a regular ceremony celebrating the sun and, by extension, the Inka rulers (D'Altroy 2002). The Itu took place when terrible events had occurred, such as earthquakes or disease, or when the emperor was heading out to war. Prior to the ceremony itself, the population of Cusco was required to fast and refrain from sex; at the appointed time the central plaza was cleared (some residents, including women, were required to leave the city), and the sacred statues of the gods were brought to the plaza. Religious personnel then performed the sacrifices of llamas and children, in order to appease the gods.

The Qhapaq Ucha took place at the installation of a new ruler, as well as at a few other specified times. Prior to the ceremony, towns across the empire were required to send several "perfect" children, around age 10, for the purposes of sacrifice. The children, dressed in finery, paraded around the city of Cusco for viewing by residents, elites, and the statues of gods and rulers, brought out for the ceremony. Priests then sacrificed the children in honor of Viracocha, Inti, and possibly other Inka deities. Death was accomplished by cutting the throat, and in many cases the heart was then extracted and offered to the god (Davies 1997). The public human sacrifice rituals were far fewer and less frequent than those carried out by the Aztecs, but they were a regularized part of Inka religious practice.

In addition to ceremonies in the plaza, human sacrifice took place on the dramatic mountaintops surrounding the Inka Empire. Early in the twentieth century, looters discovered mummified human remains atop a mountain. The mummy was accompanied by many offerings, including pottery, some precious metal items, and other adornments that ended up on the antiquities market. This alerted archaeologists to the fact that other mummies probably remained undisturbed in the high Andes, and over the last decades many have been located. Perhaps the most famous of these is known as the Ice Maiden, found at the summit of Mount Nevado Ampato (Reinhard 2005). Discoveries on other mountaintops include children of both sexes, infants, other young women, and one young man (Ceruti 2004). Due to the extreme cold and aridity on these high mountains, these human sacrifices were remarkably preserved; often laboratory tests could ascertain what the victims had consumed prior to death, how they were killed, and even, to some extent, what they looked like. Offerings left with them were also preserved, including clothing, adornments, ceramics, figurines of cloth and metal, shells, and even feathers. Children destined for these mountaintop sacrifices were probably identified through the same processes as in the Qhapaq Ucha ceremony. Spanish chroniclers report that sacrificial victims had to be beautiful, unblemished, and virginal (Ceruti 2004). It is quite possible, therefore, that young women led up the mountains for sacrifice were drawn from the aqllawasi, the "chosen women" who were dedicated to the service of Inka religion. Death came to these victims in various forms, including strangulation, suffocation, exposure, burial alive, and a blow to the head. The latter may have been the least common, as the human offerings were to be "unblemished" when given to the gods. Mountaintop sacrifices were made to the main

Inka deities Viracocha, Inti, and Illapa, but also to local mountain gods who also had important roles in controlling the weather.

The study of the 14-year-old Ice Maiden, discovered in 1996, revealed a great deal about her last hours. Archaeological remains at various points on Mount Nevado Ampato (her mummy was found at a height of 6,310 meters or nearly 21,000 feet) indicate that a procession stopped at several "camps" on their trek up the mountain. It is estimated that about 15 people, including the girl, priests, and assistants (perhaps aqllawasi), and a few other important pilgrims, ascended Mount Ampato in a several-day journey. At the summit, on a stone platform built for the purpose, offerings were made and the virgin was given a final meal, which may have included chicha, possibly to inebriate her prior to her death (Reinhard 2005). Her skull showed that she may have been killed by a blow to the head. She was then folded into a fetal position and wrapped in textiles. The girl was dressed in brightly colored clothing made of alpaca wool and then covered with a shawl held closed by a silver pin; she may have also worn a headdress (Figure 10.7). Statues of gold and silver and other items including shell and ceramics accompanied her into the afterlife. Did the Ice Maiden and others go willingly up to the mountaintops? Some archaeologists suggest that the Inkas considered it a great honor to give their children to the deities and that those old enough, such as the Ice Maiden, may be been eager to join the realm of the gods in her next life.

Figure 10.7. Artistic rendering of the Ice Maiden (far right) at the top of Mount Nevado Ampato. After she consumes the chicha she will be sacrificed. (*M. J. Hughes*)

Conclusion

There is a clear relationship between power and religion in ancient Andean civilizations, but the role of the environment is not a minor element in their belief systems. The topography and climate of the ancient Andes are dramatic. Breathtaking peaks rise above valleys and deserts, extreme cold contrasts with arid heat, and crops grown in narrow valleys barely suitable for agriculture are in constant need of adequate water. The combination of a growing elite class and the need to appeal to deities of the mountains, sky, and earth resulted in cultures that deified their rulers and people who obeyed their leaders in hopes of plentiful crops and adequate rains. An important element thrown into this mix is the veneration of ancestors, perhaps for their ability to enter the supernatural realm and influence the deities to treat their living descendants well. Among the Chavín and Moche, and especially the Inka, the most important ancestors were those from the nobility; Moche warrior priests and elites went to burial equipped to live well in the next life, accompanied by servants sacrificed to serve their masters. The Inka rulers were treated as gods after death, revered as vital connections to the deities who controlled the elements that would ensure a healthy and fertile kingdom. Respect for and obedience to Inka elites, especially the Sapa Inka, made for a ready workforce among the common population, and convinced parents that giving up their offspring to sacrifice was a sacred and even joyous duty. Among these ancient Andean cultures, religion, environment, and power were as intricately interwoven as the beautiful textiles for which the region is so famous.

USEFUL SOURCES

Gordon McEwan, *The Incas, New Perspectives*. 2006.
Michael Malpass, *Daily Life in the Inca Empire*, 1996.
Helaine Silverman, *Andean Archaeology*, 2004.

PART IV

RELIGIONS IN EUROPE

11

UPPER PALEOLITHIC AND NEOLITHIC EUROPE

FROM CAVE TO VILLAGE

As Neanderthals disappeared across Europe, and *Homo sapiens* began to inhabit the continent, new material culture began to emerge. The Upper Paleolithic (35,000–10,000 B.C.E.), the last phase of the Old Stone Age, saw the development of a vast range of tool technology, the exploitation of a wider range of resources, and, among many other innovations, the emergence of what can be called "art." This art occurs in many forms, including figurines, sculpture in relief, and paintings on cave walls.

The European Upper Paleolithic is divided into periods based on stone tool technology and tool kits. The Mousterian period (ca. 55,000–33,000 B.C.E.) sees the last remnants of Neanderthal material culture; the Aurignacian (ca. 35,000–20,000 B.C.E.) heralds the appearance of new material culture associated with archaic *Homo sapiens*. Overlapping the Aurignacian, the Gravettian period (ca. 25,000–20,000 B.C.E.) sees the earliest cave art and the creation of female figurines, both in the round and carved into cave walls. These two periods are followed by the Solutrean (ca. 20,000–18,000 B.C.E.), when more sophisticated stone tool technology develops, and cave art begins to appear regularly. The final Upper Paleolithic period is known as the Magdalenian (ca. 18,000–8,000 B.C.E.), when some of the finest examples of cave art were created.

Upper Paleolithic Europeans were hunter-gatherers, moving across the landscape to acquire their food. Hunters concentrated on reindeer, but other large mammals—such as red deer, bison, ibex, and wild ox—were also part of their diet. In addition to art on cave walls and the creation of human figurines, Upper Paleolithic humans made other objects of great beauty. These include atlatls (spear throwers) decorated with animal carvings, delicate and intricate fishhooks of bone and antler, and weapons carved with animals or other designs. While Upper Paleolithic hunting-and-gathering groups may have taken shelter inside caves during the worst of the winter months, archaeological research has shown that for substantial portions of the year small groups lived outside for weeks or months at a time in impermanent shelters. It is also possible that several groups may have aggregated once or at various times during the year, perhaps at cave sites. Such gatherings may have allowed for the transmission of information, the opportunity to visit with kin members, perhaps even to exchange goods. If such gatherings did occur at cave sites, it may have been during these times that artwork was accomplished for the purposes of religion, information recording or transmission, or for other reasons important to the artists. The beauty of the art and the quantity of figurines have generated much discussion on the meaning of the earliest human art in Europe.

The period following the Upper Paleolithic is known as the Neolithic (beginning ca. 8000 B.C.E. and lasting several thousand years). During this period the occupants of Europe developed agriculture, which resulted in more permanent settlement. Ceramics for storage and cooking were invented and animals were domesticated. Neolithic central, southern, and eastern Europeans continued to produce female figurines in even greater numbers, but male figurines also became part of the standard material culture. Some sites, such as Lepenski Vir on the banks of the Danube River, offer evidence of a rich ritual life.

Upper Paleolithic Cave Art

As noted above, much of the cave art was created in the period known as the Magdalenian, with most examples clustering between 18,000 and 12,000 B.C.E. Several hundred caves spread primarily across France and Spain offer painted images of Ice Age animals, anthropomorphs and therianthropes, geometric designs such as dots, lines, crosshatchings, and human hands in reverse relief. Some caves offer but a few examples of art, while others—such as Lascaux, Chavet, and Les Trois Frères in France, and Alta Mira in Spain (Figure 11.1)—provide entire galleries for study. In many cases animals were repainted several times, perhaps as a form of renewal, and in other cases entirely new scenes were painted over previous images. The paintings were in deep recesses of the caves, often difficult to reach and far from any natural light. They were not created for the casual viewer who might wander into a handy cave.

When locales such as Lascaux Cave were first discovered and studied in the nineteenth century, archaeologists believed the images represented aspects of the hunting way of life. Since so many caves sported paintings of animals (Figure 11.2), it was their assumption that these images must have related to the important activity of hunting, depicting the hunting triumphs of Upper Paleolithic men. In essence, it was believed these early *Homo sapiens* created art simply because they could, and they depicted what they knew—hunting. Archaeologists called this "hunter's art." Then in the early twentieth century, the *hunting magic* interpretation emerged; this theory employs Sir James Frazer's ideas on magic, suggesting that the drawings on the walls were made by men preparing for the hunt. Hunters would depict the animal(s) they wished to kill, and thereby, in a form of sympathetic magic, ensure a successful hunt. This interpretation explained why some animals appeared to have arrows or spears sailing toward them or embedded in their bodies, representing the sympathetic "killing" of the animal (Dickson 1990).

Further research turned up flaws in these interpretations. For instance, in a comparison of faunal material retrieved from Upper Paleolithic sites, it turned out that many of the animals depicted, such as cave lions, were rarely if ever eaten by Upper Paleolithic *Homo sapiens*. Besides, why were anthropomorphs and therianthropes depicted (see Figure 4.2)? And what did lines, dots, and other non-hunting-related imagery mean? Another significant problem was that only about a fifth of the animals were actually "killed" in the art. In the end, explanations like hunting magic and hunter's art were too simplistic, not to mention mono-gendered, to suffice as interpretations (Hays-Gilpin 2003).

In the 1960s, using structuralist methodology, André Leroi-Gourhan suggested that the paintings were not accomplished piecemeal by individual artists for their own purposes, but rather were composed as ensembles representing Upper Paleolithic

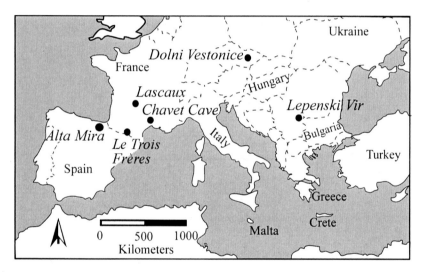

Figure 11.1. Map of sites and regions discussed in this chapter. (*S. R. Steadman*)

Figure 11.2. Artistic rendering of cave art from the "Hall of the Bulls," Lascaux Cave. (*R. Jennison*)

cosmology (1965). In an intensive study of the positioning of animals and designs on cave walls, Leroi-Gourhan advocated that certain animals and geometric designs occurred in pairs or in intentional association with one another. These systematic co-occurrences had meaning to Upper Paleolithic humans, representing important myths and principles significant in their cosmology. Image placement was a "syntax" that could be read by Upper Paleolithic viewers. Leroi-Gourhan suggested that a central concept illustrated was the male-female principle. He identified certain animals as male and others as female, and their juxtapositions conveyed important information to Upper Paleolithic viewers. However, Leroi-Gourhan's predictions about which animals and symbols should occur together have not held up in further examination of more recently discovered caves, and his complicated theory has become far less prominent in recent decades.

A few years later, Alexander Marshack came forth with alternative interpretations (1972). He suggested that the images constituted a sophisticated calendar of seasons, animal movements, and human events, all portrayed as a series of stories painted on the caves. Marshack believed Upper Paleolithic peoples were as concerned with the passage of time as modern humans. A common understanding of the symbols, notations, and images on the walls would have allowed any visitor to figure out seasonal changes in the region, migration patterns of herds, and even the movement of peoples. A simple example of this theory is the Les Trois Frères bison with zigzag markings on its body and arrows (spears) embedded in it. Marshack suggested the zigzag represents the summer moult and the spears indicate the animal can be hunted; other symbols and notations on or near the bison expressed to the Upper Paleolithic reader what season, perhaps even what month, the moulting bison was to be found in the region for hunting purposes (1995). Anthropomorphic and therianthropic images refer to ritual events at particular times of the year; in this interpretation the paintings represent both a history of what had gone before and a calendar of what was to come.

A recent theory, discussed in Chapters 3–4, was offered by David Lewis-Williams (2002) and suggests that the cave art in Europe, like that in Africa and elsewhere, depicts shamanistic activities and images seen during altered states of consciousness. In many cultures it is believed that the shaman departs this world for the other, either through water or by going underground. Lewis-Williams suggested the Upper Paleolithic people believed the walls of caves separated this world from the spiritual plane to which their shamans must travel. Anthropomorphs and therianthropes who appear to be humans adorned with animal accoutrements depict actual shamans engaged in their important activities. The various geometric forms represent the entoptic phenomena, the shapes the shaman saw as he or she entered the trance (Lewis-Williams 2002). Animals may have represented the shaman's spirit, or that of the spirit helper. In some cases the images on the cave walls may depict the mission of the shaman (to ensure a good hunt? to increase the fertility of the herd?). Lewis-Williams suggested that particular paintings, especially those rendered so that the animals appear to be part of the cave wall or even extending from it, may have played a role in a shaman's vision quest or initiation process into the shamanistic echelon (2002). A vision quest carried out in the deep and dark recesses of a cave, in which the shaman sees his own spirit or that of his helper emerging from the cave wall, was then painted on that wall as a record of the vision. While Lewis-Williams believes his theories describe much of the extraordinary art in these caves, he acknowledges that there are many images we will never be able to interpret.

These are only a few of the many interpretations that attempt to explain these amazing works. What is certain is that the act of painting and the paintings themselves were of great importance to Upper Paleolithic humans. The art must have figured prominently in their cosmology, but as beautiful as it is, the art offers us only fragments of the entire "picture" of their religion.

Female Figurines in the Upper Paleolithic

Another major category of Upper Paleolithic art is the collection of female figurines from sites in France, Italy, the Czech Republic, and Austria, and from as far east as the Ukraine and Russia. The earliest examples began to appear ca. 30,000 B.C.E., with the majority occurring between 25,000 and 20,000 B.C.E. These objects are examples of portable art (items that can be carried); figurines were carved of bone, ivory, coal, and stone and are also found as partial reliefs carved in cave walls. Figurines have been found inside caves as well as at open-air sites, often inside or near hearths. Some appear to have been intentionally buried. The figurines are consistent only in their female gender (Nelson 2001); beyond this commonality, they vary in size, attributes, and possibly in meaning. Many figurines show no clear facial characteristics, while others (Figure 11.3) have finely carved faces. Quite a few show no feet but rather come to a point, allowing them to be propped upright in sand or in a holder made for such a purpose. Others have clearly rendered legs and feet, sometimes in a flexed position, and some have almost no human anatomical features except bulbous protrusions, such as the "rod with breasts" from the site of Dolni Vestonice (Figure 11.4). Though nearly universally interpreted as female breasts, this and other similar forms could also represent male genitalia or some non-human form altogether. Some figurines have designs that may represent items of apparel or jewelry (e.g., Figure 11.5). Many figurines had been painted or sprinkled with ocher. While others have large breasts and/or buttocks, wide hips, and appear pregnant, many of those found are, according to modern standards, "normal" or even slender (Nelson 2001). There is no typical figurine that can be used as representative of the entire class of Upper Paleolithic examples.

This, however, did not stop early archaeologists from offering a monolithic interpretation. In the mid-nineteenth century, the name "Venus" was attached to these figurines, thereby associating them with love, sex, and Western-style eroticism of the female body. This in part derived from the impression that all the figurines were female, well-endowed by Western standards, and nude. It was suggested that these figurines were made by Upper Paleolithic European men, for men's purposes (Nelson 2001). The main speculation was over the reason for their creation—whether they were simply

Figure 11.3. Head of ivory figurine showing facial features, Brassempouy, France. (*R. Jennison*)

Upper Paleolithic "pin-up girls" related to sex and eroticism, or representative of fertility and the continuation of the male kin line. In this latter instance, the figurines represented the idea of Upper Paleolithic women as "vessels" to carry on the human species and provide progeny for their male counterparts. Other explanations moved closer to a more female-centered view, suggesting the figurines celebrated the institution of motherhood (Beck 2000).

As time moved on and the figurines were studied with more statistical and stylistic precision, the diversity of the shapes and renderings were noted. Some challenged the "femaleness" of many figurines, suggesting that perhaps only 60 percent could be confirmed as female (Beck 2000). Studies in the 1970s and 1980s sought to break away from androcentric interpretations and delve instead into the roles these figurines might have played in more gender-neutral or female-centered Upper Paleolithic life.

In the early 1970s, Marshack suggested that the figurines were part of the Upper Paleolithic European women's world and functioned as prompts for stories, as temporary ritual objects, or as aids to teach young women about their coming maturity and aspects of adult womanhood (Marshack 1972); the figurines were time-keepers of important women's issues and marked important milestones. He suggested that some of the figurines were made more quickly, for usage only one or a few times, while others showed long-term use (polishing from much handling, for instance). Those made for more limited use perhaps functioned as a ritual item celebrating singular events, such as a girl's first menstruation or some aspect of a first pregnancy. Figurines that

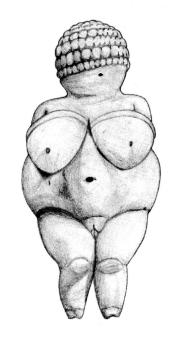

Figure 11.4. Sketch of "rod and breast" figurine from Dolni Vestonice (*S. R. Steadman*)

Figure 11.5. Limestone figurine from Willendorf, Austria. *(R. Jennison)*

were more carefully rendered and showed extensive use may have functioned more in a teaching context, showing prepubescent girls what was to come. Further, Marshack suggested that lines incised on the stomach, breast, or legs of a number of figurines served to mark the passage of time in increments. The incisions may have corresponded to the monthly occurrence of menstruation, months between birth and next pregnancy, or any other aspect of time that may have been important to Upper Paleolithic women (Marshack 1972). If not time itself, the marks may have represented rituals associated with the women's process. Further, different types of markings may have had different meaning—some related to a young woman's life (pregnancy, onset of the menses, etc.), others heralding the cessation of menstruation and the onset of the next stage of a mature woman's life.

Marshack suggested the figurines were important actors in "what we inadequately call a 'ritual,' 'ceremonial,' 'religious,' 'magic,' or 'superstitious' act" (Marshack 1972:312). Although many of Marshack's notions about the figurines were based on speculation rather than hard evidence, his observations derived from a much more thorough study than many previous theories. His book was also one of the first to place the function of the figurines squarely in the realm of the Upper Paleolithic woman's world.

Following Marshack's work in the 1970s came more studies negating the earlier "made by men, for men" theories. In the 1980s, a number of books and articles appeared identifying the figurines as representations of a "mother goddess" religion (Eisler 1988; Gimbutas 1989). The role of the mother goddess was thought to range from a focus on female fertility and pregnancy (from the female rather than the male perspective) to the fertility of the earth as giver of plant and animal life to Upper Paleolithic hunter-gatherers.

Because certain figurines appear to be pregnant, a belief in a goddess of fertility and childbirth became a leading theory among some scholars. Though we cannot determine the Upper Paleolithic infant-mortality rate or the numbers of woman who died in childbirth, we are safe in assuming that death rates would have been fairly high. Women turning to a supernatural power to see them through pregnancy and birth is not very difficult to imagine. If Upper Paleolithic women were primarily responsible for gathering plant foods, it is possible that they equated pregnancy and birth to the growing season with its fruition of edible products.

In this way these figurines could indeed represent female fertility (both human and earthen) and could be described as symbolic personifications of a "mother goddess" or, perhaps more accurately, the spirit or essence of fertility and womanhood. A belief in a magical or spiritual power that could bring an infant and its mother through the potentially dangerous birth process could have been a source of much comfort to young women in the late stages of their first pregnancy. If that same principle helped women acquire important plant resources, then this would indeed have provided a solid complement to whatever help, if any, the cave paintings provided to Upper Paleolithic hunters.

This interpretation does have some drawbacks, however. Not all figurines are "pregnant" for instance, and others, such as the "rod and breast," would hardly seem to represent any aspect of childbirth or related concepts. Likewise, the questionable femaleness of perhaps 40 percent of the figurines led many to reexamine the mother goddess concept. Some began to question whether identifying the figurines as goddesses was just as rash as earlier claims that they were "Venuses" or erotic "pin-up girls" for Upper Paleolithic men.

Several studies suggested that the figurines had no religious or spiritual meaning at all but were simply illustrative of various phases of women's lives, representing stages from pre-reproduction to post-reproduction (Rice 1981). This interpretation explains why only some of the figurines appear pregnant, some are slender like a pre-pubescent girl, and others would seem to portray women in more mature stages of their lives. Beyond representing generalized stages of life, others have suggested that the figurines are renderings of specific individual women, either self-portraits or images made by others.

A recent study suggests the figurines depicted female shamans, particularly in their role as midwives; the marks on the figurines could have represented specialized clothing worn by the shaman (Tedlock 2005:33). This interpretation offers some interesting areas for speculation. For instance, perhaps the marks were not clothing, but a tally of successful births. Perhaps each midwife-shaman carried her own figurine (those termed "well-handled" by Marshack) as well as a "temporary" pregnant figurine for each client; elements of sympathetic magic might have aided (both magically and psychologically) in a successful birth process. Non-pregnant figurines might have represented clients suffering other ills needing the shaman's help. Envisioning these figurines as representative of female shamans and their work takes their interpretation light-years away from the "pin-up girls" theory of earlier decades.

Neolithic Europe

A proliferation of figurines in the Neolithic has been used to support the existence of a well-developed mother goddess religion that fully emerged only in the Upper Paleolithic. By the Neolithic era, people were living in more permanent settlements and were engaged in agricultural pursuits. Village houses at sites in northern Greece and the Balkan region suggest residents were spending a significant portion of the year living in one place in order to tend their crops. A greater reliance on cultivated plants and a possible focus on fertility and the agricultural cycle, combined with far greater numbers of female figurines, coalesce to convince some scholars that a mother-goddess-based religion existed in Neolithic Europe.

Marija Gimbutas was one of the most vocal proponents of the claim that a Neolithic mother goddess religion existed in "Old Europe" (the region from the islands of Malta to Crete, from Greece and Italy to the Ukraine, and Hungary to the Balkans). Neolithic figurines from these regions are quite varied in size, style, form, and design. Some are seated, or "enthroned," others are in an upright position; some hold infants, others show arms holding their breasts, stomachs, or abdomens. Figurines occasionally appear pregnant, and many have very stylized faces, while others have no face at all.

The sheer diversity of Neolithic-period figurines has led to a wide-ranging discussion as to their meaning and function. In a comprehensive study of the designs carved on many figurines, Gimbutas classed them into three groups: those representing a sky goddess, those representing a vegetation goddess, and the rest centered on water. All of these recognized, in some way, the earth's fertility, the agricultural cycle and animal life, and the essential role women played in maintaining life in the Neolithic. Gimbutas suggested that the mother goddess represents the life, death, and rebirth of the earth (i.e., seasonal changes), as well as the fertility cycle of human women in their role as propagators of the human species (Gimbutas 1989, 2007).

Some scholars have examined why the mother goddess interpretation became so popular so quickly, noting that studies advocating an Old European female-centered society and belief system emerged at the same time as a more feminist-based approach to studying the present and the past (Meskell 1995). This shift also coincided with the wave of New Age religions that burgeoned in Europe and North America; the existence of an ancient mother goddess religion fit in nicely with many tenets of New Age beliefs. Thus the "mother goddess" religion of Old Europe was accepted by many, not based on archaeological data but on present-day beliefs about how the past might, or should, have been.

Recent studies offer interpretations based more on archaeological context than on the appearance of or decoration on the figurines. For instance, figurines discovered in or near graves may have represented the death or even afterlife of particular individuals buried there. Perhaps the figurines served a purpose in rituals devoted to ancestor veneration (of both males and females, since figurines of both sexes are found in the Neolithic). These figurines may have served not only as protection of family holdings against usurpers, but also as important foci of devotional activities. A study of figurines found in later Bulgarian sites (dating from the fifth to early fourth millennium B.C.E.) suggests the figurines depicted actual individuals (Bailey 1994). Many figurines were decorated with painted, incised, and pierced designs that may have indicated the social position of the individuals, including their socioeconomic rank and even societal role (e.g., religious personage, leader, farmer, etc.) (Bailey 1994).

Another study notes that many Neolithic figurines were found near ovens and hearths, essentially the "heart" of the house (Hodder 1990). There may be, therefore, a link between the figurines and the hearth, or the activities that took place near the hearth, including food processing and cooking, and textile production. The figurines, then, could represent the woman's role in the household, carrying out the activities that enabled residents to live relatively comfortable lives. This does not necessarily mean that Neolithic Europe was a matrifocal society or matriarchal in any form. Rather, the notion here is that the house and household may have been representative of womanhood or women's work, and the figurines symbolically illustrated, even celebrated, this ideology (Hodder 1990). In this explanation the figurines do not symbolize a "mother goddess" cult, but rather the space and work associated with the female half of the society. At a site called Opovo, in former Yugoslavia, female figurines appear to have been deliberately broken and placed in refuse pits; the houses in which these figurines presumably originally rested had been deliberately burned (Tringham and Conkey 1998). This leads to some speculation that the figurines represented not only womanhood and women's work, but *specific* women. Perhaps when the household cycle was completed, when the "woman of the house" died, her figurines and her house were destroyed. When taken as a whole, the evidence for a link between home, work, woman, and figurines is quite strong, though the exact symbolic meaning of that link still eludes us. If this idea is indeed correct, it is quite possible that other objects represented men's work and spaces, though these might well have been located outside the households and were perhaps made of organic materials that do not remain in the record for our review.

Lepenski Vir

A site worth exploring in some detail is that of Lepenski Vir, in eastern Serbia. Occupation at this site began in the mid-sixth millennium B.C.E. and lasted for roughly 1,000 years. The small village rests on the shores of the Danube River, and some two dozen trapezoidal houses, all with doorways, face the river (Figure 11.6). Each house had a plastered floor and an interior hearth; in some houses, small stone slabs were set into the ground in a V-shape, with the point toward the hearth (Srejovic 1972). Many

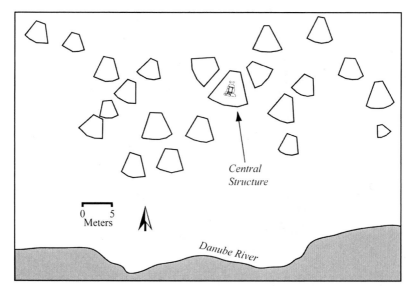

Figure 11.6. Sketch plan of Lepenski Vir village. (*S. R. Steadman*)

houses also had what the excavator described as "altars." In some cases altars resembled animals, such as the head of a deer or the shape of a fish; in others they were stones with designs carved on them (Srejovic 1972). Under the house floors were adult burials, and in almost all cases stag horns were placed in the graves. In the center of the village was a large, non-domestic building dubbed the Central Structure, which contained a hearth, altars, and unusual statues (described more fully below).

The residents at Lepenski Vir mainly hunted deer, and although they gathered the majority of their plant foods, they may have been engaged in some basic cultivation activities. Not surprisingly, they made extensive use of the river resources; fish made up a considerable portion of their diet. Along with antlers, fish bones were also found in graves, and both apparently served as offerings at household hearths. Residents made use of a range of bone and stone tools and weapons, some bearing the same types of carvings as the stone altars.

The stone sculptures are some of the most striking finds at Lepenski Vir. Boulders of varying size were sculpted into anthropomorphic figures, some looking distinctly fish-like while others appear somewhat more like humans. Some represent human heads rather than whole bodies. The statues appear to depict both males and females, and in a few specific instances the female genitalia seem to be accentuated (Figure 11.7). In some cases the sculptures do not resemble humans, animals, or fish, but rather are carved with the symbols that also appear on the stone altars. These statues are found in the back areas of many of the houses, but the finest examples are in the Central Structure, standing behind the hearth and facing the river.

Interpreting the rich iconography and symbolic representations at Lepenski Vir is indeed challenging. Clearly, residents had an active belief system that reflected many

Figure 11.7. Lepenski Vir statues that resemble fish, the one on the left displays female genitalia. (*R. Jennison*)

aspects of their life. Perhaps the simplest correlation can be made between the antlers in the burials, the offerings of antlers and fish bones, and the subsistence economy of the Lepenski Vir inhabitants. Though they surely relied on plant foods as well, the protein portion of their diet consisted mainly of deer and fish. These animals may have held important places in the Lepenski Vir cosmology.

Making offerings may have been meant to ensure the continued health and abundance of these animals and perhaps the continued success in acquiring them in sufficient quantities. If this is the case, the rituals at Lepenski Vir would be in complete accordance with the idea that religion is reflective of the culture in which it is integrated.

There are many elements at Lepenski Vir that defy interpretation. The V-shaped stone designs surrounding some hearths may well have had deep symbolic meaning, or they may have simply been decorative or even functional (e.g., trivets for hot pots?). The excavator suggests that the presence of carved stones on the eastern side of the the house hearths, and some of the designs on them, represent the sun and life, while the western side of the hearth, under which the dead were regularly buried, represents death (Srejovic 1972). The stone altars and statues that bear ornamental carvings certainly carried meaning for the inhabitants; it is tempting to associate them with clan symbols or representations of supernatural beings, but at present they cannot be at all securely explained.

Many questions remain. Should the burials, the altars, and the statues all be combined together to attempt a "package" interpretation, or are these separate and unrelated aspects of the Lepenski Vir belief system? The statues, many with a distinctly "fishy" look, recall the fish bones and the importance of this food resource. If the inhabitants did believe in a river deity or spirit, one that protected this important resource, a human-fish cast to the statues might make sense. That some statues appear female and some male may suggest that several supernatural beings were responsible for ensuring the health and vitality of the Danube and its resources.

However, additional iconography at Lepenski Vir would seem to indicate that there are more layers of belief than just recognition of river spirits. On one of the statues, and on several other stones, the representation of a vulva is clearly displayed, suggesting the importance of female genitalia, or more abstractly, the birth process. This adds the dimension of rebirth to the belief system, perhaps more generally interpreted as fertility with regard to the river's resources, and more broadly to the products of the earth. That the house entrances all face the river could suggest that rebirth and the river were linked in the cosmology.

Finally, the burials under the floors must be added to the mix, bringing in the element of death. At least one archaeologist believes that much of the belief system at Lepenski Vir revolved around the concept of death, including how to control it (Hodder 1990). One way of controlling death, of course, is to consider it only the last stop before rebirth. The burials under the house floors suggest Lepenski Vir inhabitants may have revered their ancestors; the smaller stones carved like human heads may have represented ancestors rather than spirits or deities. Perhaps the altars were meant not only for acknowledging the supernatural world, but for honoring the ancestors. These are all, of course, highly speculative suggestions, which may or may not coincide with the actual original beliefs and practices of residents at Lepenski Vir.

Conclusion

The material in this chapter confirms that the residents of Paleolithic and Neolithic Europe enjoyed rich and complex belief systems. The numerous theories surveyed indicate that there is no scholarly consensus as to what these systems were and what elements of the natural and supernatural world were most crucial to those ancient believers. Upper Paleolithic cave paintings of animals may have simply represented the food resource so crucial to a hunting population, or far more complex images of shamanic journeys into a spiritual world; in either case we see the importance animals played in the world of these residents, a sure reflection of their environment and their daily concerns for subsistence. The female figurines, initially seeming so easy to interpret, offer perhaps an even greater challenge. Interpretations range from toys or teaching dolls to a full-blown mother goddess religion; common to most theories, however, is the recognition that on some level the notion of fertility or the importance of childbirth is expressed. It is perhaps not a far leap to believe that Upper Paleolithic inhabitants were concerned about the fertility not only of people and the survival of their offspring, but perhaps of the earth itself, again a reflection of the world in which they lived; if the earth did not produce adequate resources, starvation and death were sure to follow.

The prominence of female figurines in the Neolithic may suggest the exacerbation of a need for fertility, especially as Europeans began experimenting with plant cultivation. Perhaps the important role of women's work, as residents became more sedentary, might also have been represented. At settlements like Lepenski Vir, the complex belief system may never be fully understood, but individual elements are certainly representative of the environment in which the village's inhabitants were situated. Prehistoric European religions were intricate and deeply symbolic representations of the uncertain, even dangerous world in which residents survived, and thrived.

USEFUL SOURCES

Bailey, Douglass, *Prehistoric Figurines Corporeality and Representation in the Neolithic*, 2005.
Peter Bogucki and Pam Crabtree, *Ancient Europe 8,000 B.C.–A.D. 1000*, 2004.
Gregory Curtis, *The Cave Painters*, 2006.

12

MEGALITHS AND POWER IN ANCIENT WESTERN EUROPE

M egalithic monuments are found all over the world, but perhaps nowhere are they more famous than in northwest Europe and the British Isles. Stonehenge, in particular, is known worldwide, though interpretations of who built it and why vary widely.

This chapter profiles some of the major Neolithic monuments in France and England and reviews many theories that have been generated to explain them. As is so often the case, a singular explanation for such remarkable places and structures is usually inadequate. In addition to overt uses as astronomical devices and cemeteries, European megaliths may have also functioned as symbols of power for an emerging Neolithic elite class.

Pre-Megalithic Northwestern Europe

Though residents in southeastern Europe were farming by the sixth millennium B.C.E., the cultivation and domestication of plants did not take hold in the West until several millennia later. Stone tools and camp remains indicate England was sparsely occupied in the seventh-millennium Mesolithic period and it wasn't until about 4000 B.C.E. that the British Isles became more heavily inhabited. These fourth-millennium people lived somewhat more sedentary lives and practiced the art of farming. Significant debate centers on the origins of agriculture in these islands. Some suggest knowledge of farming was transmitted from the mainland (e.g., France) which had been practicing agriculture for some centuries. Others believe that a population migration from the mainland brought farming and new inhabitants at the beginning of the fourth millennium. Whatever the method, by the beginning of that millennium inhabitants of these islands practiced farming and had successfully domesticated animals such as the pig, sheep, goat, and cow (Malone 2001). In the earlier Neolithic (the early fourth millennium), inhabitants supplemented their diets with some gathering of wild plants and hunting. However, by the later Neolithic (early third millennium), inhabitants depended on farming and animal husbandry almost entirely.

Houses in the earlier Neolithic were generally rectangular and timber-built, sometimes resting on stone footings. Roofs were thatched, and clay, mud, and animal dung were used to plaster the walls to seal the interior. By the later Neolithic, many inhabitants were building more circular rather than rectangular houses and making greater use of stone both in house and furniture construction. In some cases these circular houses later became tombs, buried under an earthen barrow (Malone 2001).

The earliest non-stone communal monuments are known as *causewayed enclosures*. Sometimes atop hills, other times in valleys, these enclosures are defined by a ditch, sometimes as deep as 2 meters, with breaks to allow passage inside, i.e., the "causeway"; the enclosed area is often quite extensive, covering many acres. The ditch was cut into the underlying layer of chalky earth, and the excavated material was then piled along the outer edge of the ditch to create a mound. The vast majority of these causewayed enclosures, more than 70 so far, occur in southern England (they are also found in France). Beginning as early as ca. 3900 B.C.E., they took numerous generations, stretching across centuries, to complete. Some enclosures show evidence of an external timber palisade built just beyond the earthen mound. Several offer domestic remains, including a few architectural remnants, suggesting people may have lived inside the enclosures. Ditches have revealed a number of items, including animal bones, human bones, and pottery. The animal bones are not ragged fragments, but rather suggest they are the remnants of feasts. The human remains are varied, with occasional specialized burials: at the Hambledon Hill enclosure, human skulls were buried in the ditches; at the enclosure known as Windmill Hill, complete child burials were recovered (Malone 2001).

Interpretations of these enormous earthworks vary tremendously. Most believe that the labor invested in creating the causewayed enclosures represents a communal belief system; the presence of human bones suggests these sites may have been used for *excarnation* (defleshing) prior to formal burial. Corpses may have been laid in the ditches or placed on scaffolding; as defleshing occurred, some bones may have escaped collection, remaining as unintentional, or perhaps intentional, deposits in the ditches. But the child burials and skulls at Hambledon Hill and Windmill Hill suggest that these places may have required some special deposition of human remains as their due. The animal bones might represent feasting either at the time of death or at some other important event associated with death. The location of causewayed enclosures on hilltops may have been meant to demarcate territories, or perhaps to highlight the importance of those living within the enclosure, representing initial elements of ranking and social stratification. If the enclosures were meant as ritual sites, then the structures within them might not have been permanent settlements but rather temporary housing for the duration of the rituals. Alternatively, a small contingent of ritual personnel may have lived there to oversee corpse excarnation and prepare the enclosure for important rituals. It is important to note that early Neolithic southern England was heavily forested; these enclosures seem to have been built in clearings, which may have represented important symbolic spaces to Neolithic inhabitants, perhaps even doorways between the human world and another plane.

Whatever the function of these causewayed enclosures, they ceased to be built or heavily used after ca. 3000 B.C.E. This coincides with the building of megalithic sites, many of which also included versions of these early earthworks.

The Culture of Megaliths

Hundreds of megalithic sites dot the landscape of Britain, Ireland, and northwestern Europe. Scholarship suggests that all were ritual sites, but many may have also been used for socioeconomic and political purposes. Only a few of the best-known sites are covered here.

Menhirs

Perhaps the simplest type of megalith is the *menhir*, or the standing stone. Menhirs are erected upright and often tower above the average human. They can stand alone or as part of a patterned grouping. It is extremely difficult to date the erection of a menhir and even harder to divine its purpose. Of course, this has not stopped archaeologists from doing either. Menhirs are found in Scandinavia and the British Isles, but the largest and most remarkable concentrations of them are in the Carnac region of Brittany, on the French coast (Figures 12.1, 12.2). There are a variety of stone monuments here, including burial structures and the largest menhir in all of Europe. The Grand Menhir Brisé once stood as high as 20 meters, weighed 350 tons, and may have been painted (Scarre 1998). It has now fallen and broken into several pieces, but its size and girth are a testament to the importance these menhirs must have had for prehistoric Europeans.

Some of the most remarkable sites in Carnac are complexes of menhirs standing in rows that stretch for up to a mile. The largest of these are at Kermario and Le Menec; each of these collections once had over 1,000 standing stones. A smaller one, known as Kerlescan, had several hundred (Scarre 1998). Today many stones are missing or fallen, but the patterns can still be discerned. Numerous interpretations of these monuments have been offered over the centuries, from the mundane suggestion that they were simply boundary markers, to the idea that they represented important individuals or marked burials. Some asserted that it was only possible for the more technologically inclined Romans to have erected so many monumental stones. By the twentieth century, most believed the Celts, specifically Druid priests, were responsible for these menhirs. However, in more recent decades excavation has determined that the stones were erected long before the Celts or the Romans. The first of the stones most likely went up sometime in the fourth millennium B.C.E., with work continuing until the mid-third millennium or even a bit later. They date, therefore, to the Neolithic period of northwestern Europe, when so many of the other megaliths were also built.

As difficult as it might be to determine the date of the Carnac menhirs, interpreting them is an even greater challenge. It is here that landscape archaeology becomes quite useful, because it allows the archaeologist to look at the entire collection of stones

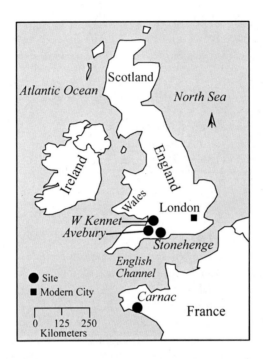

Figure 12.1. Map of sites and regions discussed in the chapter.
(*T. Edwards/S. R. Steadman*)

Figure 12.2. Photo of Carnac menhirs.
(*Claudio Giovanni Colombo/Dreamstime.com*)

in their setting. For instance, the nearly 1,100 stones in the Le Menec collection begin in 11 rows that stretch nearly a mile. The rows become narrower, and one row is deleted, as the stones march eastward. At either end of these rows are the remnants of stone circles that may have once been complete and perhaps demarcated special ritual areas. It is possible that these stone rows were meant to guide a processional of worshippers from one ritual site to the other (Scarre 1998).

This seems a good explanation for the smaller collection of stones at Kerlescan as well. Here 300 stones, smaller in the east, grow progressively larger as they march 355 meters westward. They are also quite close together in the east but fan out to the west. At the western end of the lines is a three-sided rectangular enclosure delineated by yet more standing stones, and the fourth side is a long mound that contained burials. It is possible, then, that the standing stones created processional ways to sacred places where religious activities took place, perhaps related to ancestor veneration or other rituals associated with kin or clan membership. The erection of thousands of stones seems laborious work just to create pathways to ritual areas, so it is quite probable that the stones themselves carried important symbolic meanings. Given that it took centuries to create the stone-filled landscape, it is likely that each generation took responsibility for adding to the procession. It is tempting to believe that each stone represented a deceased ancestor, especially as the Kerlescan long mound and its juxtaposition to the standing stones connects the notion of death with the menhirs. The actual meaning of each of the several thousand menhirs at Carnac, however, will remain a most fascinating puzzle for present and future archaeologists.

Henge Sites

A *henge* is an architectural structure, usually circular or ovoid, laid across a landscape (sizes range widely, but usually a henge has a diameter of at least 20 meters). Architectural components of a henge might include earthworks such as ditches or mounds, and a built boundary of stone, wood, or other material. Two of the best-known henge sites are in England, one at Avebury and the other, Stonehenge.

Avebury

Avebury, in southern England, is a henge site consisting of an outer mounded ring of earth with an interior ditch and with stone circles inside. The outer ditch and mound are a type of causewayed enclosure but on a much smaller scale than Windmill Hill (several kilometers northwest of Avebury) or Hambledon Hill. The Avebury region is a chalkland, meaning that deposits underlying the topsoil are chalky white and digging down to them creates a white scar in the earth. The building of the Avebury henge (and some subsidiary areas, mentioned below) began around 2500 B.C.E.; it probably took a number of generations to complete this enormous structure. Avebury is the largest known henge in England, with a diameter of 350 meters. The outermost stone circle consists of nearly 100 menhirs erected just inside the ditch, with two other smaller circles inside the larger one. It is not the stone component of Avebury that is so remarkable, but the earthen mound and ditch that delineate it. Originally 10 meters deep, the ditch, according to archaeologists, must have required the removal of about 4 million cubic feet of earth and chalk (Scarre 1998). The mound that borders it makes it look all the more deep. This was an enormous effort, given that in 2500 B.C.E. England was a pre-metal culture and tools consisted of wood, animal bone, antler, and stone. Not only did the builders have to dig the ditch and create the mound, they had to locate, transport, and erect the dozens of stone menhirs in the henge. Clearly, the building of Avebury was a group effort, and one deemed very important.

Four entrances into the henge, set on the cardinal points, cut through the ditch and mound. At the bottom of the ditch, archaeologists have discovered human skulls and, in one case, the burial of an adult female. All of these components suggest that the henge at Avebury was, at least in part, a place for the dead, and that the living could enter the space through the four paths. Another component to the Avebury monument may help with interpretation. Archaeologists have discovered an avenue marked by a parallel line of standing stones. This avenue meanders for 1.5 miles to the south and west and ends on a hilltop at a place that has come to be known as the Sanctuary (Pitts 2000). From this location one see the entire region; on this hilltop once stood an external stone ring, a type of "fence" with three entrances. An interior stone-and-wood ring completed the architecture; buried at the base of one of the Sanctuary megaliths was an adolescent, and a human jaw was found near another (Pitts 2000). The avenue suggests a formal procession between the large Avebury henge and the Sanctuary, but the direction, frequency, and times of processions are uncertain. One clue is that the northwest entrance to the Sanctuary has a megalith in its center. At the summer solstice, if one stands within the Sanctuary, the sun rises directly over this stone. It is possible the architecture of the Sanctuary was structured to gauge the timing of the summer solstice and possibly initiate a series of ritual activities.

A third component to the Avebury complex is Silbury Hill, a massive mound of earth, clay, and chalk. This mound stands 37 meters high and has a base diameter of 160 meters; it is the largest earthwork in Europe (Scarre 1998). It does not appear to contain burials, and its function is not at all clear, but it was constructed contemporary with, or just after, the Avebury henge, avenue, and Sanctuary. Like the henge itself, the construction of Silbury Hill required enormous effort from many laborers; it must have been of significant import for England's Neolithic inhabitants.

Stonehenge

Stonehenge, the most famous of henge sites, is in the Salisbury Plain of southern England. The history of Stonehenge stretches back to Mesolithic times, perhaps as early as the ninth millennium B.C.E., when early hunter-gatherers erected massive timbers about 250 meters northwest of where Stonehenge stands today. It appears that this location was considered a sacred place, not just by the Neolithic inhabitants of the region, but also by those who lived thousands of years before them (Burl 2007). Stonehenge has all the elements of Avebury, and more. It has a ditch cut into the underlying chalk layer and a lower mound just outside it, with the higher one on the inside; it also has an outer ring of stones inside the ditch and mound. Inside this outer ring is another set of standing stones cut specifically to carry a lintel on top, and inside this secondary ring is yet a third, also bearing lintels (Figure 12.3). This intricate pattern of stones makes Stonehenge unique among henge sites.

Stonehenge was built in stages, the first stage (consisting of the ditch and mound) beginning around 3000 B.C.E. (Burl 2007). Two entrances were created, one on the northeast side and another on the opposite side of the circle. Over the

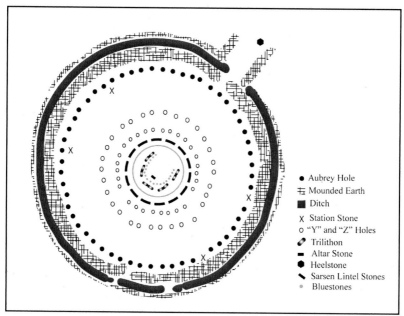

Figure 12.3. *Above:* Photo of Stonehenge. *(Stephen Inglis/Dreamstime.com)*
Below: Sketch plan of its final structure. *(S. R. Steadman)*

next several hundred years, the Stage 2 parts of Stonehenge were built; specifically, approximately 56 wooden posts were erected, probably in the circle format seen today. None of the posts remain, only the *Aubrey holes* where they once rested; these archaeological remnants are named for a seventeenth-century scholar who investigated Stonehenge.

At some point during or after the Stage 2 building phase, the Stonehenge ring began to be used for the deposition of cremations. Some are found in or near the Aubrey holes, suggesting that cremations may have been placed next to the wooden timbers that once stood at the site. Most of the cremations were found in the ditch. The earliest cremations were somewhat clumsy, in that the remains were not fully burned and large portions of bone remained, but as time and practice continued, cremations became more complete. Scholars estimate that at least 200 cremated individuals were deposited at Stonehenge during the early third millennium. Interestingly, some of the human cremation deposits also contained burned animal bones (Burl 2007). Animal remains may have resulted from feasts that took place at the time of cremation.

Stage 3 began in the mid-third millennium, when builders began using stone. That Stonehenge was an important place is demonstrated by the fact that the "bluestones" (a non-specific designation denoting stone foreign to the area) they chose to use came all the way from Wales, over 220 kilometers away. These bluestones, on average about 2 meters tall, were originally erected not in a circle, but in two curved lines facing toward the northeast entrance (Burl 2007). At the same time as the arrival of the bluestones, another type of stone known as *sarsen* (see below) was erected. This is known as the Heelstone, and it rests outside the ditch and mound circle, 24 meters out from the northeast entrance. Archaeologists have found a hole to the left of the Heelstone where it is likely that a second stone once stood. The function of the Heelstone and its purported twin is discussed below. A final use for bluestones was to erect stones known as the four Station Stones, in a perfect rectangle; if lines were drawn between these four stones (only two of which remain), they would outline perfectly the southwestern and northeastern edges of the stone circle (Burl 2007). A recent study suggests the bluestones came from a place Neolithic inhabitants believed had healing powers (Darvill 2007; Jones 2008), thereby bringing their magic to Stonehenge. The 2002 discovery of a skeleton dubbed the Amesbury Archer, and a second burial nearby, may lend credence to this theory. The archer and the other, younger, man may have been related. Both suffered from bone problems, and the archer also had knee and tooth infections (Stone 2005). It is possible that these two traveled to Stonehenge from mainland Europe to experience its healing magic (Jones 2008).

Soon after the bluestones went up, the more massive sarsen stones were transported to the site and erected. The sarsen stones, quarried from sites as much as 40 kilometers away, were far larger than the bluestones, reaching heights of 9 meters and weighing as much as 40–45 tons. These sarsen stones were erected in a continuous circle, with lintels placed atop them. Inside the circle were five more sets of lintels facing the northeast entrance, set in a U-pattern, called *trilithons*; inside these, the bluestones had been moved to create a curving U. One of the final stone pieces placed in this monument is known as the Altar Stone, a greenish sandstone that is unique at Stonehenge. To the left of the Altar Stone, a sarsen stone bears carvings of approximately 14 axes and a dagger; another figure on the same stone might be a second dagger or perhaps a crudely rendered human (Burl 2007). To the right of the Altar Stone is another sarsen pillar with carvings; high up on the stone is a rectangle with a semicircle at its top; a similar but smaller image is below it. Two of the outer rings of bluestones also bear several markings. Today the Altar Stone lies flat, but a great many scholars insist it once stood erect, and that one of its important functions was to act as a sighting point to see the midsummer sunrise over the Heelstone. Indeed, if one stands at the center of Stonehenge at dawn on the morning of the summer solstice, the sun rises on the western edge of the Heelstone; if the second "heel" stone were still standing, it would rise directly between them. Those viewing this sunrise would be able to confirm that the summer solstice, the half-year mark, and most likely an important point in the agricultural cycle, had occurred. In fact, a pathway leading from the Heelstone heads to the River Avon and is nicely aligned with the summer solstice sunrise.

While the function of the Heelstone(s) seems clear, that of the Altar Stone and Station Stones is less so. If their function was simply to track the rise of the midsummer sun, such an elaborate construction of enormous lintels was hardly necessary. The labor and time put into the building of Stonehenge would more likely be justified by a monument with multiple functions, rather than one utilized only during a single important ritual every summer. A closer examination of the Altar and Station Stones establishes even more firmly that Stonehenge was more than just a calendar device to measure the sun's movements.

The Station Stones, only two of which survive, have garnered far less consideration than the more elaborately arranged stone circle at Stonehenge. Nonetheless, a number of archaeologists have offered explanations for their presence. First, studies were undertaken to see if these four stones also served astronomical functions. Investigations in previous centuries determined that two of the four stones were in rough alignment with the midsummer sunrise, and two were in alignment with seasonal moonsets, including Beltane (on or around May 1 each year). However, these stones would have been crude observation points, and in fact the alignments with these sun and moon rises are slightly off, so astronomical observation was probably not their main purpose. Another suggestion is that the stones may have been used as engineering guides in the construction of the stone circles, since diagonal lines cross at the very center of the Stonehenge circle. Yet, if the principal function of the Station Stones was to act as an engineering template for the sarsen circle at Stonehenge, then it is reasonable to ask why they were not removed after construction. The Station Stones remain a bit of a mystery, but one archaeologist suggests that we must not discount the symbolic meaning that rectangular geometry might have held for Neolithic inhabitants (Burl 2007). In addition to its probable role as a template for the building of the stone circle, the rectangle may also have had cosmological relevance; the presence of a similar shape carved into one of the sarsen stones inside the circle may lend credence to this suggestion.

The Altar Stone offers another opportunity for various interpretations. Early scholars believed that the rising of the midsummer sunrise was sighted from the Altar Stone. However, the location of the Altar Stone is not ideal for this service, and so astronomical observation is perhaps not the most likely explanation. One of the main questions is whether it originally stood upright or was always supine. Early scholars who favored the latter imagined the placement of offerings and even human sacrifice on the stone. However, more recent and careful investigation of the probable pattern of falling sarsen stones, which likely knocked over and displaced the Altar Stone, more or less confirms that the Altar Stone once stood upright in front of the largest of the trilithon stones. Based on the proposed placement of the Altar Stone, an interesting setting emerges. An upright Altar Stone creates a space, perhaps even a "sanctum" at the apex of the trilithon (Burl 2007). Furthermore, the carvings on the trilithons were obscured from general view by the placement of the inner circle of bluestones. However, if a person stood at the Altar Stone, the carvings were visible. They were not particularly clear in plain daylight, but when the early morning sun reached them they appeared in high relief. The sarsen stones of the trilithons would tower over a human; one archaeologist suggests that they represented deities sacred to the people of Stonehenge (Darvill 2006). One important function of the Altar Stone, therefore, may not have been as an altar at all, but rather as a delimiter of particularly sacred space, perhaps accessed only by important religious practitioners or societal leaders at auspicious times, such as the midsummer solstice. What activities individuals performed there are presently lost to us.

The Builders of Stonehenge

At an archaeological site about 2 miles northeast of Stonehenge, an excavation has been investigating another henge site known as Durrington Walls, a massive circle of ditch and earthen mound with a diameter of 500 meters. A set of wooden timbers lined the interior of the henge, and the orientation of the entire structure is aligned with the winter solstice sunrise. Inside the large enclosure are the remains of two wooden structures. Post holes show that two separate circles, one to the north and one to the south, were constructed of stout timbers (Pitts 2000). Several have suggested that these timbers were sturdy enough to support a roof and that these may have been actual buildings rather than wooden circles. In addition, within the henge, several buildings have been excavated that may have belonged to elites in charge of activities at Durrington Walls. Alternatively, they may not have been houses, but rather buildings devoted to the religious activities that doubtless took place in this sacred space. Construction of the Durrington Walls monument began at the end of the fourth millennium B.C.E., and activities took place there for at least another 500 years. Many believed that the monument fell out of use when the bluestones and sarsen stones were erected at Stonehenge in the mid-third millennium, but recent archaeology suggests a new interpretation.

In 2007 the archaeological team announced the discovery of seven houses just beyond the henge, built between 2600 and 2500 B.C.E. (Alexander 2008), roughly contemporary with the Stage 3 construction of Stonehenge. Each house had an interior hearth to warm residents during cold English winter nights and to cook their food. The excavator, using magnetometry, has suggested that there may be several hundred more houses in this community, making it the largest Neolithic settlement in Britain and one of the larger ones yet discovered in Europe. In addition to these houses, archaeological work has discovered a wide avenue from this village to the Avon River. There is no doubt that it was intentionally built, as it is stone-paved and cut into the topsoil. This echoes the pathway between Stonehenge and the Avon that is aligned with the summer solstice sunrise. The pathway from Durrington Walls is instead aligned with the summer solstice sunset.

The presence of the village at Durrington Walls suggests that residents made use of the henge monument just beyond the doors of their own houses, but Stonehenge may also have been part of their ritual life. In fact, the residents at the Durrington Walls settlement may have helped to construct both sites. The proximity of the two henge sites, their pathways to the river aligned with the summer solstice, and the orientation to winter and summer solstices have led some archaeologists to suggest that both formed part of an entire sacred complex, celebrating life and death. The village located next to the wooden henge monument at Durrington Walls has revealed evidence of feasting, apparently at the winter solstice (Alexander 2008). Perhaps the feasting and a midwinter celebration honored life and vitality, while the stones at Stonehenge were markers for the concept of death. The deposit of so many cremation burials suggests that at least one of Stonehenge's functions was as a repository for the dead. While there was probably some connection between Durrington Walls and Stonehenge, whether it was simply that they marked the two opposite seasons of the year, or drew a more symbolic line between life and death, is as yet uncertain. Continued excavation at this large settlement will yield further clues, and perhaps even answers, to the questions archaeologists continue to ask about the meaning of Britain's henge monuments.

The Long Barrow Builders

Long barrows are earthen mounds that cover burial chambers. Britain is dotted with these burial places. The West Kennet long barrow is one of eight that lie near Avebury, and there are others that are even larger in other regions of southern England.

The West Kennet long barrow, constructed around 3500 B.C.E., had five burial chambers built of stone. Four flanked a passage, two on each side, with the fifth at the end of the passage (Figure 12.4); these were accessed through a doorway blocked by massive menhirs. A total of 46 people were interred in these chambers. Skeletons were not articulated, and only portions of the remains made it into the tomb. This suggests the deceased were left out in the elements for defleshing, and then the bones were collected for interment (Scarre 1998). During either the excarnation or the collection, some bones were apparently lost. There was some thought put into the placement of individuals in the tomb chambers. In the chamber at the end of the passage, only adult

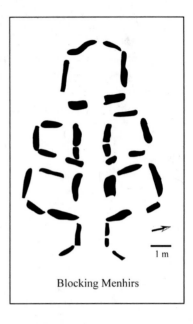

Figure 12.4. Sketch plan of West Kennet tomb. (*S. R. Steadman*)

Blocking Menhirs

1 m

males were buried, while both adult males and females were found in the two chambers across from each other nearest the back cell. In the two outer chambers, younger individuals had been interred. The mound built above the burial chambers stretches far longer than the underground burial hall itself. The mound rises from the surrounding region, easily visible and flat enough on top to support activities if they took place above the chamber beneath.

Several other interesting aspects about West Kennet are notable. First, the barrow was dug into cultivable land, which would seem to diminish the land available to farmers. This suggests that it was important to place the tomb in this area, rather than on nonarable land. Second, several of the individuals interred suffered from various medical conditions, including spina bifida and other ailments that can be passed genetically through the generations (Fagan 1998). Finally, West Kennet was used as a burial chamber for as long as five centuries. The incidence of similar or identical medical problems suggests to many that those interred in West Kennet were of the same family, and the length of usage would make West Kennet the "family vault." What is of interest, however, is the low number of burials: only 46 individuals placed in the tomb over a course of several hundred years. Clearly, some were singled out for burial in the stone-built tomb, and others were buried, or cremated, elsewhere.

There are numerous long barrow tombs in southern England, and many other types of tombs are found throughout England, including circular chambered tombs and tombs with smaller, multiple "stalls" rather than chambers. Each region seems to have had a particular style of tomb, but all required a fair amount of labor, and most received multiple interments over time.

Why Build Megalithic Monuments?

Some of the theories for monuments such as Carnac, Avebury, and Stonehenge have already been advanced. The pathways that the menhirs at Carnac created seem to have led to ritual sites, and Avebury seems to have served in part as a cemetery, as did Stonehenge. The role Stonehenge played in astronomical observations has also been explored. West Kennet and other long barrows were clearly meant as tombs. These are all solid and mostly uncontested explanations. What is not clear is why residents of Neolithic England and France went to such *effort* to build these monuments. Why stone, and why huge stones? Wouldn't wooden fences work just as well at Carnac? Wooden timbers were once used at Stonehenge; why not continue to do so? A few long barrows had wood-built chambers (now collapsed); why did most feel the need to build family tombs with stone? Most scholars who have asked these questions answer them in general by acknowledging that the enormous labor invested in building these monuments, and the hundreds or even thousands of people involved, clearly demonstrate a forceful drive to erect permanent and extraordinary monuments. The question is, for what purposes?

One of the most convincing explanations is that they served to highlight the power that some had over others—that is, smaller groups of people who could marshal larger groups to engage in the labor needed to build these monuments. Smaller groups wielding that power might be described as emergent chiefs, or elite family or lineage leaders (Hayden 2003). As Neolithic residents settled into permanent towns and population began to increase, some families may have grown more wealthy and powerful than others. These more fortunate residents may have attributed their success to their ancestors, occasioning elaborate celebrations of deceased kin and the need to construct suitable resting places for family leaders. It is possible that the most powerful leaders were even considered semi-divine, explaining why they, or their descendants, could co-opt so many participants into building these megalithic structures (Hayden 2003). In this case powerful families may have made the case that their own ancestors were capable of looking after not only their own living descendants, but everyone in the town or region, making the actual ancestors of one family the symbolic ancestors of everyone.

At important times of the year, including the solstices, feasting took place in sacred spaces such as Avebury and Stonehenge, as well as inside the tombs. These feasts may have honored both the agricultural cycle and the ancestors responsible for ensuring a successful harvest. The small and cramped quarters inside the tombs suggests that only a few individuals feasted inside with their ancestors; perhaps the ancestor's descendant family leaders were the only ones allowed into the family vault (in which only leaders and their families may have been interred). Used for centuries, tombs may have been filled and closed permanently only when that family or lineage died out (Hayden 2003). Everyone could participate in the feasts at the sacred sites such as Carnac, Avebury, or Stonehenge. Perhaps their right to participate in rituals stemmed from their contribution to the building of one or more of the monuments. It is possible the feasts were sponsored by the leading families of the region, a sort of remuneration to the people who had built the monuments honoring the ancestors. The cremations and burials at sites such as Avebury and Stonehenge, though not numerous enough to account for the entire populations of the towns in the region, may have been the family leaders, soon to become ancestors, of non-elite residents who did not have the resources to build stone tombs and long barrows.

The construction of these monuments would have served several purposes: it honored the ancestors of the powerful (and possibly divine) families, benefiting everyone; it demonstrated the power of the elites to control resources and labor; it demonstrated the wealth of the elites in their ability to build enormous structures, perhaps for the benefit of the population if the bluestones were indeed thought to possess magical healing properties; and it bound communities together in a united belief system. With everyone cooperating to build these staggering monuments, all could feel assured that the ancestors, and perhaps other supernatural beings also worshiped at these sites, were pleased with their human charges. In this explanation, the Neolithic megaliths of Britain and France are perfect examples of the successful combination of religion and power.

Conclusion

The megaliths discussed here are only a few of the many that can be found across the breadth of Britain and Ireland and in many areas on the western European mainland. The reasons for building these enduring structures are likely as myriad as their styles and shapes. Astronomical observations were clearly important, as were processions to important ritual sites where feasting and other activities took place. However, the ubiquitous burial sites, with selected individuals interred in elaborate tombs, suggests that ancestor veneration was an extremely important aspect of Neolithic religion and ritual. The power of the ancestors, and their living descendants, may have been at the heart of the construction of these monuments—testaments to the strength of fervent belief to create an extraordinary landscape.

Useful Sources

Aubrey Burl, *A Guide to the Stone Circles of Britain, Ireland, and Brittany*, 2006.
Christopher Chippindale, *Stonehenge Complete*, 2004.
Anthony Johnson, *Solving Stonehenge*, 2008.

PART V

RELIGIONS IN SOUTH AND SOUTHEAST ASIA

13

FROM HARAPPANS TO HINDUISM AND BEYOND
RELIGIONS IN SOUTH ASIA

The South Asian subcontinent is the homeland of two of today's major traditions, Hinduism and Buddhism. A number of other belief systems, such as Jainism and Sikhism, also developed there. Many aspects of Hinduism, as well as of modern Indian society, may have had roots in cultures that existed over four millennia ago—namely, in Harappan and post-Harappan societies.

The Harappan civilization (Figure 13.1) flourished along the Indus River, arising by 2600 B.C.E. and fading by roughly 1800 B.C.E. At some point before, during, or after the Harappans, a non-indigenous people known as the Indo-Aryans entered South Asia (Lahiri 2000; Mallory 1989; Renfrew 1987; Singh 1995), although some suggest they were actually indigenous to the region. The generally accepted view is that the Indo-Aryans, nomadic horse-riding pastoralists, left their homeland in the Russian Steppes, passed through Persia and Central Asia, to finally arrive in South Asia. The Indo-Aryans brought their language and belief system to South Asia, creating a mixture that resulted in the mosaic of ethnicities that makes up Indian culture today.

South Asia Today

India comprises hundreds of separate language groups and dialects, each with individualized cultural practices and economies. The languages of India fall into three primary families: Austro-Asiatic, Dravidian, and Indo-Aryan. Austro-Asiatic speakers, mainly in eastern India, consist largely of the pastoralist peoples and cultivators who live outside of urban centers. Dravidian-language speakers are found mostly in the southern half of India. The Dravidian languages are the most ancient in the Indian

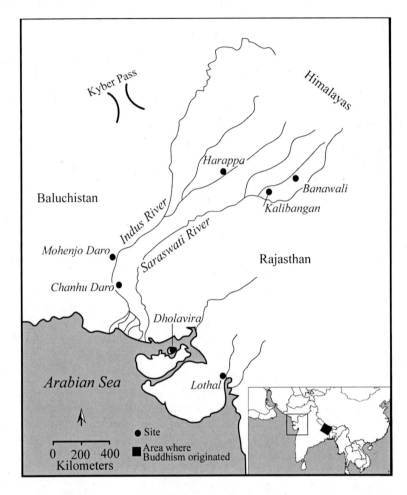

Figure 13.1. Map of Harappan sites discussed in the chapter.
(*T. Edwards/S. R. Steadman*)

subcontinent and are widely regarded as the indigenous Indian languages. Indo-Aryan languages are spoken principally in the northern region, except for Hindi, which, along with English, is spoken throughout the country. The variety of language families across India is testimony to the ancient populations and their movements thousands of years ago.

One of the best-known elements of Indian societal structure is its caste system. Since the 1950s the Indian government has taken steps to dismantle this system in favor of a "class" structure, though adherence to caste behaviors is still found in rural India today. The caste system is easily 2,000 years old but may have roots reaching even further back, as will be discussed below. India's caste system was closed to movement, meaning that once born into a caste (known as a *varna*), and more specifically a particular *jati* (occupational group within a varna), you and your offspring remained in that jati and varna (Sharma 1998). Traditionally, one married within one's caste and jati and practiced the profession of one's parents. In this way the caste structure remained stable and unchanging.

The origins of the caste system seem to be based on the perceived purity and susceptibility to pollution associated with various occupations (Sharma 1998). The four caste levels are hierarchically ranked; the highest, Brahmins, originally consisting of the priesthood, were considered the purest, based on their occupation. The lowest, or Shudra, caste included those who performed manual labor, including service jobs, farming (non-landowners), and pastoralism. Below the Brahmins were the middle two castes: the Chatrias, comprising the nobles (landowners) and warriors, and below them, the Weishas, the merchants and business-related workers (Sharma 1998). One final group is known as the Dalit; they were effectively a fifth and lowest caste (though not traditionally considered a caste in Indian society). Dalits were relegated to performing the least pure occupations, those most susceptible to pollution, such as garbage collection and street cleaning. There were numerous entrenched rules about inter-caste relations, with strict guidelines regarding the maintenance of purity at varying caste levels.

Though there are numerous indigenous traditional religions practiced, the main religion of India is Hinduism, a remarkably complex and tolerant religion encompassing thousands of major and minor deities. The roots of this religion can perhaps be traced back to the third millennium B.C.E.; over time, new rituals and deities, including those brought to South Asia by the Indo-Aryans, produced the structure of present-day Hinduism. The rise and florescence of Hinduism can be divided into four periods (however, scholars differ on the dates of transition between these period):

- The Formative period, 1500–1200 B.C.E., is when the Vedas (Hindu sacred texts written in Sanskrit, an early Indo-Aryan language) were composed.
- The Classical period begins sometime after 1000 B.C.E.
- The Post-Classical period begins by the seventh century C.E.
- The Modern period begins after 1600 C.E.

A well-known tenet of Hinduism is the concept that the human experience is a long cycle of life, death, and rebirth, with *karma* playing a role in determining the form of the rebirth (into a higher or lower being than in the previous life). The goal is *moksha*, or release from the life cycle, allowing unity with the universe. The structure of Hinduism is laid out in the Vedas, a set of four religious texts. The oldest and most important is the Rigveda, which includes hymns to Indo-Aryan gods and stories about them. Second to the Rigveda is the Atharvaveda, which details rituals to be used in the home. The Yajurveda outlines rites and sacrifices to gods, and the Samaveda contains hymns and chants for priests to recite. Each Vedic book contains four sections, and in each of the Vedas one section is called the Upanishads.

The Upanishads describe the philosophical basis of Hinduism, including the explanation of the karmic cycle and the road to moksha. The other three sections of each Vedic book are concerned with more practical issues: hymns, chants, sacrifices, and prayers. Unlike the rest of the Vedas, which are decidedly polytheistic in their outlook, the Upanishads also seem to focus more on a single entity known as Brahman. Brahman is, in the Upanishads, representative of the one reality; everything, including other deities and human existence, is simply part of that Brahmanic reality. Worship is mainly achieved through meditation rather than chants, rituals, or sacrifice; contemplation of the human relationship to Brahman is necessary to obtain release from the karmic cycle. The best contemplative attitude is the seated lotus position, allowing the mind to float free into the consideration of Brahman. Many believe that the Upanishads were not originally written as part of the Vedic literature, but rather were added as a separate compilation, perhaps deriving from a separate non-Vedic tradition (Hopfe and Woodward 2001; Morris 2006; Weisgrau 2000).

There are several thousand deities in Hinduism, but a select few of these are the most popular and considered the most important. Three of the most powerful gods are Brahma (different from Brahman), Shiva, and Vishnu, and all are considered extensions of Brahman. These three oversee all aspects of the human and earthly cycle: Brahma is the creator, Shiva the destroyer, and Vishnu the preserver. Of these, Shiva is the most popular in Classical and Post-Classical Hinduism (Hopfe and Woodward 2001). He is the god not only of death and destruction, but of dance and reproduction (plant, animal, and human) as well. In iconography Shiva is often seated in a lotus position and is regularly shown with three faces. As god of reproduction, Shiva's penis is often emphasized; this *lingus*, or phallic symbol, is part of his standard iconography. Shiva, along with other gods, exhibits a "third eye" in his forehead, which stands as a sign of an all-seeing ability and spiritual wisdom. The notion of the third eye in Hinduism relates to the attainment of higher consciousness and seeing the true reality of the universe, a concept expressed in the Upanishads. Vishnu, nearly the opposite of Shiva, stands for love and forgiveness. Vishnu is invested with the preservation of humanity and accomplishes this by appearing on earth in nine forms (called *avatars*). One of these avatars is another god named Krishna.

Krishna is known as a prankster, a playful and youthful deity who is the cowherd of the gods. He typically plays a flute and is far more interested in leisure and the ladies than in tending his herd. Krishna's name means "dark," and he is usually depicted as darker than other deities. One other deity of note here is Shakti, the goddess of fertility or female energy, and a consort of Shiva. Shakti has a close association with the notion of earth and fertility and may have had pre-Aryan roots.

Hindus worship according to the guidelines set out in the Vedas. Household altars are used for daily ritual, and temples dedicated to various deities provide public venues. There are two common factors in all religious activities, whether in house or temple: fire and water. The purifying qualities of water have long been crucial to any Hindu ritual (Lahiri and Bacus 2004). Before attending any *puja* (ritual), all participants must bathe and ritually cleanse their hands. Water is also found in the Hindu rituals at the time of death. First, to ensure karmic rebirth, the body must be cremated on a funeral pyre. Following this, the remains (bones and ashes) must be cast upon water, preferably the holy Ganges River in eastern India, but other places with sacred waters also suffice.

Fire is also used in making offerings and sacrifice rituals. Items sacrificed range from food and liquid (milk, ghee, fruits) all the way to the expansive royal "horse sacrifice" of past times. Through burning, the sacrifice reaches the deities via the rising smoke, conveyed upward by the fire god Agni. The elements of fire and water form important cores to most rituals, both in the household and in temples.

The Harappan Civilization

The Harappan, or Indus, civilization comprises large cities surrounded by towns, villages, and hamlets, stretching from Baluchistan to the modern-day city of Mumbai to the south. This culture was named Harappan after the early discovery of the city by the same name, first excavated in the late 1800s and again beginning in 1920. Following World War II, new excavations revealed much more about "Harappan" sites, though we do not know how the people of this culture referred to themselves and their region.

Harappan Settlements and Societal Structure

The major Harappan cities were stretched along the Indus and Saraswati rivers and their tributaries and showed a remarkable penchant for city planning. Among the larger known cities, including Lothal, Chanhu Daro, Kalibangan, and Dholavira, the best known is the city of Mohenjo Daro, which possibly translates to "mound of the dead men" (Possehl 2002:185). Mohenjo Daro is the largest Harappan city we know of, spanning over 200 hectares and supporting a population of as many as 40,000 people. Harappa is the second-largest known city, at over 150 hectares; other cities range in size from 80 to 100 hectares (Kenoyer 1998).

Harappan cities were laid out on a grid, with streets and buildings conforming to the four cardinal directions (a few recently discovered settlements have less structured town plans). Broad avenues cross-cut these centers, and smaller streets and alleys divided buildings into "city blocks." Many Harappan cities were built on an artificially elevated platform, to guard against inundation by spring floods, with additional mounds built on this initial platform. The cities and internal mounds were often surrounded by mudbrick walls. At first deemed defensive, many believe these walls were not for protection, but rather served other purposes, perhaps creating "neighborhoods" or providing additional flood protection (Kenoyer 1998). Cities usually had a higher area known as "the citadel," where public buildings were built. The majority of residences and craft and market areas were in the lower parts of the cities. On the citadels at Mohenjo Daro and Harappa, large buildings were originally interpreted as public granaries or storehouses, but more recent analysis suggests they may have been pillared assembly halls (Kenoyer 1998; McIntosh 2002).

Harappan houses generally conformed to a standard plan with rooms surrounding an open courtyard; walls suggest houses were at least two stories high. Each house held both a bathing room and a separate latrine. Houses varied somewhat in size, ranging from a small family home to those large enough to house a substantial extended family. The largest were those with attached outer units. A recent study of debris found scattered across floors in Mohenjo Daro indicates these small rooms may have been workshops (McIntosh 2002). Families apparently engaged in single craft production, so that a shell worker may have had a potter as a neighbor on one side and a jeweler on the other. However, larger "factory style" areas have also been found, perhaps cooperatives for those without space in their homes to carry out their crafts. Such is the case in today's India; some make their crafts at home, while others go to cooperatives or central locations. One interesting feature in the Harappan houses is the elevated doorstep, creating a kind of stoop. This allowed residents to sit or stand in front of their homes, possibly visiting with neighbors or passersby. Harappan city planners also made certain there were ample market areas, often near the gates. There may have been artisans' quarters located there as well.

Harappans were master craftmakers, working in such media as clay, metal, shell, stone, and cloth, trading their goods as far afield as Mesopotamia and the Persian Gulf. Jewelry, made of shell, metal, and beads, was very popular among the Harappans; terracotta statues, another common craft, show both men and women sporting bracelets, necklaces, earrings, and headdresses. Coppersmiths made a variety of metal tools and weapons, and artisans working in soft stones such as steatite crafted stamp seals, statues, and figurines. Harappan pottery featured painted designs of Harappan life. A commonly depicted character was the bull; other animals—stags or antelopes, birds, water buffalo and fish—were also featured.

Harappan political structure continues to be a subject of discussion (e.g., Kenoyer 1994). It is unclear whether the civilization was divided into a series of city-states each with a major center as the seat of power (Kenoyer 1995), or was led by a single ruler who dwelled at a significant city such as Mohenjo Daro; of course, any number of other political structures may also have been in place. Whether city-state or single empire, was the ruler singular—like a king or queen—or was the Indus civilization ruled by a council of elders? Were rulers secular or religious, all-powerful or guided by advisors? None of these questions are adequately answered as yet. There is one bit of evidence in the form of a statue found at Mohenjo Daro (Figure 13.2), known as the Priest-King. It depicts a bearded man wearing an embroidered robe covering one shoulder and a headband with a circular symbol on his forehead. Some suggest his narrowed eyes imply he is in a state of meditation, and the covering of one shoulder is, in later times, a sign of reverence to a deity. That the statue depicts an important person is likely; whether it represents a king who was also a priest is harder to document.

Harappan civilization is rather extraordinary because it appears to have functioned so differently from other contemporary civilizations such as Egypt, Mesopotamia, or the Shang Dynasty in China. What stands out in Harappan settlements is the seeming lack of differentiation among individuals and social groups. A few

Figure 13.2. The "Priest-King" statue from Mohenjo Daro. (*R. Jennison*)

sites, such as Dholavira's "castle" and "bailey" (possibly the house of an elite person), demonstrate large and lavish residences (Lawler 2008). With these few notable exceptions, houses were fairly uniform in size, and there is a dearth of lavish decorations or individualization inside or outside homes. Possibly, farmer, merchant, and craft producer lived side by side in similar circumstances, each with their bathrooms, courtyards, and spacious houses. It would be inaccurate to say the Indus River civilization was "egalitarian," but it certainly appears that there was a relative lack of hierarchical ranking within the society, especially as compared with contemporary cultures of similar size and complexity.

The Harappan Script

Much of our ignorance about Harappan society stems from the fact that we have not yet deciphered their script. The Harappans wrote using pictographs (Figure 13.3); at present over 400 pictographs have been identified. They probably wrote more lengthy documents on perishable organic materials such as paper or skins. The main examples that remain are steatite seals that comprise a mixture of pictographs and iconographic symbols, some of which may have religious connotations. A few other examples, such as a "sign board" found at the Dholavira city gate, perhaps the city name or a type of "welcome" sign, round out the samples of Harappan script. Most scholars believe Harappan was a Dravidian language, but this is not at all certain.

Harappan Religion

Architecture and Clues to Beliefs

One of the best-known architectural features in Harappan civilization is the so-called Great Bath on the citadel at Mohenjo Daro. The Great Bath is situated between the

Figure 13.3. Example of Harappan pictographic writing. (*R. Jennison*)

building known as the Warehouse/Granary (which was probably an audience hall) and another structure known as the College, along with other buildings at either end. The pool itself was surrounded by small cubicles and slightly larger rooms. Some of these appear to be bathing rooms with drainage systems. The pool measures 12 × 7 meters and is over 2 meters deep. It was absolutely watertight, with an underlying layer of bitumen topped by tightly fitted bricks that were carefully plastered. One entered the water at either end via a set of stairs, to a final low platform for sitting or standing. A second story once existed, built of wood, but it probably covered only the sides and left the bath open to the sky. The effort that went into building this astonishing structure is considerable and suggests it was much more than the local swimming spot (Figure 13.4). As one archaeologist says, "most scholars agree that this tank was used for special religious functions where water was used to purify and renew the well-being of the bathers" (Kenoyer 1998:64). Thus far, the Great Bath at Mohenjo Daro is unique among Harappan cities (a larger tank at Harappa is probably for water storage [Kenoyer 1998]). Lustral (purification) baths may well have existed at other Harappan settlements but await further excavations.

Next to the Great Bath at Mohenjo Daro was the structure dubbed the College of the Priests by one excavator. This is a complex of rooms defined by early excavators as the cells of monks or priests who oversaw the ablutions in the Great Bath. However, lacking evidence to support this interpretation, more recent analyses have suggested this building may have functioned as the large residence of an official (secular or religious), or a multi-person residence or guest house (Possehl 2002).

One of the remarkable aspects of Harappan cities is the lack of identifiable public temples. No large-scale religious structures, other than the Great Bath, have been unearthed. There is a higher building on the citadel that archaeologists once thought was a Buddhist *stupa* (religious building) built centuries after the end of Harappan society; recent work has reevaluated the date of the building and suggests it might have been a Harappan temple (Lawler 2008). It is possible that large open spaces may have served the function of the city temple, as areas where public gatherings could take place. One such area was found just in front of the citadel at Dholavira. Large open areas might also have been marketplaces, but these were more commonly located near gates at Harappan sites. A single structure in the Mohenjo Daro residential area, known as House HR1, has been described as a possible neighborhood temple or perhaps a priest's house (Ratnagar 2001). The courtyard featured two staircases flanking what

Figure 13.4. Artistic rendering of ritual bathing in the Mohenjo Daro Great Bath.
(*M. J. Hughes*)

may have been a tree. However, no altars or other clearly religious paraphernalia were found in this structure, so its role as a religious building remains speculative.

In addition to the Great Bath and open areas, Harappan cities featured *fire altars* which were intentionally built to support fires, perhaps for sacrifice. The clearest examples are found at Kalibangan, both on the citadel and on a lower mound. These are plastered mudbrick structures set into the ground, usually circular or oval in shape. Ashy remains, including burned animal bones, indicate material was burned in these installations. Fire installations have been found at other sites, including Lothal, Rakhigarhi, and a site called Banawali. However, some believe these are not necessarily altars, but rather were used as kilns or for other, more prosaic functions. The identification of these features as fire altars at Kalibangan, however, seems very secure, and as one scholar notes, such small ritual structures are "probably in other towns and cities" but as yet unexcavated (McIntosh 2002:110).

Seals, Figurines, Supernatural Beings, and Priests

Other materials that offer clues to Harappan religion include seals, figurines, and statues. A common element on the seals is the presence of plants; and perhaps most often depicted is the pipal tree (a type of Indian fig tree). This tree has heart-shaped leaves and seems to appear in association with a number of figures that might be deities. Depictions of this tree or its leaves are found not only on seals, but on ceramics and terracotta tablets. Sometimes humans water the tree, in other cases a deity sits within its branches. Kenoyer suggests that the pipal tree may have been the "temple" for Harappans, open-air sacred locales where people could make offerings to this sacred representative of nature (Kenoyer 1998). Several scholars have suggested that the sacred nature of the pipal and banyan tree in modern Hinduism stretches back to Harappan times (Chakrabarti 2001; Ratnagar 2001).

The common representation of animals, on seals and pottery and in terracotta form, prompts some to suggest an animal cult was practiced in the Indus civilization, or at least that animals figured prominently in Harappan mythology (Kenoyer 1998; Ratnagar 2001). Commonly depicted are tigers, bulls, water buffalo, and the occasional elephant. In some scenes on seals, there appears to be a man fighting or mastering animals; the man sometimes has a headdress and may be some sort of deity in a "master of the animals" setting. Kenoyer describes these seals and plaques with human and animal depictions as "narrative scenes" of Harappan myths (1998:115). In addition, cattle bones have been found in fire altars, indicating cows were sacrificed. Most scholars agree that bovines were sacred to ancient Harappans, perhaps along with other animals such as the tiger.

One seal image that has elicited substantial discussion depicts a male, sitting on a platform, bearded and wearing a horned headdress. This figure is three-faced and seated in the yogic position (Figure 13.5) with his penis evident. This figure has been identified by some as a Proto-Shiva. The present-day Shiva is often represented associated with animals or riding the sacred bull Nandi; he also typically holds a trident and is seated in the yogic position, with phallic (lingus) representation, and a multi-faced presentation. Many suggest that the Harappan seals have too many similarities to later images of Shiva to ignore the possibility that an early version of this powerful Hindu god is depicted. The Proto-Shiva headdress has been interpreted as either the forerunner of the trident or a representation of a bull or water buffalo—and thus a possible Proto-Nandi. Further Harappan evidence suggestive of some sort of Proto-Shiva is the discovery of numerous objects identified as *lingam*, or phallic symbols (McIntosh 2002). The lingus is one of the well-recognized iconographic symbols of the Hindu Shiva; stone pedestals, associated with fire altars at Kalibangan, and stones that appear "unmistakably phallic" at sites such as Mohenjo Daro and Dholavira, all contribute to this theory (Chakrabarti 2001).

Terracotta female figurines are fairly numerous and often sport bangles on their arms, headdresses, elaborate necklaces and earrings, and a kilt or short skirt. A number have had a red wash applied for coloring, and some carry an infant. Female figurines are more numerous than male examples, and the majority of both have come from Mohenjo Daro. Whether this is because of more extensive excavations there, or because they were, in fact, produced in greater quantities, is unknown. The standard interpretation of the figurines is that they represent a goddess-based religion with a focus on fertility, possibly used as votive offerings or in household-based rituals (Possehl 2002). However, aside from these female figurines, there is not much other evidence to indicate the presence of a powerful female-oriented belief system. Find spots of the figurines are not clearly associated with areas considered religious in Indus settlements, nor in hearths or other important domestic locations. Rather, many were recovered as part of street debris or in other inauspicious contexts (Ratnagar 2001). The same is true of the ubiquitous terracotta and stone or faience figurines of animals, including bulls, rams, squirrels, and rhinos, though many of these have perforations allowing them to be worn as amulets or carried suspended on string. These "nonreligious" find spots lead some to believe that the female and animal figurines

Figure 13.5. Seal depicting a three-faced figure seated in a yogic position—a possible Proto-Shiva. (*R. Jennison*)

were merely toys, dolls, or objects for other nonreligious uses. An alternative explanation for their curious find spots is that they did indeed serve as votive offerings, but during a single ritual or ceremony; after the completion of that particular event, the sacred nature of the figurine was dispensed with, and they could indeed become toys or even be discarded.

A seal featuring a female with elaborate jewelry and headdress has also received some attention. The central female sits in a pipal tree, and before her kneels a goat and a human figure. In the register below her are seven female figures, perhaps in a procession headed to the female in the tree. Some have suggested that this female deity is an early version of the fertility goddess Shakti, who remains popular in rural India today (Elgood 2004). Evidence indicates that a female deity representing fertility has been common in village worship for at least two millennia (Elgood 2004; Lahiri and Bacus 2004). Shakti (and the goddess Durga, one of Shakti's manifestations) is sometimes associated with seven attendants, derived from the myth that Durga resulted from the merging of seven mothers. The identity of the kneeling male is entirely speculative, but Shakti/Durga's association with Shiva suggests he is a possible candidate.

Other notable items are the "masks" of a horned human. Several examples of these have been found at both Harappa and Mohenjo Daro (Figure 13.6). One is small enough to have functioned as an amulet, but all depictions seem to be of a mask with a human face, probably male, sporting horns, perhaps representing a bull. On some seals a human figure with horns is also seen, perhaps the full-bodied version of the terracotta mask representations. The Harappan reverence for cattle is well documented and previously discussed. The question here is the identity of this masked figure, described as a "probable deity" by scholars; but without additional evidence, this is as far as we can go. It is interesting to note, however, the later popularity of the Hindu god Krishna, the cowherd. Krishna was and remains a popular god in rural India and has very ancient roots. Perhaps we see a type of "proto-Krishna" here, represented in his role as caretaker of the sacred cows.

Harappan stone statuary constitutes the last category of items that might yield clues to Harappan religion. The most provocative of these is the already mentioned statue known as the Priest-King from Mohenjo Daro (Figure 13.2). The bearded male figure wears a headband with a circular symbol on his forehead, a similar band on his upper arm, and a garment with trefoil and circle designs. The garment's designs once held red pigment, and holes in the statue's neck indicate a necklace or headdress was once attached. The eyes contained shell inlay, and their half-closed rendering may represent a meditative state. Early excavators suggested this statue represents a priest, a king, or both; however, there is no evidence to support such claims, and thus the identity of the figure remains hidden. Two aspects of the statue are worth noting, though. The contemplative or meditative attitude of the face would imply that such practice, common in later Hinduism, may have been part of Harappan ritual behavior. Second, the headband with the circle on the forehead invites one to consider the Hindu beliefs involving the "third eye" of Shiva as representative of transcendent understanding of universal reality. Other stone and terracotta statues of males have been found, also

Figure 13.6. Horned mask found at Mohenjo Daro. (*R. Jennison*)

wearing beards and headbands, and some of these have the "meditative" look found on the Priest-King's face.

Reflections on Harappan Religion

Though our understanding of this civilization's religion is still fragmentary, some trends can perhaps be identified. The Great Bath at Mohenjo Daro suggests that water was a principal element in religion and ritual. The frequent appearance of bovids or cow iconography on seals, pottery, and masks highlights the importance of cattle and perhaps their presence in the cosmology. The Harappans lived in a flood-plain where the annual rise of the Indus and Saraswati rivers was certainly crucial to successful agriculture. Central components to farming, water, and cattle for draft labor may have also been deeply rooted in Harappan religious beliefs, offering a clear reflection of Harappan religion and the environment in which believers lived.

One other point worth noting is the potential link between Harappan religion and sociopolitical structure. The curious lack of extensive socioeconomic stratification in Harappan settlements seems equally reflected in their religion. Harappans may have worshipped not in temples that limited admittance only to elites, but in open areas and in homes. Substantive evidence of an elevated "priestly" class, or caste, is limited, as is clear demonstration of a palace and royal/ruling elite. Although Harappan society may well have been hierarchical (Lawler 2008), it was not ranked in a traditional sense; the differences between elites and commoners were as much symbolic as material. This lack of differentiation with respect to wealth, power, and prestige appears in the religion that was itself relatively unranked with regard to supernatural beings, access to ritual areas, and opportunities for worship. The notion that a society's religion is reflective of its social structure would seem to be well demonstrated in the ancient Indus civilization.

The End of Harappan Civilization and the Arrival of the Indo-Aryans

Explanations for the end of Harappan civilization are numerous and inconclusive. By 1800 B.C.E. the civilization had broken up into regional polities, as shown in changing material culture and social structure. Early theories postulated external attack, with the most oft-cited perpetrators being the arriving nomadic Indo-Aryans. Others advanced hydrological disaster, flooding, and subsistence destruction as leading culprits. As is so often the case, even for smoothly operating empires, internal factors in complex and cascading sequences are usually at the core of systemic collapse. Kenoyer suggests that "overextended networks of trade and political control were easily disrupted by changes in river patterns, flooding, and crop failure" (1998:174). Adding to other problems, the Saraswati River was drying up, possibly causing a crisis in food production and a population relocation. The social disruption created by these and other factors may have led to the demise of the Harappan civilization after it had flourished for 500 years. This ushered in a Late Harappan era (ca. 1900–1300 B.C.E.), a period of small city-states or chiefdoms, with changing subsistence technologies, smaller and more regionally based trade networks and political structures, and new material culture (Kenoyer 1998).

An Indo-Aryan Arrival?

During the Late Harappan period, evidence of a non-Harappan and non-Dravidian population began to emerge in the form of the Vedic texts produced most likely by Indo-Aryans. When Indo-Aryans entered South Asia is unclear, but they had arrived by ca. 1200 B.C.E. because this is when the Rigveda was written in Sanskrit. However, the date that sacred texts are written down does not always coincide with their oral composition, which may have been much earlier. Unfortunately, archaeological evidence is mainly mute on the Indo-Aryan issue; burials featuring horses (animals important in Indo-Aryan culture) date to the second millennium but do not themselves prove an Indo-Aryan presence; nor does the skeletal record suggest the sudden appearance of a new ethnic group (Kennedy 1995). Some, therefore, have suggested that Sanskrit speakers arrived in the third millennium, or earlier, and slowly settled among Harappan cultivators (Allchin and Allchin 1982; Renfrew 1987). Others have suggested that Indo-Aryans were, for all intents and purposes, *indigenous* to South Asia, having arrived long before the Harappan civilization ever emerged (Bryant 2001; Lal 1997; Singh 1995). Therefore, it is unclear whether Indo-Aryans and indigenous (Harappan) systems of belief intermingled for hundreds of years or were thrown together shortly before the appearance of the Vedas.

Our knowledge of original Indo-Aryan culture is limited. A cautious outline can be built using burial evidence and other material culture from contemporary cultures cognate with the Indo-Aryans (Bryant 2001). Practicing nomadic pastoralism as they traveled through West, Central, and South Asian landscapes, Indo-Aryans probably continued to rely on animal husbandry even after settling in India and engaging in cultivation. Stock breeding was a staple economic endeavor, and a reliance on the horse is clear (Allchin and Allchin 1982). Indo-Aryans existed within a ranked societal organization, featuring elites, warriors, and possibly religious personnel, with probable lower classes that might have included merchants, craftsmen, and, at the bottom rung, laborers (Fairservis 1995; Hiebert 1995; Renfrew 1987). Comparative linguistic analysis suggests the presence of patrilineal kinship with a possible clan-based tribal structure, with male heads of households (Allchin and Allchin 1982; Mallory 1989).

We are on somewhat more secure ground describing Indo-Aryan religion, using some archaeological evidence combined with clues from the Vedas. With almost no exceptions, Indo-Aryan deities were male. Storm, sky, and mountain gods were of great importance; the Vedas describe major deities such as Indra, Varuna, Agni, and others, many of whom have ancient Persian and West Asian counterparts. The Vedas also recount the creation of humans in which Brahmins, or priests, spring from the head of "Primeval Man," a deified figure. The warriors, the Chatrias, who were men of strength and action, came from his shoulders, and from the thighs came Weishas, the merchants; finally, the laborers, or Shudras, came from his feet. In this myth, those doing the "purest" work, the clerics, came from the head, which is farthest from the ground, while the part of the body most likely to be defiled, the feet, produced those in the most impure professions. Herein, it is thought, is the explanation of the caste structure that pervaded Indian society for millennia.

Other aspects of Indo-Aryan religion and culture are also captured in the Vedas. Chants, prayers, and rituals outlined in the Rigveda were clearly central to worship. Animal sacrifice, not surprising in a pastoralist society, was prominent, including the grand and expensive royal horse sacrifice. Sacrifice often included fire as a method of conveying the offering to the gods. What is conspicuously absent is overt instructions for the building of temples or grand edifices for worship. The Indo-Aryans were more accustomed to open-air or non-permanent ritual locales, perhaps to be expected in an originally nomadic culture. From the combination of Indo-Aryan and Harappan religions came the complex and fascinating religion of Hinduism.

Harappans, Indo-Aryans, and the Rise of Hinduism

There is no doubt that the Hinduism practiced today is substantially different from that practiced 2,000 years ago. New deities and avatars, and more regularized worship in temples, might very well make today's Hinduism somewhat strange to someone who lived in the past. However, there are elements of Hinduism that appear to be extremely ancient and perhaps even had their roots in the pre-Hindu cultures of India.

There are three important elements found in both Harappan and Indo-Aryan religions that can be considered to connect the two cultures: fire, animals, and sacrifices. Fire altars with evidence of (occasionally animal) sacrificial offerings at sites such as Kalibangan and Lothal demonstrate the use of both fire and animal sacrifice in

Harappan religion. Furthermore, the cow, found in so many Harappan contexts, highlights the importance of this animal. When we turn to the Vedas, we find fire playing a crucial role as the proper method to make sacrifice to the gods. Indo-Aryans, originally nomadic pastoralists, would have certainly recognized the role animals played in their world; arriving in South Asia and finding a similar reverence, along with the recognition of fire as an important actor in worship, might have made them feel right at home.

The absence of buildings for public worship (i.e., temples) may have been a further point of intersection. Such is perhaps to be expected among nomadic pastoralists who would more likely set up portable altars as needed. However, in a civilization the size of the Harappans, the apparent absence of monumental buildings for worship would seem to suggest Harappans enjoyed a more individualistic approach to their deities. Household shrines or altars, perhaps visits to the Great Bath or other bathing-related locations, and the occasional public gathering in open areas may have characterized Harappan methods of worship. Non-temple worship may have seemed familiar to Indo-Aryans.

Other aspects of the original Harappan religion seem to have made their way into modern Hinduism. The pipal tree, still sacred today, was certainly a powerful symbol in ancient Harappan cosmology. In like fashion, the importance of water remains a core factor, stretching from ancient Harappan society to Hindu beliefs today. When analyzing specific deities, a slightly higher level of guesswork enters the equation. Perhaps one of the most secure identifications is that of Shiva. His possible early appearance as the three-faced god in yogic position on Harappan seals would seem to be a likely precursor to the very popular god of destruction in Hinduism today. Although less certain, the importance of a female deity in ancient Harappa could well be the Shakti/Durga of later Hinduism. Finally, most speculative is the identity of the male masked figure with bovine horns. A connection between this figure and the playful and popular Krishna, avatar of Vishnu, is also worthy of consideration.

A Few Other Considerations: Caste and Consciousness

Many scholars have commented on the great differences between the Vedas and the Upanishads. In contrast to the clearly pantheistic Vedas, the Upanishads teach an all-encompassing consciousness of yogic meditation as a form of worship and the proper path toward ultimate attainment of oneness with Brahman. That two such different messages would operate side by side in the same sacred text is unusual and leads one to speculate that Brahman, meditation, and the karmic cycle were elements of Harappan beliefs, whereas pantheism derived from the Indo-Aryans. Was the "Priest-King" meditating, demonstrating the correct Harappan path to moksha? Is the symbol on his forehead a reminder of the "third eye of consciousness" expressed in the Upanishads? Certainly, with the current state of evidence we cannot even begin to answer these questions. But asking them is all part of the archaeology of religion.

Entire books have discussed the origins of the Indian caste structure, so it is unlikely a paragraph or two here will satisfactorily deal with the topic. However, what little we do know about Harappan and Indo-Aryan societies lends itself to some speculation. Harappans had an unusual approach to societal organization: social groups included farmers and herders, craftsmen and merchants, apparently some sort of defenders or warriors, and elites (religious or secular, or both). That ranked *classes* of these groups are not easily detected is what makes Harappan society so interesting (Coningham and Young 1999). A hierarchical society may well have been in place, but one's placement at a "lower" level may not have been disadvantageous. Let us, for a moment, image a society where, once born into an occupation, that of one's parents, that role was set for one's life and for one's children as well. The farmer would see few differences between his own home and that of his neighbor, the merchant, and his other neighbor, the city guard. In this way a well-ordered and smooth-running society would be achieved, with no lack of individuals to carry out important roles. Farmers would not give up farming to become merchants; city guards would not incite coups to take over the rule of the city.

Now consider a nomadic pastoralist society with elites, warriors, and "lower classes," all ranked and privileged according to their position within the society. What if two such systems met and merged—the Harappan one tailor-made for ranking but unranked, the Indo-Aryan one heavily ranked but perhaps needing a bit of structure and permanence to their system? A ranked caste system would ensure that Indo-Aryan elites maintained their positions even upon settling in a new land. The likely greater number of Dravidian indigenous South Asians, engaged in farming, herding, and craft-making, would remain in the lower echelons of society and thus would be more easily controlled by a smaller number of indigenous and Indo-Aryan elites. The roots and organization of India's ancient caste system were surely far more complicated than described here, but the intersection of the Harappan's peculiar undifferentiated society and the Indo-Aryan ranked system may very well have played an important role.

Classical-Period Hinduism and the Origins of Buddhism

In the early first millennium B.C.E., northern India was divided into small chiefdoms controlled by leaders empowered though kinship ties (Embree 1988). By this time Hinduism and a hierarchical caste structure were firmly entrenched in north Indian society. Temples dedicated to major deities such as Shiva and Vishnu were becoming common, and focus on female deities had deceased. This may have coincided with the relegation of the woman's prominent role in the household to a secondary one, a status division present in modern Indian society.

Vedic styles of worship were carefully followed by this time, and sacrifice figured prominently in the Hindu liturgy. Along with the newly important temples, priests were now required at most rituals; they were supported by the people through offerings and payments for services. Those with greater wealth could perform rituals more often and make more notable sacrifices (such as animals), while those in the lower echelons of society could not show their devotion as regularly or with such elaborate offerings. The notion of pollution and purity became an even more powerful distinction in the caste divisions and more firmly separated the wealthy and powerful from those in the lower castes (Weisgrau 2000). Some suggest it was at this time that the "untouchables," the Dalits, emerged in response to a need for people to perform the most polluted and undesirable tasks of a growing society.

By the sixth century B.C.E., old tribal allegiances had weakened and more politically oriented kingdoms began to emerge (Embree 1988). Not only were those in the lower castes more permanently set in their jatis, but those who had been powerful elites found themselves in less strategic positions with the emergence of centralized power structures (Robinson and Johnson 1997). These alterations in the basic structure of society in northern and northeastern India resulted in the development of at least two new religions, Buddhism and Jainism. There may have been others, but these are the two that survive into modern times. Both religions offer alternative paths to moksha, avoiding the sacrifice-heavy route practiced in Classical Hinduism and making moksha accessible to all believers, without distinctions according to caste or possession of wealth. In this way Buddhism and Jainism can be viewed as responses, and even rebellions, to a societal structure and a religion that had become repugnant enough to invite change. The origins of Buddhism well illustrate the gap this religion appeared to fill in first-millennium B.C.E. India.

The Origins of Buddhism

The term *Buddha* means "awakened one" and refers to the concept of achieving enlightenment or *nirvana* (a form of moksha). The Buddha, originally a man named Siddhartha Gautama, became awakened through a path other than that prescribed in the Vedas; this path emerged into the religion now known as Buddhism. Siddhartha Gautama was born somewhere between the mid-sixth century and the early fifth century B.C.E. and died approximately 80 years later (Trainor 2001a). The details of The Buddha's life are vague because chroniclers wrote about him several hundred years after his death, relying on oral tradition while also glorifying his life on earth. Archaeologists have excavated various sites in the region of the upper Ganges River and Himalayan foothills (see Figure 13.1), where Siddhartha Gautama probably lived and Buddhism began (Allen 2003). His family apparently belonged to the Chatrias caste, and his father was an important tribal leader in the region; however, the area was absorbed into a kingdom, and so Siddhartha Gautama's family, like many other elites, may have been experiencing the type of social displacement discussed above.

The Buddha's birth is recounted in the context of miraculous events and sacred indicators heralding the birth of a great leader. Accounts speak of an aged sage who examined the infant and declared the child would become either a great monarch or a religious leader, the latter only if he left the palace to wander the world. To encourage the former, the story goes, Siddhartha's father forbade the child to leave the grounds of the compound, and built high walls to prevent his son from seeing the outside world. Siddhartha was surrounded by peace and solitude, with healthy people who were happy, with music and dance and all the pleasures of life. It was in this way that his father hoped to groom him to be a great monarch and avoid the life of poverty that he would experience should he dedicate his life to religion. As a young man, however, Siddhartha was curious about the world beyond the walls, and one day he set out to see the royal gardens. Some accounts suggest that his father cleared the road of all indicators of unpleasantness (i.e., disease, infirmity, poverty) so that Siddhartha would continue to be blinded to life's realities. But supernatural beings known as *devas*, those who have achieved nirvana, appeared to Siddhartha as diseased old men, and one even posed as a corpse. Another appeared as a wandering ascetic, a man at peace because he had renounced his burdens; Siddhartha realized it was this life of simplicity that called to him as well. At the age of 29 or 30, he left the palace, his wife, and his child and began his life as an ascetic to achieve peace and eventually nirvana. For six years Siddhartha lived in the forest with other ascetics, wearing the saffron-colored robe characteristic of these holy men. He wandered and lived a life of abject poverty. One day, on the point of starvation and death, Siddhartha accepted food and renounced the life of asceticism (Trainor 2001a). He sat down under a pipal tree and began to meditate. During this period of meditation he became a *bodhisattva*, one who is very close to achieving enlightenment. After three days he became The Buddha, the enlightened one, and began his ministry.

The Allure of Buddhism

During his enlightenment Buddha came to several realizations which formed the underpinnings of Buddhism: the earth-bound physical body is caught up in an endless cycle of birth, death, and rebirth. In part, this cycle is perpetuated by ignorance, human cravings, clinging to the notion of humanness, and, above all, suffering. Enlightenment frees the body from these things and allows the karmic cycle to be broken and replaced with advancement into nirvana. As Buddha began his teachings, these concepts emerged as the *Four Noble Truths* of Buddhism (Smith 1994):

- Life is *dukkha* (imperfectly translated as "suffering").
- Dukkha is caused by *tanha*, i.e., ignorance, cravings, desire.
- To avoid dukkha one must overcome tanha.
- To overcome tanha one must follow The Eightfold Path.

The Eightfold Path is a set of behaviors that, according to Buddha, will allow humans to reach the hoped-for release to nirvana. The proper behavioral and ideological codes in the first four paths are (1) knowledge; (2) aspiration; (3) speech; and (4) behavior, this last offering a set of rules which should not be broken. The second four pathways include (5) livelihood, meaning one should join a monastic order for some part of one's earthly existence; (6) effort, meaning an active exertion to throw off tanha; (7) mindfulness, the mental attempt to do the same; and (8) absorption, which refers to the meditative process leading the propitiant to nirvana.

The Buddha quickly attracted followers, including his old companions, the ascetics of the forest; he soon gained over 60 followers, and these he sent out to proclaim his teachings. Many others were attracted to his message of equality among believers;

status and expensive sacrifices had no place in this new message. Some followers became monks and nuns, others lay practitioners. New Buddhists were drawn from both the elite and commoner levels of society; males, and soon after, females, could become full-fledged "renunciants" or followers of the Buddhist tradition (Hopfe and Woodward 2001; Trainor 2001a). All were attracted to the concept of compassion for all humans regardless of caste, gender, or social designation (Robinson and Johnson 1997).

The Buddha died when he was 79 or 80 years old, and the monks and nuns spread out to establish monastic communities across northeastern India and into Nepal. However, the prescription that one must give up earthly goods and join a monastic community in order to achieve enlightenment (lay practitioners could only hope to attain a higher birth in the karmic cycle) kept the religion from achieving widespread popularity much beyond the north. Thus, Hinduism remained the dominant religion among residents of South Asia, with only a minority practicing Buddhism. This might have remained the norm until today, and Hinduism might have ended up absorbing Buddhism completely, had not a Buddhist ruler come to the throne of the Mauryan Kingdom of northeastern India in the third century B.C.E. The emperor Ashoka was responsible for ensuring not only the survival of Buddhism in India for centuries, but for its spread eastward as well.

Ashoka did not insist his people convert to Buddhism, and thus Hindus and Buddhists existed side by side. Ashoka undertook three methods to spread the religion of Buddhism through India and beyond, two of which are easily documented archaeologically. One major endeavor was Ashoka's building campaign. When The Buddha died, his remains were cremated and then divided into eight parts and taken across the region to form the foundation of the eight original *stupas*, the rounded sacred buildings that house Buddhist relics (Robinson and Johnson 1997). Unlike Hindus, Buddhists did not have "temples" at which they might focus their devotion and engage in meditation and prayer. Ashoka therefore commissioned the building of stupas and pillars across his kingdom to provide a sacred place for Buddhists of each region to visit. Ashoka built these monuments in stone rather than wood, so many still stand today, in spite of later defacements by Hindus and Muslims (Willis 2001). A second undertaking included the creation of statues and images of Buddha, placed at stupas, in monastic cave sites, and other places sacred to worshippers (Barnes 1995). These statues, which may have been inspired by Alexander the Great and the Classical Greek artistic ideals he brought in the previous century, functioned not as idols to be worshipped in and of themselves, but as inspiration to follow the Four Noble Truths. The early images of Buddha showed him as emaciated and without possessions, yet meditative and at peace. To gaze upon the countenance of their religion's founder while contemplating the path they must follow helped to retain existing Buddhists and draw new adherents to the faith. Ashoka's third innovation was not in material culture but in human agency. He was responsible for sending missionaries to regions beyond India, including to Sri Lanka and Myanmar (Burma) (Hopfe and Woodward 2001). These missionaries were aided by the development of bodhisattvas, who became known as beings that had nearly achieved nirvana but had turned back to assist believers in their struggle to become enlightened. The notion that divine beings existed to help overcome the dukkha of human life served to draw even more believers to the Buddhist religion. During the centuries following Ashoka, Buddhism continued to spread toward the east, eventually making its way to Southeast Asia and beyond.

Buddhism: A Quiet Rebellion

Ironically, Buddhism advocates nonviolence, but the word *rebellion* is an appropriate one to apply to the religion's origins. Buddhism, like contemporary religions such as Jainism, arose in response to a societal situation that many in mid-first-millennium B.C.E. northern India found untenable. The confines of caste society, and the burdens of achieving Hindu moksha in what seemed an increasingly elite-friendly religion, drove many into the arms of a more forgiving and economically manageable belief system. That it later all but disappeared in the land of its birth has less to do with the religion itself and more with societal forces of the time. The legacy of Buddhism lived on, however, in regions to the north and east of the South Asian subcontinent, becoming the major religion practiced in much of Southeast Asia today.

USEFUL SOURCES

Raymond Allchin, *The Archaeology of Early Historic South Asia*, 1995
Dilip Chakrabarti, *An Archaeological History*, 1999.
Tom Lowenstein, *The Vision of the Buddha*, 1996.
Gregory Possehl, *The Indus Age: The Beginnings*, 1999.

14

FROM HUNTER-GATHERER TO EMPIRE
RELIGIONS IN SOUTHEAST ASIA

The geographical term *Southeast Asia* covers a vast area, including the modern countries of Malaysia, Indonesia, Vietnam, Laos, Cambodia, and Thailand. The discussion here centers on the region that stretches from the Red River to the Chao Phraya Delta (Figure 14.1), and southeastward to encompass the Mekong River region. Today this peninsula includes Vietnam, Thailand, Cambodia, and Laos, but numerous empires and smaller-scale cultures transcended the boundaries of these modern nations. It is a region with a rich prehistory and tantalizing ritual practices ideal for speculation.

Neolithic Hunter-Gatherers and Bronze Age Farmers

Archaeologists have discovered early sites all over Southeast Asia, but some of the most extensive information has come from the Chao Phraya River region in northern Thailand, where early sites such as Spirit Cave were occupied from about 9000 to 5500 B.C.E. (Higham 2002). Residents at Spirit Cave practiced hunting and gathering, exploited a wide range of plants and animals, and used an extensive stone tool kit. They also experimented with pottery production. Unfortunately, no burials or evidence of ritual behavior was recovered from the cave. The residents of Spirit Cave and other rock shelters in the region must have carried out activities related to their belief system while away from their homes, or in ways that do not appear in the archaeological record.

Khok Phanom Di and Life on the Water

Several thousand years after the abandonment of Spirit Cave, Khok Phanom Di, a coastal site near the Gulf of Thailand, emerged and now offers us much more evidence about ancient Southeast Asian religion. The people at Khok Phanom Di (2000–1500 B.C.E.) practiced a hunting-gathering economy, even while other regions practiced rice cultivation and metal production. The Khok Phanom Di area offered access to

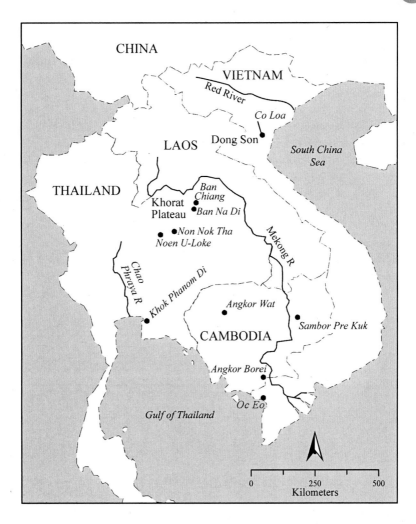

Figure 14.1. Map of sites and regions discussed in the chapter.
(*T. Edwards/S. R. Steadman*)

marine resources in the gulf, freshwater river fish and shellfish, intertidal and mangrove plants and animals, and forest areas close by. It is not surprising that these coastal residents found that the hunting-gathering life entirely suited their needs.

Some abrupt environmental changes affected the region, and these are reflected in the Khok Phanom Di mortuary rituals. Numerous interments were discovered under domestic areas at the site. In the earliest mortuary phases (MP 1–2), Khok Phanom Di people exploited the marine environment and hunted pig and macaque in the intertidal mangrove forest (Higham 2002); heavy upper-body musculature evidenced on male burial remains suggests men were frequent canoers and hunters. At death both males and females were buried covered in red ocher and wrapped in a shroud; burial goods consisted of pottery, shell disc beads, and other shell jewelry (including exotic cowrie shells in one burial), jewelry made of fish vertebrae, and tools such as stone adzes and burnishing stones for pottery (Figure 14.2). In spite of a rich food supply, residents suffered high infant-mortality rates due to an inherited blood disease that caused a deadly anemia.

Halfway through the 500-year occupation (in the MP 3–4 periods), the environment began to change, and the Khok Phanom Di residents no longer had easy access to marine resources. Instead they had to rely on freshwater foods and hunt more regularly in the forest lands (Higham 1996). Their food supply had altered, and so too did their food-acquisition techniques. Burial goods no longer featured shell ornaments, but rather granite hoes and shell knives used for harvesting grasses. Men and women received different burial goods, a distinction not found in earlier phases. Decorated turtle carapaces accompanied men, while women received clay anvils, used in pottery production. One final difference from earlier periods was a much lower infant-mortality rate, perhaps due to different food sources and daily activities that kept parents closer to home and available for more constant child care.

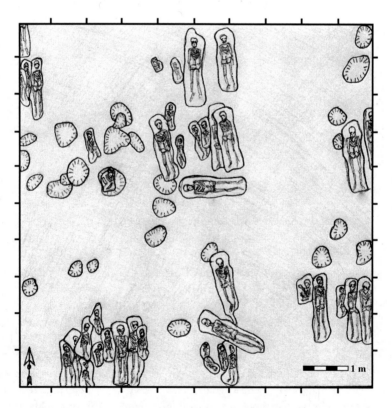

Figure 14.2. Sketch plan of Khok Phanom Di MP 2 burials. (*R. Jennison*)

In the final, MP 5 period, the environment shifted back to favor a marine-based subsistence. Burials became extremely wealthy, no longer featuring agricultural tools, but rather shell jewelry, ceramics, and pottery production materials, and other exotic, possibly imported goods such as ivory. Burials were individual, rather than clustered as in earlier phases. Women as well as men received significant grave goods. Musculature evidence on the hands of female skeletons indicates women may have been the potters.

The evidence from the Khok Phanom Di mortuary sequence is rich in both physical data derived from the skeletal material and economic data gleaned from the burial goods. During the MP 1–3 phases, residents suffered high infant-mortality rates and ate marine-based foods; men spent long hours in canoes, hunting and probably trading shells and marine resources with inland and other estuary neighbors. By MP 4, a shift in the environment to freshwater resources and rice cultivation created healthier infants and an emphasis on ceramic production; ceramics replaced shells as a major trade item (Higham 1996). All these data are supported by the evidence, but what can we say about the Khok Phanom Di belief system?

We can begin by relying on the premise that their beliefs would have coincided strongly with their economic pursuits, which, of course, were related to their original marine environment. We can infer a belief in animistic spirits who oversaw hunting in the mangrove forest and fishing and water-related activities. Perhaps both men and women collected marine-based foods; therefore both sexes received similar treatment at death. However, by MP 4, these spirits of the marine world had failed their believers, and the spirits of the land and forest became more prominent. The power of these land-based spirits was demonstrated by the fact that children survived more frequently; burial goods recognizing farming and ceramic production perhaps commemorated this power. By then, women and men had different jobs; women's pottery production and its role in the economy are highlighted in their rich burials. Further speculation is impossible, but we can be certain that over the course of the 500-year habitation of Khok Phanom Di, residents experienced abrupt changes in their ecological setting and economy; it is likely these environmental changes found their way into the belief system as well.

Farmers in the Bronze Age

Nomadic hunters and gatherers of Neolithic Southeast Asia began to settle into communities based on rice cultivation between 4500 and 4000 B.P. Around this time, people speaking Austronesian languages, who were also practicing rice cultivation, spread southward from Taiwan and southern China. In the Southeast Asian peninsula, they created new language dialects, culturally distinct communities, and a lively network of farming and animal husbandry (Higham 2002). Over the succeeding centuries, additional migration created the rich complex of cultures, languages, and religions that characterize Southeast Asia today.

Neolithic rice cultivators made use of the major rivers for trade networks and communication routes. These populations began developing various crafts, including a significant metallurgical industry, drawing on skills possibly derived from southern China. A few hundred years after the emergence of Neolithic rice-farming communities, bronze production began, ushering in the Bronze Age, beginning shortly after 2000 B.C.E. and lasting until ca. 500 B.C.E., when the region moved into the Iron Age (Higham 1989).

Many Bronze Age sites are located on the Khorat Plateau of northeastern Thailand, just south of the upper Mekong River. Sites such as Ban Chiang, Non Nok Tha, and Ban Na Di, inhabited between ca. 1600 and 800 B.C.E., offer significant archaeological data. Residents settled on slightly elevated ground near regions suitable for rice and grain farming; access to fresh water was crucial. Domesticated animals included dog, pig, chicken, and cattle; residents hunted wild pig, deer, and other animals, and supplemented their diets with fish and turtle (Higham 1996). The combination of a wet climate and wooden building materials has resulted in a nearly complete lack of architectural data. However, as was the case at Khok Phanom Di, burial evidence has given insights into societal structure and ritual behavior.

Post holes and the presence of hearths over burials indicate that the cemetery may have been located under the village. Burials tended to be clustered and included adult men and women, children, and infants. Some clusters had burials laid one on top of another, indicating later burial on top of "ancestors" (Higham 2002). Many of the burial goods were items reflecting daily activities, including ceramics, clay anvils, stone adzes, metal tools, spindle whorls, crucibles and moulds, as well as shell, metal, and stone jewelry. There was little distinction in awarding grave goods to males versus females, but different burial clusters appear to be "richer" or "poorer," indicating some wealth stratification in these Bronze Age cultures.

Items indicative of mortuary ritual include animal bones, animal figurines, and pots with food remains, found in both adult and child burials at all of the Khorat Plateau sites. Child burial 8 at Non Nok Tha contained three pots; the rear limbs and jaw of a pig were placed on the child's chest, and the skeleton of an adult dog lay at the child's feet (Higham 2002). Burial 14 at the same site contained a child covered by a pigskin shroud upon which were laid smashed pots, creating a blanket of sherds. Burial goods included four pots, shell beads, an entire pig and remains of a second, and the forelimb of a cow (Higham 2002). Burials at Non Nok Tha and other Bronze Age sites included chicken skeletons, ox skulls, deer antlers, and fish bones; one infant at Ban Na Di was interred under a crocodile-skin shroud. Far less common were clay animal figurines, usually cattle, but deer and elephant representations were also found. These tended to occur in the graves deemed more "wealthy," based on the number of items and their relative value.

Most archaeologists working in this region and period concur that the clustering of burials, and the sequentiality of placement indicate the existence of kin groups, possibly unilinear in descent (it has been suggested that matrilineal descent was the norm at Khok Phanom Di [Higham and Bannanurag 1990]). Furthermore, there appears to be some economic stratification at these sites; some burials received more substantial grave goods than others. The placement of food within the graves could represent offerings for the deceased in the afterlife, or remnants of ritual feasting at the time of burial. It is also possible that the numerous empty vessels may have stood, symbolically, for food offerings (Parker Pearson 1999), or they may have been used for the burial feast and then placed in the graves. All of these interpretations suggest that Bronze Age inhabitants believed in venerating ancestors, at least at the time of death. Should settlement data ever become more ubiquitous, the investigating archaeologist would be wise to keep an eye out for household altars or other indicators of ancestor veneration by kin descendants. A final note relates to the animal figurines, uncommon but present nonetheless. Such items may have been used as toys, or decoration, or for other secular functions. However, the presence of animal remains not intended for consumption (e.g., deer antlers), and animal-skin shrouds, combined with the occasional figurine, bring to mind the notion of totemistic ancestors. The importance of animals in later Asian religions, whether as totems, spirits, or gods, may well be traced back to the earliest farmers responsible for domesticating them in the first place.

The Arrival of Hinduism and Buddhism in Southeast Asia

In the last centuries of the first millennium B.C.E., residents in coastal settlements began to engage in longer-distance trade, especially with India and China. At this time the overland Silk Road, a trade route stretching from China to the Mediterranean, developed southern extensions into Southeast Asia.

Peoples, crafts, and ideologies accompanied the goods traveling along these trade routes. In the early centuries of contact, Indians began appearing in Southeast Asian contexts; one is even credited with founding the first Southeast Asian empire. By this time Hinduism had entered its Classical period (see Chapter 13), with a fully developed pantheon, structured rituals, and the practice of building temples for worship of the deities. Archaeological and textual evidence indicates that elements of the Hindu religion were appearing in Southeast Asian contexts by the early centuries C.E. Hinduism, by this time an ancient religion, possessed an extensive pantheon into which local Southeast Asian deities could be inserted; they appeared as avatars of existing gods or as new deities with mythologies fashioned to connect them to Shiva, Vishnu, Brahma, or others (Snellgrove 2004). Although a relatively new religion, Buddhism was also making its way into Southeast Asia.

The Mauryan King Ashoka, who ruled northeastern India in the mid-third century B.C.E. (see Chapter 13), had converted to Buddhism and engaged in a concerted effort to spread the word of his religion. He sent out Buddhist missionaries, first to Sri Lanka and later to Central Asia, and possibly as far out as Southeast Asia (Trainor 2001b). Solid evidence of Buddhism in Southeast Asia, however, is not documented until the Funan Empire period (discussed below), sometime during the first centuries C.E. Silk Road trade between Sri Lanka and Southeast Asia (via maritime routes) was surely a main mechanism by which both Hinduism and Buddhism arrived in the Southeast Asian peninsula. By the fifth century C.E., Buddhist *stupas* (sacred buildings) and stone carvings of the Buddha were present in Southeast Asian settlements (Higham 2002). However, religious iconography indicates that the practice of Hinduism was far more prevalent than Buddhism and remained so until the twelfth century C.E.

The Iron Age and the Rise of Empires

From the Red River Delta to the Khorat Plateau, extraordinary metalcraft, favorable agricultural conditions, and access to well-used trade routes led to the development of iron technology and the roots of what would later be the empires of Southeast Asia. Though preservation is poor for both architectural and human remains in this area, extensive cemeteries and their goods have offered some information on early chiefdoms such as the Dong Son culture.

Settlements in these regions were built as a series of ramparts surrounded by moats. One Dong Son settlement, Co Loa, was at least 600 hectares in size, indicating a significant population existed there (Higham 2002). As many as 2,000 people may have inhabited Khorat Plateau sites such as Ban Chiang and Ban Na Di (Higham 1996). Settlements were located at strategic points to control important natural resources, such as salt flats and metal ore sources. Burial evidence from Dong Son and Khorat Plateau sites shows increasing wealth differentiation among residents. In Dong Son sites, some individuals were buried in wooden coffins fashioned from boats and were provided with very fine grave goods, such as metal drums, jewelry, and weapons (Figure 14.3). Other burials held only basic tools from daily work activities. Dong Son ceramics and metal drums bear scenes of daily life and episodes of warfare. Khorat Plateau sites revealed individuals buried with weapons embedded in their bones. Archaeologists believe this was a period defined by warfare in which rival leaders sought to increase the size of their chiefdoms.

Stratigraphically excavated burials at Noen U-Loke on the Khorat Plateau show an interesting trend in mortuary ritual. Five phases of burials (MP 1–5) date from 300/200 B.C.E. to 300 C.E. or somewhat later (Higham 2002). In the earliest phases (MP 1–2), coinciding with the beginning of the Iron Age, burials contained food-related offerings including complete pig skeletons and dog bones. This practice, also found in earlier Bronze Age sites on the plateau, may have been related to ancestor recognition and veneration. By MP 3, a new mortuary practice began: deposition of white rice in quantities substantial enough to completely cover the dead and partially fill the grave. This practice may be related to the present-day ritual of making rice offerings to the spirits (Higham 2002). Adding rice to the burial at Noen U-Loke, then, may indicate that non-ancestral spirits had become as important as the ancestors. By MP 4, burials no longer included the placement of animal-based food, and by MP 5 rice was no longer present. One possible interpretation of such changes in mortuary practice can be linked to increasing complexity and the development of chiefdoms. A decrease in the importance of ancestors, followed by a complete break with ancestor veneration, would coincide with an increase in complexity and the importance of individual societal position vis-à-vis family social status and economic standing. Rituals recognizing non-ancestral spirits may have become commonplace, occurring in temples on a regular basis. Public areas of worship would have been the destination of rice or other offerings for spirits and/or deities, alleviating the need for rice offerings in burials. It is not long before the belief systems practiced in these Iron Age chiefdoms became the basis of large-scale empires.

The Emergence of Empires

The earliest documented empire in Southeast Asia is known as the Funan Empire. The Funan state is centered in the Mekong Delta region of Vietnam and Cambodia. In the mid-third century C.E. a Chinese emperor sent two cultural ambassadors to Southeast Asia on a fact-finding mission. There they encountered the Funan trading empire founded, according to sources, by an Indian man in the first century C.E. The existence of a state-level society in this region has been confirmed by archaeological excavations at the sites of Oc Eo and Angkor Borei, two settlements linked by a canal. Oc Eo was surrounded by ramparts and moats; travel within the city itself and to outlying settlements was accomplished by canal boats (Higham 2002). Artifacts from Oc Eo, settled sometime in the late first century B.C.E., demonstrate that residents were trading with the Roman Empire to the west, the Chinese Empire to the north, and were also linked to India and other regions on the Asian continent. At least one temple stood in the city of Oc Eo, but its location under a modern temple has hindered investigation into the nature of the Funan temple's function.

Angkor Borei, founded as early as the fifth century B.C.E., may have been the main Funan center, using Oc Eo as its port city. Angkor Borei later became part of the

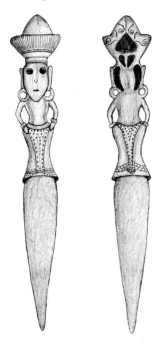

Figure 14.3. Example of Dong Son bronze dagger with elegant hilt. (*R. Jennison*)

Khmer Empire (see below), and it is only recently that pre-Khmer periods at the site have been investigated. A legend associated with this area of Cambodia recounts the story of a female ruler who was conquered by a man from the west (possibly India) who then married her and founded a kingdom (Stark 2003). Thus the first known Southeast Asian kingdom may well have begun at Angkor Borei, as a result of foreign influence. The religion practiced by the Funan culture is still poorly understood. Residents were still burying their dead with grave goods, but cremation had become a regular practice (Stark 2003). One interesting hint about Funan religion comes from a few inscriptions containing verses in Sanskrit and some small statuary and other relics that are indicative of both Hindu and Buddhist belief systems (Glover 1998; Stark 2003). Whether or not the "Indian founder" of the Funan Empire brought his religion with him, it is certain that both Hinduism and Buddhism arrived in Southeast Asia via the extensive trade network that was the nerve center of the Funan economy.

By the sixth century C.E. the Kingdom of Chenla was established, but the transition from Funan to Chenla is not clearly understood. Chinese sources suggest that a people speaking the Khmer language conquered the Funan and established a state called Chenla (Snellgrove 2004). Sambor Prei Kuk was a major Chenla city, possibly its capital; it featured moats, ramparts, and temples. The settlement was divided into three areas, each with a large sanctuary or temple. These temples were built of bricks rather than wood, allowing much improved preservation. Temples were set on raised platforms, on which a single walled room contained the statue of the deity (Higham 2002). The statue appears to have consisted primarily of a *lingus* (stone pedestal) reminiscent of Hindu phallic representations of Shiva. Relief decorations on the walls of the temples display motifs and figures also found on contemporary Hindu sacred buildings in India (Higham 2002); there is little doubt that Hinduism is well ensconced in Southeast Asia by the time of the Chenla Kingdom. Inscriptions further document this fact by detailing the names of Chenla rulers who generally took the name of a local or Hindu deity and then attached the affix *varman*, meaning "protected by" in Sanskrit (e.g., "Bhavavarman," and "Isanavarman").

However, Hinduism was not the only, or even the predominant, religion practiced in the Chenla culture. Hinduism appears to have been the primary state religion; temples at Angkor Borei feature Hindu motifs and worship, and rulers presented themselves as devotees of Hindu deities. Buddhism, although known and apparently practiced, was very much a minor religion at this time; the major state deities appear to have been Shiva, Vishnu, Krishna, and Rama (Snellgrove 2004). Textual evidence, however, reveals that non-elites did not necessarily practice Hinduism. The majority of people living outside the major centers were farmers who bore Khmer rather than Sanskrit names. Farmers were required to make "donations"—perhaps, more accurately, taxation duty—to fund the building of local temples, which were dedicated to either Hindu or local deities. Regional leaders, who carried the title *pon* attached to their names, used these donations to construct and equip the temples as well as to build up surplus food for redistribution. Chenla records indicate that in these outlying regions, wealth and power were transmitted through the female line

(Vickery 1998), suggesting that matrilineality may have been the norm in Southeast Asia. Many local female deities received offerings and temples were built to honor them; texts describe veneration of ancestors as well, indicating this ancient practice was still carried out, at least in individual homes.

While Hinduism and Buddhism were practiced as state religions in the Chenla Empire, most people continued to practice their indigenous beliefs, including worship of local gods and goddesses and ancestor veneration. Though most ancestral shrines and small local temples were built of wood and are therefore lost, written documents make it clear that they were a norm in Chenla settlements. While some people may have converted to the "new" religions, it is probable that many practiced their traditional beliefs while also publicly recognizing Hinduism, and possibly Buddhism, as state religions. Hinduism as an all-encompassing religion may have absorbed local deities into the Hindu pantheon, binding the two belief systems into one. Buddhism's flexibility in allowing most types of worship to suffice as methods toward enlightenment would make this religion easy to ensconce in Southeast Asia as well. Thus, during the Chenla period, non-elites were careful to make their public and required offerings to the Hindu city temples and attend public ceremonies and rituals; in their own villages and homes, however, it appears that traditional worship of age-old deities, and lineage ancestors, was alive and well.

Chenla was only the most powerful of many fifth- to eighth-century Southeast Asian kingdoms that existed in a continual state of friction with one another, vying over control of lands and people. Each probably practiced its local and Hindu religions, with some presence of Buddhism as well. Thus, people across the Southeast Asian landscape were familiar with Hinduism and Buddhism, and probably treated the deities of both with reverence, while maintaining their own indigenous belief systems. One subtle change in attitude and practice comes to us from textual evidence. The title *pon* for regional leaders became less common in the later seventh century, and by the early eighth century it had been replaced by the title *mratan* (Higham 2001). This Khmer term could only be conferred by a king, suggesting that regional leaders no longer arose from within the ranks of their home populations, but rather were appointed by the ruler; the conclusion from this is that kings were seeking to concentrate more and more power into their own hands by controlling the landscape and the population through a cadre of trusted and hand-picked mratan. These kings continued to allow their subjects to practice local religions, although this liberal religious policy came to a halt with the establishment of the Khmer Empire in the early ninth century.

The Khmer Empire: Royal Religion and the Power of Kings

In 802 C.E., Jayavarman II gained the throne of a small Khmer kingdom in central Cambodia. He consolidated lands into a single empire that eventually stretched from the Gulf of Thailand in the west, through much of southeast Thailand including the

Khorat Plateau, to the southern reaches of Laos. Khmer kings built regional centers, water works and causeways, palaces, hundreds of major temples, and many more smaller ones. Most of these buildings were constructed of stone; work was carried out by the king's subjects who received little compensation for their labor.

Khmer society was divided into a two-class structure of elites and commoners, each with various internal divisions. The elite class included the ruling family, large-scale landowners, and high administrators. In the commoner group was the majority of the population, including farmers, artisans, small-scale landowners, merchants, and slaves. Those assigned to religious duties, who were not considered high administrators, were also in the commoner class (Stark 2004). The Khmer Empire depended on a rice-growing economy, supplemented by trade, taxation of regional polities, and military expansionism. Most important, however, was the surplus from rice farming, which explains the substantial investment the Khmer kings made in building water transport and storage systems (canals, dikes, moats, and reservoirs). This hydrological system, supplemented by the natural rainfall, enabled substantial rice production; it also freed a large portion of the farming population to act as *corvée* laborers (unpaid workers laboring at the behest of the king). Elite landowners who desired to build a temple or other monumental structure directed commoners to undertake the building as part of their duty to the landowner and the king. Commoners, including farmers and slaves, may well have been engaged in building projects as well as in trying to keep their rice fields intact through much of the year. Artisans, especially stoneworkers, found themselves applying their skills to enhance the façade of temples in service to the king; their artistic abilities served not to enhance their own economic standing, but rather impoverished them as they toiled for free on royal projects. One major reason why the population appeared willing to submit to the demands of the king can be found in the religious belief system established by the Khmer rulers.

Deified Kings

Jayavarman II's accession to the throne is recorded on a stela discovered in a Khmer temple. Apparently he installed himself in the capital city of a small kingdom, and from there he launched military campaigns to consolidate much of the region under his own rule. By 802 he had amassed a large empire and established his rule at a place called Hariharalaya (Stark 2004). He commissioned a ceremonial public installation of himself as king of the Khmer Empire. What is important about this event is that Jayavarman II underwent the traditional "crowning" of the king by a Brahmin priest, a process undertaken by earlier kings of the various regions, but in a parallel rite he was also made "the god who is king." This second ritual advanced Jayavarman II's status beyond that of merely being "protected" by the god(s), to that of *representing* the god.

As already noted, Hinduism functioned as the state religion of many Southeast Asian kingdoms. In many cases the focus of Hindu worship was the god Shiva, most often represented by the phallic stone pedestal, the lingus. He was thus often called Shiva-Linga. Jayavarman II reinforced this state god and the worship of him throughout the kingdom; the new ceremony that linked Jayavarman II with Shiva-Linga was intended to convey the oneness of human and god and Jayavarman II's earthly representation of Shiva-Linga.

Jayavarman II took his personal *Devaraja* (translated "god-king," a small Shiva-Linga stone) wherever he traveled, again emphasizing his oneness with Shiva (Snellgrove 2001). The role of the *Shiva-Linga Devaraja* is to keep the Khmer people safe from attack and from any other disasters, natural or human-wrought. The linking of Jayavarman II with Shiva-Linga Devaraja required that the people worship not only Shiva, but the king as well. Should he become displeased or suffer in any way through their neglect, then disaster would certainly strike. By acceding to Jayavarman II's every wish, the people felt assured that he, in concert with Shiva-Linga, would keep balance and harmony in their universe.

Once Jayavarman II had deified the Khmer kingship, his successors followed suit. Most continued the linkage with Shiva, but a few chose Vishnu. The deification of the king, and the threat hanging over the people if the divine king was not properly worshipped and obeyed, allowed the Khmer kings to accomplish astonishing building projects. The rulers following Jayavarman II commissioned projects that glorified the king, the god, and the empire. In addition to reservoirs and canals, it became the norm to build a temple to the deified royal ancestors (of which Jayavarman II was one), a palace, and a temple that served as the current king's mausoleum at his death. This temple became the holiest of temples during the king's reign in that it held the lingus representing the god with whom the king was linked. The temple mausoleum was a symbolic representative of Mount Meru, the home of the gods in Hindu mythology; a reservoir surrounding the temple symbolized the sacred waters around Mount Meru. The message, then, was that at his death the king went to reside on Mount Meru with the rest of the gods, a compelling reminder to the people that the king was indeed divine. The entire temple and palace complex was usually covered with stone reliefs portraying scenes of everyday Khmer life and images from Hindu mythology, combining the king's role as earthly ruler and deity.

The best-known and largest temple complex is Angkor Wat, and the largest and most elaborate capital city is nearby Angkor Thom. King Suryavarman II, who came to the Khmer throne in 1113 C.E., expanded the Khmer Empire to its greatest extent; he began construction of Angkor Wat early in his reign (Figure 14.4). He built a number of stone temples dedicated to both Shiva and Vishnu, but Suryavarman II was thoroughly devoted to Vishnu as his personal god. Angkor Wat, meant to serve as Suryavarman II's tomb, is built on an artificial rise and surrounded by a 200-meter-wide moat. It also served as the main state temple dedicated to Vishnu. It is laid out on a square plan, with two lower levels that contain beautiful stone carvings depicting Hindu sacred stories and events, as well as scenes from Suryavarman II's kingly duties and military exploits. Inscriptions relate his deeds, his work to keep the Khmer Empire healthy and rich, and his punishments of those defying him or his counterpart Vishnu. The highest platform contains the actual edifice, a temple with five towers, the highest representing Mount Meru and the lower four symbolizing smaller peaks in the

Figure 14.4. Photo of Angkor Wat.
(*Shirley Hu/Dreamstime.com*)

mountain complex. Suryavarman II was buried in the central tower, where the lingus dedicated to Vishnu resided. The builders, architects, and artisans who created Angkor Wat are unknown to us. Their work is not signed, nor are their names recorded. The focus was on the king and the creation of a beautiful home for the Hindu gods. Whether the creators of these beautiful temples were rewarded in any way is unclear, but their labor and expertise, to be given regularly and without complaint, was certainly expected.

Jayavarman VII took the throne in 1181 C.E. and immediately began construction of a new capital known as Angkor Thom. This city was surrounded by a wall nearly 13 kilometers in length, with a 160-meter-wide moat filled with crocodiles. Angkor Thom, laid out according to the cardinal compass points, housed Jayavarman VII's mausoleum, which also served as the royal temple called the *Bayon* (the royal palace). The roads into Angkor Thom were flanked by statues of gods and demons; many of the statues and carvings adorning Angkor Thom were once covered in gold or silver. The many towers of the Bayon show a face gazing out over the countryside. Most interpret this as Jayavarman VII's countenance, a reminder to the people of his power over their fortunes (Figure 14.5). In addition to Angkor Thom, Jayavarman VII sponsored many other building projects across his kingdom, including hospitals, shrines and temples, and a large temple dedicated to his father. All of this was accomplished by the people in their service to king and gods. Although Jayavarman VII and his predecessors built reservoirs, hospitals, and other structures

Figure 14.5. Photo of Bayon at Angkor Thom. (*Timurk/Dreamstime.com*)

that were overtly for "the people," the benefits derived from all royal endeavors served to strengthen and enrich the Khmer elites, on the backs of the common population.

Jayavarman VII, unlike his predecessors, practiced Buddhism. However, his city and mausoleum are covered with scenes from the Hindu cosmology, in like fashion to earlier temples and buildings, accompanied by his kingly exploits. A few small Buddha images can be found in the corners of some galleries in Angkor Thom, but these are rare in comparison with the overwhelming Hindu theme (Snellgrove 2001). This might seem strange given that Jayavarman VII was clearly a devotee of Buddhism. Several interpretations for the lack of Buddhist imagery in his capital city and royal temple can be suggested. It is entirely possible that the artisans required to decorate Angkor Thom simply did not know how to represent Buddhist themes and therefore did not do so. An equally likely possibility is that Jayavarman VII, an astute and successful king, knew that the population was accustomed to worshipping Hindu gods and the king as their divine representative; thus, reminding the Khmer people that he was a Buddhist may have weakened his position of power and control over their labor. Serving both the Hindu religion and a personal devotion to Buddhism may have seemed the best action. He could retain the reverence of the people while also acknowledging a small but growing devotion to Buddhism in Southeast Asia.

The Collapse of the Khmer Empire

Jayavarman VII's belief in Buddhism legitimated the religion, and thereafter it gained a foothold in Southeast Asia, particularly among the Khmer population. In fact, the growing popularity of Buddhism is shown by the actions of Jayavarman VIII, who came to power in 1243. He ordered the Buddhist-style faces and any other Buddhist elements of Angkor Thom defaced, and replaced with Shiva-Linga, in an effort to reassert the Hindu religion in the minds of his people (Snellgrove 2001). But by the late thirteenth century, under a king named Indravarman III, Buddhism became the state religion, and texts suggest that the ceremony linking the king with a Hindu deity no longer took place. It was under Jayavarman VIII, the last Hindu Khmer king, that the final major building project took place. He built a temple near Angkor Thom dedicated to Vishnu. After Jayavarman VIII's reign, the Khmer Empire entered economic and political decline. Eventually it was overcome by more powerful Thai neighbors in the mid-fifteenth century.

There is never one cause for the collapse of an empire as vast and powerful as the Khmer. That the neighboring Thai state was growing in power was certainly one factor that contributed to the downfall, though the Thai attack and defeat of the Khmers in the mid-fifteenth century was only the final straw in an entire haystack of problems. Jayavarman VII's extensive building campaign may have strained the royal coffers beyond their capacity, using up wealth that was needed for other imperial agendas, such as maintaining the military and the extensive water system. If the water reservoirs and canals were not maintained and siltation occurred, crops could not be irrigated and would fail, causing food shortages (Stark 2004). Though not the single cause of the Khmer collapse, concern about providing sufficient food to the people, not to mention the soldiers, would put a ruler and his people on edge. The combination of all of these factors would certainly be sufficient to cause the slow and steady collapse of an empire.

What cannot be ignored, however, is the role religion may have played, not only in the power wielded by Khmer kings, but in the waning of that power. In pre-Khmer times, under the Chenla dynasty, Hinduism became the state religion, but people continued to practice their indigenous beliefs, including ancestor veneration. With Jayavarman II and the deification of the Khmer kings, this balance seems to have changed. Hinduism not only continued as the state religion, but was imposed onto the lives of the commoners. No matter where they turned, there was a Hindu shrine or temple at which they might (must?) worship, and certainly they contributed, by tax or labor, to its building and decoration. The Khmer version of Hinduism became the pervasive belief system, with the deified king at its head; any ancestor veneration or local religion was clearly secondary to the religion sanctioned by the state. It was under these conditions that the Khmer kings were able to command a labor force capable of building thousands of temples, palaces, public buildings, canals, and other water works, for very little return compensation except the assurance that the king and gods would be pleased and the state and cosmological universe would remain balanced and strong. Shortly after the zenith of this building campaign, under Jayavarman VII in the late twelfth century, the empire began its two-century descent toward disintegration.

It cannot be a coincidence that at the same time as Buddhism became a widely accepted religion and Khmer kings ratified it as the new state religion, the Khmer Empire ceased its building campaign and began its decline. Less emphasis on the military and more interest in peaceful trade contacts became the agenda in the last two centuries of the Khmer Empire. Kings who were simply humans, not gods, did not command the people to build temples, monasteries, or palaces. The reason for this might be twofold. Buddhist values of equality, respect, and nonviolence, internalized by king and commoner alike, may have made practices such as corvée labor and forced taxation abhorrent to the Khmer rulers. At the same time, kings who were no longer gods held no sway over the very universe in which the people lived; they had lost their ability to command free labor from unwilling farmers and artisans. Had the Khmer kings been able to fend off attacks from Thailand and elsewhere, rectify problems with the water system, and rebuild their stocks of wealth through legitimate taxation, a Buddhist-based Khmer Empire might still exist in Cambodia today. However, the practices of a regime that used religion as a whip to control a population, that deified its kings and held royal and divine power over the heads of the commoners, and who used this power to strip the kingdom of every vestige of its wealth and security did not leave a legacy strong enough for the continuance of an empire no longer ruled by fear of the king and his gods. Thus, the great Khmer Empire is known to us only through the texts, inscriptions, and the great stone monuments built on the backs of a people who, through their rejection of one religion and acceptance of another, simultaneously broke free from royal control and initiated the death of an empire.

Useful Sources

Michael Coe, *Angkor and the Khmer Civilization*, 2003.
Ian Glover and Peter Bellwood (eds.), *Southeast Asia*, 2005.
Charles Higham and Rachanie Thosarat, *Prehistoric Thailand*, 1998.

PART VI

RELIGIONS IN AFRICA AND THE MIDDLE EAST

15

RELIGION AND EMPIRE IN EGYPT AND GREAT ZIMBABWE

Ancient Egypt is a favorite topic for those interested in early civilizations and ancient religions. We know an extraordinary amount about the Egyptians, due to a long history of archaeological exploration and the many texts and illustrations detailing Egyptian life. The empires of sub-Saharan Africa are somewhat less known, but no less impressive. One of these is Great Zimbabwe, a kingdom that flourished in the twelfth–fifteenth centuries C.E.

Ancient Egypt

Northeastern Africa is dominated by desert landscape cut vertically by the Nile River, which flows over 6,000 kilometers from its origin to empty into the Mediterranean Sea. The only arable land is along the Nile floodplain, a 10- to 20-kilometer-wide ribbon of land that stretches from the Nile Delta in Lower Egypt (the north) to Upper Egypt (in southern Egypt) and into Nubia (in northern Sudan). Rich Nile mud was deposited in spring floods, making this extremely fertile soil for cultivation.

Dates in the Egyptian chronology are still debated, but most agree on the divisions of the most ancient periods into five categories: Predynastic, Protodynastic, Early Dynastic, Old Kingdom and Middle Kingdom. A sixth period, known as the New Kingdom, takes history down nearly to the end of the second millennium B.C.E. These periods, except for Predynastic Egypt, feature sequentially numbered dynasties from 0 to 20 (see Table 15.1). Interspersed are "Intermediate Periods" during which time Egypt experienced difficulties, including invasions, dynastic collapse, or other ill fortunes.

TABLE 15.1. EGYPTIAN CHRONOLOGYY

Period	Dynasties	Dates	Pharaohs Mentioned in Chapter
Predynastic	N/A	ca. 5000–3100 B.C.E.	
Proto/Early Dynastic	0–2	ca. 3000–2750 B.C.E.	Narmer (Menes?)/ Menes/Aha (?); Djet
Old Kingdom	3–6	ca. 2750–2250 B.C.E.	Sneferu; Khufu; Khafre; Menkaure
First Intermediate Period	7–11	ca. 2250–2025 B.C.E.	
Middle Kingdom	11–13	ca. 2025–1630 B.C.E.	
Second Intermediate Period	14–17	ca. 1630–1540 B.C.E.	
New Kingdom	18–20	ca. 1539–1075 B.C.E.	Ramesses III

Predynastic Egypt

In the sixth millennium B.C.E., inhabitants hunted and gathered along the Nile banks, and by roughly 5000 B.C.E., small communities of food producers had emerged, growing wheat and barley and keeping domesticated animals (Hoffman 1991). Over the next millennium, settlements multiplied and expanded, and small chiefdoms or petty kingdoms developed in what is commonly called "Predynastic" Egypt. Data from this early period is minimal, since most settlements, located in the Nile floodplain, have been either washed away or lie under meters of alluvial deposit. The majority of information about Predynastic Egypt comes from cemeteries, as these were typically located away from the farming belt in slightly higher locales. Such data suggests that Upper Egypt, south of the delta, was experiencing some political consolidation by the early fourth millennium.

Leaders at towns such as Hierakonpolis and Naqada were vying for control of lands and people, but these may not have been the only regions in conflict (Figure 15.1). Upper Egypt at this time may have been divided into a series of petty chiefdoms or small kingdoms, each with a ruler anxious to expand his territories. The political situation in Lower Egypt, especially the delta region, is more difficult to track since most sites are buried under meters of Nile mud. Material culture excavated at the site of Buto in the delta region suggests residents interacted with the Levant and Upper Egypt (Davies and Friedman 1999). Whether Buto and other Lower Egypt settlements were political polities or kingdoms is less certain.

The status of Upper Egypt in the Predynastic period has been more fleshed out, based on data from excavations at Hierakonpolis. This settlement (ca. 4000–2650

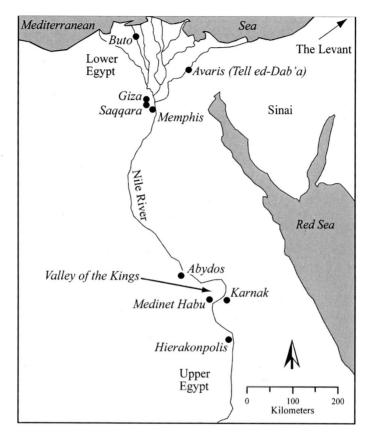

Figure 15.1. Map of ancient Egyptian sites and regions. (*T. Edwards*)

B.C.E.) was one of the first urban centers in ancient Egypt; it featured neighborhoods inhabited by craftsmen and merchants, farmers and administrators (Shaw 2003). A temple structure stood in the town's center, with an oval courtyard laid out in front of it; the temple consisted of three rooms fronted by four massive wooden pillars, perhaps obtained from as far away as Lebanon (Davies and Friedman 1999; Friedman 1996). A pole in the center of the oval courtyard may have featured a statue of the falcon god, later known as Horus, to which the city was dedicated. Hierakonpolis demonstrates that even prior to the founding of Pharaonic Egypt, temple-based religion was an important part of Egyptian society.

Hierakonpolis is important not only for the information it provides about Pre-dynastic Egyptian political and religious structure, but also for the discovery of the Narmer Palette. This slate palette shows King Narmer on both sides engaged in battle with various foes. In each he triumphs and dons the crown of the region, Upper Egypt on one side and Lower Egypt on the other. The Upper Egyptian crown is a white cone-shaped headpiece, while the Lower Egyptian crown is red with a protruding frontal symbol. In Pharaonic Egypt, the pharaoh wore these two as a "double crown," symbolizing his rule over Upper and Lower Egypt. Accompanying Narmer on the palette is a falcon with a papyrus plant in its talons, a symbol of Egypt and its people. The entire scene suggests that a king of Hierakonpolis, aided by his patron god, Horus the falcon, succeeded in uniting Upper and Lower Egypt into one kingdom. Narmer (in early scholarship thought to have actually been a ruler known as Menes), the king ancient Egyptians considered responsible for the unification of Egypt, was the last king in what archaeologists call Dynasty 0.

Early Dynastic Egypt

The first king to rule after Narmer was known as Aha ("Fighter"; some now identify Aha with Menes, seeing Narmer as having preceded this ruler). Aha, founder of the first Egyptian dynasty, moved the capital of the new united empire to Memphis in order to seat power at a point where the two regions intersected. However, due to the shifting Nile channel and alluvial and aeolian deposits, the first Egyptian capital city still rests under meters of overburden. Some information about the first dynasty comes from Abydos, where early kings, including Dynasty 0 rulers, were buried. Abydos was considered very sacred in ancient Egypt, particularly since it was dedicated to Osiris, god of the underworld. Kings selected Abydos as their burial site in Dynasties 1–2; in Dynasty 3, pharaohs began to build the pyramids for which Egypt is so famous.

These Dynasty 1–2 tombs were entirely underground. They consisted of a large room that held the deceased ruler and multitudes of material goods that would be needed in the next life. Flanking the main tomb were subsidiary tombs, much smaller in size, in which the king's servants and administrators, and possibly family members, were buried, sacrificed by poisoning at his death (Galvin 2005). Earth was then mounded over the complex, still in a subterranean structure, so that little was visible on the surface. Near the tombs were, remarkably, fourteen wooden boats, ranging from 60 to 75 feet in length. These were viable boats that could have sailed the Nile but were instead buried with Dynasty 1 pharaohs. Whether the boats were meant to ferry the kings in their afterlife or were there for symbolic reasons has yet to be discovered.

Abydos burials demonstrate that even in early dynastic Egypt, rulers could command not only extensive labor from their people, but their actual lives. The effort to move enough earth to build and bury tombs and boats, and stock them with fabulous goods literally fit for a king, was enormous. These practices set the tone for the succeeding millennia of Egyptian rule.

The Pyramids and Pyramid Builders

Without doubt, it is the pyramids in the Egyptian landscape that have made this ancient society one of the most famous in all of world history. The pyramidal structure evolved over many dynasties of pharaohs, only to disappear, sacrificed to underground tombs in the New Kingdom. Scholars still argue over many aspects of these enormous structures, including how they were built, by whom, and what they really meant to the ancient Egyptians.

The Earliest Pyramids

The famous pyramids at Giza were not the earliest ones built by pharaohs. The first above-ground pyramid was built at Saqqara around 2650 B.C.E. by King Djoser, a Third Dynasty ruler. Djoser's pyramid was built in steps representing a series of *mastabas*. Mastabas are the large underground flat-topped tombs built by earlier rulers. Though the tomb was actually underground, Djoser built a stone mastaba above ground and then created successively smaller ones, one atop the other; this resulted in an enormous structure rising 60 meters above the Egyptian sands. Djoser's pyramid survives because it was built of stone rather than mudbrick, a modification conceived of by the famous Egyptian architect Imhotep, who built many structures during Djoser's reign (Hawass 1997). Djoser's tomb was underground, centered under the pyramid. The founder of the Fourth Dynasty, Sneferu, built several pyramids, including the "Bent Pyramid" at a site, south of Saqqara. Initially Sneferu wanted a "true" pyramid, one with straight sides soaring to a point, but attempts at such collapsed, resulting in the Bent Pyramid, which stands 105 meters high. Sneferu's pyramids were the bridge to the building of the Giza "true pyramids," the first built by his son, King Khufu (also known as Cheops), ca. 2585–2560 B.C.E. (Figure 15.2).

Khufu's pyramid is the largest in all of Egypt and is commonly called the Great Pyramid. Khufu's pyramid stands 147 meters high and consists of over three million limestone blocks, each weighing approximately 2.5 tons. The king's burial chamber was actually inside the pyramid rather than underground, reached by a series of narrow corridors. Alongside the pyramid are numerous mastabas built for Khufu's officials and family members, as well as temples and causeways connecting the pyramid complex to the Nile Valley where other temples stood a kilometer away. Satellite pyramids in the Khufu complex either housed Egyptians queens (including Khufu's mother) or were empty and may have been meant to house the pharaoh's spirit or to function in ceremonies honoring his reign (Hawass 1997). Two more Fourth Dynasty kings succeeding Khufu—Khafre and Menkaure—built pyramids at Giza. Khafre's pyramid (ca. 2555–2532), nearly as large as Khufu's, is best known for the Great Sphinx that rests at the causeway leading up to it. The smallest of the three, Menkaure's pyramid (ca. 2532–2510), had to be completed by his son, as Menkaure died during construction; perhaps this explains its smaller size. The burial chambers for both these pyramids are found underground rather than inside the structure. Burial chambers contained the sarcophagus of the king, with his embalmed mummy inside, and the multitudes of objects necessary for daily use in his next life. Walls of tomb chambers were carved and painted with colorful scenes of Egyptian daily life, religious events, and scenes of the entombed person's life, sometimes accompanied by inscriptions. Some also contained biographies and descriptions of events; one tomb inscription described the payment given to the workers who built it.

The enigmatic Great Sphinx has elicited much discussion (Figure 15.2), but its purpose remains obscure. The colossal statue was built by King Khafre, and his features can be seen on the sphinx's human face, which rests on a lion's body (Hawass 1997). Lions were guardian symbols in ancient Egypt, and thus the sphinx may have

Figure 15.2. Photo of the "true" pyramids at Giza (*Holger Mette/Dreamstime.com*) and of the Great Sphinx. (*Jordan Tan/Dreamstime.com*)

been meant simply to stand as guardian to the pyramid complex. Others suggest that the sphinx's position, with head standing between the Khufu and Khafre pyramids, resembles the hieroglyph for "horizon"; perhaps this complex played an important role in Egyptian beliefs associated with the sun (Hawass 1997).

By the Middle Kingdom, kings still built pyramid complexes but they were substantially smaller. The outer facing was limestone, but the interior of these pyramids consisted of mudbrick, requiring less cost and somewhat less labor. Pyramid interiors had a maze of rooms and passages, all decorated with funerary texts (detailed more extensively below). Unfortunately, the mudbrick interior did not support the stone outer-casing over the ages, and many have collapsed into inarticulate mounds of dirt.

By the New Kingdom period, Egypt had suffered invasion and episodes of imperial collapse. Advertising the location of one's royal tomb had lost its appeal, and instead kings were buried in secret tombs dug deep beneath the valley floor. This practice led to the famous region known as the Valley of the Kings, where countless royal tombs lie underground or cut into the living rock. Many were looted in antiquity, but a startling number remain intact. It was here that Howard Carter and Lord Carnarvon discovered the tomb of Tutankhamun in the 1920s.

The Meaning of the Pyramids

Two remarkable aspects of Egyptian pyramids are the effort it took to build them, and the meaning and function attributed to them by the ancient Egyptians. Pyramids represented several important symbols in Egyptian cosmology. Their mountain-like shape stood for the mound that first arose from the watery chaos called *Nun*. From this mound the sun god Ra-Atum began to create the world that eventually became Egypt. By associating the pyramid with the creation of earth, the pharaoh, by burying himself within the pyramid, linked himself with the sun god Ra-Atum. This fits well with the other important function of the pyramid: as a vehicle to the sun. In ancient Egypt pharaohs were considered gods on earth, descended directly from the sun god. When ready to move to his next life, then, the king was simply returning to his celestial family. The pyramids served as a "ramp" to the sun and thus to the sun god (Hawass 1997). The initial stepped pyramids may have represented a staircase to the sun; the true pyramids were meant to convey the idea of a smooth ascension. The boats buried by earlier tombs may have symbolized the carriages that would convey early kings to the celestial realm. The temples associated with the pyramid complex may have been where the preparation of the king's body was carried out, and served as places for rituals honoring him after his burial. Archaeologists have also uncovered areas known as *pyramid cities*, where the builders of the pyramids, and the artisans who decorated them, lived while carrying out their work. The associated workshops produced equipment as well as food and beer necessary to supply workers. After the pyramid complex was completed, the pyramid city was occupied by those who maintained the area and the cult of the pharaoh after his entombment.

The Pyramid Builders

The laborers who created the pyramids are of as much interest as the buildings themselves. The effort required to build such edifices was enormous; pharaohs and administrators must have employed a vast workforce to accomplish these feats. What motivated the workers to build these massive buildings and associated structures? Was the population coerced, in the same fashion as laborers and artisans in the Khmer Empire (Chapter 14) appear to have been, through threat of religious retribution for failure to serve the king and state? Was building the pharaoh's tomb a type of "tax" levied on the population, similar to the system employed by the Inkas, or was the Egyptian workforce employed at fair pay rates for their daily labor? The building of such monuments was surely costly.

Evidence for who built the Egyptian monuments comes to us from texts, paintings, and archaeological excavation of what appear to be workers' tombs and a workers' village. These data sets offer a picture of a well-organized and hierarchical labor force, with ranks of laborers, skilled craftworkers, supervisors, and overseers; those at the top probably included representatives of the pharaoh and the architect(s) responsible for the project. Egyptians who built the pyramids, temples, and other monuments were paid in rations of consumable commodities: food, drink, fish, cakes, and sometimes household goods. The most common provisions given to workers were rations of bread and beer, in amounts determined by one's rank in the labor system. Beer was awarded in units of "jugs"—so, for instance, an overseer might receive sixteen loaves of bread and eight jugs of beer for his daily labor, surveyors six loaves and three jugs, and carpenters, masons, and artisans, one jug and two loaves per day (Smith 2004). Overseers and surveyors were probably full-time employees of the state, while those performing the actual labor may have been only seasonal employees or were called in as needed. Records of payment to workers, their daily efforts, and the materials they moved and used were kept by scribes, who could then make recommendations about delinquent workers or additional or fewer materials needed. These precise records made construction projects ultra-efficient and were as important to the building of the pyramids as the "overseer's lash or the engineer's ingenuity" (Kemp 2006:180).

How did the pharaoh acquire the enormous workforce (tens of thousands of people) to build his pyramids, temples, and other structures? The somewhat meager payment in beer and bread, and the extraordinarily difficult work that was carried out, suggest to many that the workers were slaves who had no choice but to work for the state for whatever recompense was given them. Others suggest that a conscription or "draft" process brought in workers for periods of time. This would perhaps correspond to the tax Inka kings levied on their people. Once service was rendered, conscripts could return to their homes and families. Another theory suggests that the majority of labor was carried out in the agricultural off-season, when fields were flooded by the Nile. Since farmers could not farm, they sought out work for the state that would sustain them until the planting cycle began again (Kemp 2006). In actuality, the labor force may have consisted of workers from all these categories. That some were concerned about their own labor being usurped by the state becomes clear in several texts. By Middle Kingdom times, those who could afford to place a "spell" on their coffins dictated that in the afterlife they would not be coerced into labor; rather, a statue (known as the *shabti*) accompanying the deceased in his tomb would be sent in his place. Another text reports that a woman who "ran away" from state service had been recovered and would be punished, and that her family, apparently imprisoned in her absence, could be released (Kemp 2006). Such texts imply a level of coercion in the state's organization of the substantial labor force.

Not far from the Old Kingdom Khufu pyramid complex were areas with workshops used for construction and decoration of the pyramids, as well as places for breadmaking and beer production (presumably for the workforce) and housing for the workers. Excavation is ongoing in the workers' village, where a mapping project and associated excavations will give insight into the lives of those who built the pyramids (Lehner 2006). A portion of these areas was turned into a cemetery for those who participated in the "pyramid cult," which included both the building of the complex and the maintenance of it afterward. Two sets of tombs, those for the lower ranks of workers, and those who were in supervisory or even elite roles, are undergoing excavation. Some tombs included spouses and children, suggesting multi-generational work in the pyramid cult. Many tombs had simple inscriptions, identifying occupants and their skills. Physical anthropological studies of skeletal material found in the simpler tombs reveal lives filled with hard work; arthritis, joint degeneration, and broken and healed bones were common traits in the remains (Smith 2004). The more elaborate tombs were larger and better built, with more paintings and inscriptions, and goods. These tombs belonged to such individuals as the "Inspector of the Craftsmen" and the "Overseer of the Masons" (Davies and Friedman 1999). It is clear from the efforts put into these tombs that the Egyptian concern for death and the afterlife was not limited to the pharaoh and his entourage.

For 2,000 years, pharaohs who ruled Egypt managed to extract enormous labor resources from their people. That Egyptians, pharaoh and commoner alike, were deeply religious people is not at all in doubt. Evidence from every corner of Egyptian life suggests that the ancient people of Egypt believed completely in the power of their gods and that their pharaoh had a special place among them, during life and certainly after death. The power of the religion and the pharaoh's role in it made possible the building of these monumental structures, meant to glorify Egypt's gods and her leaders.

The Temples of Egypt

In addition to pyramids and tombs, pharaohs commissioned the construction of temples, built by the same labor force responsible for the pyramids. There are three basic categories of temples in ancient Egypt: those constructed to honor local deities such as patron gods, those to honor the sun god Ra, and "mortuary" temples dedicated to the pharaoh. The only Egyptians who entered the temples were those working there, administrators, priests, and a few chosen elites.

Early Dynastic temples, mostly built of mudbrick, have not survived, decimated by time and Nile floods. By Old Kingdom times, pharaohs built temples of sandstone, and later temples were carved from the living rock stretching the length of the Nile. Buildings today appear monochrome, but they once displayed brightly painted surfaces highlighting the carvings and scenes depicting Egyptian mythology.

We know little about smaller temples dedicated to local gods, which have survived the least well in the archaeological record. Besides as places to worship the state god Ra, the Sun Temples functioned as distribution centers for tons of supplies dedicated to the temples. Texts suggest that vast amounts of bread, beer, cakes, and animals were brought to the temples each year. Some of these were redistributed to temple employees and some dedicated to the god. Many of these donations came from lands owned by the temple, but a significant portion also came from the common farming population who worshipped Ra as the main god in the Egyptian pantheon. The spectacular temples built in later periods at places such as Karnak and Luxor attest to the wealth and power wielded by religious elites in ancient Egypt.

In the Old and Middle Kingdoms, temples were built in proximity to the pyramids, creating an entire mortuary complex. These temples were places where the cult of the deified pharaoh could be maintained. Since the dead pharaoh resided with the gods in the afterlife, it was essential to recognize him as regularly as any other Egyptian deity. Priests and temple administrators lived in or near the temples and kept the cult alive for decades, even centuries, after the death of the pharaoh. Many of those dedicated to the cult of the pharaoh constructed their own modest tombs in the complex as well.

During the New Kingdom, when pharaohs no longer constructed pyramids but were entombed in the surrounding valleys, mortuary temples took on even greater importance, as these were the only visible evidence of the dead pharaoh's greatness. One of the best-known of these is the temple dedicated to Ramesses III at Medinet Habu (1100–1070 B.C.E.). Ramesses III built an enormous temple accompanied by a ceremonial palace, as well as storerooms, temples dedicated to other gods, and buildings to house administrators. It is essentially a city dedicated to a deceased pharaoh, built by his people and maintained long after his death.

Gods and Goddesses of Egypt

There are far too many deities in the ancient Egyptian pantheon to deal with even a fraction of them in any detail. Estimates suggest that ancient Egyptians worshipped over 700 gods and goddesses, but only a few of these were at the pinnacle of the pantheon. We know the names and attributes of the main Egyptian deities from the ubiquitous tomb paintings, stone reliefs, and rarer papyrus texts that have survived the ages. Most of the Egyptian deities sought to aid their human charges, but if crossed, they could cause enormous destruction and harm to the land and its people. There were a few supernatural beings that can safely be called *demons* in that their goal was to create havoc; it was the job of Egyptians, through propitiation of the beneficial deities, to keep the demons from succeeding.

Chief among the Egyptian deities were the sun god, Ra-Atum; Horus, the falcon-headed god who protected the pharaoh; and Osiris, the god of the dead and the netherworld (Figure 15.3). Osiris and Anubis, the jackal-headed god of necropolises and embalming, were important actors in the Egyptian death cult (discussed in more detail below). An important female deity was Isis, considered the consort of Osiris; she personified the throne and is the goddess of the reign. Ma'at was the daughter of Ra-Atum, the sun god, and she oversaw justice, equilibrium, and balance. She also played a very important role in the death cult and in the human passage to the afterlife. It is Ma'at's purview of balance and equilibrium that had to be maintained during the pharaoh's reign. Another deity, Seth, identified with the crocodile, causes nothing but trouble for these other deities. Demonic deities included the snake-like Apep, who constantly sought to prevent the sun from rising, and Ammut the "devourer," who dwelled in the passage between this life and the next. Ammut represented divine retribution for the wrongs an Egyptian committed during his or her life and was certainly feared by living Egyptians; he was portrayed as a composite of various creatures, including a dog, crocodile, lion, and hippopotamus.

An important myth in Egyptian cosmology concerned the life of Osiris. He was one of the original gods of Egypt and became the deity overseeing the entire earth; he married his sister Isis and together they ruled Egypt. Their brother, Seth, was jealous of Osiris's power and undertook to betray him. Seth imprisoned Osiris in a coffin and threw him in the Nile, where Osiris died and went to the underworld. Isis recovered the body of Osiris, but Seth again intervened and cut it up into pieces which he scattered across Egypt. Isis gathered up the scattered parts and took them to Anubis who, in effect, brought Osiris back to life. Osiris became the god of the underworld, but the throne of kingship was therefore empty. Isis had conceived and borne Osiris's son, Horus, who had to battle Seth for the right to the throne. No matter how badly Horus was injured, Isis's power protected him and he was healed. At one point Seth struck Horus's eye out, but Thoth, the Ibis-headed god of wisdom, restored it. Horus eventually defeated Seth and became god of kingship and the pharaohs. Embedded in this

Figure 15.3. Egyptian gods discussed in the chapter: *a*, Thoth; *b*, Ma'at; *c*, Isis; *d*, Osiris; *e*, Horus; *f*, Anubis; *g*, Seth; *h*, Ammut. (*R. Jennison*)

myth are explications of the roles of these important gods: Osiris ruled the underworld, while his son carried on his father's role as god of kingship; Anubis became the overseer of death; and Isis the defender and protector of Egypt and her king.

In addition to gods, ancestors could also be called upon for help. Because the dead went on to an afterlife associated with the Egyptian gods, dead ancestors were believed to have supernatural power. They could appeal to the gods to help living family members, to rectify a problem, or even exact revenge on someone who had caused harm. Ancestors were contacted via small shines in the household; a "letter" accompanying the offerings gave the ancestor details of what was needed (Davies and Friedman 1999).

Pharaohs, who were considered sons of the sun god Ra, were responsible for the secular rule of the state and functioned as liaison between the people and the gods. Pharaoh kept the cosmos in harmony with the earth, which would descend into chaos without his constant work. Not only was the pharaoh a divine being during his rule of Egypt, but in his afterlife he would have the ear of the gods as he argued for his former people. It was, therefore, essential that the pharaoh be pleased with his people throughout his rule, and that he be prepared perfectly for his afterlife so that he could be their advocate forever more. This belief in the divine nature of the king explains the temples built near the pyramids; Egyptians needed to continue showing their dedication to previous deceased pharaohs even while they were ruled by a newly enthroned king.

The Egyptian Death Cult and Funerary Texts

Each culture has a unique attitude to human death; some fear it and seek to prolong earthly life for as long as possible; others see death as only a rite of passage to another stage of life. The Egyptians might be said to have been obsessed with the concept of death. The cultic behavior surrounding death, eventually producing mummified remains entombed in pyramids and sarcophagi, is evidence enough of a culture deeply consumed with the life beyond earthly existence. Fortunately for us, the Egyptians were quite concerned with proper preparation of the deceased for entrance into the afterlife. They wrote detailed instructions on the funeral process, and the Egyptian *Book of the Dead* describes the difficult path to the Hall of Justice and how to achieve success while there to move on to eventual afterlife.

Embalming the Dead

The proper preservation of the body was an essential component to a successful afterlife. Several embalming scenes painted on tombs and coffins offer clues to how the procedure worked. During the process Egyptians believed that the embalmer became one with Anubis, ensuring that each stage was done correctly. The embalming process took centuries to perfect and, in fact, was passed orally from one embalmer to the next. Our information about the process comes from Herodotus, not the Egyptians themselves. Early rulers and Egyptians were simply buried in the desert sands to achieve desiccation; but by the beginning of the Old Kingdom, a combination of naturally occurring chemicals (a salt compound called *natron*) was used to achieve a mummy that would remain more-or-less preserved to the present day.

The embalming process took approximately 70 days if done correctly (only wealthy Egyptians could afford the entire process). First the brain was removed, either through the nasal cavity or a hole in the skull; it was then discarded as unimportant. The vital organs, the intestines, and the stomach were removed and placed in separate vessels (*canopic jars*) and would accompany the deceased into the tomb. Several goddesses were charged with protecting these organs, and often the jar's lid portrayed the iconography of the protector goddess (Figure 15.4). The heart was left in the body because it was considered the organ responsible for emotion, intelligence, and reason. The cavities left in the body were packed with natron, and then the body itself was covered with natron in order to achieve desiccation. After 40 days the body was washed and anointed with unguents (accompanied by the proper prayers), the cavity was packed with linens soaked in resin, and the face, desiccated by the chemicals, was plumped up to look more natural (with plaster or sawdust); later mummies had a mask placed over the face for the same purpose. The body was wrapped in linens within which amulets were placed to aid the deceased in the afterlife. One of these amulets, a "heart" scarab, was placed over the heart, which played a vital role in the coming ordeal in the Hall of Justice. The corpse was then placed in a coffin.

Following the 70-day process, the coffin was transported to the burial site. If the wealth of the deceased warranted, this was an event of great importance. The coffin was placed in a boat, carried by mourners, so that it seemingly "glided" along waters to

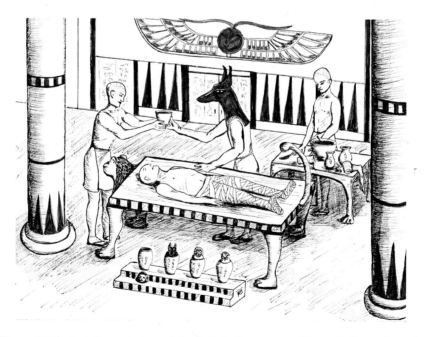

Figure 15.4. Artistic rendering of the embalming process. The embalmer, dressed as Anubis, hands an internal organ to an assistant for placement in a canopic jar. (*M. J. Hughes*)

the burial place. In the tomb chamber, the coffin was laid in a stone sarcophagus (if one had been commissioned by the deceased). The canopic jars were also placed in the tomb, which was already heavily stocked with items needed in the next life. Rituals and prayers were performed, and finally the tomb was closed to leave the deceased to travel on to the afterlife.

Sacred Texts to Counsel the Dead

The ultimate goal of every Egyptian, king and commoner alike, was to successfully enter the Field of Reeds ruled by Osiris. This netherworld was thought to be an earth-like place where the next life could be spent in peace and happiness. It was there that kings would join in the cyclical movement of the sun, symbolically becoming one with father Ra. To accomplish this goal, the Egyptians took sacred texts with them into the tomb. These served as a "how-to" manual for navigating the troubled waters to the next life. We see some of the earliest versions of what later become texts written on papyrus and linen, inscribed on the walls of royal tombs.

These *pyramid texts* give information on what should be included in the tomb (food, drink, provisions) but also offer advice for safe travel to Osiris's netherworld. By Middle Kingdom times, individuals had spells and instructions inscribed on the interior of their wooden coffins for easy viewing. These *coffin texts* were explicit in their instructions to the deceased. One common text was known as *The Book of the Two Ways*, which mapped out the route to the Hall of Justice, the last stop before entering the afterlife. This route was plagued with demons that had to be successfully bypassed. Coffin texts detailed exactly how to accomplish the necessary tasks for safe passage. Texts vital to the pharaohs included *The Book of Gates* and *Amduat*, both of which described the sun god's nightly journey through the underworld. In these books, Ra traversed the twelve divisions (corresponding to the twelve hours of night-time) in his solar boat. He had to defeat enemies to continue on so that the sun would rise the next day. The texts informed the king about the sun god's journey and the difficulties the deity would face; the king should help aid Ra along this journey, and instructions for doing so were contained in these books. In this way the king would help his own case for entering the Field of Reeds.

The best-known Egyptian funerary text is the New Kingdom–period *The Book of the Dead* (in Egyptian, "The Book of Going-Forth by Day"), which is a compilation of nearly 200 spells. Many of these were also contained in the coffin texts; they help the deceased avoid demons such as Apep the snake (who also plagues the sun god in his nightly journey). *The Book of the Dead*, as it is now known, was written on papyrus or linen and was most commonly found in non-elite graves and tombs. People took as much of this document into the tomb as they could afford. Poor people could only take a few spells along for the journey. If a choice had to be made, nearly everyone took Spell 125, which detailed the proper behavior in the Hall of Justice. After navigating the passages and gates to the hall, avoiding demons and pitfalls, the propitiant had one last task before entering the Field of Reeds: judgment by the gods (Figure 15.5). The deceased would only be able to enter the hall if the embalming process has been done correctly. Led into

Figure 15.5. The judgment scene in the Hall of Justice. (*R. Jennison*)

the hall by Anubis, the deceased faced Osiris and a panel of 42 judges representing the lands of Egypt. The goddess of justice, Ma'at, was also an important part of the process. The deceased's heart was placed on a scale, for which the counter balance was the feather from Ma'at's headdress. Each of the 42 judges then asked the deceased one question about his or her behavior when alive. The *Book of the Dead* instructs that the correct answer is always "no," meaning that injustice or bad behavior was never to be admitted by the deceased; it was permissible to try to deceive the judges here in order to pass through the hall. The questions and answers were recorded by Thoth, who stood by the scale. If the deceased passed this test and the heart remained balanced with the feather, he or she was declared "true" and "justified" by Osiris and was awarded a place in the afterlife with the Egyptian gods. If the heart weighed heavy, however, and the deceased failed the test, the heart was consumed by the demon Ammut, who waited below the scale. The deceased died a "second death" from which recovery was impossible. Those who failed were sent to the Egyptian version of hell, where they were tortured and forced to eat blood and excrement. This was certainly a fate all ancient Egyptians wished to avoid.

Conclusion

The ancient Egyptians offer perhaps one of the clearest illustrations of the role religion can play in empowering the ruling elite. The deification of the pharaoh surely allowed him to command labor and tribute (both symbolic and material) from his people, not only during his life, but after his death as well. Were people coerced into this labor, grudgingly, toiling for an all-powerful deified leader while their families got by as best they could, or did they happily build Egypt's famous monuments in service to their pharaoh, perhaps for generous remuneration? As work continues at sites along the Nile, these and other questions may well be answered. What is certain is that the power of Egypt's royal elites was inextricably tied to the complex religion of this ancient civilization.

The Great Zimbabwe Kingdom

Far to the south, and hundreds of years after the might of ancient Egypt had faded, another African kingdom rose to prominence. In the present-day country of Zimbabwe, stone ruins stand as testament to a powerful kingdom that achieved its zenith in the twelfth–fifteenth centuries C.E. This kingdom, known as Great Zimbabwe, rested on a plateau between the Limpopo and Zambezi rivers (Figure 15.6) and is named for the nearly 300 stone enclosures, or *zimbabwes*, that dot the countryside. This word from the Bantu language translates to "sacred house" or "ritual seat of a king," highlighting the importance of religion in this empire (McIntosh 1998). In the fourteenth century, the kingdom's main settlement, Great Zimbabwe, may have had a population of 18,000 people living, working, and worshipping there.

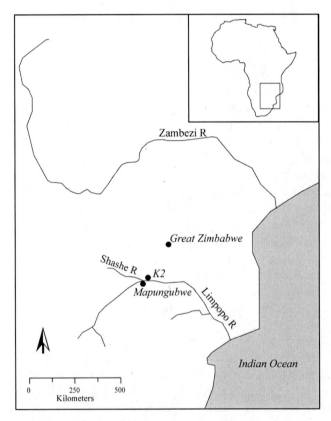

Figure 15.6. Map of Great Zimbabwe sites discussed. (*T. Edwards*)

Precursors to Great Zimbabwe

The Limpopo Basin was not heavily occupied until about 900 C.E. because the landscape is not very suitable for agriculture, nor is water for cattle-herding plentiful. By

1000 C.E., a subtle shift in climate and higher rainfall levels allowed a large settlement, known today as K2, to emerge. Residents at K2 spoke an earlier form of the Shona language, the major language family in the region today (Huffman 2005). By 1200 C.E., approximately 1,500 people lived at K2; the chief lived in the largest house, a circular structure built of *daga*, a mud and dung mixture, with clay and gravel floors and possibly a veranda (Huffman 2005). There may have been additional huts in the compound serving as women's spaces (with kitchen and storage), and for unmarried male and female kin members. Near the complex of dagas would have been the *kraal*, or fenced area, for the chief's herd. The rest of the K2 residents would have had similar but far smaller housing compounds and kraals.

A common religious rite, still practiced today, was the ritual for rainmaking. During the rainy season, in September and November, rainmakers carried out rituals to ensure the arrival of sufficient rainfall. The rituals took place on hills, thereby bringing the practitioners closer to the clouds that would issue the rain (Huffman 2005). K2 residents worked in fields that provided food for the entire community; essentially these were "state-owned" rather than individual fields. At harvest time the chief presided over a feast, using the food from these fields to celebrate the agricultural cycle. K2 functioned as the capital city of the Limpopo Basin from about 1000 to 1200 C.E. By the mid-thirteenth century, however, a new and larger capital had been established.

The Mapungubwe settlement consisted of a large hill on which the ruler lived; below the hill was an apron of land higher than the surrounding terraces. The royal family resided on this apron; everyone else lived on the lower terraces to the south, east, and north, including commoners and administrators (Huffman 2005). The Mapungubwe hill was one of the rainmaking hills on which rituals were carried out; by establishing his residence there, the king made a connection between himself and this important aspect of Limpopo River Basin life: the bringing of rains and the success of the agricultural cycle.

At its height, as many as 5,000 people lived at Mapungubwe. Using a combination of ethnographic and archaeological data, archaeologists believe the king's residence consisted of a large zimbabwe arranged so that the king resided at the back. Those wishing to see the king had to report to the messenger at the entrance of the zimbabwe. From here the potential visitor entered the office of the diviner, who could assess the intentions of the visitor. If evil was intended, the visitor went no farther; if the visitor passed the diviner's scrutiny, then he was escorted to the audience chamber where he could present his case to the king. Almost certainly the visitor did not speak directly to the king, but rather to an intermediary, and the visitor did not call the king by name but probably used some word symbolizing "mountain." Nor, probably, did direct visual contact take place, as the visitor may have kept his head bowed, or there may have been a curtain between visitor and king (Huffman 2005). In this way the king was not only physically but also ritually secluded from his people, making him seem a very powerful and perhaps mysterious leader. In the back section of the zimbabwe, away from the more public front areas, was the king's house, including a ritual area where rainmaking rituals took place. Also in the back was the residence of the senior sister, the main female in the lineage. She was probably present at many of the ritual ceremonies and therefore resided in the palace. The king had many wives, some of whom had a residential area outside the palace but on the hill, while others lived in their own settlements outside of Mapungubwe, carrying out the king's work and serving as host if he had reason to travel to the area (Huffman 2005). Golden objects found in elite graves, and the efforts put into the building of the Mapungubwe zimbabwe and other structures, demonstrate the wealth and power of the king in this emergent trading state. By the beginning of the fourteenth century, the climate changed again, limiting rainfall in the Limpopo Basin and making the agriculture and herding economy a more risky venture at Mapungubwe. As the region was abandoned and Mapungubwe faded in power, a new regional center to the north, known as Great Zimbabwe, grew to even greater size and power than Mapungubwe.

Great Zimbabwe

Great Zimbabwe gained wealth and prominence due to its location on important trade routes. As contacts with the Arab world grew, many in the region turned from cattle-herding to trade. By the thirteenth century, residents had constructed a magnificent stone city at Great Zimbabwe, composed of two parts: the Hill Complex at the top of a steep cliff, and the Great Enclosure at its base. Several centuries later, after the kingdom had collapsed and its material culture had been looted or destroyed, European visitors believed the ruins had been built by the ancient Egyptians, or perhaps by other foreign trading empires (McIntosh 1998). As archaeologists in the twentieth century began their explorations of this kingdom, its indigenous African origins came to light. Today the region is occupied by the Karanga culture (renamed Shona in colonial times); most assert Great Zimbabwe was inhabited by the ancestors of the Karanga, but the notion of "the ancients," a lost African culture, also persists (Pikirayi 2001).

The Hill Complex and the Great Enclosure

Besides the difference in elevation, the Great Enclosure and Hill Complex are separated by an area known as the Valley Complex. In this valley region were smaller zimbabwes surrounding thatch-roofed houses and storage areas. These may have been the residences of commoners and administrators who served the royalty and worked within the kingdom's center to facilitate the vast trading network. The rest of the 18,000 people who made up the Great Zimbabwe Empire lived in the outlying regions, where they could more easily engage in cattle-herding and agriculture.

The Hill Complex rests on a granite shelf 300 feet above the valley and commands a view of the entire region. The complex is composed of small stone-built enclosures connected by narrow passages. At either end were two walled areas: the larger, Western Enclosure and, roughly 200 feet east, the Eastern Enclosure. From this latter enclosure one could climb up to another area known as the Balcony, from which the entire valley could be seen. Below the Eastern Enclosure is a cave whose acoustical qualities make any sounds produced in the cave audible to the valley below. The king most likely resided in the Western Enclosure, which may also have functioned as an audience hall. As at Mapungubwe, there was probably no direct contact between visitor and king, though they may both have been in the audience hall at the same time. A senior sister's residence was also located on the Hill Complex. Another hut, decorated with snake imagery, probably belonged to a diviner (Huffman 1996). The Eastern Enclosure was not residential but was rather meant for ceremonial and ritual performances. Bronze and iron items, including iron gongs, and beautiful bird effigies carved of soapstone and mounted on pedestals were some of the discoveries in the Eastern Enclosure.

In the valley, one large area served as the housing area for the king's wives, of which there may have been hundreds. One of the largest and oldest enclosures probably belonged to the king's first wife. In this structure were numerous objects of great value, made of gold, ivory, metal, and glass. Iron gongs like those found in the Eastern Enclosure were also present; these were symbols of the king's office and are good evidence that this house belonged to someone in the royal family, likely the senior wife. Nearby was another zimbabwe that held a carved soapstone bird like those found in the Eastern Enclosure on the cliff. This building was most likely the location where the senior wife carried out rituals.

At the outer edge of this area was the Great Enclosure, the largest stone-built structure in the southern region of Africa. The massive outer wall stretches over 800 feet in length, reaches a height of 32 feet, and is, in some places, 17 feet thick. The top of the outer wall is decorated by delicate chevron friezes. Inside the Great Enclosure area were a number of smaller interior zimbabwes connected by passages, several circular raised platforms (known as *chikuva* in the Shona language), and one conical tower near the outer wall on the southeastern side. This tower is approximately 30 feet high and 18 feet in diameter. The top of this stone structure is also decorated with a pattern. A platform, the largest one found at Great Zimbabwe, rests next to a doorway leading to the conical tower.

Most of the material culture remnants were missing from Great Zimbabwe when modern investigations began at the site. However, oral tradition from the present-day Shona-speaking population, combined with historical data, has offered some excellent insights into the political, social, and religious structures of the Great Zimbabwe kingdom.

Religion and Power in the Zimbabwean Past and Present

Much of what we understand about the belief system at Great Zimbabwe comes from today's Shona-speaking Karanga culture which inhabits the Great Zimbabwe area between the Limpopo and Zambezi rivers. The Karanga believe in a range of supernatural beings, the most important of which are their ancestor spirits. Ancestors serve as guardians of the living, helping their descendants where possible, deflecting witchcraft and fending off evil intentions. Only those who were elderly at death, produced children, and who had lived honorable lives become ancestor spirits (Shoko 2007). However, the ancestors can also bring punishment for the evil actions of their descendants, such as stealing, adultery, and other infractions; punishment might come in the form of disease, injury, or lack of rain. Ancestors are honored by gifts of millet, beer, and rituals. An area at the back of a Karanga house is dedicated to the ancestors; the *chikuva* platform in this area symbolizes the connection between living and ancestral spirits (Shoko 2007). One of the most important rituals involves rainmaking and takes place at the beginning of the rainy season. As was true at K2, the chief oversees the ceremony and offerings are made to the ancestors. The chief then arranges a feast after the harvest, celebrating a successful season.

The Karanga chief serves as both political and religious leader. In Karanga oral tradition, the crocodile is a powerful symbol of the chief because its character is considered dangerous, fearless, and powerful. In past times, chiefs, prior to their installation, were required to capture and kill a crocodile and then consume food cooked by heated stones taken from its belly; in this fashion the chief symbolically became a crocodile himself (Huffman 1996). In Karanga iconography, crocodiles are symbolized by nested diamonds, pits and bumps (to imitate its skin), and chevrons. In earlier Karanga times, the senior sister, sometimes called the *ritual sister*, served as an advisor for political and social affairs (Huffman 1987). The Karanga ritual sister was an important representative of the women and was the keeper of sacred medicines that were crucial to the health of the king; she also symbolized the fertility of the people, especially the women. Because of her importance, the Karanga ritual sister lived in or near the chief's palace and was treated with equal respect.

Besides the crocodile, another important animal in Karanga iconography is the snake, which is associated with rain and fertility and, in some cases, women. Snake and crocodile symbols (snakes are represented by zigzag and diagonal line patterns) are found on divination dice in present-day cultures as well as at Great Zimbabwe. Based on ethnographic analogy, it is believed that the chief needed to ensure that his people lived in a balanced and just world, that the land and people were fertile, and that everyone was strong and healthy. His power was believed to derive from the link between the land and his ancestral spirits (Shoko 2007), thereby making the chief's ancestors of vital importance to the entire population. Besides his role as ruler of the people, he also had to propitiate the ancestral guardian spirits on behalf of his people. To this end he arranged ritual feasts, such as the one at the end of the harvest season. When a chief died, power passed to his male heir. The chief then became an important ancestor who had joined the rank of spirits offering guardianship and aid to the people.

An important task of the ancestors is to communicate with Mwari, the supreme god in Karanga religion, who is crucial to the bringing of rain. One Karanga oral tradition suggests that Mwari led people to Great Zimbabwe, making it a "promised land" for them (Shoko 2007:38). Mwari is regularly entreated for rain at sites that are sacred to him, many of them in cave settings. Petitioners approach the cave and give their requests to the mediums who serve Mwari. A voice issues from the cave, often unintelligible to the petitioners, and the message is interpreted by Mwari's mediums. Mwari is consulted on any subject of concern to the people, whether climatic, political, or social. Although today it is primarily mediums that act as the intercessors between the god and the people, in the past chiefs acted as priests who spoke to Mwari for their people (Shoko 2007). Much of Karanga religion explains the archaeological remains found at Great Zimbabwe.

Religion at Great Zimbabwe

As is the case among the Karanga today, recognition and propitiation of ancestor spirits at Great Zimbabwe seem to have been a central part of the belief system. The chief's ancestors were of crucial importance, as they were in a very influential position to bring rain, wealth, fertility, and balance to the people. The ritual seclusion of the chief—spatially, by placing his palace on the cliff, and visually, in the audience hall— added to the sense of power and sanctity invested in the office and the man himself.

Karanga culture and earlier oral tradition help us interpret the buildings in the Western Enclosure of the Hill Complex. To meet with the chief, a visitor had first to negotiate with the messenger at the front gate, after which he approached the diviner who served as escort to the king's audience chamber. At the back of the Western Enclosure was the king's hut, and beyond that a *chikuva* platform, very likely the place where he interacted privately with his ancestors. The chikuva was flanked by a stone tower and three natural monoliths that extended out from the cliff face. There were also carved soapstone beams decorated with chevrons and diamonds, symbolizing the crocodile and thus leadership. The platform was decorated with ridges that may have represented the crocodile's skin (Huffman 1987). Another important item resting there was a carved soapstone bird standing on a pillar near the chikuva. Archaeologists discovered a bronze hoe and spearhead in this area, both of which were deemed more ceremonial than utilitarian, given their delicacy. These may have served as symbols of the king's office and his responsibilities for ensuring a fertile harvest and protecting the people and their well-being. The other resident of the Western Enclosure was probably the senior ritual sister, who was an important actor in both ritual and political events.

It was in the Eastern Enclosure where the more public rituals probably took place. At the front was a sizable bench, perhaps for those invited to the ceremonies. Symbols representing the crocodile decorated the eastern door; perhaps the king entered the enclosure here. The senior sister and her attendants (possibly some of the king's wives) entered from the western door. Material culture found inside the Eastern Enclosure probably had ritual functions. A stone cylinder is decorated with bumps and circular lines that resemble a crocodile's skin, but the most remarkable objects found there were the six soapstone birds (Figure 15.7). The carvings are approximately 30 centimeters tall and stand on the top of pillars at a height of at least a meter (Huffman 1987). There appear to be two general representations of birds, both of which are probably raptors; it is notable that these birds all have five toes, suggesting an anthropomorphic element. In Karanga oral tradition, birds are considered messengers who carry information between the ancestors and their living descendants. Since both the king and the ritual sister attended, and perhaps conducted, ceremonies in the Eastern Enclosure, it is possible that the two styles of birds represent male and female humans or ancestors; the king's ancestors were concerned with the fertility of the land and the sister's with the fertility and well-being of the people (Huffman 1987). It is unclear if each individual bird represented a specific ancestor, or if different birds were dedicated to different messages (such as rain, fertility, or other problems such as security). Certainly many other interpretations for the use of these statues are also possible, but it seems clear that birds served as symbols of ancestral royalty and the sacred duty of the king and the ritual sister to look after the well-being of their people. This would explain the discovery of the carved soapstone bird in the apparent senior wife's ritual enclosure in the lower settlement area. Perhaps she also made use of the spiritual birds for communicative purposes, or they may have been meant to symbolize the king's power when he visited her residence.

The cave located below the Eastern Enclosure may have also played a role in the religion of Great Zimbabwe. The noises made in the cave can be heard out in the valley below; it is possible that it was used as a device for imparting messages to the people from the supernatural world. Karanga oral tradition suggests that the Mwari cult began at Great Zimbabwe; the cave may have been used as a vehicle through which Mwari spoke to the people of the land (Huffman 1996). That a supreme deity emerged in the Great Zimbabwean belief system more or less simultaneously with the institution of a very powerful king is not at all surprising. The fortuitous natural acoustics of the cave, adjacent to the king's residence, may have served the dual purpose of allowing the king, and the emergent supreme god, to impart important information to the people, including guidelines for behavior and service to their king and god.

The greatest controversy surrounding the Great Enclosure concerns its function. Though some have suggested it was the king's palace, the lack of domestic remains negates the likelihood it was a residence. The immensity of the outer wall points to its

Figure 15.7. Two examples of the Great Zimbabwe birds. (*R. Jennison*)

importance in the settlement, leading others to advocate it was the settlement's temple, even though state rituals took place on the Hill Complex. The structures inside the Great Enclosure are enigmatic on first glance. Two doorways are on the northern side of this elliptically shaped structure. One doorway, with internal buttresses, led into a squarish enclosure where two stone monoliths stood; in present-day cultures, standing stones like these represent male symbolism. The other doorway was accessed by an external passageway, connected to the first wife's residence. These two doorways have therefore been interpreted as male and female entrances, respectively. Opposite the doorways, on the southeastern side, the wall is thicker and taller, almost fortress-like. Activities that took place in this part of the enclosure may have needed protection from prying eyes (Huffman 1987).

In the eastern area of the Great Enclosure is a daga platform that once stood approximately a meter high, with steps leading to its summit; it may have been a platform designed for someone to address listeners standing or sitting below. Clay figurines of animals and humans, metal objects, and other nondomestic items were found scattered around it, and stone monoliths with carvings and paint, some illustrating snakes, once surrounded it (Huffman 1996). At the southeastern end of the enclosure is a conical stone tower with a grain bin resting next to it. In front of this tower is a stepped stone platform resembling a pulpit. The top of the tower had a stone chevron decoration, representing the male crocodile symbol; the grain bin perhaps represented women, as they were responsible for the grain and bins in the household (Huffman 1996). Just inside the female entrance was a stone cairn that had been covered in ash and cattle bones and has thus been labeled the "sacrificial cairn." Also near the female entrance was a second circular stone enclosure with a hut inside. Anyone inside this smaller enclosure or in the hut would not see activities within the larger Great Enclosure.

The unusual collection of architecture and objects within the Great Enclosure may be explicable as belonging to a type of instructional area, a school of sorts, where young men and women underwent their initiation into adulthood (Huffman 1987). The male and female symbolism built into the structures or painted on them (snake and crocodile patterns), and the various locations within the area where a teacher, or initiator, might stand to address a group, make sense within such a setting. In present-day Karanga initiation ceremonies, figurines of animals and humans are used as instructional devices (Huffman 1996). That such objects were found near the large daga platform lends even more credence to the idea that the Great Enclosure was a place where one entered as a child and left as a young adult. Perhaps the hut in the internal enclosure was where family visited with a child undergoing the initiation period (which may have been days or even weeks long). Perhaps visitors, family members, or the initiates themselves made sacrifices to the ancestors and other gods at the stone cairn near the entrance. Given that it is near the female entrance, we might assume that either it was dedicated to female ancestors (perhaps of the ritual sister) or that only women made sacrifices. If the Great Enclosure was indeed the place of initiation, the effort and care put into building it is representative of the importance of properly educating the young among the ancient residents of Great Zimbabwe.

The Fading of Great Zimbabwe

By the mid-fifteenth century the Great Zimbabwe area was in decline, as other regions of Africa grew in importance and diverted traders and merchants to their own territories. In the sixteenth century the Portuguese arrived and told stories of the abandoned city; by the nineteenth century, speculation about who had built the ruins arose. It was not until the twentieth century that archaeologists and historians insisted to the world that the magnificent buildings at Great Zimbabwe were built by a great African kingdom rather than by Egyptians or people from elsewhere. While we must continue to work on unraveling the religion and culture of the Great Zimbabwe kingdom, the architectural patterns and ethnographic data paint a picture of a deeply religious people and a ruler dedicated to their health and welfare. Unlike in earlier empires such as the Egyptian dynasties, it does not appear that the king of Great Zimbabwe used his close connection with his ancestors and with Mwari to demand enormous labor or other tribute from his people. Rather, he provided feasts and rituals for them. Perhaps he commissioned, and paid for, the building of the Great Enclosure as a service to the youth of his kingdom. Though much about the lives of those who inhabited Great Zimbabwe remains hidden, it is clear that their spirituality was deep and their trust in their king to lead them properly and protect them from harm was utter and absolute.

Useful Sources

Peter Garlake, *Great Zimbabwe*, 1973.
T. G. H. James, *Ancient Egypt*, 2005.
Mark Lehner, *The Complete Pyramids*, 1997.

16

ANCIENT SUMER AND RELIGIONS IN ANCIENT MESOPOTAMIA

S outhwest Asia, more commonly called the Middle East (and in archaeological circles termed the Near East), stretches from Iran to the Mediterranean, and from
the southern shores of the Black Sea to the Persian Gulf. It is the birthplace of many
religions, including three that are practiced by more than half of the world's population today: Christianity, Islam, and Judaism. The cultures and beliefs of ancient
Mesopotamia (Figure 16.1) played an important role in the shaping of early Israelite
religion, later known as Judaism, which emerged in the Levant several millennia later.
These earliest Near Eastern religions are explored here.

Ancient Sumer and the Religion of Mesopotamia

Ancient Southwest Asia has been a focus of archaeological work since the inception of
the field. In spite of this, or perhaps because of it, we have many questions about the
earliest roots of civilization in the "land between the rivers," or Mesopotamia. One of
the most remarkable aspects of this earliest civilization is that it arose in a region with
quite limited resources. Southern Mesopotamia is a vast alluvial plain; 7,000 years ago,
in the Ubaid period, when some of the earliest settlements were established, the Tigris
and Euphrates rivers offered ample fresh water in a very fertile land. Irrigation agriculture allowed people to build settlements and farm successfully; their houses were built
of mudbrick, their agricultural tools made from clay, and their baskets and pots sealed
by bitumen, a tar-like substance found in the region. Most other goods in their houses,
however, came to them through trade. Ubaid villages contained buildings that probably served as temples, and as the population grew it may have been temple personnel
who facilitated trade and managed land and surplus grain resources, offering clerics
some overarching importance in the community and some level of economic control
(Pollock 1999). In the Uruk period, beginning in the early fourth millennium (and
lasting until approximately 3100 B.C.E.), the Sumerian civilization emerged. The
period between 3500 and 3100 B.C.E. was known as the Uruk Phenomenon, so-called
because cities in southern Mesopotamia, especially Uruk itself, rose to such power, size,
and economic prominence in such a short period. Though there were other cities in

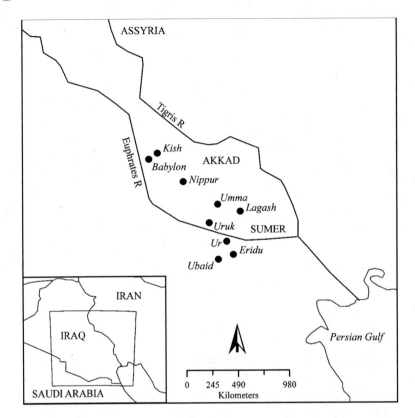

Figure 16.1. Map of sites and regions discussed in the chapter. (*T. Edwards*)

southern Mesopotamia at this time, it would appear that Uruk was the unofficial "capital" of this fourth-millennium civilization. It is not necessarily accurate to describe this civilization as a "kingdom," as there is no certain evidence that Uruk or other cities were ruled by kings; rulership may have been seated in the temple system rather than in any secular position. By 3100 B.C.E., trade contacts were beginning to crumble, and sociopolitical and economic powers outside southern Mesopotamia were emerging.

Following the Uruk period is a century-long phase known as the Jemdet Nasr, when the Uruk system reorganized into a different political structure. Beginning in roughly 3000 B.C.E., a new phase known as the Early Dynastic period began and lasted until the Akkadian Empire was established in 2350 B.C.E. It is during the Early Dynastic period that writing achieved its full-fledged form, and the greatest architectural monuments were built in Sumerian cities. The southern Mesopotamian cultures became known as Sumerian, due to the language and later texts that described the region as "the land of Sumer," though we do not know how residents referred to themselves. In the Early Dynastic period, Mesopotamia was divided into city-states in which one main city ruled the region surrounding it, each vying for power with occasional eruptions of warfare between different regions. During the Early Dynastic centuries, some city-states grew to great prominence only to eventually fade in the face of even more powerful foes. These city-states were ruled by kings who commanded armies and wielded secular power but who were also deeply intertwined with Sumerian religious affairs. The temples were administered by priests and priestesses, many duly appointed by the king, and rulers were responsible for overseeing important religious ceremonies on a regular basis. Therefore, although kingship had been established by the Early Dynastic period, "separation between church and state" was certainly not in effect.

The Sumerian Civilization in the Uruk and Early Dynastic Periods

By the mid-fourth millennium B.C.E., a major urban center had developed on the banks of the Euphrates River. The city of Uruk covered an area of 250 hectares and supported a population of perhaps 50,000 people, growing to twice this size by ca. 3100 B.C.E. Excavations at Uruk and at other Sumerian cities have demonstrated complex social and economic hierarchies and the presence of a class structure that included wealthy and powerful elites (Matthews 2003). The ecological setting of southern Mesopotamia allowed its cities, especially those in the deep south, to flourish. Besides fertile land and access to fresh water for irrigation, the southern marshes provided ample fish and fowl. The rich land produced a variety of foods, including cereals and fruits (such as dates), and smaller gardens may have provided other plant food items. Domesticated animals (sheep and goat) provided milk products as well as wool and hair for clothing and textiles.

Economy and Politics in Ancient Sumer

While the vast majority of the Sumerian population was involved in agriculture, there was certainly a group who dedicated their time to craft production. Crafts ranged from utilitarian and (probably mass-produced) textiles, metal goods (such as tools), and ceramics to those more accurately labeled "luxury" or non-utilitarian items, such as cylinder seals, which came into use by the late fourth millennium. Cylinder seals are small objects of bone, stone, or other materials that were carved so that when rolled across a soft surface, they left an impression; carved images were unique to an individual or to an office, thereby acting as a type of signature. Usually about 3 centimeters tall and 1–2 centimeters wide, they often had a hole through their center so they could dangle from a pin or be carried on a string, perhaps as a necklace. Seals were an important administrative tool, useful for marking the ownership of goods by rolling them across the wet clay used to seal a container. Other objects needed in the growing city included art and decoration for religious buildings, statuary for use in temples (discussed in more detail below), and luxury items such as jewelry and symbols of office fashioned of precious and semiprecious stones and metals.

   With the expansion of craft production and a growing population came the need for managers to control the movement of goods. It was not long before an administrative class developed that was responsible for the organization of craft production, keeping track of goods coming into the city, and managing the redistribution of those goods to the city's residents. The economy seems to have revolved around temple centers in Sumerian cities (Matthews 2003), a system that may have had roots in the preceding Ubaid period. In the Uruk period, goods were dedicated to deities and their temples. Sumerian temples consisted of huge buildings within which these goods could be stored until their redistribution. The administrative class was responsible for keeping track of what goods came into the temple, who had contributed them (and who still owed), and later how goods should be reallocated. As this system became larger and more complex, with increasing volumes of agricultural and trade products, administrators required a more sophisticated accounting system, the development of which eventually led to the origins of writing.

In the largest settlements such as Uruk, at least a portion of the goods dedicated to the temple were redistributed to the administrators and other city residents associated with the daily running of the temple. This may have been a fairly significant number of people, given the size of these structures and the important role they played in Sumerian religion and economy. Farmers were probably required to contribute to the temple but depended far less on any redistributive goods coming back to them. It is less clear how much craft workers depended on the redistribution of goods from the temple, but at least some were employed as temple workers. The Sumerian population, then, consisted of a socioeconomic hierarchy of classes, with elites at the pinnacle and farmers and herders at the bottom (with a possible slave group below this). Intermediary classes of religious personnel, administrators, craftspersons, and other workers associated with the temple made up the rest of the population. Though farmers and herders may have rested at the bottom of the hierarchy, they were least dependent on receiving support from a redistributive temple economy, while those at higher ranks received a portion, or even a majority, of their daily needs from this system. However, as the city grew and the elite class expanded, the amount of tribute required for dedication to the temple also increased, placing added burdens on farmers, artisans, and administrators alike (Pollock 1999).

The political structure of ancient Uruk settlements is not entirely understood. The temple clearly functioned as an important economic center in Sumerian settlements. Monumental secular buildings are at a bare minimum in these cities, and no "palace" structure has been found. This does not suggest, however, that there was no centralized leadership. A document known as the "Standard List of Professions" offers an account of titles of officials and their duties, as well as lists of workers and their jobs (such as "gardener," "herder," and "farmer"). At the top of this list is an individual who is the highest administrator in the land. In later versions of this text, this individual carried the title *king*, but in these earlier stages the title is not clearly understood; some have suggested the Uruk leaders were "priest-kings" who drew their power through close association with the temple. While archaeologists and other scholars are still debating the exact nature of the ancient Uruk ruling structure, it is clear that rulership was intimately associated with the temple.

By the Early Dynastic period (3000–2350 B.C.E.), the Sumerian landscape, and the population on it, had altered substantially. Most people had moved from the countryside to cities, perhaps because of growing tribute demands from Uruk-period cities and temples. This forced an economic reorganization that resulted in what some call an *oikos* economy (Pollock 1999). In the Early Dynastic system, cities were organized into productive units known as *oikoi* (plural of *oikos*), or "households." All of the products needed for survival, and beyond (i.e., luxury goods if the oikos was wealthy enough), were produced by individuals in the oikos structure. The head of the oikos was responsible for distributing goods back to members, and each was given rations based on hierarchical rank (using such factors as social standing, gender, and age) (Pollock 1999). Those in higher-ranking positions received proportionately more, maintaining a socioeconomic stratification in Early Dynastic cities. The largest and most extensive oikos structures were headed by royal elites and the temples. Each member of the royal family (including children) had his or her own oikos, which may have included hundreds of members, all toiling to produce goods for that oikos. Not only did the god or goddess to whom a temple was dedicated function as the head of an oikos, but the spouse of the deity also had one. It is likely that temple officials also stood at the head of oikoi. Therefore, while there were numerous oikoi independent of the royal and temple systems, it is clear that a significant portion of the Early Dynastic populations were economically dependent on secular and religious elites.

The leadership of Early Dynastic cities is clearly defined in the texts. By this period, kingship was established, and palaces, separate from temples, were built in Mesopotamian cities. Kings and their families were still deeply involved in religious duties, but temples were headed by priests and priestesses, and kings controlled the armies and performed other secular duties associated with running the state. We know about the lives and exploits of some Early Dynastic kings from the texts written about their endeavors. The emergence of secular kings may have begun several hundred years earlier, when various regions began contentious conflict over land and resources. The commander of the army may have become quite important, eventually becoming the ultimate secular leader. In early phases of the Early Dynastic period, each city had two important leaders, the king, who resided in his palace with the royal family, and the main priest of the temple dedicated to the city's patron deity. By the later phases, however, a merging of divine and secular power had occurred. Kings claimed that their power was given by the god of the city and that the seat of kingship had descended from the realm of the deities. The king essentially had claimed divine status and ruled over city, military, and temple. A king could launch building campaigns, military campaigns, or undertake economic or political reorganizations by claiming he acted on behalf of the gods who sanctioned his kingship (Pollock 1999). As kings increasingly became the primary Sumerian rulers, it was more difficult for temple officials, or anyone else, to curb their behavior. Over the course of a thousand years, then, the Mesopotamian power structure had changed from one seated in the religio-temple realm, to dual leadership between king and temple, to supreme power wielded by a divinely sanctioned king.

The wealth and power commanded by elites is perhaps best demonstrated by the burials known as the Royal Tombs of Ur. A cemetery outside this city held several thousand graves dating to the Early Dynastic period. Seventeen of these were remarkable in that they had beautiful tomb architecture and fabulous burial gifts, some of which have become hallmark symbols of ancient Mesopotamia (Figure 16.2). The excavator of the cemetery, Leonard Woolley, believed these to be the tombs of a royal family, but there is no firm evidence of this; it is certain that those buried here were wealthy elites of the city of Ur. Besides grave goods such as jewelry, weapons, games, statues, musical instruments, and vessels made of the finest materials (gold, ivory, lapis lazuli, and electrum, to name just a few), those buried in the tombs took their servants with them as well. In one area, 74 victims of sacrifice were discovered—killed, presumably, to serve their masters in the next life. The tombs at Ur may be a unique occurrence in Early Dynastic Sumer, but they are indicative of the power of the elites in this period.

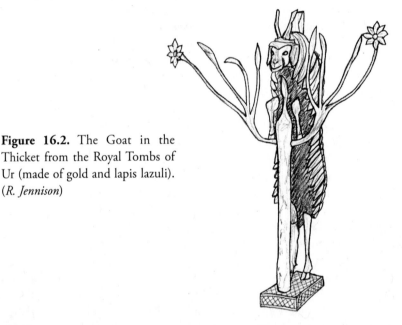

Figure 16.2. The Goat in the Thicket from the Royal Tombs of Ur (made of gold and lapis lazuli). (*R. Jennison*)

Writing and Early Texts

The dynamic and complex Sumerian economy required a sophisticated record-keeping system that was the spur to the earliest writing system in the world. Sumerians may have originally used small tokens of clay, in different sizes and shapes, to keep track of the movement of goods in and out of city temple storage areas. This developed into the use of clay tablets with markings on them, alleviating the need for numerous small pieces of clay. Eventually even this system was insufficient, and Sumerians developed the earliest-known writing system to keep track of their economic endeavors. This earliest system was pictographic and emerged in the late fourth millennium. Sumerians impressed a counting symbol to indicate an amount and then drew pictures of the idea they wished to record. Eventually greater efficiency and flexibility were needed, which led to the creation of cuneiform writing, a system using signs impressed on clay by a stylus. Sumerian was no longer ideographic (representative of an idea), but rather used signs to create words and sentences. By the mid-third millennium, a full-fledged Sumerian writing system, with grammatical structure and hundreds of signs, was used to record quasi-historical documents along with the standard economic texts. Other tablets recorded far more than just economic information; myths, temple hymns and rituals, and various royal inscriptions also became part of the corpus of texts (Pollock 1999). It was not long before literary texts, such as the *Epic of Gilgamesh*, were composed.

Literacy was not commonplace in ancient Sumer, and in fact it is unlikely that elites themselves could read the texts that recorded their wealth and stories. A class of scribes, perhaps trained from childhood, learned the elaborate writing system and the language that went with it. Sumerian may have differed considerably from the daily spoken language; possibly it was a separate written language, perhaps with deeply ancient roots, used for the formal record-keeping, and later, literature. Scribes would have held a certain status in Sumerian society for their esoteric knowledge (Ross 2009). However, ultimate power was held by those who could command what the scribes should record, and this right almost certainly belonged to Sumerian elites, including religious and secular leaders (Pollock 1999).

Sumerian texts have given us a great deal of information about Mesopotamian culture. The *Epic of Gilgamesh* is the earliest piece of literature yet discovered; it eventually (in later centuries) comprised twelve chapters, which contained references to a great flood. Gilgamesh was, according to the story, a great king of Uruk who built the city walls and the temple precinct. (Gilgamesh was probably an actual figure who may have ruled Uruk sometime in the earlier third millennium.) Gilgamesh was a bit too fond of Uruk's young women, and he worked its young men hard building the city's wall. The gods were entreated to curb Gilgamesh's behavior, and they sent Enkidu, a man-beast, to fight Gilgamesh. These two heroes wrestled but then became the best of friends and headed out to accomplish great deeds together. After several adventures, Enkidu died, causing Gilgamesh great anguish. In addition to mourning his friend, Gilgamesh feared his own mortality and wished to avoid death. He went to see Ut-napishtim to learn the secret of long life. Ut-napishtim and his wife had survived a great flood, becoming immortal in the aftermath. Ut-napishtim recounts the flood story to Gilgamesh in chapter 11; it bears a striking resemblance to the story in the book of Genesis in the Bible, composed later, in which Noah and his family survive a flood on an ark (McCall 1990). In the Gilgamesh story, the gods decided to create a great flood to eradicate humans. Ea (god of fresh waters) warned his favorite human Ut-napishtim of the coming disaster and told him to build a boat, complete with measurements and what should be brought on board (precious metals, animals, and Ut-napishtim's family). After a week of flooding, Ut-napishtim sent out a dove and then a swallow to search for land, but they both returned. Lastly he sent a raven, which did not return, signaling land had emerged from the floodwaters. The gods made Ut-napishtim and his wife immortal, but Gilgamesh failed to achieve immortality. The *Epic of Gilgamesh* was copied numerous times, and fragments of tablets with the myth are found all over Mesopotamia and beyond, indicating it was a widely known story. The style of writing suggests it might have been read publicly (McCall 1990), perhaps at festivals or other ceremonies.

In contrast, the *Epic of Creation* is written in a very formal style and does not offer exciting passages or great adventures. It tells of a time when two deities created generations of gods and eventually, after internal battles, created humans as well. This epic is in an elevated hymnic style and is full of repetition; it may have been used in formal ceremonies inside important temples, rather than read to the public at large gatherings (McCall 1990).

Other myths describe the actions of the gods and simultaneously explain the Sumerian world. The *Descent of Ishtar* recounts how the goddess went to visit the underworld. She became trapped or imprisoned there and had to be rescued by Ea. The underworld demons, however, demanded a replacement for her, and so Ishtar sent her lover, Dumuzi, in her place. Dumuzi could only ascend to earth for six months of the year, which corresponded to the Mesopotamian growing season. The Sumerians believed everything was orchestrated by the gods, including good fortune and disaster, and their myths explain the how and why of these events.

In addition to religious texts, other documents recount historical information. One of the most important of these is the *Sumerian King List* (SKL). This document lists the names of early Mesopotamian cities, their rulers, and the length of their reigns, and offers a short description of their accomplishments. The SKL was copied and recopied through the ages in city after city, so we have several versions, often with conflicting information. The SKL begins with the statement that kingship descended from heaven, thereby acknowledging the semi-divine nature of rulers. It divides kings into *antediluvian* ("pre-flood") and those who ruled after the flood. Kings who ruled before the flood lived fantastically long lives, sometimes in the thousands of years. Those listed immediately after the flood, and thereby closer in time to the actual composition of the list, were probably historical figures with increasingly more normal life spans and reigns. Gilgamesh, who ruled not long after the flood, had a reign of 126 years. Later kings held reigns that are independently documented as accurate. The SKL is fascinating on a number of levels, not least of which is its echoing of the existence of the flood recounted in the *Epic of Gilgamesh*, as well as the recognition of a king of Uruk with that name. The oft rewriting of the SKL would seem to indicate Sumerians, and later Mesopotamian cultures, believed it an important document. Some or much of it may have been known outside of scribal circles, and residents in individual cities may have been aware of the portions that described the dynastic successions of kings.

Sumerian Religion

Our understanding of Sumerian religion derives both from archaeological discoveries and from textual evidence such as the myths and hymns noted above. Sumerians were deeply religious and expended a great deal of wealth and effort to gain the support from the many gods and goddesses in whom they believed. Their religion was polytheistic, with different deities overseeing patron cities as well as different aspects of human affairs. Each Sumerian city boasted a significant temple dedicated to the patron god or goddess, but other temples were also built so that almost no deity went unrecognized. For instance, a text dating to the early third millennium states that no fewer than twenty temples were to be found in the city of Lagash (Pollock 1999); many of these, if not all of them, certainly existed in the fourth-millennium Uruk period. Good examples of Uruk-period city temples are found at the city of Uruk itself, which, perhaps because of its size and power, had two principal patron deities: Anu (the sky god) and Inanna (the goddess of love and war, also known as Ishtar), who was worshipped in the Eanna precinct. Sumerian temples were enormous, colorful places. Temples were built of mudbricks which were then plastered and decorated. The White Temple at Uruk (named for the white gypsum plaster clinging to the walls; Figure 16.3), most likely dedicated to the city god Anu, rested on a platform that could be mounted by staircase. Later texts state that these platforms were made of "clean sand" brought in from outside the city so that temples could be built upon unsullied foundations. Traces of earlier temples underlay the late fourth-millennium White Temple, indicating this particular part of the city had been dedicated to religious worship for generations. The White Temple had three parts (known as *tripartite* architecture), with walls that were niched and buttressed to give them texture and monumentality. Inside the temple was an altar and a place to make offerings. Uruk's Eanna precinct was a bit more elaborate, with pillared halls, several tripartite, niched and buttressed temples, and large courts (Figure 16.3). Several buildings were decorated with "clay nails," large golf-tee-shaped baked clay objects that were inserted into walls and columns, the heads of which were painted various colors to create decorative designs.

Inside the temples were statues of the deity to which the building was dedicated. These statues were made of wood and then covered in gold. The statue was believed to be a living representative of the god or goddess and was treated with great respect, bathed and then clothed in finery each day, and fed the finest of foods drawn from the offerings made to the temples. That these statues were considered animate, and the deities essential to the welfare of the city, is demonstrated in later times when attackers would "carry off the gods" to their own cities. Later texts lament of Mesopotamian cities that had lost their patron gods and were therefore bereft and at the mercy of any ill fortunes that might befall them.

In addition to these large and elaborate temples, smaller buildings in residential neighborhoods may have served as ritual structures for the non-elite population (Pollock 1999). These smaller structures may not have been temples, but rather a place to pay homage to the city god or other deity. Some rituals were carried out only in the city temples, attended perhaps only by the elites, while other festivals took place in more public settings where most residents could participate.

In the Early Dynastic period, when palaces began to appear, the Mesopotamian *ziggurat* emerged. Ziggurats were stepped structures with sacred buildings resting on

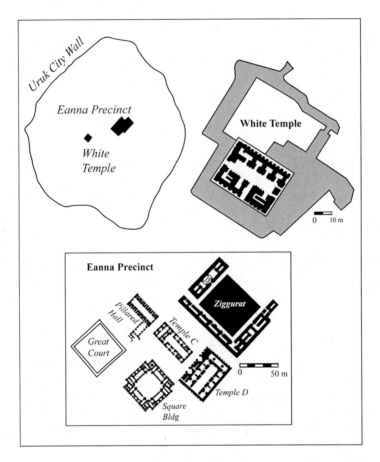

Figure 16.3. Plans of the White Temple and Eanna precinct at Uruk.
(*S. R. Steadman*).

the top platform. Each platform was like an increasingly smaller layer of cake, built with a sand interior and mudbrick exterior. The ziggurat dedicated to Anu at Uruk likely required hundreds of daily workers for a period of several years to complete the structure (Matthews 2003). These monuments were visually impressive and demonstrated the power of the god, as well as the power of those who could command the labor to build them. That each city boasted a number of temples, and some featured several ziggurats, is evidence of a powerful elite and religious class capable of marshaling an astonishing amount of labor.

Temples were decorated with carvings, decorative objects such as large vases, and perhaps other organic elements now lost to us. One interesting standard element inside Sumerian temples was the *votive statue*. Commissioned by Sumerians who could afford to have them made, these portray Sumerian people, standing with eyes wide and hands held in a specific fold or holding a cup (Figure 16.4). Once completed, these votive statues, often bearing the name of the person they were meant to repre-

Figure 16.4. Examples of Sumerian votive figurines giving "perpetual worship" in the temple. (*R. Jennison*)

sent, were taken into the temple and placed on a bench or in a wall niche to face the cult statue of the temple's god or goddess. The clasped hands signified an attitude of prayer or respect, the cup a libation to be offered; the statues stood in perpetual admiration of the deity. Those from wealthier classes could command larger and more elaborate statues made of expensive materials, thereby impressing the deity with their dedication and devotion.

Religion in the Sumerian period formed the foundation of religious belief for the next several millennia in Mesopotamia and beyond. Different regions worshipped deities of different names, but these gods and goddesses lived in city temples built by the rulers and city elites. Patrons stocked the temples with goods, and statues of various types were placed inside in attitudes of worship. The legacy of kingship, established in the Early Dynastic period, was handed down as well, with ever more powerful kings who deemed themselves divine and justified in their actions by the pantheon of the gods.

The Akkadian Empire

By the later third millennium, two city-states had become extremely powerful. One of these was the Sumerian city of Ur. The other was farther to the north, in a region later known as Babylonia. Here a city named Akkad sat at the center of an increasingly powerful kingdom. Akkad came to prominence because Sargon the Great, a king of the city of Kish who came to power in 2334 B.C.E., moved his capital to this previously little known settlement. Unfortunately, Akkad has not been located or excavated, so the records that were certainly generated by Sargon's scribes are still absent from the record. However, because Sargon became such a famous and accomplished ruler, many texts were written about him in later generations, giving us a quasi-historical account of his reign. Sargon may not have been in the Kish dynastic lineage, as his name translates to "legitimate king," a telltale sign that he was not. However, Sargon grew to be a very popular king who expanded his Akkadian empire to stretch from the shores of the Mediterranean to the Persian Gulf. Along the way he conquered Uruk, Ur, and most other Sumerian cities. Sargon was famous not just because of his enormous empire, but for his personal accomplishments as well. During his 56-year reign, various stories were apparently circulated about him that made their way into later documents. One of the best-known describes his origins and serves to explain his presence in the royal house of Kish. The story tells of Sargon as a baby, who was rescued from a reed basket floating on the river. He was taken into the royal house where he was a "cup-bearer" to the king. Because the goddess Ishtar loved Sargon, she helped elevate him to kingship and made his empire powerful. In this story, therefore, there is a legitimate explanation for Sargon's presence in the royal house, and his reign is sanctioned by a powerful goddess. Perhaps these stories were circulated by administrators and religious personnel during Sargon's reign to counter claims that he had no right to the throne. They seem to have worked because Sargon became known as a great king, and later rulers took his name to signify their own greatness.

Sargon took several actions that changed the nature of key Mesopotamian customs. He appointed his daughter, Enheduanna, to be high priestess of the temple dedicated to Nanna, the moon god and patron deity at Ur. This began a tradition of appointing women, especially daughters, to important religious positions. Enheduanna was a powerful priestess who was prolific in her composition of hymns, poems, and prayers to Nanna. Because we have not securely located Akkad, we do not know what the city temple, dedicated to the patron goddess Ishtar, looked like, but Sargon was well known for his building projects across his empire. Sargon was responsible for erecting large temples and palaces in several of the cities he conquered, but most have disappeared under later building projects. These architectural monuments were probably decorated with stelae and statues, only fragments of which are left to us today. The power of the Sargonic throne, enhanced by the goddess Ishtar, enabled the king to command a great deal of labor and obedience from his people.

During his long reign, Sargon also accomplished a shift in the official language used by the Akkadian state. Texts dating to Sargon's time and afterward were written in a language now known as Akkadian, rather than in the Sumerian used for a millennium. Akkadian is a Semitic language and is thus a relative to Arabic and Hebrew. It was originally theorized that Sargon was from a different ethnic and language group, thus speaking a Semitic rather than Sumerian language. If this is true, then he was the first Semitic king and established a Semitic language as the lingua franca of Mesopotamia, which has persisted essentially to the present day. However, some scholars have suggested that Akkadian was actually the language of "the people" even during Sumerian times, and the Sumerian found on earlier texts was a type of state or administrative language no longer spoken by Mesopotamians (Pollock

1999). Whether Sargon was a usurper, and brought Semitic language and ethnicity to the forefront of Mesopotamia, or whether he was simply responsible for shifting the language of the state to one actually spoken by everyone, he established the first written Semitic language in the Middle East, a region that saw the florescence of many others over the succeeding millennia.

Sumer, Akkad, and the Power of Religion

Sumerians and their successors, Akkadians, were clearly deeply religious. To please their deities, and apparently at the behest of their secular and religious rulers, residents dedicated the products of their labor, and their labor itself, to the glorification of the city and its gods and goddesses. This resulted in landscapes with enormous buildings dedicated to various deities, some of which were large temples capable of storing enormous quantities of goods which then made their way into the hands of those who served the temple. The construction of the towering ziggurats required untold hours of human labor which was seemingly freely given in exchange for sustenance. With the establishment of divine kingship, the palace emerged, built by the hands of those who possessed the least in society. In exchange, the king and priests ruled the city in accordance with the gods' wishes, ensuring health and prosperity for all. That the king could intercede with the city god must have been reassuring to his people, further encouraging them to carry out his edicts and building projects. At least at Ur, the power of the elite class was such that several dozen servants could be sacrificed in order to continue on into the next life with their masters. Public ceremonies and festivals, perhaps sponsored by the temple or palace, gave the public the opportunity to worship and hear the myths and epics recited from the sacred texts. Inside the great temples, high-level ceremonies, probably closed to the public, celebrated other aspects of the cosmology, such as the creation of the entire world. Between these public festivals the common population could carry out daily or regular worship at neighborhood temples. In this way they could be certain that the gods were propitiated at every level: by the king, by the city temples and priests, and by each individual resident. This approach proved successful, as Mesopotamian empires remained powerful players in ancient Near Eastern history for millennia.

USEFUL SOURCES

Harriet Crawford, *Sumer and the Sumerians*, 2004.
J. Nicholas Postgate, *Early Mesopotamia*, 1994.
Marc Van de Meirop, *History of the Ancient Near East*, 2003.

17

LEVANTINE RELIGIONS AND THE ORIGINS OF JUDAISM

There are probably more controversies, debates, and excavation reports written about this small region than any other comparable area of the world. The Levant, the coastal region that stretches from modern Syria to the border of modern Egypt (Figure 17.1), is the homeland to two of the five major world religions of today: Judaism and Christianity. The wealth of archaeological sites in the region, and the detailed descriptions of places, people, and events reported in sacred texts, have produced innumerable debates about the origins of these two religions. Some textual and excavated data mesh nicely, providing a firm basis for understanding the events that shaped the people and their religions; more often, the two do not match, or there is no archaeological evidence available at all. It is at these junctures that scholarly debate about how to understand the development of the religions, and the major figures in them, ensues.

The text sacred to these two religions is known as the Bible and is divided into numerous books. The Bible is comprised of two sections: the Hebrew Bible (also known as the Old Testament) which describes the creation of humans and their world, and the events surrounding the emergence of Judaism; and the Greek Bible (the New Testament), which focuses on the emergence of Christianity. An earlier discussion (see Chapter 1) touched on ethics and the unfortunate tendency, in the past, to use excavated materials to "prove" sacred texts. This was a particular problem in earlier Levantine archaeology but is much less so today (Schmidt 2007). The following explores the archaeological evidence for the various belief systems, including early Judaism, in the ancient Levant.

The First Patriarchs Emerge

The first book of the Hebrew Bible, Genesis, begins with the creation of the world and all its inhabitants. It goes on to list the descendant generations of the first humans, describing individuals with exceedingly long life spans (e.g., Methuselah who lived 969 years and others who fathered children at an advanced age—as old as 182).

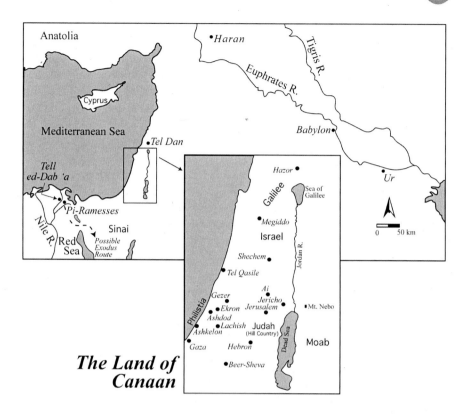

Figure 17.1. Map of sites and regions discussed in the chapter. (*S. R. Steadman*)

It also describes a great flood that destroyed the earth, except for some selected humans (Noah and his family) and animals. The flood story is remarkably similar to the one in the Gilgamesh epic described in Chapter 16; the two texts may have derived from peoples who shared versions of this myth, perhaps in ancient Mesopotamia. Genesis records that after the flood people lived shorter lives, until they eventually had life spans similar in length to those we consider normal today; this progression, of incredibly long lives prior to the great flood and more normal ones afterward, parallels the Sumerian King List also described in Chapter 16. The notion that humans who lived long ago, before the flood, were virtually immortal seems to have been a common conception in many areas of the ancient Near East.

After the flood myth, Genesis goes on to describe a man named Abraham who was born in Ur, in southern Mesopotamia, but he moved to Haran, located today in southern Turkey. While there, a god instructed Abraham to take his family and move to the Land of Canaan, which today is constituted by the modern states of Israel and western Jordan and the regions known as the West Bank and Gaza. In Canaan, Abraham had a son named Isaac, and Isaac had two sons named Esau and Jacob. Genesis reports which cities these individuals and their families lived in or near, and archaeologists have excavated many of these. The exact chronological period when these events might have taken place is entirely uncertain; most believe that they should be placed at some point in the first half of the second millennium B.C.E. (Table 17.1), but a more exact date is difficult to pinpoint. However, during the Middle Bronze periods, and even in Late Bronze I, many of the settlements described in Genesis were not inhabited, presenting a prime opportunity for debate. One likely solution is that the texts describing these early patriarchs were composed many centuries later than when these settlements were inhabited; thus forgotten names of Abraham's and Isaac's home towns were substituted with those existing at the time that the oral tradition became written word (Grabbe 2007).

TABLE 17.1. POSTULATED CHRONOLOGY OF EVENTS IN GENESIS

Middle Bronze I–II	ca. 2000–1550 B.C.E.	Abraham arrives in Canaan
Late Bronze I	ca. 1550–1400 B.C.E.	Patriarchs in Canaan—enslaved in Egypt
Late Bronze II	ca. 1400–1200 B.C.E.	Exodus and Conquest of Canaan
Iron IA	ca. 1200–1150 B.C.E.	Israelites Settle in Canaan
Iron IB	ca. 1150–1000 B.C.E.	Hostilities with Philistines—Saul emerges
Iron IIA	ca. 1000–925	Kingdoms of David & Solomon
Iron IIB	ca. 925–720	Divided Monarchy

In the second half of Genesis, circumstances took Abraham's descendants, led by Jacob (and his ten brothers), to live in Egypt. At this point these descendants are called the Israelites, meaning the people faithful to the god who spoke to Abraham. The Israelites remained in the Nile Valley for several generations, becoming quite a large population. According to the texts, at some point the Israelites became slaves of the Egyptian monarchy. It is in the freeing of these slaves, and their return to the Land of Canaan, that the finer points associated with the practice of early Judaism began to be established.

The Exodus and Wandering in the Wilderness

The Egyptians were excellent record-keepers and often painted scenes of daily life on their tombs and temple walls. These would be promising clues to the experiences of the Israelites in Egypt had these people been written about or depicted, but unfortunately they were not. This does not mean, however, that there isn't archaeological evidence that coincides with portions of the biblical narrative. One example of this is the Egyptian account of the invasion by a people known as the Hyksos in the mid-second millennium (ca. 1670–1570 B.C.E.). Archaeological work on Hyksos sites in Egypt has demonstrated that they may not have come from a distant land, but rather from

Canaan (Finkelstein and Silberman 2001). The Hyksos seem to have taken control of Egypt for a short time and set up their capital city, Avaris, in the Nile Delta. However, the Egyptians quickly regained power, and by the later sixteenth century, records claim Egypt "expelled" the Hyksos and destroyed Avaris. Archaeological data shows that from approximately 1520 to 1450 B.C.E. Egyptians marched on Canaanite cities and destroyed a number of them (Dever 2003). It is possible, therefore, that the Israelites may have been the remnants of the Hyksos who didn't flee back to Canaan, subsequently becoming the Bible's enslaved Israelites in the post-Hyksos Egyptian empire.

Archaeology in the Nile Delta has identified Avaris (Tell ed-Dab'a), and material culture confirms it was a Canaanite city. There was, therefore, a powerful Canaanite ("Hyksos") presence in Egypt in the mid-second millennium. Tell ed-Dab'a did suffer a destruction, in accordance with Egyptian records detailing the expulsion of the Hyksos. The biblical texts report that the enslaved Israelites were ordered to build two cities, Pithom and Pi-Ramesse. Recent work at Tell ed-Dab'a suggests that there was a rebuilding of this city in the thirteenth century; this rebuilding has tentatively been identified as having been commissioned by the pharaoh Ramesses II, who wished to have a city named after himself (Dever 2003). However, archaeologists have yet to locate the site of Pithom.

Most archaeologists and biblical historians agree that Ramesses II (1290–1224 B.C.E.) was the "pharaoh of the Exodus," the period when the Israelites escaped from Egypt. Ramesses II was a very powerful pharaoh in Nineteenth Dynasty Egypt, and he did mount a rigorous building campaign. Even more evidence comes from his successor, Merneptah, who commissioned the making of a stela inscribed with his exploits, including the areas he attacked and (possibly) conquered. The stela, erected in ca. 1207 B.C.E., mentions "Israel," suggesting that by the end of the thirteenth century the land previously known as Canaan was settled and even ruled by the people of Israel—that is, the Israelites (Grabbe 2007). Therefore, most place the events surrounding the Exodus in the mid or later thirteenth century B.C.E., during the reign of Ramesses II.

According to the Bible, the instigator of the exodus was an Israelite who had been raised in a royal Egyptian house. As a baby he had been set afloat on the Nile in a reed basket and retrieved by a woman of the royal household and raised as her son. This story explains why an Israelite named Moses was raised as a powerful and wealthy Egyptian until his early adulthood. The story is very similar to that told of Sargon, king of the Akkadians (see Chapter 16); in both cases the baby-afloat-in-the-basket story explains why the most unlikely of men came to hold such positions of power. The biblical narrative reports that Moses committed a crime in defense of the Israelites and then fled to the desert. While there, his god revealed to Moses that he, Moses, would lead the Israelites out of Egypt back to their homeland in Canaan. After returning to Egypt, Moses tried to reason with the pharaoh to release the Israelites; when this failed, Moses' god brought about ten plagues, which finally convinced the Egyptians to rid themselves of these troublemakers. As might be expected, there is little in the way of archaeological or textual evidence to document these events.

Once the Israelites had left the cities of Egypt, the pharaoh changed his mind and pursued them into the desert. It is here that one of the most famous miracles in the biblical narrative occurs, the "parting of the Red Sea." The Israelites passed through this body of water, but their god closed the waters on the Egyptians. While archaeology is silent on this event, textual study does aid somewhat. The Hebrew word used in the book of Exodus translates not as "Red" Sea, but "Reed" Sea, which might refer to a marshy area north of the tip of the actual Red Sea. Tidal movements, or the pure muddiness of a marsh, might have allowed lightly clad people to pass through but would surely bog down chariots and heavily armored soldiers. Herein may lie the explanation of the successful escape of the former slaves from the might of Egypt.

The next set of events in the biblical narrative describes the long period of "wandering" the escaped slaves endured on their way back to Canaan. The account takes up the next three books in the Bible (Leviticus, Numbers, and Deuteronomy), which frequently break away from the narrative to offer codes of behavior and methods of worship that are the backbone of modern Judaism.

The period of wandering, almost certainly in the Sinai Desert, is one that is difficult to track archaeologically, since at this point the Israelites were essentially mobile pastoralists, leaving little material culture behind. Nonetheless, many attempts to document the Israelites in the wilderness have been undertaken, as it is during this period that very important events took place. During the wanderers' time in the desert, the god of the Israelites revealed the laws by which they should live (now known as the Ten Commandments) and finally offered them a name by which they could call him: Yahweh (Hebrew for "I exist" or "I am"). Yahweh reaffirmed the promise, first made to Abraham, that the Land of Canaan would be their land and that he would guide and support them if they were true to him. The Ten Commandments were written on stone tablets that instantly became sacred. The Israelites built a holy container, an *ark*, for them, and wherever they camped they erected a *tabernacle*, or temple (probably a tent) to house these sacred stones (Figure 17.2). So, for the first time, the Israelites had a name for their god, rules to live by, and a place to worship him. In this time of wandering, then, the first concrete framework for the structure of Judaism was created.

Figure 17.2. Artistic rendering of Israelites worshipping the Ark during the "wandering" in the wilderness. (*M. J. Hughes*)

The Conquest of Canaan

According to the Bible, after their long period in the wilderness, the Israelites finally reached the border of Canaan, and they prepared to take the land by force. They camped in the land of Moab, today in the country of Jordan, on the east side of the Jordan River. Moses died in Moab, and leadership fell to another man named Joshua. The biblical narrative describes a Joshua who is a skilled tactical commander, leading the Israelites against city after city in Canaan. Their very first conquest was the city of Jericho, a heavily defended settlement near the Jordan River. After a week of marching around it, and perhaps laying siege to Jericho, the Israelite god Yahweh caused the walls around the city to collapse. This was followed by a very violent defeat of the city of Ai, where the Israelites slaughtered all inhabitants and hanged the king of Ai from a tree. These early defeats of Canaanite cities caused other Canaanite kings to forge alliances with one another to fight against the Israelites. Nonetheless, the Israelites, with the help of their god, defeated city after city, including Hazor, a very important city in the south. After five years of battles, the Israelites took residence in their promised land and began to rebuild it.

Archaeologists are fairly certain the period of the conquest must have been in the late thirteenth century (the Late Bronze II period). Because the Bible is so specific about which towns were conquered, archaeologists have been able to locate and excavate many of them. As might be expected, archaeology offers conflicting data that has given rise to a number of theories on the reentry of the Israelites into Canaan.

Proposed in the 1920s, the *conquest model* offers a scenario not dissimilar from that described in the Book of Joshua in the biblical text; this model was widely believed until the last few decades. More recent excavations determined that a number of the settlements "conquered" by the Israelites in the Late Bronze II period were not even inhabited at that time, not least of which was Jericho (Dever 2003). While Jericho had suffered a major destruction, it was centuries earlier and came at the hands of the Egyptians; by the thirteenth century the settlement was abandoned. The same is true for the second settlement on the Israelite itinerary, Ai. Other cities in the biblical list, including Hazor, were indeed destroyed in the late thirteenth century, but excavation cannot confirm it was Israelites who did the destroying (Ben-Tor and Zuckerman 2008); besides the Egyptians, other empires had carried out campaigns in Canaan during this time, and destruction may have come at the hands of any of these powerful kingdoms (Finkelstein and Silberman 2001). Most archaeologists now suggest the evidence does not support a violent conquest model to describe the entry of Israelites into Canaan.

A second theory, diametrically opposed, suggests a *peaceful infiltration*. In this model, nomadic, animal-herding Israelites (much like today's Bedouins of the Middle East) slowly moved into Canaan, settled, and took up farming side by side with other residents. Eventually their numbers and the force of their culture prevailed and the region became "Israel." This theory was also proposed in the 1920s and was celebrated as an excellent contrast to the more violent, even genocidal, account found in the biblical narrative. A major flaw, however, is in the description of how pastoral nomads act.

Ethnographic work on Bedouins and other nomadic pastoralists finds them resisting settlement and avoiding confining areas where large cities and heavily populated land-scapes are the norm (Dever 2003). The peaceful infiltration model was built on the belief that, given half a chance, Bedouins would always choose settlement over the nomadic life, an ethnocentric conception not borne out in ethnographies of present-day pastoral nomads. Further, the adjustment from herding to farming would have taken generations rather than just a few years, and such a difficult transition would be unlikely to yield a powerful kingdom just a decade or two later. The peaceful infiltration model has therefore also faded in popularity.

A third model, sometimes called the *peasant revolt model*, suggests that either indigenous Canaanites or Yahwistic Israelites revolted against oppressive rulers and founded a new system more to their liking. There has not been a great deal of support for this theory, and it is not demonstrated archaeologically either. One of the main flaws in all three models is the effort to find one central explanation that describes a complex process of settlement by a people who later became the rulers of the region. Rather than wholesale destruction, undetectably subtle settlement of pastoralists, or an internal revolt, archaeology suggests a long-term development that involved socioeconomic and political shifts which eventually led to the establishment of the Israelite kingdom.

Recent scholarship combining both textual and archaeological data argues that to understand the rise of Israel requires a broader view of the Levant in the thirteenth-century Mediterranean world. The Late Bronze II period was one in which empires rose and fell, including the Mittani in Syria, the Hittites in Anatolia, and the Assyrians in northern Mesopotamia; always crouching to the south of Canaan was the great Egyptian empire. Late in the thirteenth century, invasions of groups known as the "Sea Peoples" caused disruption from Egypt to Anatolia. The chaos instigated by the Sea People invasions (Sea Peoples may have come from Crete, Cyprus, Western Turkey, or even from points farther west) caused a ripple effect across Western Asia, disrupting trade and commerce, and resulting in the violent destruction of key cities. This socioeconomic chaos may have caused a significant movement of peoples from the lowlands of Canaan into the hill country (regions known as Judah and Samaria), where they resettled in smaller towns and villages. Some of these people may have included pastoralists who were forced to abandon traditional lifeways that were no longer possible in the changing political landscape of late thirteenth-century Canaan (Finkelstein and Silberman 2001). Archaeology demonstrates that by the Iron I period (early twelfth century), there was significantly more settlement in the hill country regions, indicating either a new influx of people from elsewhere, or a reorganization of settlement structure within Canaan, or both.

Others suggest the Sea People invasions and economic instability resulted in the collapse of the Canaanite city-states at the end of the thirteenth century. This may have been exacerbated by a decreasing yield of agricultural crops near cities with large populations. In response, people moved out of cities into smaller settlements, in order to farm less heavily used land and to avoid what may have been anarchical chaos in populated areas; some of these populations moved to the hill country. Numerous ethnic groups may have occupied thirteenth-century Canaan, some called 'Apiru by Egyptians and others (perhaps the later "Hebrews"), and who were sometimes considered upstarts and troublemakers. One possibility is that as Canaanite city-states disintegrated, the Israelites/'Apiru resettled the hill country, allowing them to coalesce into a more distinct ethnic/tribal entity over time (Dever 2003). As new arrivals from various quarters entered Canaan, some of whom perhaps were escaped Semitic slaves from Egypt, they may have chosen to settle with the Israelites with whom they shared ethnic ties (Killebrew 2006). Over time, these groups may have organized something of a tribal political structure that slowly, or perhaps quickly, developed into a more elaborate and far-reaching entity, resulting in the first Israelite kingdom.

Canaanite Religion and the Philistines

Whether the Israelites entered Canaan violently, peacefully, or were always there, they were surrounded by people practicing a polytheistic religion, who attended rituals and ceremonies in temples and worshipped idols representing gods and goddesses. The biblical texts make reference to two groups with whom the Israelites dealt frequently, the Canaanites and the Philistines.

The Canaanites and Their Religion

The Canaanite culture had been practiced in the Levant at least since the Middle Bronze period, if not much earlier. Canaanites built the cities that biblical texts say the Israelites destroyed in their conquest of Canaan. Material culture in the form of temples, idols, jewelry, and glyptic art such as cylinder seals offer evidence of Canaanite beliefs. These are bolstered by non-biblical textual evidence that describes Canaanite deities and their roles.

Three of the most important Canaanite deities were El, his son Baal, and Asherah (also known as Astarte or Ishtar), who appears to be Baal's sister. Asherah was associated with love, fertility, and apparently war, while Baal was a powerful storm god (Mazar 1990). The supreme Canaanite god was El, a creator god at the head of the Canaanite pantheon. Canaanites built temples that held cult statues of the divinities. The temples, found in Middle Bronze II levels at such sites as Megiddo, Hazor, and Shechem, were rectangular in shape with a single entrance at one of the short ends (Figure 17.3); extremely thick walls suggest the temples stood at some height, making them visible across the city. At the back of the interior large room was either a niche or a dais where the statue of the deity rested (Mazar 1990). Some of these temples had entrances flanked by two pillars or projections which may have had symbolic meaning. Biblical texts make reference to cultic prostitution in Canaanite religion, perhaps associated with temples dedicated to Asherah, though no extra-biblical confirmation of such practice has been discovered (Grabbe 2007). The temples were located in the center of most settlements and may have been open to any who wished to worship there. A number of temples were situated near open courts or cultic areas

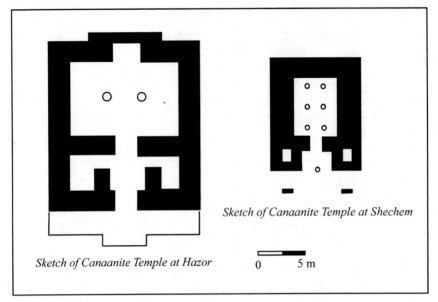

Sketch of Canaanite Temple at Shechem

Sketch of Canaanite Temple at Hazor

0   5 m

Figure 17.3. Examples of Canaanite temple styles. (*S. R. Steadman*)

that could hold large groups during public ceremonies. At some of these open areas, large stones (known as *massebot*) were erected, perhaps to symbolize various deities in the Canaanite pantheon. It is possible that any Canaanite could make an offering or libation in these open areas at any time, thereby making public worship immediately available to everyone, even if the temple was closed or unavailable for visitation.

Canaanites made small statues and images of their deities that could function as objects of worship at other locations. A number of statues of a female, probably Asherah, have been discovered. These are often made of metal and are sometimes in a dagger shape, perhaps representing her role as a war goddess (Figure 17.4). Other examples illustrate her partially or fully nude, probably in recognition of her role as a fertility and love goddess. Baal is found on cylinder seals, often standing beside an important figure (such as a prince); he wears a horned headdress

Figure 17.4. Example of Canaanite Asherah dagger (thin gold metal piece). (*R. Jennison*)

and is also shown in association with a crescent moon. The horns may be representative of a bull. Several examples of calf statues have been recovered in ritual locations, perhaps representing Baal or his father, El. Statues were discovered at the massebot in the high open areas near the temples, as well as inside the temples. Canaanites could apparently wear images of their goddess to show their devotion and dedication.

The Philistines

Another group with whom Israelites apparently had to contend was the Philistines. The Philistines were most likely descendants of the "Sea Peoples" who menaced Egypt and the Levant in the Late Bronze Age. Within a very few generations, those who had settled in the Levant adopted Canaanite styles of language and script, but held onto a vaguely Aegean-style material culture that set them apart from their Canaanite and Israelite counterparts. The Philistines also appeared to adapt readily to the notion of polytheistic beliefs, probably having come from such a tradition in the west. They lived mainly in the southern coastal region and developed a thriving economy based on maritime trade as well as agricultural production in the inland coastal areas.

Philistine settlements, such as Gaza, Ashkelon, Ashdod, and Tel Miqne-Ekron, are mainly identified by their material culture, including their unique pottery (which displays Greek influences), their various burials in anthropoid coffins, and their unusual glyptic art on cylinder seals (bearing styles associated with Cyprus and points west). Our best information about Philistine worship comes from the site of Tel Qasile, where several Philistine temples were discovered. Early Philistine temples do not look at all like their Canaanite counterparts, but after a century of rebuilding, temples took on a form similar to but not exactly like Canaanite examples. The interior of Philistine temples held a platform upon which the cult statue of the deity could rest, with interior benches that may have been for parishioners or cult objects donated to the temple.

We know far less about Philistine deities, in part because the Philistines adopted much of Canaanite religion not long after their arrival. One of their main gods was named Dagon, who may have been an indigenous god that was combined with a Canaanite god. Several rulers of Philistine cities had *Dagon* as part of their name, perhaps allying them with this important god. Dagon may have been associated with fertility and successful agriculture, a crucial endeavor for Philistines even though they lived mainly along the coast. In fact, as they settled more firmly into the Levantine region, they apparently prospered and their population grew, causing them to expand northward and somewhat inland. This brought them into more consistent contact with both Canaanites and Israelites, the latter living primarily in the hill regions of the Levant. At Ekron, the Philistines apparently worshipped a patron deity named Baal-Zebul ("Princely Lord") who may have derived from Canaanite Baal. In biblical texts this name was corrupted to *Baal-Zebub*, which means "Lord of the Flies," clearly showing Israelite contempt for the gods of their Philistine neighbors (Laughlin 2000). The Philistines also worshipped a goddess whose name was Ashtoreth, again a derivation of the Canaanite goddess Asherah. While both the Philistines and Canaanites had polytheistic religions, temples, statues, and public rituals, it was with the

Philistines that the Israelites came into close and constant conflict at the beginning of the first millennium B.C.E.

The First Israelite Empire

According to the biblical tradition, after their entry into Canaan, Israelites had trouble remaining faithful to their god. In the book of I Samuel, the Israelites are described as worshipping "foreign gods" and making offerings at "high places" (perhaps at Canaanite massebot). Some believed selecting an Israelite king would be beneficial for the people, but their religious leader Samuel disagreed. Nevertheless, according to Yahweh's wishes, he anointed a king when the time came.

In the late second/early first millennium, the Israelite political structure may have consisted of small chiefdoms, each with a leader who wished to be a king. Eventually, according to biblical texts, a man named Saul emerged as the appropriate choice for Israel's first king, perhaps in the late eleventh century B.C.E.; he was anointed by Samuel and and then set out to expand the kingdom of Israel militarily.

Even before Saul became king, the Israelites were experiencing problems with the Philistines. The book of I Samuel reports a bitter battle in which the Philistines attacked the Israelites and managed to make off with the Ark that held the sacred Ten Commandments. The Philistines destroyed several Israelite cities as well, which firmly cemented hatred between the two peoples. According to the Bible, wherever the Philistines took the Ark, problems occurred; eventually they decided to rid themselves of this troublesome sacred object and set it on a cow-drawn cart to be taken out of their territories. It eventually was retrieved by the Israelites. Another myth describes the love story between Samson, an Israelite, and Delilah, a Philistine. These two married and went to live in a Philistine city. Delilah betrayed her new husband by cutting his hair (in which his extraordinary strength lay) and blinding him. Samson's god Yahweh restored his strength, however, and Samson destroyed a temple of Dagon in Gaza, killing Delilah and several thousand Philistines. These stories show the significant rivalry between the two cultures in the early stages of the first Israelite kingdom.

David, Solomon, and the First Temple

According to the Bible, the troubles with the Philistines apparently continued, with several pitched battles between the two peoples. In one battle, the Israelites lost and Saul was mortally wounded, ending his kingship quite early in his reign. After the defeat of the Israelite army and the death of Saul, the continued sovereignty of the Israelite kingdom hung in the balance. Into this difficult situation stepped a man named David, who had slain a Philistine warrior named Goliath in a previous battle during Saul's reign. Goliath was a huge and well-armored man, and David, only a young man (perhaps a teenager) at the time, killed him with a simple slingshot. Saul had invited David to become a leading warrior in his court, but there was rivalry between the two, and eventually, after Saul tried to kill him, David went into exile to the south where he built a rather impressive kingdom. Not long after Saul's death, David united the north and south regions so that all of the different Israelite tribes were now part of one kingdom; the traditional date for the establishment of the United Monarchy is approximately 1000 B.C.E.

Archaeology has yet to find evidence of Saul; traces of David's kingdom are few, and they are controversial. During the eleventh and tenth centuries B.C.E., Philistine and Israelite cities and settlements suffered destructions, but whether these resulted from armed conflict between the two is still beyond our grasp archaeologically. In one of David's most important battles, he took the city of Jerusalem. According to the Bible, he chose this city to be his capital and moved the Ark there to make it a center of political and religious power. David embarked on a building campaign across his kingdom and especially in Jerusalem, which became a great city. Archaeological evidence of these endeavors has not yet come to light despite consistent efforts to document physical evidence of David's reign. A point of controversy is whether Jerusalem was even more than just a small town in the tenth century. Survey data, population models, and minimal archaeological evidence make for a range of interpretations. Some argue that Jerusalem was little more than a village in the tenth century, thereby refuting biblical claims that it became David's capital. Others assert that survey data shows a rapid population increase in the Judaean hill country surrounding Jerusalem and in the city area itself, confirming that the location became a center of political and economic activity. Taken together, the evidence suggests that Jerusalem in the tenth century was a modest town that was growing rapidly, and "it exhibits the characteristics of a regional administrative centre or the capital of a small, newly established state" (Grabbe 2007:72). More specific archaeological evidence of David's reign, however, is not yet attested. One interesting item of evidence is a stone inscription excavated at Tel Dan in 1993. This inscription probably dates to the ninth century and reports a king's successes in battle. The king asserts that he killed someone who was "king of the House of David." This would indicate that a historical figure named David founded a dynasty that had at some point ruled an Israelite kingdom.

According to biblical tradition, the third king was Solomon, son of David, who was famous for his wisdom, his wealth, and his building campaigns. During his 40-year reign, Solomon fortified the cities of Hazor, Megiddo, Gezer (reported in I Kings), Jerusalem, and a number of other cities. Unfortunately, though wise, Solomon apparently couldn't resist using his royal power to ensure these projects were completed. He coerced people who were not "Israelites"—that is, those the Israelites had conquered—to construct the fortifications and buildings in his cities. This scenario echoes the Israelite experience in Egypt.

Solomon's most famous endeavor was his construction of the first Yahweh temple in Jerusalem. Several biblical stories attest to Solomon's fame as a wise ruler, and this is also shown by his desire to build his people a temple. The numerous Canaanite temples and idols encouraged frequent worship of and obedience to their deities. The Yahwistic prohibition against idolatry may have made the god of the Israelites seem less accessible, a situation exacerbated by the absence of a place to dedicate offerings or to make prayers for help or solace. Israelites, as reported in the biblical texts, were continuously drifting to Canaanite methods of worship and even visiting their temples and sacred high places. King Solomon built a temple for his people so that they, too, would have a place to worship their god. The building housed the sacred Ark of the Covenant, provided a central location for public rituals, and served as a constant reminder of the true god of the Israelites.

As is the case with nearly everything else in biblical history, the archaeological record offers conflicting evidence of these Solomonic building campaigns. Archaeology has indeed uncovered evidence of new fortifications built at the cities of Megiddo, Hazor, and Gezer, as well as at Lachish and the Philistine city of Ashdod. The gates at these cities, particularly at Megiddo, Hazor, and Gezer, are remarkably similar. They have six chambers, which sets them apart from the four-chambered gates of previous centuries. When these gates were initially discovered, archaeologists believed they were proof that Solomon had commissioned an architect to design them, and they were promptly labeled the "Solomonic Gates." However, further investigation has offered some obstacles to this interpretation. First is the fact that the gates have different types of structure. Those at Hazor and Gezer have front towers, but the one at Megiddo does not. All three are of different sizes and built of different construction materials. Furthermore, many archaeologists have examined the stratigraphy of these gates and assert that not only were they built at different times, but they are later than the traditional mid- to late tenth-century time of Solomon (Finkelstein and Silberman 2006). A further problem is that similar gates were found at cities outside of Solomon's kingdom, such as at Ashdod, a Philistine city. It is unlikely that Solomon would have rebuilt *their* city, though it is perhaps reasonable to believe that his architect might have copied a gate system that seemed innovative and well structured. Therefore, the evidence of David and Solomon's kingdom has two very different interpretations; in one case archaeologists argue that the population around Jerusalem was increasing in the tenth century and that the building campaigns at cities such as Hazor, Gezer, and Megiddo are commensurate with Solomon's kingdom, and other scholars argue the direct opposite. It is a clear case of a need for further work, which certainly continues today.

One last aspect of Solomon's reign that needs discussion is his building of the first temple. Solomon had been commanded by Yahweh to build a temple, and its construction and description are reported in great detail in I Kings Chapters 6–7. The exact measurements and even description of construction materials (i.e., "cedars from Lebanon") lend credence to the belief that such a structure was indeed built in the early decades of the United Monarchy. That a temple did stand is not in dispute, since it was destroyed in the sixth century by a Babylonian invasion. The question is whether it was built during the time of a king named Solomon, in the tenth century. Not surprisingly, the Yahweh temple looked a great deal like a Canaanite temple, with a rectangular structure and a doorway in one of the short ends (Figure 17.5). At the other end was the holy of holies, which held the Ark of the Covenant. At the front of the temple was a portico flanked by two freestanding columns, perhaps meant to mimic columns found in front of Canaanite temples dedicated to Baal and Asherah. Solomon had craftsmen involved in building the temple who were Canaanite rather than Israelite, and the description of the temple suggests that Canaanite architecture and styles were visible in this first sacred temple. The interior might have held an altar or a place for offerings, but unlike the Canaanite temples, no statue of the Israelite god would be found.

Evidence for this temple is entirely lacking, because the area where the temple would have stood has suffered repeated destruction and rebuilding episodes, almost certainly eradicating any evidence of a tenth-century temple. In 586 B.C.E. the Babylonian king Nebuchadnezzar marched on Jerusalem and destroyed the entire city, including the Temple Mount. Nebuchadnezzar not only destroyed the city and its temple, but enslaved and deported many of its inhabitants to Babylon, ushering in a period known as the Babylonian Exile. Prior to this (perhaps even decades earlier), tradition says the Ark of the Covenant had been secretly removed to keep it safe from invaders as well as from a renegade Israelite king who had allowed Canaanite gods to be worshipped in the Israelite temple. The Israelites constructed the so-called Second Temple in the later part of the sixth century; this stood until 70 C.E., when it was utterly destroyed by the Romans (it is unclear if the Ark was returned to this temple). Prior to this destruction, the Second Temple had been greatly enhanced. In approximately 20/19 B.C.E., Herod the Great, ruler of Judaea (the region that

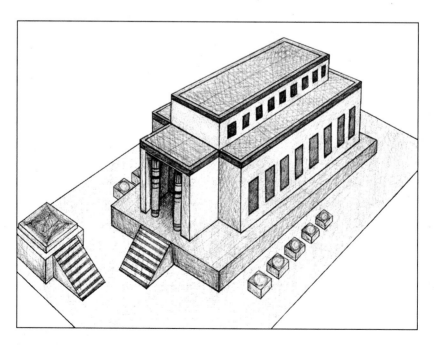

Figure 17.5. Artistic reconstruction of Israelite temple built by Solomon.
(*R. Jennison*)

included Jerusalem), commissioned the renovation of the Second Temple complex. He had an enormous platform built upon which rested an enlarged and more grandiose Second Temple. This rebuilding almost certainly wiped out most of the traces of the First Temple destroyed centuries before. After the Second Temple was destroyed in 70 C.E., no temple replaced it until the Muslims built the Dome of the Rock on the Temple Mount. The presence of this sacred building prevents any archaeological investigation of earlier religious structures.

The Divided Monarchy

Though Solomon appears to have made some fine decisions for his people, including building them a temple, he showed poor judgment in other ways. The United Monarchy was composed of two parts, tribes that lived to the north (previously ruled by Saul) and those in the south that had been part of the Kingdom of David. When David united the two regions, he treated each equally, appointing a head priest for each region and attempting to be fair to the needs of all. Under David, Canaanite religion was frowned upon, and the people of his kingdom were strongly encouraged to maintain their Yahwistic beliefs. Solomon, however, was not quite so even-handed. He expelled the priest representing the north, and even went so far as to cede some of the northern lands to the king of Lebanon (who had given cedars for the building of the temple). Though he built the temple, Solomon was far more lenient about which gods his people worshipped, riling the priests of the land who struggled to keep the Israelites true to their own god. The Bible even reports that in his old age Solomon worshipped some of the foreign gods followed by his many wives. The kingdom that his father, David, had built with war, hardship, and single-minded focus on Yahwistic religion, became a very different place under Solomon. While David built the power of the United Monarchy, Solomon simply inherited that power and used it, at times injudiciously, over his people. This was to have monumental consequences after his death.

Upon Solomon's death, Rehoboam, his son, came to the throne but was rejected by the northern tribes, who declared a different man, Jeroboam, to be their king. Their rejection of the House of Solomon stemmed from his treatment of them during his 40-year reign. They wished to reestablish Yahweh as the only deity in the kingdom, regain the lands given away by Solomon, and avoid forced labor assignments under Solomon's successor. Therefore, in ca. 931 B.C.E., after a short-lived United Monarchy, the "Divided Monarchy" began, with Judah in the south and Israel in the north; a bitter rivalry between the two regions was established. A divided kingdom invited imperial invasion, first from Egypt and later from Assyria. For the next thousand years, Israel and Judah were often controlled by various foreign rulers, and they fought with each other as well. Besides political and military difficulties, the religious leaders struggled mightily to keep their people from drifting to the many other temples and deities available for worship. In spite of military conquests and seductive religions, the people of Judah and Israel managed to hang onto their identity as the people of Yahweh and created the foundation of the religion today known as Judaism.

Conclusion

Much of what we know about the origins of Judaism come from the single text holy to its believers. Decades of archaeology have offered volumes of data on what life was like during these centuries, but the "confirmations" of biblical events that some believers seek are few and far between. The lack of such findings does nothing to negate the tenets of the religion and the power of belief in it.

The story of Judaism is one in which a lone deity led a people through centuries of trial and tribulation to the final establishment of their first temple. In many ways the origins of Judaism embody all of the theoretical threads advanced in this book. In its infancy the religion of Abraham was one ideally practiced by a mobile pastoralist people; rituals could be carried out on high places with nothing more than a standing stone as an altar. Temples were unnecessary, and elaborate artistic renderings, for which you might need craft producers in an established and sedentary community, were forbidden. These early elements are certainly reflective of the people who later became known as the Israelites and draws on the environmental setting in which they lived. Desert, water, and animals all played a significant role in the rites and rituals of early Judaism.

When Abraham was called by his god, it was not to rebel against the polytheistic religions of the ancient Near East. However, throughout the history reported in biblical literature, Israelites clung to their beliefs, even when they were enslaved by Egyptians, continuously seduced by Canaanite temples, attacked by Philistines, and finally, exiled to Babylonia. Even under Roman rule, Jews managed to maintain their beliefs. It was, in their own minds, the fact that they practiced this monotheistic faith that made them targets for enslavement, exile, and other ill treatments. Rather than succumb to the gods of more powerful states, they used their religion to maintain their identity as a believing people; it was, in effect, a rebellion against the power of others who targeted them for the very thing that they would not give up. Their beliefs allowed them, and their religion, to survive.

The United Monarchy under Solomon was certainly a time of great triumph for the Israelites. They had an independent state and were free to worship their god in their own way. The negative aspect was that a king meant control over them, and control was indeed exerted. Solomon launched building projects and other endeavors that required the sometimes unwilling service of his people. His position as monarch enabled him to command their labor and their taxes. Defying Solomon may have seemed tantamount to defying Yahweh, especially when their god had dictated that Solomon build the first Israelite temple ever erected. The power the elites derived from their association with religion is clearly demonstrated in Solomon's reign; the disaster this can sometimes wreak is shown in the dissolution of the United Monarchy after his death.

USEFUL SOURCES

William G. Dever, *Did God have a Wife?* 2008.
Jonathan Golden, *Ancient Canaan and Israel*, 2004.
Beth Alpert Nakhai, *Archaeology and the Religions of Canaan and Israel*, 2001.

18

REVITALIZING THE PEOPLE
THE ORIGINS OF CHRISTIANITY AND ISLAM

The religions that are today known as Christianity and Islam had origins hundreds of years apart but developed in somewhat similar circumstances. In each case, religious, political, and socioeconomic strife created a world in which many were anxious about the present and the future. In both religions, a single man offered a message of hope, a new set of practices and beliefs that were, he asserted, the path to a good life both on earth and beyond. In each case, a few followers became many, and before long both religions became the foundations of powerful empires. The following chapter explores the social, political, and economic circumstances in place when these religions were founded. Both Christianity and Islam developed in turbulent times; that each religion should be understood not only as an early cult, but one that emerged out of a need to revitalize a people, is explored.

The Roman Levant and the Origins of Christianity

In the first century B.C.E., the Levant was under the control of the Seleucid Monarchy, a Romanized empire based in Syria; by 63 B.C.E. the region had become part of the Roman Empire. Prior to this date, infighting between leading Jewish families had created a chaotic and unstable region. When Rome took control, Judaea, as it was then called, was recast as a territory (Figure 18.1). Some of its northern cities and all of the territory east of the Jordan River were placed in the province of Syria. The governor of Syria was given temporary control over Judaea and ensured that it paid tribute to Rome. A provincial ruler was appointed by the Syrian government to oversee Judaean affairs. This ruler, known as an *ethnarch* because he was of Jewish heritage, was generally drawn from the Hasmonean dynasty, a prominent royal Jewish family. In 37 B.C.E., however, Herod, an Idumean (not of royal ancestry), was elected by the Roman senate to be "King of the Jews." This election took place after several murder plots, assassinations, and challenges to the standing ethnarch. The Judaean population was not pleased with the appointment of Herod because he was not of royal lin-

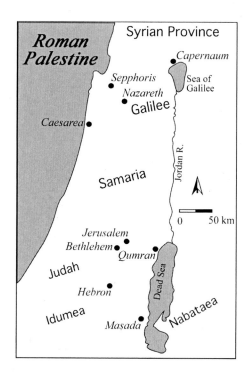

Figure 18.1. Map of Roman Palestine/Judaean sites and regions discussed in the text. (*S.R. Steadman*)

eage and was viewed as loyal to Rome rather than to his religion and his people. Nonetheless, Herod, known as "Herod the Great," ruled Judaea for 34 years.

Herod the Great had to walk a fine line between remaining loyal to Rome and preventing open revolt from his Jewish population. Another chronic problem was that the Hasmoneans believed they should be in control of Judaea, and there was constant pressure for a new "legitimate" king to be named. In order to celebrate Rome but to also please his subjects, Herod launched enormous building projects. He expanded and renovated the Jerusalem Temple to curry favor among his people. He also worked at maintaining strong ties with the more powerful Jewish sects which helped him maintain his power base. These methods were extremely successful during his reign, but upon his death in 4 B.C.E., chaos descended on Judaea.

After Herod's death there were many claimants to the throne, including his sons and members of Hasmonean families. The following summarizes the state of Judaea in these years:

> In the interim, serious disturbances erupted in Judaea . . . [including] rival claims over the kingship aimed at promoting various Herodians or less conventional claimants, some with anti-Herodian and anti-Roman programmes. Roman reprisals were severe and a legion was installed to garrison Jerusalem. Protests against Herodian rule were also voiced in Rome by Jewish representatives with requests for the incorporation of Judaea into the province of Syria. (Pearce 2002:470)

Eventually one of Herod's sons was appointed ethnarch and ruled until 6 C.E. After his ineffective and apparently cruel reign, Rome decided to put Judaea under direct Roman rule, and a series of prefects were appointed; they were less tolerant of the Jewish religion and imposed increasingly high taxes on the Judaeans. The best known of these prefects was Pontius Pilate (26–36 C.E.), who instituted a savage rule; he was eventually suspended by the Roman government on charges of cruelty and claims that he had engineered at least one massacre (Pearce 2002).

The political situation in the first centuries B.C.E./C.E. in the Roman Levant, especially in the Jewish state of Judaea, was troubled, even violent at times, laced with cruelty and often unstable. At virtually no time was a ruler in place who had the people's best interests at heart; their most peaceful time was under Herod the Great. However, even during his reign, Roman religion crept into Judaea; at one point images representing the Roman Empire (such as the eagle) were placed in the Jerusalem Temple, inciting a riot. The common population of Judaea did not feel they could turn to their rulers if they were troubled about their daily lives and the futures of their children.

Jewish Sectarianism in the Roman Levant

By the first century B.C.E., Judaism was a firmly established religion with standard practices and methods of worship known to all believers. There were, however, some very clear divides among the Jews of the Roman Levant; contemporary historians such as Josephus, and others, report the names of several Jewish sects: Pharisees, Sadducees, Essenes, Zealots, among others.

Each of these sects promoted different behaviors with regard to the practice of Judaism within the context of Roman rule. The Pharisees and the Sadducees were the two most powerful groups, with the greatest number of political connections. The Pharisee approach to religion was strict observance of Mosaic law as it was written in the Torah (the first five books of the Hebrew Bible). They maintained strict levels of purity in their work and eating habits, and they saw themselves as the holiest of the Jewish people (Nickelsburg 2003). In general, the Pharisees ignored Roman rule, believing that strict observance of their religion would allow them to outlast any foreign ruler or gods. Nonetheless, they did have political ties which caused them to be either in conflict with, or closely connected to, the ruling elites of Judaea. The Pharisees regularly attempted to convince their fellow Jews that theirs was the only correct path, and those who denied it risked condemnation by Yahweh.

The Sadducees constituted the priestly aristocrats, the elites of Jewish society. They saw the Pharisee beliefs as verging on radical; they did not believe in the type of afterlife espoused by the Pharisees and also vied with them for political positioning. The Sadducees seem to have been responsible for the temples and public Jewish rituals, which gave them a high profile in the Roman Levant and possibly promulgated a strong relationship between them and the Roman rulers. Commoners may have been at the center of a very powerful tug-of-war between the Pharisees and Sadducees in the first century B.C.E.

A third group, known as the Essenes, was described by the historian Josephus and others. Like the Pharisees, the Essenes believed their interpretation of the Torah was the correct one. They lived lives bound by strict rules of purity and ritual holiness and believed that these were the key to eternal life with Yahweh. In fact, they believed that they had become his chosen people and that other Jewish sects, as well as nonbelievers, were doomed. For this reason, they removed themselves from society and lived in isolated communities away from those who did not believe as they did (Nickelsburg 2003). One such community may have been located at the site of Qumran, in the Judaean desert. It is the occupants of the Qumran community that are credited with authorship of the Dead Sea Scrolls found in the mid-twentieth century (see below). Given that several historians mentioned the Essenes, it is clear they were not a little-known sect.

A fourth sect mentioned by Josephus is the Zealots, who became far better known after their revolt against Rome in 66 C.E. They managed to wrest Jerusalem from Rome and held it until 70 C.E., when the Romans retook the city and destroyed the temple that had been embellished by Herod. The Zealots retreated to the Roman fortress at Masada, which they took and held for three years in spite of repeated Roman assaults. When the Romans finally breached the walls, they found the Zealots had committed suicide rather than live under Roman rule. What is unknown is how well organized and outspoken the Zealots were earlier in the first century C.E. Zealots may have been involved in earlier rebellions against Rome, including one that occurred in 6 C.E. against the imposition of the Roman Imperial Cult in Judaea. Even if the Zealots were not completely organized in the early first century C.E., it is clear that there were a number of people unhappy with Roman rule and willing to take subversive action against it.

In addition to these four groups, scholars have suggested that first-century C.E. Roman Palestine contained even more Jewish sectarian groups, each with its own beliefs about proper behavior, attitudes to Roman rule, and views on the future. Commoners may have felt pressure to adhere to one group or another, to reject Roman rule or go along with it, or perhaps to ignore it altogether and retreat from mainstream society. Many probably just hoped that they could eke out enough of a living to support themselves and their families, pay Roman taxes, and avoid violence. The early first century of the new era was fraught with socio-religious uncertainty and political instability, and harbored an underlying stratum of unrest and incipient rebellion.

Jesus and the Origins of Christianity

The founder of the Christian faith was a man named Jesus whose biography is reported in the first four books of the Greek portion of the Bible (also called the New Testament). These four books, Matthew, Mark, Luke, and John (known as the Gospels), offer great detail on Jesus' ministry, but lack much detail on the earlier years of his life. Two books, Matthew and Luke, chronicle the birth of Jesus, but they offer conflicting accounts. Matthew's account suggests Jesus was born during the reign of Herod the Great, around 4 B.C.E. or earlier, while his birth date in Luke is more comfortably placed in 6 C.E., when a census mentioned in Luke was ordered by the new Roman ruler. Both authors agree that Jesus was born in Bethlehem, but whether in his parent's house (Matthew reports Jesus' parents lived in Bethlehem) or in a stable after traveling to Bethlehem (as reported by Luke) is unknown. Given the lack of detail regarding the exact whereabouts of Jesus' birthplace in Bethlehem, it is next to impossible for archaeology to attest to the actual "house" or "stable" where it might have taken place. The "Church of the Nativity" in Bethlehem was first constructed in the fourth century C.E. over a cave that was said to be the birth location. That church still stands today.

Very little is known about the youth and early adulthood of Jesus. The Gospels concentrate on the period of Jesus' ministry, somewhere around the date of 30 C.E., when he was in his late 20s or perhaps 30 years of age. As an adult, he appeared at the Jordan River to be baptized by a well-known figure called John the Baptist. Following his baptism, Jesus went to the desert where he triumphed over temptation and returned ready to begin his ministry. John the Baptist is mentioned by all four Gospel authors, and he is also mentioned by the historian Josephus as having had a wide following. The places where he performed baptisms cannot be attested archaeologically, but the various documents that describe him suggest he was indeed a historical figure. Naturally there is no way to track Jesus' time in the desert archaeologically.

From the desert, Jesus returned to a region known as the Galilee, in the north of what is today the country of Israel. Jesus settled for a time in a town called Capernaum. He attracted the first of his *disciples* (his close followers) who were Galilee fishermen. At first Jesus gave sermons in synagogues in the Galilee region, but when the crowds grew too large he preached on hillsides and in open areas. Jesus also began to perform miracles of healing, as well as other feats such as turning water into wine, feeding huge crowds with very little food, walking on water, and later, raising a man from the dead. When speaking in the synagogues, Jesus probably had Pharisees and Sadducees in his audience. However, most of his audience in the open arenas were commoners—the farmers and fisher folk who made up a large percentage of the Jewish population in Roman Palestine. It was to them that Jesus directed his sermons, which included stories commonly called *parables*.

Jesus' parables recounted stories about farmers, herders, the poor, and the downtrodden. In these stories Jesus advocated attitudes of peace and enduring love for human beings, not only from their god, but between one another. He hammered out notions of pure justice and asserted that if someone had erred, if truly repentant, he was equal to the most righteous person (Smith 1994). He suggested that the poor and those who had fallen into difficulties were also loved by god and would be able to enter his "kingdom of heaven" upon their deaths. Jesus did not instruct people to stay true to Mosaic codes of behavior, as did the Pharisees; nor did he appear to cater to the power of the Romans. He counseled against violence and did not urge his followers to withdraw from society, but rather to spread the word of his god to as many as possible. Jesus' message, contained within his parables, was different from that offered by the other Jewish sects of the day. It was one that professed hopefulness to commoners, who understood the points of the simple stories about people like themselves. His messages about justice and repentance were appealing to many who felt they had not, for many reasons, been able to practice "proper" Judaism, according to one sect or another.

After months of traveling the hinterlands of Roman Palestine, Jesus and his disciples entered the city of Jerusalem. Here Jesus, according to the text, undertook several endeavors that gained him notice by the Sadducees who controlled the Sanhedrin, or the council of judges, in Jerusalem. The Book of Mark reports that the head of the Sanhedrin, Caiaphas, ordered Jesus arrested; Jesus was brought to the house of a member of the Sanhedrin (perhaps Caiaphas') to be questioned. Caiaphas sentenced Jesus to death for blasphemy against Judaism and the codes of the land. The ultimate decision to carry out the sentence fell to the prefect, Pontius Pilate. Jesus and two others (thieves) were then crucified to death, a process that took several days. Upon his death Jesus was buried in the rock-cut tomb of a wealthy follower who subscribed to Jesus' teachings; the tomb was located just outside Jerusalem. It is the events after his death that essentially elevated Jesus to the level of founder of a new religion. The Gospels report that after three days, Jesus arose from the dead (both physically and spiritually) and ascended to heaven to be with his god. Witnesses of this event, to whom Jesus spoke after his death, would go on to report this final episode of Jesus' life, sparking an even deeper belief in the messages offered by Jesus during his travels in the region. From these events arose the religion we today call Christianity.

Was Jesus an Essene? Archaeology and Qumran

In 1947 one of the greatest discoveries concerning the biblical world was made by accident. In the mountainous desert terrain by the Dead Sea, a Bedouin boy was tossing stones into a cave while minding his goats. When he heard a pot break he investigated the cave and discovered what are now known as the Dead Sea Scrolls. These texts, written on leather "paper," offer a variety of ancient literature, including recountings of the books in the Hebrew Bible, instructions on ritual and purity, and accounts of people and events both known and new, by authors known and unknown. They were rolled and placed in ceramic vessels, which were then capped to preserve the scrolls. The translation of these scrolls took decades, due to delayed access to them and political issues regarding "ownership" of both territory and scrolls. All this resulted in wild speculation as to the date, authorship, and content of the scrolls. Today, after over a decade of open access and scholarly investigation, some questions have been answered. Most scholars believe the scrolls were written between the second and first centuries B.C.E., but their authorship is still a matter of dispute. Some believe the scrolls, authored by Sadducee priests, had been originally housed in Jerusalem, but then were removed and secreted in the Dead Sea caves during the 66 C.E. Jewish Revolt, to keep them safe during the expected Roman backlash. Those who support this interpretation point to scrolls that describe elements of rituals and codes of purity that conform to Sadducee interpretations of Mosaic law (Martinez 2000).

Others assert that the scrolls were written by the Essene sect who lived in the Qumran community, not far from the discovery site of the scrolls. There is controversy over whether Qumran housed an Essene sect; some suggest it was a Roman villa, or some other nonreligious structure. The main body of scholarship, supported by archaeological discovery, suggests that the ruins at Qumran housed a religious community where

Essenes—possibly a dissenting sect of Essenes—lived and copied the sacred scrolls (Martinez 2000). Since *monasticism* is a Christian concept, it is perhaps not accurate to describe the Qumran community as a "monastery"; many scholars do suggest, however, that this complex housed a group of religious people who had indeed withdrawn from mainstream society to practice their beliefs. The Essenes believed the inaccuracy of temple rituals practiced by Sadducees and Pharisees in Jerusalem would delay or prevent the coming of a *messiah* (savior). They therefore withdrew into the desert where they could perform the rituals properly. They also set themselves the task of preserving the written literature, now known as the Dead Sea Scrolls. Archaeology has demonstrated that the pots in which the scrolls rested in the caves were identical to the ones produced in the Qumran community, virtually confirming a connection between the residents at Qumran and the scrolls (Magness 2002). The residents at Qumran apparently hid the scrolls in the caves for the same reason as it was assumed the Sadducee priests might have: to save them from destruction by the Romans. Indeed, the Qumran community was destroyed in 68 C.E. by the Romans during the Jewish Revolt.

Archaeological excavations at Qumran have revealed a complex that housed a community of 150–200 people who lived their lives according to strict ritual codes of purity. At one end of the complex was the ritual bath; at the other end were the latrines, strictly separating ritual activities from profane bodily functions. A section of the complex was devoted to a potters' workshop, and other areas housed cloth production and other crafts. A meeting hall, eating and cooking areas, and a possible "scriptorium" where the scrolls were composed, round out the main components of this self-sufficient complex (Magness 2002).

One line of scholarship suggests Jesus was actually an Essene (another suggests John the Baptist, not Jesus, was the Essene), and that the messages Jesus preached to the people are found in the scrolls. However, there are other elements in the Qumran community and Essene traditions that are distinctly different from Jesus' ways. One similarity between them is that both the Essenes and Jesus believed in an approaching apocalypse, that the world would end with the coming of a messiah. This commonality leads some scholars to suggest Jesus may have been trained as an Essene; some even suggest that during his time in the wilderness, he was actually in the Qumran community. However, many of Jesus' practices were distinctly un-Essene; he dealt with women, Romans, Sadducees, and Pharisees, all groups the Qumran community had rejected. Jesus also did not really follow the strict ritual practices that were so important to the Qumran community.

The Archaeology of Jesus

A section on "the archaeology of Jesus" will be short because archaeology is not about finding individuals, but rather revealing cultures. This does not mean there is no archaeology from the time of Jesus; indeed there is, and it has a bearing on our understanding of the historical events of the time. Most notable are the massive engineering projects commissioned by Herod the Great and his son Herod Antipas. Excavations at sites such as Caesarea, Sepphoris, and Masada show the enormous labor put into constructing these first-century B.C.E./C.E. sites built in Roman style with theaters, military fortifications, and decorations celebrating Roman themes. There is little doubt that these works, described by Josephus and referenced in biblical texts, were built by these Jewish rulers.

Jesus' birthplace is not attestable archaeologically, despite Bethlehem's "Church of the Nativity." However, some scholars also ask, "which Bethlehem?" The biblical story describes a journey that Jesus' parents, Joseph and Mary, undertook from Nazareth in the Galilee to Bethlehem in Judaea, a very long journey for a pregnant woman. Non-biblical texts mention a Bethlehem in the Galilee, causing some to wonder if it was not this Bethlehem to which Joseph and Mary journeyed (Chilton 2006), as this would be an easier journey for one in Mary's condition. The Galilean Bethlehem has not been found archaeologically.

At the beginning of his ministry, Jesus lived in a place known as Capernaum, on the shores of the Sea of Galilee. One of his chief disciples, Peter, also lived there, as did other of Jesus' disciples. In the mid-twentieth century, two Franciscan priests excavated an octagonal-shaped fifth-century C.E. church on the shores of Lake Galilee, in a town identified as Capernaum; textual evidence in the sixth century identified this as a church that stood over Peter's house. Beneath this structure was a fourth-century church, though built more like a simple house than an octagonal basilica. At the lowest level was the courtyard of a first-century C.E. house; an inscription on a plaster fragment may contain the name "Peter" (Charlesworth 2006). Many are convinced that this is the site of Peter's house, a structure that Jesus is reported to have been in on a number of occasions and from which Jesus delivered some of his parables (Figure 18.2). At least by the fourth century, the Christians of the region believed the site to be important, and by the fifth century it was worthy of the construction of a significant church.

As noted earlier, Jesus' disciples were commoners, rather than from the more powerful Pharisee or Sadducee sects. Peter himself was a fisherman piloting a boat with several fishermen, several rowers, and their catch. In 1986, a severe drought lowered the Sea of Galilee, exposing lakeshores that had not been visible for centuries. A few miles from Capernaum the remains of a boat were found and excavated on the lakeshore. It measured 8 feet wide and 26 feet long; it was able to hold a crew of eight or nine along with a cargo of fish (Crossan and Reed 2001). Dated to the first century C.E., the boat is colloquially known as the "Jesus Boat." Though perhaps not the boat in which Peter and Jesus traveled, it does attest to the existence of boats in Galilee such as are described in biblical texts.

Archaeology in Jerusalem has also offered some clues to life during Jesus' time. There are many churches in Jerusalem commemorating the various events in Jesus' life leading up to his death. For instance, the "Church of All Nations" in the region known as Gethsemane is said to mark the place where Jesus was arrested by agents of the Sadducees. In another part of the city stands the "Shrine of the Holy Sepulchre" that reputedly marks the location of Jesus' tomb. Though it was built very early (begun during the reign of Constantine in the fourth century C.E.), there is no archaeological evidence to indicate that the church marks the exact tomb in question.

Archaeology has, however, made some exceedingly interesting discoveries. In the 1970s excavations sponsored by the Hebrew University of Jerusalem took place on the western hill of the Old City, an area that offered a direct view of the Temple Mount. Here excavations revealed several large houses dating to the first century C.E.; textual sources suggest that it was in this area that the Sadducee high priests dwelled (Crossan and Reed 2001). One house was of "palatial" dimensions, covering approximately 6,000 square feet, with a large courtyard and numerous rooms decorated with frescoes on the walls and mosaics on the floors. These houses of the high priests attest to their wealth and power in first-century C.E. Jerusalem. In the Gospels, Jesus was arrested and brought to the "courtyard" of the high priest's house, probably Caiaphas. With Caiaphas were other priests and scribes, the former to assist Caiaphas in the assessment of Jesus' crimes and the latter to record the proceedings. It would have taken a large courtyard, such as that found in the most palatial of the homes discovered, to hold such a crowd. Whether Jesus was sentenced in this palatial house or not, excavations have demonstrated that houses such as those described in the Gospels certainly existed.

Figure 18.2. Artistic rendering of "Peter's house" at Capernaum, the fishing boat, and Jesus' recruitment of his apostles (*M. J. Hughes*)

Another discovery related to Caiaphas is an *ossuary*, or stone coffin, that bears this name. In 1990 investigations in a cave outside of Jerusalem's Old City revealed a family tomb in which several ossuaries were discovered, most with names common to Jewish families in the first century C.E. The name *Caiaphas*, however, was not particularly common, and it was this name that was etched on the finest of the ossuaries (Figure 18.3). This stone box was beautifully carved and must have been commissioned by someone of wealth and power. It is likely that this was the family tomb of Caiaphas the Sadducee high priest, most famous for sentencing Jesus to death, though some do question the validity of this assertion (Evans 2006).

The method of Jesus' execution—crucifixion—is not in dispute, as there is ample textual evidence to document that the Romans were fond of this method for "lower-class" criminals (Crossan and Reed 2001). Crucifixion was very public, meant to act as a deterrent to others who might contemplate actions against Roman law. Crucified victims were generally left to rot where they died, slowly decaying, aided by carrion eaters and the hot and dry weather. For those of Jewish faith, they feared not only this horrible and sometimes days-long process of death, but also the fact that they would not be properly buried, a necessity for a successful afterlife. Some scholars have suggested that the biblical story describing the burial of Jesus in a rock-cut tomb could not be accurate, given that crucified victims weren't buried. Had Jesus not been buried, the story describing his resurrection several days later, one of the linchpins of Christianity, would be in jeopardy. However, in 1968 a cave with several ossuaries was discovered. In one of these was a man whose name, inscribed on his coffin, was "Yehochanan." Yehochanan's ankle was attached, by nail, to a piece of wood. Upon examination, archaeologists determined that Yehochanan had been crucified; when the nail was driven through his ankle into the wood of the cross, it bent and could not be extracted. Therefore, after his death, this portion of the beam was cut from the cross so that family members could remove him from his death place for burial in the family tomb. This discovery documented that in some cases victims of crucifixion could be removed from the cross and buried, as is recounted in the biblical story of Jesus' death.

Figure 18.3. The "Caiaphas ossuary." (*R. Jennison*)

Conclusion

Scholarship on the emergence of Christianity, whether archaeological, textual, or religious, includes a vast and complicated set of documents that raise as many controversies as they solve. What is clear, however, is that first-century C.E. Roman Palestine was a difficult and chaotic place, and many Jewish sects offered a possibly unappetizing array of methods to deal with religion, Romans, taxation, and lives of hardship. Into this mix, biblical texts tell us, walked a man who offered a different path for the poor and less fortunate; he described a god that did not discriminate between "haves" and "have nots," one who did not seem as concerned with the strict rituals of the Pharisees and the priestly Sadducees. This god did not propose violence as an answer, nor utter rejection of society. Rather, humans were meant to trust in their god, love and respect one another, and work hard. These were principles many in Roman Palestine could understand and accomplish, and so they followed this Jesus and his messages and eventually, after Jesus' death, they followed his growing number of disciples.

Christianity began as a cult-like movement, a newly developed sect of Judaism which quickly emerged as a full-blown alternative religion. In its infancy, Christianity was not only a cult, but might also be described as a revitalization movement. Many within the Jewish population of first-century Roman Palestine believed that life could not get much worse, and perhaps the world was even nearing its end. The messages from the god of Jesus gave them hope and strength to continue—an essential component in a revitalization movement. Such movements combine elements of the previous, pervasive beliefs, and new elements as well, certainly a valid description of early Christianity. Though initially Christianity began simply as a cult-like defection away from the Judaism of the time, the foundations laid by the figure known as Jesus did eventually lead to a rejuvenated community of people who built a religion that has become the most widely practiced in the world today.

Muhammad and the Origins of Islam

The prophet Muhammad lived in sixth- to seventh-century C.E. southern Arabia and, like Jesus before him, inspired a new religion; Islam is the second most widely practiced faith in today's world. Archaeologically we know even less about Muhammad and his time than we do about Roman Palestine, but text-based histories offer a detailed account of his adult life. As was the case in first-century C.E. Roman Palestine, the sixth and seventh centuries in Arabia were somewhat unstable, and many, including Muhammad, sought a more peaceful and humane world. The following section examines the possibility that Islam should be considered a type of revitalization movement that moved far beyond its cultish beginnings.

Pre-Islamic Arabia

Our knowledge of pre-Islamic Arabia is extremely minimal, in part owing to limited excavations and the widespread Islamicization of the peninsula by the early Muslims. The majority of our information comes from inscriptions that name gods and goddesses, and from records from non-Arabian peoples (e.g., Romans, Byzantines, and Persians). Texts and some archaeological remains confirm that pre-Islamic Arabia was polytheistic and that some of the deities worshipped had connections to Greek, Syrian, and Persian gods and goddesses. Temples in the Arabian towns and cities held idols dedicated to these deities; residents made sacrifices and offerings and attended public rituals celebrating them. Some of the principal Arabian deities included Hubal, Al-Lat, Manat, and Al-Uzza. Hubal was a god of fertility and agriculture; he was worshipped at Mecca and elsewhere. The other three deities were female and were considered sisters; Al-Lat was goddess of the moon, Manat was associated with death and fate, and Al-Uzza with war. These three goddesses were the daughters of a powerful, even supreme, god known as Al-Lah. Tribal kin groups worshipped particular deities as their patron god or goddess. The Quraysh tribe, into which Muhammad was born, recognized Al-Uzza as their patron goddess.

All of these deities, and perhaps hundreds more, had statues erected in temples across Arabia. This was particularly true in Mecca, an important cult center and the destination of important pilgrimages each year. The most important temple in Mecca, the Ka'aba, housed the idols of numerous deities. There were also other cities and temples that served as pilgrimage destinations; during an important pilgrimage, hostilities ceased and everyone was allowed safe passage to perform their sacred duties.

By the late sixth century, there were two major empires on the Middle Eastern map: the Byzantine and the Sassanian (Figure 18.4). The Christian Byzantine Empire, inheritors of the Roman Empire, controlled Anatolia, the Levant, and Egypt, and had allies in northern Arabia. The Sassanians, a Persian empire, stretched from Iraq to Central Asia and included part of eastern Arabia; this empire encompassed many religions, including Zoroastrianism. Though neither empire ruled western and southern Arabia, the conflicts between the two behemoths did affect Arabian trade and diplomacy; the Byzantine zeal to spread the Christian faith had also begun to make inroads on the Arabian Peninsula. Missionaries had converted Arab tribes in the northern part of the peninsula and had created significant Christian communities in Sudan and Ethiopia, which also spilled over into Yemen in southwestern Arabia.

Sixth-century Arabia was populated by city-dwellers and nomadic Bedouin pastoralists. Both Bedouin and settled groups were organized in tribal confederations based on family, economic, and political associations; rivalries between tribes were common and were occasionally exacerbated by the political maneuverings of surrounding empires. As early as the fifth century C.E., Meccan merchants made arrangements with tribal leaders (including the Bedouins) to allow safe passage for goods traveling from Mecca to elsewhere, and for protection of the caravans. In return, the caravans would carry tribal goods as well, and bring wealth back to the tribal leaders who ensured safe passage (Ibrahim 1982). It was Muhammad's tribe, the Quraysh, that had made these arrangements with the neighboring Bedouins, a century before his birth.

These trade arrangements resulted in very lucrative returns for all. Routes to Syria, Egypt, and the Mediterranean were established, and merchants moved goods without fear of attack or theft; strong ties developed between the Quraysh family of Mecca and tribesmen across the peninsula. Meccan merchants established trade with both Byzantine and Sassanian merchants and regularly traversed the Red Sea to trade with African businessmen as well. By the sixth century C.E., Mecca had become an important player in the international market (Ibrahim 1982).

The Bedouins had their own strict codes of behavior which differed from those followed by city-dwellers, whom the Bedouins believed lived "soft" lives where corruption, stinginess, and underhandedness thrived. The general, the Arabian attitude was that the best virtues were preserved in the Bedouins' ancient nomadic lifestyle, including generosity to those in need, the trustworthiness of their word, and a strong sense of honor. The Bedouins were known for their poetry and oral traditions, fierce loyalty to tribal affiliations and kin, and deep knowledge of the desert. The Bedouins believed in, or at least acknowledged, many of the deities whose idols stood in the city temples. Their more immediate focus was on the supernatural beings, closer to

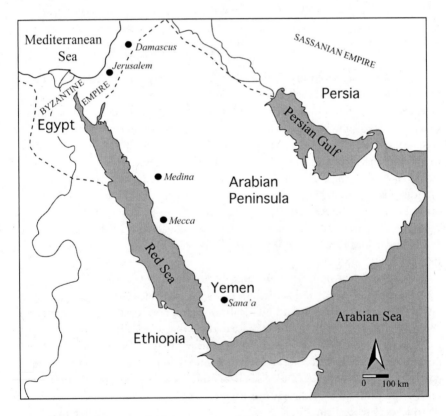

Figure 18.4. Map of Arabian sites and regions discussed in the chapter.
(S. R. Steadman)

spirits than gods, that lived within the Bedouin landscape. Certain places, such as mountains, oases, caves, or other remarkable natural features, were particularly sacred.

By the later sixth century C.E. the Quraysh tribe had grown wealthy and powerful and had become one of the leading families of the Meccan trading center. Those involved in the upper echelons of trade, including the Quraysh, were wealthy and growing wealthier, while at the same time many poor were thrust into even greater poverty. As Mecca became more wealthy and powerful, it drew a growing population of merchants anxious to engage in the thriving economy, and others seeking work in the many different sectors needed to produce goods and support an increasingly large city. Many of these laborers were indebted to merchants and came to Mecca to work off their debt; they severed their tribal ties so that their personal debt did not fall onto the shoulders of their kin (Ibrahim 1982). As debt piled up on individuals, slavery became increasingly common, as did a growing class of poor; Mecca became a heavily stratified class society, with powerful families such as the Quraysh at the pinnacle. As class stratification and concerns over the attainment or retainment of wealth became paramount, kin and tribal ties were weakened; merchants could not always be trusted, nor could wage laborers, based only on tribal affiliations. In addition, the plight of the poor and destitute increased, as the wealthy were less inclined to spend their earnings on those who were less fortunate than they; this became especially prominent as tribal loyalty eroded (Ibrahim 1982). The late sixth century in Mecca was a time of some political instability, as empires competed for territory and worked to spread their own religious faiths. Arabia was a place in which the possession of wealth was quickly becoming one of the most important values.

Muhammad and the Birth of Islam

The traditional year of Muhammad's birth is 570 C.E. During the first five or six years of his life, the Sassanians and the Byzantines fought battles over Arabian territories, and Mecca was actually under the control of each empire for a short while. Muhammad's father died before his birth, and his mother when he was 6 years old. One tradition suggests that until the age of 6, Muhammad lived among the Bedouins, perhaps to absent him from the troubled political chaos of Mecca, but also to allow the boy to absorb the virtues and codes of behavior for which the Bedouins were known. After his mother died, Muhammad first lived in his grandfather's household, but two years later he went to his uncle after his grandfather died. Young Muhammad may have once again lived among the Bedouins as they traveled the trade routes to places such as Syria, perhaps as a representative of his uncle's merchant endeavors.

At the age of 25, Muhammad was ready to lead his own caravan, and he did so, escorting the goods of a widow named Khadija who was from another leading merchant family in Mecca. Muhammad and Khadija then married, and Muhammad became the head of her merchant family, combining the power of the Quraysh tribe with that of Khadija's. Muhammad began to take long sojourns in the desert, seeking out caves where he would meditate, sometimes for days at a time. During these times, he fasted and gave what food he had to the poor who visited him in his solitude. Muhammad was troubled by the state of human affairs around him, including the political chaos of imperial gamesmanship, but especially by his fellow tribesmen's concern for wealth and the erosion of human social relationships. As Muhammad meditated on the corruption and lust for wealth that had become commonplace among his people, he began to question the religion he had known all his life. He pondered the existence of multiple deities, and wondered whether there wasn't a better path.

The next events are recorded in the Muslim holy book known as the Qu'ran. In approximately 610 C.E., during one of his seclusions in a cave outside Mecca, Muhammad was visited by an angel named Gabriel, who ordered him to recite a message from the god Al-Lah. Subsequent visits and many recitations resulted in the holy book known as the Qu'ran, which translates to "recitation," recalling the original method of its composition. These recitations revealed to Muhammad the true path that would take his people back to purity and morality, to the worship of the one true god named Al-Lah, and to a world of peace, loyalty, and care for the poor. Out of the recitations came the Five Pillars of Islam: belief in the one true god, prayer, fasting, giving alms (support) to the poor, and making a pilgrimage to Mecca. Following these tenets, said Muhammad, would lead people back to morality, honesty, loyalty to family and tribe, and the proper belief in the one deity that existed in the supernatural world. Muhammad's belief system became known as Islam, meaning "submission" to the will and guidance of the god known as Al-Lah. Part of Islamic belief dictated that idolatry was wrong, and Muhammad advocated for the destruction of the hundreds of idols in the temples throughout Arabia, particularly in Mecca. This did indeed happen in post-Islamic Arabia, explaining the scarcity of archaeological evidence for earlier periods. The ancient practice of the pilgrimage, however, remained an essential element in the new religion, and it is one of the most sacred events in present-day Islam, known as the *Hajj* to Mecca (Figure 18.5).

At first Muhammad attracted only a few followers. They were persecuted in Mecca and eventually fled to the city of Yathrib, later known as Medina (this fleeing is known as the *Hijra*), where Muhammad and his beliefs were accepted and Islam began to spread. By the time of Muhammad's death in 632 C.E., Meccans, and numerous tribal groups to the north and south of Mecca and Medina, subscribed to Islamic beliefs. The successors to Muhammad continued to spread the religion, until little more than a century later, Islam had spread to North Africa and well into Western and Central Asia.

Conclusion

Like Jesus, Muhammad was troubled by the world around him—a world filled with political chaos, warring tribes, corruption, and mistrust. The values and codes of honor and generosity Muhammad learned as a boy were eroding away among the city-dwellers of his adulthood. Muhammad sought a better world, one that was not as confusing and dangerous, and one in which wealth was not the most important

Figure 18.5. Photo of Mecca and the modern pilgrimage.
In the center is the holy Ka'aba. *(Aidar Ayazbayev/Dreamstime.com)*

measure of a human. Like early Christianity, early Islam also began as a cult movement; initially followed by only a few, both then spread with rapidity. The growth of Islam brought cohesion and vitality to the people of Arabia and eventually regions well beyond. The tenets of Islam appear to combine elements of the ancient beliefs in morality and compassion, with newer ideals laid out in Muhammad's recitations. These offered a pathway to a faith in which a single god oversaw all aspects of human life, and simple acts such as prayer and a strong moral code would result in a pure existence and a rewarding afterlife.

We tend to think of "cults" as short-lived fringe movements that cease after the death, or occasionally the imprisonment, of the cult leader. It is hard to imagine that present-day cults might have future impacts that rival Christianity and Islam. Were these religious founders and their followers more charismatic than cult leaders today? Were people in greater need of guidance and religious direction in the past than today? Did the world seem far more dire, more on the edge of chaos, in the past than today? Perhaps all of these elements, combined with many more, created settings in which small cult-like revitalization movements, one about 2,000 years ago and one about 600 years later, succeeded where many others had failed. Archaeology can only give us a narrow glimpse into the world in which these earlier believers dwelled; the rest of our understanding must come from our willingness to step into the belief systems of these ancient peoples and see their world through the lenses of the past.

USEFUL SOURCES

Jonathan L. Reed, *Archaeology and the Galilean Jesus*, 2000.
Ian Wilson, *Jesus: The Evidence*, 1996.
Robert Hoyland, *Arabia and the Arabs*, 2001.

REFERENCES

Akazawa, T., Muhesen, M., Dodo, Y., Kndo, O., and Mizoguchi, Y.
  1995 "Neanderthal infant burial." *Nature* 377:585–86.
Aldhouse-Green, Miranda, and Aldhouse-Green, Stephen
  2005 *The Quest for the Shaman*. London: Thames and Hudson.
Alexander, Caroline
  2008 "If the stones could speak: Searching for the meaning of Stonehenge." *National Geographic* 213.6:34–59.
Allchin, Raymond
  1995 *The Archaeology of Early Historic South Asia*. Cambridge: Cambridge University.
Allchin, Bridget, and Allchin, Raymond
  1982 *The Rise of Civilization in India and Pakistan*. Cambridge: Cambridge University.
Allen, Charles
  2003 *The Search for the Buddha. The Men Who Discovered India's Lost Religion*. New York: Carroll and Graf.
Anderson, David G.
  2005 "Pleistocene human occupation of the Southeastern United States: Research directions for the early twenty-first century." In *Paleoamerican Origins: Beyond Clovis*, edited by Robson Bonnichsem, Bradley T. Lepper, Dennis Stanford, and Michael R. Waters, pp. 29–43. College Station: Texas A&M University.
Anderson, William L.
  1991 *Cherokee Removal: Before and After*. Athens: University of Georgia.
Arnold, Philip P.
  1999 "Eating landscape: Human sacrifice and sustenance in Aztec Mexico." In *Aztec Ceremonial Landscapes*, edited by Davíd Carrasco, pp. 219–32. Boulder: University Press of Colorado.
Arsuaga, Juan Luis, and Martínez, Ignacio
  2006. *The Chosen Species: The Long March of Human Evolution*. London: Blackwell.
Atkins, Nancy J.
  2003 "The burials of Pueblo Bonito." In *Pueblo Bonito: Center of the Chacoan World*, edited by Jill E. Neitzel, pp. 94–106. Washington, DC: Smithsonian Books.
Atran, Scott
  2002 *In Gods We Trust: The Evolutionary Landscape of Religion*. New York: Oxford University.
Aveni, A. F., Clanek, E. E., and Hartung, H.
  1988 "Myth, environment, and the orientation of the Templo Mayor of Tenochtitlan." *American Antiquity*, 53.2:287–309.

Bahn, Paul G.
  2001   "Save the last trance for me: An assessment of the misuse of shamanism in rock art studies." In *The Concept of Shamanism: Uses and Abuses*, edited by Henri-Paul Francfort and Roberte N. Hamayon, pp. 51–93. Budapest: Akadémiai Kiadó.

Bailey, Douglass W.
  1994   "Reading prehistoric figurines as individuals." *World Archaeology* 25.3:321–31.
  2005   *Prehistoric Figurines: Corporeality and Representation in the Neolithic*. London: Routledge.

Balzer, Marjorie M.
  2003   "Sacred genders in Siberia. Shamans, bear festivals, and androgyny." In *Shamanism, A Reader*, edited by Graham Harvey, pp. 242–61. London: Routledge.

Barnes, Gina L.
  1995   "An introduction to Buddhist archaeology." *World Archaeology* 27.2:165–82.

Beck, Margaret
  2000   "Female figurines in the European Upper Paleolithic: Politics and bias in archaeological interpretation." In *Reading the Body: Representations and Remains in the Archaeological Record*, edited by Alison E. Rautman, pp. 202–14. Philadelphia: University of Pennsylvania.

Ben-Tor, Amnon, and Zuckerman, Sharon
  2008   "Hazor at the end of the Late Bronze Age: Back to basics." *Bulletin of the American Schools of Oriental Research* 350:1–6.

Belfer-Cohen, Anna, and Hovers, Erella
  1992   "In the eye of the beholder: Mousterian and Natufian burials in the Levant." *Current Anthropology* 33:463–71.

Bergquist, Anders
  2001   "Ethics and the archaeology of world religions." In *Archaeology and World Religion*, edited by Timothy Insoll, pp. 182–92. London: Routledge.

Berndt, Catherine, and Berndt, Ronald
  1983   *The Aboriginal Australians: The First Pioneers*. London: Pitman.

Bertemes, François, and Biehl, Peter F.
  2001   "The archaeology of cult and religion: An introduction." In *The Archaeology of Cult and Religion*, edited by Peter F. Biehl, François Bertemes, and Harald Meller, pp. 11–24. Budapest: Archaeolingua.

Binford, Lewis R.
  1983   *In Pursuit of the Past: Decoding the Archaeological Record*. London: Thames and Hudson.

Bogucki, Peter I., and Crabtree, Pam J.
  2004   *Ancient Europe 8000 B.C.–A.D 1000: Encyclopedia of the Barbarian World*. London: Charles Scribner's.

Bourget, Steve
  2001   "Children and ancestors: Ritual practices at the Moche site of Huaca de la Luna, north coast of Peru." In *Ritual Sacrifice in Ancient Peru*, edited by Elizabeth P. Benson and Anita G. Cook, pp. 93–118. Austin: University of Texas.
  2006   *Sex, Death, and Sacrifice in Moche Religion and Visual Culture*. Austin: University of Texas.

Bowen, John R.
  2005   *Religions in Practice: An Approach to the Anthropology of Religion*. Third edition. New York: Allyn and Bacon.

Bowie, Fiona
2006   *The Anthropology of Religion.* Revised edition. Oxford: Wiley-Blackwell.

Boyd, Carolyn E.
1998   "Pictographic evidence of peyotism in the Lower Pecos, Texas Archaic." In *The Archaeology of Rock-Art*, edited by Christopher Chippindale and Paul S. C. Taçon, pp. 229–46. Cambridge: Cambridge University.

Boyer, Pascal
2001   *Religion Explained: The Evolutionary Origins of Religious Thought.* New York: Basic Books.

Bradley, Richard
1998   "Daggers drawn: Depictions of Bronze Age weapons in Atlantic Europe." In *The Archaeology of Rock-Art*, edited by Christopher Chippindale and Paul S. C. Taçon, pp. 130–45. Cambridge: Cambridge University.
2002   *The Past in Prehistoric Societies.* London: Routledge.

Broda, Johanna
1991   "The sacred landscape of Aztec calendar festivals: Myth, nature, and society." In *Aztec Ceremonial Landscapes*, edited by Davíd Carrasco, pp. 74–120. Boulder: University Press of Colorado.

Brown, James A.
1997   "The archaeology of ancient religion in the Eastern Woodlands." *Annual Review of Anthropology* 26:465–85.

Brown, Michael F.
1989   "Dark side of the shaman." *Natural History* (November):8–10.
2000   "The New Age and related forms of contemporary spirituality." In *Religion and Culture: An Anthropological Focus*, edited by Raymond Scupin, pp. 421–32. Upper Saddle, NJ: Prentice-Hall.

Bryant, Edwin
2001   *The Quest for the Origins of Vedic Culture. The Indo-Aryan Migration Debate.* Oxford: Oxford University.

Burger, Richard L.
1992   *Chavín and the Origins of Andean Civilization.* London: Thames and Hudson.

Burl, Aubrey
2007   *A Brief History of Stonehenge.* New York: Carroll and Graf.
2006   *A Guide to the Stone Circles of Britain, Ireland and Brittany.* Second edition. New Haven: Yale University.

Carr, Christopher, and Case, D. Troy (eds.)
2006   *Gathering Hopewell: Society, Ritual and Ritual Interaction.* New York: Springer

Carrasco, Davíd
1990   *Religions of Mesoamerica.* San Francisco: Harper and Row.
1998   *Daily Life of the Aztecs: People of the Sun and Earth.* Westport, CT: Greenwood.
1999   *City of Sacrifice: The Aztec Empire and the Role of Violence in Civilization.* Boston: Houghton Mifflin.
2000   *Quetzalcoatl and the Irony of Empire.* Revised edition. Boulder: University Press of Colorado.

Ceruti, Constanza
2004   "Human bodies as objects of dedication at Inca mountain shrines (North-Western Argentina)." *World Archaeology* 36.1:103–22.

Chakrabarti, Dilip
1999   *India — An Archaeological History.* Delhi: Oxford University.

2001   "The archaeology of Hinduism." In *Archaeology and World Religion*, edited by Timothy Insoll, pp. 33–60. London: Routledge.

Challis, William
2005   "'The men with rhebok's heads; they tame elands and snakes': Incorporating the rhebok antelope in the understanding of southern African rock art." *South African Archaeological Society Goodwin Series* 9:11–20.

Charlesworth, James H.
2006   "Jesus Research and Archaeology: A New Perspective." In *Jesus and Archaeology*, edited by James H. Charlesworth, pp. 11–63. Grand Rapids: Eerdmans.

Chase, Philip G., and Dibble, Harold L.
1987   "Middle Paleolithic symbolism: A review of current evidence and interpretations." *Journal of Anthropological Archaeology* 6:263–96.

Chilton, Bruce
2006   "Recovering Jesus' *Mamzerut*." In *Jesus and Archaeology*, James H. Charlesworth, pp. 84–110. Grand Rapids: Eerdmans.

Chippindale, Christopher
2001   "Studying ancient pictures as pictures." In *Handbook of Rock Art Research*, edited by David S. Whitley, pp. 247–72. Walnut Creek, CA: AltaMira.
2004   *Stonehenge Complete*. Third edition. London: Thames and Hudson.

Choi, Chungmoo
2003   "The artistry and ritual aesthetics of urban Korean shamans." In *Shamanism, A Reader*, edited by Graham Harvey, pp. 170–85. London: Routledge.

Clendinnen, Inga
1985   "The cost of courage in Aztec society." *Past and Present* 107:44–89.

Clottes, Jean
1998   "The 'three Cs': Fresh avenues toward European Palaeolithic art." In *The Archaeology of Rock-Art*, edited by Christopher Chippindale and Paul S. C. Taçon, pp. 112–29. Cambridge: Cambridge University.
2002   *World Rock Art*. Translated from the French by Guy Bennett. Los Angeles: Getty.

Coe, Michael D.
2003   *Angkor and the Khmer Civilization*. London: Thames and Hudson.

Cock, Guillermo
2002   "Inca rescue." *National Geographic* 201.5:78–91.

Coningham, Robin, and Young, Ruth
1999   "The archaeological visibility of caste: An introduction." In *Case Studies in Archaeology and World Religion*, edited by Timothy Insoll, pp. 84–93. BAR International Series 755. Oxford: Archaeopress.

Conkey, Margaret W.
1989   "The structural analysis of Paleolithic art." In *Archaeological Thought in America*, edited by C. C. Lamberg-Karlovsky, pp. 135–54. Cambridge: Cambridge University.
2001   "Structural and semiotic approaches." In *Handbook of Rock Art Research*, edited by David S. Whitley, pp. 273–310. Walnut Creek, CA: AltaMira.

Connah, Graham
2004   *Forgotten Africa: An Introduction to Its Archaeology*. London: Routledge.

Cordy-Collins, Alana
2001   "Blood and the moon priestesses: *Spondylus* shells in Moche ceremony." In *Ritual Sacrifice in Ancient Peru*, edited by Elizabeth P. Benson and Anita G. Cook, pp. 35–53. Austin: University of Texas.

Crapo, Richley H.
    2003   *Anthropology of Religion: The Unity and Diversity of Religions*. New York: McGraw-Hill.

Crawford, Harriet
    2004   *Sumer and the Sumerians*. Second edition. Cambridge: Cambridge University.

Crossan, John Dominic, and Reed, Jonathan L.
    2001   *Excavating Jesus: Beneath the Stones, Behind the Texts*. New York: HarperCollins.

Curtis, Gregory
    2006   *The Cave Painters: Probing the Mysteries of the World's First Artists*. New York: Knopf.

Curry, Andrew
    2008   "Ancient excrement." *Archaeology* 61.4:42–45.

D'Altroy, Terence N.
    2002   *The Incas*. Oxford: Blackwell.

Darvill, Thomas
    2006   *Stonehenge: The Biography of a Landscape*. Stroud: Tempus.
    2007   "Towards the within: Stonehenge and its purpose." In *Cult in Context. Reconsidering Ritual in Archaeology*, edited by David A. Barrowclough and Caroline Malone, pp. 148–57. Oxford: Oxbow.

David, Bruno
    2002   *Landscapes, Rock-Art and the Dreaming. An Archaeology of Preunderstanding*. London: Leicester University.

Davies, Nigel
    1997   *The Ancient Kingdoms of Peru*. London: Penguin.

Davies, Vivian, and Friedman, Renée
    1999   *Egypt*. London: British Museum.

Davis, Wade
    1995   "Ethnobotany: An old practice, a new discipline." In *Ethnobotany: Evolution of a Discipline*, edited by Richard E. Schultes and Siri von Reis, pp. 40–51. New York: Champan and Hall.

DeBoer, Warren R.
    1997   "Ceremonial centres from the Cayapas (Esmeraldas, Ecuador) to Chillicothe (Ohio, U.S.A.)." *Cambridge Archaeological Journal* 7:225–53.

Dever, William G.
    2003   *Who Were the Early Israelites and Where Did They Come From?* Grand Rapids: Eerdmans.
    2008   *Did God have a Wife?* Grand Rapids: Eerdmans.

Devlet, Ekaterina
    2001   "Rock art and the material culture of Siberian and Central Asian shamanism." In *The Archaeology of Shamanism*, edited by Neil Price, pp. 43–55. London: Routledge.

Dickson, Bruce D.
    1990   *The Dawn of Belief: Religion in the Upper Paleolithic of Southwestern Europe*. Tucson: University of Arizona Press.

Diehl, Richard A.
    2004   *The Olmecs. America's First Civilization*. London: Thames & Hudson.

Dillehay, Tom D., Rossen, Jack, Andres, Thomas, and Williams, David E.
    2007   "Preceramic adoption of peanut, squash, and cotton in northern Peru." *Science* 316. 5833 (2007):1890–93.

Donnan, Christopher B., and McClelland, Donna
    1979   "The burial theme in Moche iconography." *Studies in Pre-Columbian Art and Archaeology* 21:5–46.

Douglas, Mary
  1966   *Purity and Danger: An Analysis of Concepts of Pollution and Taboo.* New York: Praeger.
  1973   *Natural Symbols: Explorations in Cosmology.* New York: Vintage.
Dowson, Thomas A.
  1998a   "Rain in Bushman belief, politics and history: The rock-art of rain-making in the south-eastern mountains, southern Africa." In *The Archaeology of Rock-Art,* edited by Christopher Chippindale and Paul S. C. Taçon, pp. 73–89. Cambridge: Cambridge University.
  1998b   "Like people in prehistory." *World Archaeology* 29.3:333–43.
Dumiak, Michael
  2006   "The Neanderthal code." *Archaeology* (November/December):22–25.
Durkheim, Emile
  1915·   *The Elementary Forms of Religious Life.* Oxford and New York: Oxford University.
Edwards, David N.
  2003   "The archaeology of religion." In *The Archaeology of Identity. Approaches to Gender, Age, Status, Ethnicity and Religion,* edited by Margarity Díaz-Andreu, Sam Lucy, Stasa Babi´c, and David N. Edwards, pp. 110–28. London: Routledge.
Eisler, Riane
  1988   *The Chalice and the Blade: Our History, Our Future.* San Francisco: HarperCollins.
Elgood, Heather
  2004   "Exploring the roots of village Hinduism in South Asia." *World Archaeology* 36.3: 326–42.
Elkin, A. P.
  1977   *Aboriginal Men of High Degree.* Second edition. St. Lucia: University of Queensland.
Embree, Ainslie
  1988   *Sources of Indian Tradition.* New York: Columbia University.
Emerson, Thomas E.
  1997a   "Cahokian elite ideology and the Mississippian cosmos." In *Cahokia Domination and Ideology in the Mississippian World,* edited by Timothy R. Pauketat and Thomas E. Emerson, pp. 190–228. Lincoln: University of Nebraska.
  1997b   *Cahokia and the Archaeology of Power.* Tuscaloosa: University of Alabama.
Emerson, Thomas E., Hughes, Randall E., Hynes, Mary R., and Wisseman, Sarah U.
  2003   "The sourcing and interpretation of Cahokia-style figurines in the Trans-Mississippi South and Southeast." *American Antiquity* 68.2:287–313.
Emerson, Thomas E., and Lewis, R. Barry (eds.)
  1999   *Cahokia and the Hinterlands: Middle Mississippian Cultures of the Midwest.* Champaign: University of Illinois.
Emerson, Thomas E., and Pauketat, Timothy R.
  2008   "Historical-processual archaeology and culture making: Unpacking the Southern Cult and Mississippian religion." In *Belief in the Past. Theoretical Approaches to the Archaeology of Religion,* edited by David S. Whitley and Kelley Hays-Gilpin, pp. 167–88. Walnut Creek, CA: Left Coast.
Erickson, Paul A.
  1998   *A History of Anthropological Theory.* Orchard Park, NY: Broadview.
Evans, Craig A.
  2006   "Excavating Caiaphas, Pilate, and Simone of Cyrene: Assessing the literary and archaeological evidence." In *Jesus and Archaeology,* edited by James H. Charlesworth, pp. 323–40. Grand Rapids: Eerdmans.
Evans-Pritchard, E. E.
  1937   *Witchcraft, Oracles and Magic among the Azande.* Oxford: Clarendon.

1940　*The Nuer: A Description of the Modes of Livelihood and Political Institution of Nilotic People*. Oxford: Clarendon.

1956　*Nuer Religion*. Oxford: Clarendon.

1965　*Theories of Primitive Religion*. Oxford: Clarendon.

Fagan, Brian M.

1998　*From Black Land to Fifth Sun*. Reading: Perseus.

2005　*Chaco Canyon: Archaeologists Explore the Lives of an Ancient Society*. Oxford: Oxford University Press.

Fairservis, Walter A.

1995　"Central Asia and the Rgveda: The archaeological evidence." In *The Indo-Aryans of Ancient South Asia: Language, Material Culture and Ethnicity*, edited by George Erdosy, pp. 206–12. New York: Walter de Gruyter.

Fedorova, Natalia

2001　"Shamans, heroes and ancestors in the bronze castings of Western Siberia." In *The Archaeology of Shamanism*, edited by Neil Price, pp. 56–64. London: Routledge.

Finkelstein, Israel, and Silberman, Neal Asher

2001　*The Bible Unearthed. Archaeology's New Vision of Ancient Israel and the Origin of Its Sacred Texts*. New York: Simon and Schuster.

2006　*David and Solomon: In Search of the Bible's Sacred Kings and the Roots of the Western Tradition*. New York: Free Press.

Firth, Raymond

1996　*Religion: A Humanist Interpretation*. London: Routledge.

Flannery, Kent V., and Marcus, Joyce

1993　"Cognitive archaeology." *Cambridge Archaeology Journal* 3:260–70.

Flood, Josephine

1983　*Archaeology of the Dreamtime. The Story of Prehistoric Australia and Her People*. Honolulu: University of Hawaii.

1997　*Rock Art of the Dreamtime*. Sydney: Angus and Robertson.

Fogelin, Lars

2008　"Delegitimizing religion: The archaeology of religion as . . . archaeology." In *Belief in the Past: Theoretical Approaches to the Archaeology of Religion*, edited by David S. Whitley and Kelley Hays-Gilpin, pp. 129–41. Walnut Creek, CA: Left Coast.

Fowler, Melvin L.

1991　"Mound 72 and Early Mississippian at Cahokia." In *New Perspectives on Cahokia: Views from the Periphery*, edited by J. B. Stoltman, pp. 1–28. Madison: Prehistory Press.

Frazer, James

1922　*The Golden Bough: A Study in Magic and Religion*. New York: Macmillan.

Fraktin, Elliot

2004　"The Laibon diviner and healer among Samburu pastoralists of Kenya." In *Divination and Healing: Potent Vision*, edited by Michael Winkelman and Philip M. Peek, pp. 207–26. Tucson: University of Arizona.

Freud, Sigmund

1961 [1927]. *The Future of an Illusion*. Translated edited by J. Strachey. New York: Norton.

2000 [1913]. *Totem and Taboo: Resemblances between the Psychic Lives of Savages and Neurotics*. Amherst, NY: Prometheus Books.

Friedman, R.

1996　"The ceremonial centre at Hierakonpolis, Locality HK29A." In *Aspects of Early Egypt*, edited by A. J. Spencer, pp. 16–35. London: British Museum Press.

Galvin, John
    2005   "Abydos. Life and death at the dawn of Egyptian civilization." *National Geographic* 207.4:106–21.
Gargett, Robert H.
    1989   "Grave shortcomings: The evidence for Neandertal burial." *Current Anthropology* 30.2: 157–90.
Garlake, P. S.
    1973   *Great Zimbabwe*. New York: Stein and Day.
    2001   "Sub-Saharan Africa." In *Handbook of Rock Art Research*, edited by David S. Whitley, pp. 637–64. Walnut Creek, CA: AltaMira.
Geertz, Clifford
    1973   *The Interpretation of Culture*. New York: Basic Books.
Gibson, Jon
    2000   *The Ancient Mounds of Poverty Point: Place of Rings*. Gainesville: University Press of Florida.
Gimbutas, Marija
    1989   *The Language of the Goddess: Unearthing the Hidden Symbols of Western Civilization*. San Francisco: Harper & Row.
    2007   *Gods and Goddesses of Old Europe, 7000–3500 B.C.* Updated edition. Berkeley: University of California.
Glover, Ian C.
    1998   "The role of India in the late prehistory of Southeast Asia." *Journal of Southeast Asian Archaeology* 18:21–49.
Glover, Ian, and Bellwood, Peter (eds.)
    2005   *Southeast Asia*. London: Routledge.
Golden, Jonathan M.
    2004   *Ancient Canaan and Israel: New Perspectives*. Santa Barbara: ABC/Clio.
Goody, Jack
    2004   "Is image to doctrine as speech to writing? Modes of communication and the origins of religion." In *Ritual and Memory: Toward a Comparative Anthropology of Religion*, edited by Harvey Whitehouse and James Laidlaw, pp. 49–64. Walnut Creek, CA: AltaMira.
Grabbe, Lester L.
    2007   *Ancient Israel. What Do We Know and How Do We Know It?* New York: T & T Clark.
Graulich, Michel.
    1997   *Myths of Ancient Mexico*. Translated by B. R. Ortiz de Montellano and T. Ortiz de Montellano. Norman: University of Oklahoma.
Grim, John A.
    1983   *The Shaman. Patterns of Siberian and Ojibway Healing*. Norman: University of Oklahoma.
Hall, Robert L.
    1977   "An anthropocentric perspective for Eastern United States Prehistory." *American Antiquity* 42.4:499–518.
    1997   *An Archaeology of the Soul: North American Indian Belief and Ritual*. Champaign: University of Illinois.
Hamayon, Roberte N.
    2003   "Game and games, fortune and dualism in Siberian shamanism." In *Shamanism, A Reader*, edited by Graham Harvey, pp. 63–68. London: Routledge.
Harner, Michael
    1968   "The sound of rushing water." *Natural History* 77.6 (June/July):28–33, 60–61.

1977 "The ecological basis for Aztec sacrifice." *American Ethnologist* 4.1:117–35.

Harris, Marvin

1974 *Cows, Pigs, Wars & Witches: The Riddles of Culture.* New York: Random House.

1977 *Cannibals and Kings: The Origins of Cultures.* New York: Random House.

Harvey, Graham (ed.)

2002 *Readings in Indigenous Religions.* London: Continuum.

Hawass, Zahi

1997 "The pyramids." In *Ancient Egypt,* edited by David P. Silverman, pp. 168–91. Oxford: Oxford University Press.

Hayden, Brian

1993 *Archaeology: The Science of Once and Future Things.* New York: W. H. Freeman and Co.

2003 *A Prehistory of Religion: Shamans, Sorcerers and Saints.* Washington, DC: Smithsonian.

Hays-Gilpin, Kelley

2003 *Ambiguous Images: Gender and Rock Art.* Walnut Creek, CA: AltaMira.

2008 "Archaeology and women's ritual business." In *Belief in the Past: Theoretical Approaches to the Archaeology of Religion,* edited by David S. Whitley and Kelley Hays-Gilpin, pp. 247–58. Walnut Creek, CA: Left Coast.

Heinze, Ruth-Inge

2004 "Divination in multireligious Southeast Asia: The case of Thailand." In *Divination and Healing: Potent Vision,* edited by Michael Winkelman and Philip M. Peek, pp. 167–80. Tucson: University of Arizona.

Hiebert, Fredrik T.

1995 "South Asia from a Central Asian perspective." In *The Indo-Aryans of Ancient South Asia: Language, Material Culture and Ethnicity,* edited by George Erdosy, pp. 192–205. New York: Walter de Gruyter.

Higham, Charles

1989 *The Archaeology of Mainland Southeast Asia.* Cambridge: Cambridge University.

1996 *The Bronze Age of Southeast Asia.* Cambridge: Cambridge University.

2001 *The Civilization of Angkor.* Berkeley: University of California.

2002 *Early Cultures of Mainland Southeast Asia.* Chicago: Art Media Resources.

Higham, Charles, and Bannanurag, R.

1990 "The princess and the pots." *New Scientist* 126(1718):50–54.

Higham, Charles, and Thosarat, Rachanie

1998 *Prehistoric Thailand.* Bangkok: River Books.

Hitchcock, John T.

2001 "Remarkably good theater." In *Shamans through Time. 500 Years on the Path to Knowledge,* edited by Jeremy Narby and Francis Huxley, pp. 200–206. New York: Tarcher/Penguin.

Hitchcock, Robert D., and Koperski, Thomas

2007 "Genocides of indigenous peoples." In *The Historiography of Genocide,* edited by Dan Stone. London: Palgrave.

Hitchcock, Robert D., and Osborn, Alan J. (eds.)

2002 *Endangered Peoples of Africa and the Middle East: Struggles to Survive and Thrive.* Westport, CT: Greenwood.

Hively, Ray, and Horn, Robert

1984 "Hopewellian geometry and astronomy at High Bank." *Astroarchaeology* 7:85–100.

Hodder, Ian

1990 *The Domestication of Europe.* Oxford: Blackwell.

Hodder, Ian, and Hutson, Scott
  2003   *Reading the Past: Current Approaches to Interpretation in Archaeology.* Third edition. Cambridge: Cambridge University.
Hoffman, Michael A.
  1991   *Egypt before the Pharaohs: The Prehistoric Foundations of Egyptian Civilization.* Revised edition. Austin: University of Texas.
Hopfe, Lewis M., and Woodward, Mark R.
  2001   *Religions of the World.* Eighth Edition. Upper Saddle River, NJ: Prentice-Hall.
Hoyland, Robert G.
  2001   *Arabia and the Arabs. From the Bronze Age to the Coming of Islam.* London: Routledge.
Howells, William W.
  1948   *The Heathens: Primitive Man and His Religions.* Garden City: Doubleday.
Huffman, Thomas N.
  1987   *Symbols in Stone: Unravelling the Mystery of Great Zimbabwe.* Johannesburg: Witwatersrand University.
  1996   *Snakes & Crocodiles: Power and Symbolism in Ancient Zimbabwe.* Johannesburg: Witwatersrand University.
  2005   *Mapungubwe: Ancient African Civilisation on the Limpopo.* Johannesburg: Wits University Press.
Hutton, Ronald
  2001   *Shamans. Siberian Spirituality and the Western Imagination.* London: Hambledon & London.
Ibrahim, Mahmood
  1982   "Social and economic conditions in pre-Islamic Mecca." *International Journal of Middle Eastern Studies* 14.3:343–58.
Ingham, John M.
  1984   "Human sacrifice at Tenochtitlan." *Comparative Studies in Society and History* 26.3: 379–400.
Insoll, Timothy (ed.)
  1999   *Case Studies in Archaeology and World Religion.* BAR International Series 755. Oxford: Archaeopress.
  2001   *Archaeology and World Religion.* London: Routledge.
Insoll, Timothy
  2001   "Introduction: The archaeology of world religion." In *Archaeology and World Religion,* edited by Timothy Insoll, pp. 1–32. London: Routledge.
Isaacson, Rupert
  2001   *The Healing Land. The Bushmen and the Kalahari Desert.* New York: Grove.
James, T. G. H.
  2005   *The British Museum Concise Introduction to Ancient Egypt.* Ann Arbor: University of Michigan.
Johnson, Anthony
  2008   *Solving Stonehenge: The New Key to an Ancient Enigma.* London: Thames and Hudson.
Johnson, David, Proulx, Donald, and Mabee, Stephen B.
  2002   "The correlation between geoglyphs and subterranean water resources in the Rio Grande de Nasca drainage." In *Andean Archaeology I—Art, Landscape and Society,* edited by Helaine Silverman and William H. Isbell, pp. 307–32. New York: Kluwer Academic/Plenum Press.

Johnson, Paul C.

2003   "Shamanism from Ecuador to Chicago. A case study in New Age ritual appropriation." In *Shamanism, A Reader*, edited by Graham Harvey, pp. 334–54. London: Routledge.

Jones, Andrew

2001   *Archaeological Theory and Scientific Practice*. Cambridge: Cambridge University.

Jones, Dan

2008   "New light on Stonehenge." *Smithsonian* 39.7:36–46.

Joralemon, Peter D.

1976   "The Olmec Dragon: A study in Pre-Columbian iconography." In *Origins of Religious Art and Iconography in Preclassic Mesoamerica*, edited by H. B. Nicholson, pp. 27–71. Los Angeles: Ethnic Arts Council of Los Angeles.

Jordan, Paul

1999   *Neanderthal*. Phoenix Mill, England: Sutton.

Kantner, John

2004   *Ancient Puebloan Southwest*. Cambridge: Cambridge University.

Kehoe, Alice Beck

1989   *The Ghost Dance: Ethnohistory and Revitalization*. New York: Holt, Rinehart and Winston.

2000   *Shamans and Religion. An Anthropological Exploration in Critical Thinking*. Prospect Heights, IL: Waveland.

Kemp, Barry J.

2006   *Ancient Egypt Anatomy of a Civilization*. Second edition. London: Routledge.

Kendall, Laurel

1985   *Shamans, Housewives and Other Restless Spirits: Women in Korean Ritual Life*. Honolulu: University of Hawaii.

Kennedy, Kenneth A. R.

1995   "Have Aryans been identified in the prehistoric skeletal record from South Asia? Biological anthropology and concepts of ancient races." In *The Indo-Aryans of Ancient South Asia: Language, Material Culture and Ethnicity*, edited by George Erdosy, pp. 32–66. New York: Walter de Gruyter.

Kenoyer, Jonathon M.

1994   "The Harappan state: Was it or wasn't it?" In *From Sumer to Meluhha: Contributions to the Archaeology of South and West Asia in Memory of George F. Dales, Jr.*, edited by Jonathon Mark Kenoyer, pp. 71–80. Wisconsin Archaeological Reports 3. Madison: University of Wisconsin.

1995   "Interaction systems, specialized crafts and culture change: The Indus Valley tradition and the Indo-Gangetic tradition in South Asia." In *The Indo-Aryans of Ancient South Asia: Language, Material Culture and Ethnicity*, edited by George Erdosy, pp. 213–57. New York: Walter de Gruyter.

1998   *Ancient Cities of the Indus Valley Civilization*. Karachi: Oxford University.

Kent, Sue

1992   "The current forager controversy: Real versus ideal views of hunter-gatherers." *Man* 27: 45–70.

Killebrew, Ann

2006   "The emergence of ancient Israel: The social boundaries of a 'mixed multitude' in Canaan." In *"I Will Speak the Riddles of Ancient Times": Archaeological and Historical Studies in Honor of Amihai Mazar on the Occasion of His Sixtieth Birthday*, edited by

Aren M. Maeir and Pierre de Miroschedji, pp. 555–72. Winona Lake, IN: Eisen-brauns.

Kimball, Charles
  2003   *When Religion Becomes Evil*. San Francisco: HarperCollins.

Klassen, Michael A.
  1998   "Icon and narrative in transition: Contact-period rock-art at Writing-On-Stone, southern Alberta, Canada." In *The Archaeology of Rock-Art*, edited by Christopher Chippindale and Paul S. C. Taçon, pp. 42–72. Cambridge: Cambridge University.

Klein, Richard G., and Edgar, Blake
  2002   *The Dawn of Human Culture*. New York: John Wiley and Sons.

Lahiri, Nayanjot (ed.)
  2000   *The Decline and Fall of the Indus Civilization*. Delhi: Permanent Black.

Lahiri, Nayanjot, and Bacus, Elisabeth A.
  2004   "Exploring the archaeology of Hinduism." *World Archaeology* 36.3:313–25.

Lal, B. B.
  1997   *The Earliest Civilization of South Asia: Rise, Maturity, and Decline*. New Delhi: Aryan Books International.

Laughlin, John C. H.
  2000   *Archaeology and the Bible*. London: Routledge.

Lawler, Andrew
  2008   "Boring no more, a trade-savvy Indus emerges." *Science* 320:1276–85.

Lawlor, Robert
  1991   *Voices of the First Day. Awakening in the Aboriginal Dreamtime*. Rochester, VT: Inner Traditions.

Layton, Robert
  1992   *Australian Rock Art. A New Synthesis*. Cambridge: Cambridge University.
  2001   "Ethnographic study and symbolic analysis." In *Handbook of Rock Art Research*, edited by David S. Whitley, pp. 311–31. Walnut Creek, CA: AltaMira.

Lee, Richard B.
  1984   *The Dobe !Kung*. New York: Holt, Rinehart and Winston.

Lehmann, Arthur C., Myers, James E., and Moro, Pamela A. (eds.)
  2005   *Magic, Witchcraft, and Religion: An Anthropological Study of the Supernatural*. Sixth edition. New York: McGraw-Hill.

Lehner, Mark
  1997   *The Complete Pyramids*. New York: Thames and Hudson.

Lehner, Mark (ed.)
  2006   *Giza Reports. The Giza Plateau Mapping Project*. Brighton, MA: Ancient Egypt Research Associates.

Lekson, Stephen H.
  1999   *The Chaco Meridian: Centers of Political Power in the Ancient Southwest*. Walnut Creek, CA: AltaMira.
  2004   "Architecture: The central matter of Chaco Canyon." In *In Search of Chaco: New Approaches to an Archaeological Enigma*, edited by David G. Noble, pp. 23–32. Santa Fe: School of American Research.

Lekson, Stephen H. (ed.)
  2007   *The Architecture of Chaco Canyon, New Mexico*. Salt Lake City: University of Utah.

Leroi-Gourhan, Andre
  1965   *Treasures of Prehistoric Art*. New York: Harry Abrams.

Lewellen, Ted C.
  2003   *Political Anthropology: An Introduction.* Westport, CT: Praeger.
Lewis, I. M.
  2003   *Ecstatic Religion. A Study of Shamanism and Spirit Possession.* Third edition. London: Routledge.
Lewis-Williams, David
  1981   *Believing and Seeing: Symbolic Meanings in Southern San Rock Paintings.* New York: Academic.
  2001   "Southern African shamanistic rock art in its social and cognitive contexts." In *The Archaeology of Shamanism,* edited by Neil Price, pp. 17–39. London: Routledge.
  2002   *The Mind in the Cave.* London: Thames and Hudson.
  2008   "Religion and archaeology: An analytical materialist account." In *Belief in the Past. Theoretical Approaches to the Archaeology of Religion,* edited by David S. Whitley and Kelley Hays-Gilpin, pp. 23–42. Walnut Creek, CA: Left Coast.
Lewis-Williams, David, and Dowson, Thomas
  1988   "The signs of all times: Entoptic phenomena and Upper Palaeolithic art." *Current Anthropology* 29:201–45.
Lévi-Strauss, Claude
  1963   *Structural Anthropology.* Harmondsworth: Penguin.
  1966   *The Savage Mind.* London: Weidenfeld & Nicolson
  1969   *The Raw and the Cooked.* Volume 1 of *Introduction to a Science of Mythology.* New York: Harper & Row.
Lowenstein, Tom
  1996   *The Vision of the Buddha.* Boston: Little, Brown.
Magness, Jodi
  2002   *The Archaeology of Qumran and the Dead Sea Scrolls.* Grand Rapids: Eerdmans.
Malinowski, Bronislaw
  1954 [1925]. *Magic, Science and Religion: And Other Essays.* Garden City, NY: Doubleday.
Mallory, J. P.
  1989   *In Search of the Indo-Europeans.* London: Thames and Hudson.
Malone, Caroline.
  2001   *Neolithic Britain and Ireland.* Stroud: Tempus.
Malpass, Michael A.
  1996   *Daily Life in the Inca Empire.* Westport, CT: Greenwood.
Malville, J. McKim
  2004   "Sacred time in Chaco Canyon and beyond." In *In Search of Chaco: New Approaches to an Archaeological Enigma,* edited by David G. Noble, pp. 87–92. Santa Fe: School of American Research.
Marshack, Alexander
  1972   *The Roots of Civilization. The Cognitive Beginnings of Man's First Art, Symbol and Notation.* New York: McGraw-Hill.
  1995   "Images of the Ice Age." *Archaeology* (July/August):28–39.
Martinez, Florentino Garcia
  2000   "The great battles over Qumran." *Near Eastern Archaeology* 63.3:124–30.
Matthews, Roger
  2003   *The Archaeology of Mesopotamia: Theories and Approaches.* London: Routledge.
Mauss, Marcel
  2001 [1924]. *The Gift.* London: Routledge.

Mazar, Amihai
    1990   *Archaeology of the Land of the Bible 10,000–586 B.C.E.* New York: Doubleday.
McCall, Henrietta
    1990   *Mesopotamian Myths.* Austin: University of Texas.
McEwan, Gordon
    2006   *The Incas, New Perspectives.* Santa Barbara: ABC/Clio.
McIntosh, Jane R.
    2002   *A Peaceful Realm: The Rise and Fall of the Indus Civilization.* Boulder: Westview.
McIntosh, Roderick.
    1998   "Riddle of Great Zimbabwe." *Archaeology* 51.4 (July–August):44–49.
Mehrer, Mark W.
    1995   *Cahokia's Countryside. Household Archaeology, Settlement Patterns, and Social Power.* DeKalb: Northern Illinois University.
Meskell, Lynn
    1995   "Goddesses, Gimbutas and 'New Age' archaeology." *Antiquity* 69:74–86.
Millon, Rene
    1976   "Social relations in ancient Teotihuacan." In *The Valley of Mexico*, edited by Eric R. Wolf. Albuquerque: University of New Mexico.
Milner, George R.
    1998   *The Cahokia Chiefdom. The Archaeology of a Mississippian Society.* Washington, DC: Smithsonian Institution.
    2005   *The Moundbuilders: Ancient Peoples of Eastern North America.* London: Thames and Hudson.
Mitchell, William E.
    1987   *The Bamboo Fire: Field Work with the New Guinea Wape.* Second edition. Prospect Heights: Waveland.
Moctezuma, Eduardo Matos
    2003   "Aztec history and cosmovision." In *Moctezuma's Mexico: Visions of the Aztec World*, edited by Davíd Carrasco and Eduardo Matos Moctezuma, pp. 3–97. Boulder: University Press of Colorado.
Morgan, Lewis Henry
    2000 [1877]   *Ancient Society.* New Brunswick, NJ: Transaction.
Morris, Brian
    1987   *Anthropological Studies of Religion: An Introductory Text.* Cambridge: Cambridge University.
    2006   *Religion and Anthropology: A Critical Introduction.* Cambridge: Cambridge University.
Morwood, M. J.
    2002   *Visions from the Past. The Archaeology of Australian Aboriginal Art.* Crows Nest, NSW: Allen & Unwin.
Moseley, Michael E.
    2001   *The Incas and Their Ancestors: The Archaeology of Peru.* Revised edition. London: Thames and Hudson.
Mulvaney, John, and Kamminga, Johan
    1999   *Prehistory of Australia.* Washington, DC: Smithsonian.
Nakhai, Beth Alpert
    2001   *Archaeology and the Religions of Canaan and Israel.* Boston: American Schools of Oriental Research.

Narby, Jeremy

2001 "The understanding deepens." In *Shamans through Time. 500 Years on the Path to Knowledge*, edited by Jeremy Narby and Francis Huxley, pp. 75–78. New York: Tarcher/Penguin.

Narby, Jeremy, and Huxley, Francis (eds.)

2001 *Shamans through Time. 500 Years on the Path to Knowledge.* New York: Tarcher/Penguin.

Nelson, Sarah

2001 "Diversity of the Upper Paleolithic 'Venus' figurines and archaeological mythology." In *Gender in Cross-Cultural Perspective*, edited by Caroline B. Brettell and Carolyn F. Sargent, third edition, pp. 82–89. Englewood Cliffs, NJ: Prentice-Hall.

Nickelsburg, George W. E.

2003 *Ancient Judaism and Christian Origins.* Minneapolis: Fortress.

Ortiz de Montellano, Bernard R.

1978 "Aztec cannibalism: An ecological necessity?" *Science* 200.4342:611–17.

O'Shea, John M.

1984 *Mortuary Variability. An Archaeological Investigation.* London: Academic.

Parker Pearson, Mike

1999 *The Archaeology of Death and Burial.* College Station: Texas A&M.

Pauketat, Timothy R.

1994 *The Ascent of Chiefs. Cahokia and Mississippian Politics in Native North America.* Tuscaloosa: University of Alabama.

Pauketat, Timothy R., and Emerson, Thomas E. (eds.)

1997 *Cahokia: Domination and Ideology in the Mississippian World.* Lincoln: University of Nebraska.

Pearce, Sarah

2002 "Judaea under Roman rule: 63 BCE–135 CE." In *The Biblical World*, edited by John Barton, Vol. I, pp. 458–91. London: Routledge.

Pearson, James L.

2002 *Shamanism and the Ancient Mind.* Walnut Creek: AltaMira.

Pelly, David F.

2001 *The Sacred Hunt.* Seattle: University of Washington.

Pikirayi, Innocent

2001 *The Zimbabwe Culture.* Walnut Creek, CA: AltaMira.

Pitts, Mike

2000 *Hengeworld.* London: Arrow.

Plog, Stephen

2008 *Ancient Peoples of the American Southwest.* London: Thames and Hudson.

Pollock, Susan

1999 *Ancient Mesopotamia.* Cambridge: University of Cambridge.

Possehl, Gregory L.

1999 *Indus Age: The Beginnings.* Philadelphia: University of Pennsylvania.

2002 *The Indus Civilization: A Contemporary Perspective.* Walnut Creek, CA: AltaMira.

Postgate, J. N.

1994 *Early Mesopotamia: Society and Economy at the Dawn of History.* London: Routledge.

Price, Barbara J.

1978 "Demystification, enriddlement, and Aztec cannibalism: A materialist rejoinder to Harner." *American Ethnologist* 5.1:98–115.

Price, Neil S. (ed.)
  2001   *The Archaeology of Shamanism*. London: Routledge.
Proulx, Donald A.
  2001   Ritual uses of trophy heads in ancient Nasca society." In *Ritual Sacrifice in Ancient Peru*, edited by Elizabeth P. Benson and Anita G. Cook, pp. 119–36. Austin: University of Texas.
Puttick, Elizabeth
  1997   *Women in New Religions: In Search of Community, Sexuality, and Spiritual Power*. New York: St. Martin's.
Rak, Y., Kimbel, W. H., and Hovers, E.
  1994   "A Neanderthal infant from Amud Cave, Israel." *Journal of Human Evolution* 26: 313–24.
Rappaport, Roy
  1967   "Ritual regulation of environmental relations among a New Guinea people." *Ethnology* 6:17–30.
  1968   *Pigs for Ancestors: Ritual in the Ecology of a New Guinea People*. New Haven: Yale University.
  1999   *Ritual and Religion in the Making of Humanity*. Cambridge: Cambridge University.
Ratnagar, Shereen
  2001   *Understanding Harappa. Civilization in the Greater Indus Valley*. New Delhi: Tulika.
Reed, Jonathan L.
  2000   *Archaeology and the Galilean Jesus: A Re-examination of the Evidence*. Harrisburg: Trinity.
Reichel-Dolmatoff, G.
  1976   "Cosmology as ecological analysis: A view from the rain forest." *Man* 11:307–18.
Reinhard, Johan
  2005   *The Ice Maiden. Inca Mummies, Mountain Gods, and Sacred Sites in the Andes*. Washington, DC: National Geographic.
Renfrew, Colin
  1987   *Archaeology and Language. The Puzzle of Indo-European Origins*. Cambridge: Cambridge University.
  1994   "The archaeology of religion." In *The Ancient Mind. Elements of Cognitive Archaeology*, edited by Colin Renfrew and Ezra B. W. Zubrow, pp. 47–54. Cambridge: Cambridge University.
  2004   "Chaco Canyon: A view from the outside." In *In Search of Chaco. New Approaches to an Archaeological Enigma*, edited by David Grant Noble, pp. 101–6. Santa Fe: School of American Research.
Rice, Patricia C.
  1981   "Prehistoric Venuses: Symbols of motherhood or womanhood?" *Journal of Anthropological Research* 7.4:402–16.
Rick, John W.
  2004   "The evolution of authority and power at Chavín de Huántar, Peru." *Archaeological Papers of the American Anthropological Association* 14.1:71–89.
Robinson, Richard H., and Johnson, Willard L.
  1997   *The Buddhist Religion: A Historical Introduction*. Fourth edition. New York: Wadsworth.
Rogers, Spencer L.
  1982   *The Shaman: His Symbols and His Healing Power*. Springfield, IL: Charles C. Thomas.

Romain, William F.

2000   *Mysteries of the Hopewell: Astronomers, Geometers, and Magicians of the Eastern Woodlands.* Akron, OH: University of Akron.

Ross, Jennifer C.

2009   "The scribal artifact: Technological innovation in Uruk period Mesopotamia." In *Agency and Identity in the Ancient Near East: New Paths Forward*, edited by Sharon R. Steadman and Jennifer C. Ross. London: Equinox, forthcoming.

Rowe, Marvin W.

2001   "Dating by AMS radiocarbon analysis." In *Handbook of Rock Art Research*, edited by David S. Whitley, pp. 139–66. Walnut Creek, CA: AltaMira.

Rozwadowski, Andrzej

2008   "Centering historical-archaeological discourse: The prehistory of Central Asian/South Siberian shamanism." In *Belief in the Past. Theoretical Approaches to the Archaeology of Religion*, edited by David S. Whitley and Kelley Hays-Gilpin, pp. 105–17. Walnut Creek, CA: Left Coast.

Ryan, Robert E.

1999   *The Strong Eye of Shamanism.* Rochester, VT: Inner Traditions.

Scarre, Christopher

1998   *Exploring Prehistoric Europe.* Oxford: Oxford University.

Scarre, Christopher, and Scarre, Geoffrey (eds.)

2006   *The Ethics of Archaeology: Philosophical Perspectives on Archaeological Practice.* Cambridge: Cambridge University.

Schmidt, Brian B. (ed.)

2007   *The Quest for the Historical Israel. Debating Archaeology and the History of Early Israel.* Atlanta: Society of Biblical Literature.

Sebastian, Lynne

1992   *The Chaco Anasazi: Sociopolitical Evolution in the Prehistoric Southwest.* Cambridge: Cambridge University.

Seeman, Mark F.

1979   *The Hopewell Interaction Sphere: The Evidence for Interregional Trade and Structural Complexity.* Prehistory Research Series 5.2. Indianapolis: Indiana Historical Society.

Sharma, Anuradha

1998   *Caste in India.* Delhi: Satish Garg.

Shaw, Ian

2003   *Exploring Ancient Egypt.* Oxford: Oxford University.

Shreeve, James

1995   *The Neandertal Enigma: Solving the Mystery of Modern Human Origins.* New York: William Morrow and Co.

Shoko, Tabona

2007   *Karanga Indigenous Religion in Zimbabwe.* Burlington, VT: Ashgate.

Silverblatt, Irene

1987   *Moon, Sun, and Witches: Gender Ideologies and Class in Inca and Colonial Peru.* Princeton: Princeton University.

Silverman, Helaine

2002   *Ancient Nasca Settlement and Society.* Iowa City: University of Iowa.

2004   *Andean Archaeology.* Oxford: Wiley-Blackwell.

Silverman, Helaine, and Proulx, Donald A.

2002   *The Nasca.* Oxford: Blackwell.

Singh, Bhagwan
    1995   *The Vedic Harappans*. New Delhi: Aditya Prakashan.
Smirnov, Yuri
    1989   "Intentional human burial: Middle Paleolithic (Last Glaciation) beginnings. *Journal of World Prehistory* 3.2:199–233.
Smith, Claire
    1999   "Ancestors, place and people: Social landscapes in Aboriginal Australia." In *The Archaeology and Anthropology of Landscape*, edited by Peter Ucko and Robert Layton, pp. 189–205. London: Routledge.
Smith, Craig B.
    2004   *How the Great Pyramid Was Built*. Washington, DC: Smithsonian.
Smith, Huston
    1994   *The Illustrated World's Religions*. HarperCollins: San Francisco.
Smith, Michael E.
    2003   *The Aztecs*. Second edition. Oxford: Blackwell.
Snellgrove, David L.
    2001   *Khmer Civilization and Angkor*. Bangkok: Orchid.
    2004   *Angkor—Before and After: A Cultural History of the Khmers*. Bangkok: Orchid.
Sofaer, Anna
    1997   "The primary architecture of the Chacoan culture: A cosmological expression." In *Anasazi Architecture and American Design*, edited by B. H. Morrow and V. B. Price, pp. 88–132. Albuquerque: University of New Mexico.
Solecki, Ralph
    1975   "Shanidar IV, A Neanderthal flower burial in northern Iraq." *Science* 190:880–81.
Solomon, Anne
    1998   "Ethnography and method in southern African rock-art research." In *The Archaeology of Rock-Art*, edited by Christopher Chippindale and Paul S. C. Taçon, pp. 268–84. Cambridge: Cambridge University.
    2001   "What is an explanation? Belief and cosmology in interpretations of southern San rock art in southern Africa." In *The Concept of Shamanism: Uses and Abuses*, edited by Henri-Paul Francfort and Roberte N. Hamayon, pp. 161–77. Budapest: Akadémiai Kiadó.
Sørensen, Jesper
    2007   "Malinowski and magical ritual." In *Religion, Anthropology, and Cognitive Science*, edited by Harvey Whitehouse and James Laidlaw, pp. 81–104. Durham, NC: Carolina Academic.
Srejovic, Dragoslav
    1972   *New Discoveries at Lepenski Vir*. New York: Stein and Day.
Stanish Charles
    2001   "The origin of state societies in South America." *Annual Review of Anthropology* 30:41–64.
Stanner, W. E. H.
    1987   "The Dreaming." In *Traditional Aboriginal Society: A Reader*, edited by W. H. Edwards, pp. 225–36. Melbourne: Macmillan.
    1998   "Some aspects of Aboriginal religion." In *Religious Business. Essays on Australian Aboriginal Spirituality*, edited by Max Charlesworth, pp. 1–23. Cambridge: Cambridge University.
Stark, Miriam
    2003   "Angkor Borei and the archaeology of Cambodia's Mekong Delta." In *Art & Archaeology of Fu Nan: Pre-Khmer Kingdom of the Lower Mekong Valley*, edited by J. Khoo, pp. 87–106. Bangkok: Orchid Books.

2004 "Pre-Angkorian and Angkorian Cambodia." In *A Cultural History of Southeast Asia: From Earliest Times to the Indic Civilizations*, edited by P. Bellwood and I. Glover, pp. 89–119. New York: Routledge Curzon.

Steadman, Sharon R.
2005 "Reliquaries on the landscape: Mounds as matrices of human cognition." In *Archaeologies of the Middle East: Critical Perspectives*, edited by Susan Pollock and Reinhard Bernbeck, pp. 286–307. Oxford: Blackwell.

Stein, Rebecca L., and Stein, Philip L.
2005 *The Anthropology of Religion, Magic, and Witchcraft*. Boston: Pearson.

Stone, Richard
2005 "Mystery Man of Stonehenge." *Smithsonian* 36 (August):62–67.

Stringer, Christopher
1990 "The emergence of modern humans." *Scientific American* (December):98–104.
2003 "Human evolution: Out of Ethiopia." *Nature* (423):692–95.

Stringer, Christopher, and Andrews, Peter
2005 *The Complete World of Human Evolution*. London: Thames & Hudson.

Stringer, Christopher, and Gamble, Clive
1993 *In Search of the Neanderthals: Solving the Puzzle of Human Origins*. London: Thames and Hudson.

Stuart, David E.
2000 *Anasazi America*. Albuquerque: University of New Mexico.

Stutley, Margaret
2003 *Shamanism, An Introduction*. London: Routledge.

Sutherland, Patricia D.
2001 "Shamanism and the iconography of Palaeo-Eskimo art." In *The Archaeology of Shamanism*, edited by Neil Price, pp. 135–45. London: Routledge.

Swain, Tony
1998 "On 'understanding' Australian Aboriginal religion." In *Religious Business. Essays on Australian Aboriginal Spirituality*, edited by Max Charlesworth, pp. 72–93. Cambridge: Cambridge University.

Swanson, Guy E.
1969 *The Birth of the Gods: The Origin of Primitive Beliefs*. Ann Arbor: University of Michigan.

Tainter, Joseph A.
1978 "Mortuary practices and the study of prehistoric social systems." In *Advances in Archaeological Methods and Theory I*, edited by Michael Schiffer, pp. 106–43. New York: Academic.
1980 "Behavior and status in a Middle Woodland mortuary population from the Illinois Valley." *American Antiquity* 45.2: 308–13.

Tattersal, Ian
1995 *The Last Neanderthal: The Rise, Success, and Mysterious Extinction of Our Closest Human Relatives*. New York: Macmillan.

Tattersall, Ian, and Schwartz, Jeffrey
2000 *Extinct Humans*. New York: Westview.

Taube, Karl
1993 *Aztec and Maya Myths*. Austin: University of Texas.

Tedlock, Barbara
2005 *The Woman in the Shaman's Body. Reclaiming the Feminine in Religion and Medicine*. New York: Bantam.

Thorne, Alan G., and Wolpoff, Milford H.
   1992   "The multiregional evolution of humans." *Scientific American* (April):76–83.
   2003   "The multiregional evolution of humans, revised paper." *New Look at Human Evolution. Scientific American*, edited by M. Fischetti, 13(2):46–53.

Toll, H. Wolcott
   2004   "Artifacts in Chaco. Where they came from and what they mean." In *In Search of Chaco: New Approaches to an Archaeological Enigma*, edited by David G. Noble, pp. 33–40. Santa Fe: School of American Research.

Townsend, Joan B.
   1997   "Shamanism." In *Anthropology of Religion: A Handbook*, edited by Stephen D. Glazier, pp. 429–69. London: Westport, CT: Greenwood.

Townsend, Richard F.
   1991   "The Mt. Tlaloc project." In *Aztec Ceremonial Landscapes*, edited by Davíd Carrasco, pp. 26–30. Boulder: University Press of Colorado.
   2000   *The Aztecs.* Revised edition. London: Thames & Hudson.

Trainor, Kevin
   2001a   "The career of Siddhartha." In *Buddhism, The Illustrated Guide*, edited by Kevin Trainor, pp. 22–39. Oxford: Oxford University.
   2001b   "Theravada Buddhism." In *Buddhism, The Illustrated Guide*, edited by Kevin Trainor, pp. 120–31. Oxford: Oxford University.

Tringham, Ruth, and Conkey, Margaret
   1998   "Rethinking figurines: A critical view from archaeology of Gimbutas, the 'goddess' and popular culture." In *Ancient Goddesses: The Myths and the Evidence*, edited by Lucy Goodison and Christine Morris, pp. 22–45. Madison: University of Wisconsin.

Trinkaus, Erik
   1983   *The Shanidar Neandertals.* New York: Academic Press.

Trinkaus, Erik, and Shipman, Pat
   1992   *The Neanderthals: Of Skeletons, Scientists, and Scandal.* New York: Vintage.

Tunbridge, Dorothy
   1988   *Flinders Ranges Dreaming.* Canberra: Aboriginal Studies Press.

Turnbull, Colin
   1972   *The Mountain People.* New York: Simon and Schuster.

Turner, Edith
   2006   *Among the Healers: Stories of Spiritual and Ritual Healing around the World.* Westport, CT: Praeger.

Turner, Victor
   1967   *The Forest of Symbols: Aspects of Ndembu Ritual.* Ithaca: Cornell University.
   1969   *The Ritual Process: Structure and Anti-Structure.* New York: Aldine De Gruyter.

Tylor, Edward B
   1961 [1871] *Primitive Culture.* New York: Harper.

Ucko, Peter J.
   1969   "Ethnography and archaeological interpretation of funerary remains." *World Archaeology* 1:262–80.

Urton, Gary
   1999   *Inca Myths.* Austin: University of Texas.

Van de Meirop, Marc
   2003   *History of the Ancient Near East: Ca. 3000–323 B.C.* Oxford: Blackwell.

Van Dyke, Ruth M.

2004 "Chaco's sacred geography." In *In Search of Chaco: New Approaches to an Archaeological Enigma*, edited by David G. Noble, pp. 79–86. Santa Fe: School of American Research.

Van Turenhout, Dirk, and Weeks, John

2005 *The Aztecs: New Perspectives.* Oxford: ABC/Clio.

Vickery, Michael

1998 *Society, Economics and Politics in Pre-Angkor Cambodia.* Tokyo: Centre for East Asian Cultural Studies for UNESCO.

Vinnicombe, Patricia

1976 *People of the Eland. Rock Paintings of the Drakensberg Bushmen as a Reflection of Their Life and Thought.* Pietermaritzburg: University of Natal.

Vitebsky, Piers

1993 *Dialogues with the Dead: The Discussion of Morality among the Sora of Eastern India.* Cambridge: Cambridge University.

1995 *The Shaman. Voyages of the Soul Trance, Ecstasy, and Healing from Siberia to the Amazon.* Boston: Little, Brown and Company.

Vitelli, Karen

1996 *Archaeological Ethics.* Walnut Creek, CA: AltaMira.

Weber, Max

1922 [1963] *The Sociology of Religion.* Translated by E. Fischoff. Boston: Unwin.

Weisgrau, Maxine K.

2000 "Vedic and Hindu traditions." In *Religion and Culture: An Anthropological Focus*, edited by Raymond Scupin, pp. 225–48. Upper Saddle River, NJ: Prentice Hall.

Whitehouse, Harvey

2000 *Arguments and Icons: Divergent Modes of Religiosity.* Oxford: Oxford University.

2004a *Modes of Religiosity: A Cognitive Theory of Religious Transmission.* Walnut Creek, CA: AltaMira.

2004b "Theorizing religions past." In *Theorizing Religions Past: Archaeology, History, and Cognition*, edited by Harvey Whitehouse and Luther H. Martin, pp. 215–32. Walnut Creek, CA: AltaMira.

Whitehouse, Harvey, and Laidlaw, James (eds.)

2004 *Ritual and Memory. Toward a Comparative Anthropology of Religion.* Walnut Creek, CA: AltaMira.

2007 *Religion, Anthropology, and Cognitive Science.* Durham, NC: Carolina Academic.

Whitehouse, Harvey, and Martin, Luther H. (eds.)

2004 *Theorizing Religions Past: Archaeology, History, and Cognition.* Walnut Creek, CA: AltaMira.

Whitley, David S. (ed.)

2001 *Handbook of Rock Art Research.* Walnut Creek, CA: AltaMira.

Whitley, David S.

1994 "By the hunter, for the gatherer: Art, social relations and subsistence change in the prehistoric Great Basin." *World Archaeology* 25.3:356–77.

1998 "Finding rain in the desert: Landscape, gender and far western North American rock-art." In *The Archaeology of Rock-Art*, edited by Christopher Chippindale and Paul S. C. Taçon, pp. 11–29. Cambridge: Cambridge University.

2000 *The Art of the Shaman: The Rock Art of California.* Salt Lake City: University of Utah.

2005   "The archaeology of religion." In *Handbook of Archaeological Method and Theory*, edited by H. Maschner and A. Bentley. Walnut Creek, CA: AltaMira.

2006   *Introduction to Rock Art Research*. Walnut Creek, CA: Left Coast.

2008   "Cognition, emotion, and belief: First steps in an archaeology of religion." In *Belief in the Past. Theoretical Approaches to the Archaeology of Religion*, edited by David S. Whitley and Kelley Hays-Gilpin, pp. 85–103. Walnut Creek, CA: Left Coast.

Whitley, D. S., Dorn, R. I., Simon, J. M., Rechtman, R., and Whitley, T. K.

1999   "Sally's rockshelter and the archaeology of the vision quest." *Cambridge Archaeological Journal* 9:221–47.

Whitley, David S., and Hays-Gilpin, Kelley (eds.)

2008   *Belief in the Past: Theoretical Approaches to the Archaeology of Religion*. Walnut Creek, CA: Left Coast.

Willis, Michael

2001   "Ashoka the builder." In *Buddhism, The Illustrated Guide*, edited by Kevin Trainor, pp. 52–55. Oxford: Oxford University.

Wills, W. H., and Windes, Thomas C.

1989   "Evidence for population aggregation and dispersal during the Basketmaker III Period in Chaco Canyon, New Mexico." *American Antiquity* 54:347–69.

Wilson, Ian

1996   *Jesus: The Evidence*. San Francisco: HarperCollins.

Winkelman, Michael

2008   "Cross-cultural and biogenetic perspectives on the origins of shamanism." In *Belief in the Past. Theoretical Approaches to the Archaeology of Religion*, edited by David S. Whitley and Kelley Hays-Gilpin, pp. 43–66. Walnut Creek, CA: Left Coast.

Wylie, Alison

2002   *Thinking from Things: Essays in the Philosophy of Archaeology*. Berkeley: University of California.

Yates, Robin D.

2001   "Cosmos, central authority, and communities in the early Chinese empire." In *Empires. Perspectives from Archaeology and History*, edited by Susan E. Alcock, Terence N. D'Altroy, Kathleen D. Morrison, and Carla M. Sinopoli, pp. 351–68. Cambridge: Cambridge University.

Yerkes, Richard

1988   "The Woodland and Mississippian traditions in the prehistory of Midwestern North America." *Journal of World Prehistory* 2.3:307–58.

Zimmerman, Larry J., Vitelli, Karen D., and Hollowell-Zimmerman, Julie (eds.)

2003   *Ethical Issues in Archaeology*. Walnut Creek, CA: AltaMira.

INDEX

Page numbers in *italics* refer to illustrations and photographs.

ABOUT THE AUTHOR

Sharon R. Steadman is an Associate Professor of Anthropology at the State University of New York, Cortland. She has focused on Near Eastern archaeological work across the Middle East, with a concentration on Turkey in the last fifteen years. She is the field director of the Çadır Höyük archaeological project in central Turkey, and is the director of the Rozanne M. Brooks Ethnographic Museum at SUNY Cortland.